THE COLD WAR AND THE MIDDLE EAST

The Cold War and the Middle East

Edited by
YEZID SAYIGH
and
AVI SHLAIM

CLARENDON PRESS · OXFORD
1997

Oxford University Press, Great Clarendon Street, Oxford OX2 6DP

Oxford New York
Athens Auckland Bangkok Bogota Bombay
Buenos Aires Calcutta Cape Town Dar es Salaam
Delhi Florence Hong Kong Istanbul Karachi
Kuala Lumpur Madras Madrid Melbourne
Mexico City Nairobi Paris Singapore
Taipei Tokyo Toronto
and associated companies in
Berlin Ibadan

Oxford is a trade mark of Oxford University Press

Published in the United States
by Oxford University Press Inc., New York

British Library Cataloguing in Publication Data
Data available

Library of Congress Cataloging in Publication Data
The Cold War and the Middle East / edited by Yezid Sayigh and
Avi Shlaim
1. Middle East—Politics and government—1979–   I. Ṣāyigh, Yazīd.
II. Shlaim, Avi
DS63.1C57   1997   956.04—dc21   96–30043
ISBN 0–19–829099–3

1 3 5 7 9 10 8 6 4 2

Typeset by Hope Services (Abingdon) Ltd.
Printed in Great Britain
on acid-free paper by
Biddles Ltd.,
Guildford & King's Lynn

ACKNOWLEDGEMENTS

This book originated in a series of lectures given at the Middle East Centre of St Antony's College, Oxford, in Michaelmas term 1994. A workshop was held at the Centre in mid-January 1995 to discuss the draft papers. We would like to thank the Social Studies Faculty Board for financial support, Derek Hopwood for his advice and encouragement, Charles Tripp for his help in planning this project, Tim Barton, Dominic Byatt, and Sophie Ahmad of Oxford University Press, together with Sarah Barrett, for their editorial support, and Elizabeth Anderson and Marga Lyall for their excellent secretarial assistance. Yezid Sayigh edited the papers and wrote his own contribution while a grantee of the Program on International Peace and Cooperation of the John D. and Catherine T. MacArthur Foundation. Avi Shlaim did his share of the writing and editing of this book while holding a British Academy Research Readership, and he would like to thank the British Academy for their support.

Y.S.
A.S.

Oxford
June 1996

CONTENTS

LIST OF CONTRIBUTORS

SHAHRAM CHUBIN is Executive Director, Research, at the Geneva Centre for Security Policy. He has taught at the Graduate Institute for International Studies since 1981. From 1977 to 1981 he was Director of Regional Studies at the International Institute for Strategic Studies. He is the author of *Iran's National Security Policies* (1994) and 'Does Iran Want Nuclear Weapons?' (1995), and co-author with Charles Tripp of 'Iran–Saudi Relations and Persian Gulf Security', Adelphi Paper No. 304, London, IISS, 1996.

ADEED DAWISHA is Professor of Government and Politics at George Mason University in Fairfax, Virginia. While in England he taught at the Universities of Lancaster and Keele, and was Deputy Director of Studies at the Royal Institute of International Affairs. In the United States he has been a recipient of a Fulbright fellowship and a fellowship from the Woodrow Wilson International Center for Scholars. In addition he has written numerous articles, his books include, *Egypt in the Arab World* (1976), *Syria and the Lebanese Crisis* (1979), *The Soviet Union in the Middle East* (1981), *Islam and Foreign Policy* (1983), *The Arab Radicals* (1986), *Beyond Coercion* (1992), and *The Making of Foreign Policy in Russia and the New States of Eurasia* (1995).

FAWAZ A. GERGES is a Professor of International Affairs and Middle Eastern Studies at Sarah Lawrence College, New York. He has been Visiting Fellow at Harvard and Princeton Universities. He is the author of *The Superpowers and the Middle East: Regional and International Politics, 1955–1967* (1994), and *New Threat from the East? American Foreign Policy Toward Political Islam: From Carter to Clinton* (forthcoming). His articles have appeared in *Foreign Affairs, Middle East Journal, British Journal of Middle Eastern Studies, Journal of Palestine Studies, Washington Post, Christian Science Monitor, Los Angeles Times, Al-Hayat*, and in other journals and edited books.

WILLIAM HALE is Reader in Politics with special reference to Turkey at the School of Oriental and African Studies, University of London. He is the author of *The Political and Economic Development of Modern Turkey* (1981) and *Turkish Politics and the Military* (1994), besides numerous articles on the politics and international relations of modern Turkey. In collaboration with Dr Philip Robins, he is currently preparing a book on Turkey's international relations since the end of the Cold War.

FRED HALLIDAY is Professor of International Relations at the London School of Economics. He is the author of many books, including *Arabia Without Sultans* (1974), *Iran: Dictatorship and Development* (1978), *Threat from the East? Soviet Policy from Afghanistan and Iran to the Horn of Africa* (1982), *The Making of the Second Cold War* (1983), *Cold War, Third World* (1988), *Revolution and Foreign Policy: The Case of South Yemen, 1967–1987* (1990), *Rethinking International Relations* (1994), and *Islam and the Myth of Confrontation: Religion and Politics in the Middle East* (1996).

EFRAIM KARSH is Professor and Head of the Mediterranean Studies Programme at King's College, University of London. He has held teaching and/or research positions at Columbia University, the International Institute for Strategic Studies in London, the Kennan Institute for Advance Russian Studies in Washington, DC, and the Jaffee Center for Strategic Studies at Tel Aviv University. He has published extensively on Middle Eastern affairs, Soviet foreign policy, and European neutrality. His recent books include *The Making of the Modern Middle East, 1789–1995* (forthcoming), *The Gulf Conflict 1990–1991: Diplomacy and War in the New World Order* (with Lawrence Freedman), *Saddam Hussein: A Political Biography* (with Inari Rautsi), *Soviet Policy Towards Syria Since 1970, Neutrality and Small States*, and *The Cautious Bear: Soviet Military Engagement in the Middle East Wars in the Post-1967 Era*.

YEZID SAYIGH is Assistant Director, Centre of International Studies, University of Cambridge. From 1991 to 1994 he acted as an adviser and negotiator for the Palestinian delegation to the bilateral Middle East peace talks with Israel, and headed the Palestinian delegation to the Working Group on Arms Control and Regional Security in the multilateral peace talks. His books include *Armed Struggle and the Search for State: The Palestinian National Movement, 1949–1993* (forthcoming), *Arab Military Industry: Capability, Performance and Impact*, and *Confronting the 1990s: Security in the Developing Countries*. His articles have appeared in *International Affairs, Middle East Journal, Third World Quarterly, Maghred-Mashreq*, and *Politique Étrangère*, among others.

PATRICK SEALE is a writer and former foreign correspondent for Reuters and *The Observer*. His books include *The Struggle for Syria, French Revolution, 1968, Philby: The Long Road to Moscow, Abu Nidal: A Gun for Hire*, and *Asad of Syria: The Struggle for the*

Middle East. Most recently, he helped HRH Prince Khaled bin Sultan write his Gulf War memoirs, *Desert Warrior.*

AVI SHLAIM is Professor of International Relations and Fellow of St Antony's College, Oxford. He is author of *The United States and the Berlin Blockade 1948–1949: A Study in Crisis Decision-Making* (1983), *Collusion across the Jordan: King Abdullah, the Zionist Movement and the Partition of Palestine* (1988), *The Politics of Partition* (1990), and *War and Peace in the Middle East: A Concise History* (1995).

LAWRENCE TAL is a Research Fellow at the International Institute for Strategic Studies in London and a former John M. Olin Fellow. He has published widely on Middle Eastern issues, and his work has appeared in various publications, including *Foreign Affairs, Middle Eastern Studies,* and *The Times Literary Supplement.* He is completing a book on *Politics, the Military, and National Security in Jordan, 1955–1967.*

CHARLES TRIPP is Senior Lecturer in Politics with reference to the Near and Middle East in the Department of Political Studies at the School of Oriental and African Studies, University of London. He has published, with Shahram Chubin, a book on the Iran–Iraq War, and has edited a number of books on Egyptian politics and one on the Iraqi invasion of Kuwait. He is presently working on a political history of Iraq.

CHRONOLOGY

23 Mar. 1945	Arab League formed.
12 Mar. 1947	Anti-communist Truman Doctrine proclaimed.
29 Nov. 1947	UN resolution for the partition of Palestine.
14 May 1948	Proclamation of the State of Israel.
15 May 1948– 7 Jan. 1949	First Arab–Israeli War.
Feb.–July 1949	Arab–Israeli armistice agreements signed.
25 May 1950	Britain, France, and US adopt Tripartite Declaration on regulating the supply of arms to the Middle East.
23 July 1952	Free Officers' revolution in Egypt.
9 Mar. 1953	Death of Stalin.
May 1953	Dulles trip to Middle East heralds new US policy.
17 Apr. 1954	Nasser becomes Prime Minister of Egypt.
July 1954	Big Four summit conference, Geneva.
19 Oct. 1954	Britain signs Suez base evacuation agreement with Egypt.
24 Feb. 1955	Iraq and Turkey sign the Baghdad Pact.
28 Feb. 1955	Israeli raid on Gaza.
5 Apr. 1955	Britain joins the Baghdad Pact.
18–24 Apr. 1955	Bandung conference of Asian and African states.
27 Sept. 1955	Nasser announces the Czech arms deal.
Dec. 1955	Baghdad Pact crisis in Jordan.
19 June 1956	British complete evacuation of their forces from Suez.
26 July 1956	Egypt nationalizes the Suez Canal Company.
22 Oct. 1956	Defensive Alliance signed by Egypt, Syria, and Jordan.
29 Oct.–7 Nov. 1956	The Suez War.
5 Jan. 1957	Anti-communist Eisenhower Doctrine proclaimed.
1 Feb. 1958	Syria and Egypt merged to form the United Arab Republic (UAR).
14 July 1958	Revolution in Iraq.
July 1958	American deployment to Lebanon; British deployment to Jordan.
28 Sept. 1961	Syrian coup leads to dissolution of UAR.
8 Mar. 1963	Ba'thist coup in Syria.
13–17 Jan. 1964	First summit meeting of Arab leaders in Cairo.
29 May 1964	Creation of the Palestine Liberation Organization (PLO).

23 Feb. 1966	Left-wing coup in Syria followed by increased PLO activity against Israel.
13 Nov. 1966	Israeli raid on West Bank village of al-Samu.
5–10 June 1967	The Six-Day War.
1 Sept. 1967	Arab League summit at Khartoum.
22 Nov. 1967	UN Security Council passes Resolution 242.
21 Mar. 1968	Battle of al-Karameh.
Mar. 1969– Aug. 1970	The Israeli–Egyptian War of Attrition.
9 Dec. 1969	Rogers Plan announced.
19 June 1970	The second Rogers initiative.
7 Aug. 1970	Israeli–Egyptian cease-fire under Rogers initiative.
Sept. 1970	Jordanian civil war, 'Black September': Jordan crushes Palestinian *fedayeen*.
28 Sept. 1970	President Nasser dics and Anwar Sadat succeeds.
22–6 May 1972	Nixon–Brezhnev summit meeting in Moscow.
July 1972	Sadat expels Soviet military advisers.
6–26 Oct. 1973	The Yom Kippur War.
22 Oct. 1973	UN Security Council Resolution 338 calls for direct negotiations.
21 Dec. 1973	Geneva peace conference.
18 Jan. 1974	Israeli–Egyptian disengagement agreement.
31 May 1974	Israeli–Syrian disengagement agreement.
26–9 Oct. 1974	Arab League summit at Rabat recognizes PLO as 'the sole legitimate representative of the Palestinian people'.
13 Apr. 1975	The outbreak of the Lebanese civil war.
1 Sept. 1975	Israeli–Egyptian interim agreement, Sinai II.
1 June 1976	Syrian military intervention in Lebanon.
17 May 1977	Rise to power in Israel of right-wing Likud Party.
1 Oct. 1977	Joint statement by the US and USSR for reconvening the Geneva peace conference.
19 Nov. 1977	Sadat visits Jerusalem.
2–5 Dec. 1977	Arab Front of Steadfastness and Opposition meets in Tripoli.
14 Mar. 1978	Israeli army invades south Lebanon.
19 Mar. 1978	UN Security Council Resolution 425 calls for Israeli withdrawal from Lebanon.
17 Sept. 1978	Israel and Egypt sign Camp David Accords.
2–5 Nov. 1978	Arab League summit at Baghdad denounces the Camp David Accords.
1 Feb. 1979	The Islamic revolution in Iran.
26 Mar. 1979	Egyptian–Israeli peace treaty signed.
25 Dec. 1979	Soviet invasion of Afghanistan.
17 Sept. 1980	Outbreak of war between Iraq and Iran.
6 Oct. 1981	President Sadat is assassinated and Husni Mubarak succeeds.
26 Apr. 1982	Israeli withdrawal from Sinai completed.

6 June 1982	Israeli invasion of Lebanon.
21 Aug. 1982	PLO leaves Lebanon for Tunisia.
June–Aug. 1982	Israeli siege of west Beirut.
1 Sept. 1982	The Reagan plan for Middle East peace.
17 May 1983	Israel and Lebanon sign agreement.
10 June 1985	Israel withdraws from Lebanon, but forms 'security zone' in the south.
15 Apr. 1986	American attack on Libya.
9 Dec. 1987	Outbreak of the *intifada.*
23 Feb. 1988	George Schultz launches his peace plan.
18 July 1988	End of Iran–Iraq War.
31 July 1988	King Hussein announces Jordan's disengagement from the West Bank.
15 Nov. 1988	Palestine National Council in Algiers conditionally accepts UN Resolutions 181, 242, and 338.
14 Dec. 1988	Arafat accepts US terms for talks with the PLO.
Feb. 1989	Soviet withdrawal from Afghanistan.
10 Oct. 1989	James Baker presents his five-point plan.
12 Oct. 1989	Ta'if accord to end the Lebanese civil war.
22 May 1990	Proclamation of the Republic of Yemen, a merger of the north and south.
20 June 1990	US suspends dialogue with the PLO.
2 Aug. 1990	Iraq invades Kuwait.
16 Jan.–28 Feb. 1991	The Gulf War.
Mar. 1991	President Bush announces major new Middle East peace initiative.
30 Oct. 1991	Madrid Peace Conference, followed by Washington peace talks.
25 Dec. 1991	Dissolution of the USSR.
23 June 1992	Labour defeats Likud in Israeli elections.
25 July 1993	Israel launches Operation Accountability in south Lebanon.
13 Sept. 1993	Israel–PLO Declaration of Principles on Palestinian self-government.
4 May 1994	Israel and PLO reach agreement in Cairo on the application of the Declaration of Principles.
25 July 1994	Washington Declaration ends state of war between Israel and Jordan.
26 Oct. 1994	Israel and Jordan sign peace treaty.
2 Feb. 1995	First summit between leaders of Egypt, Jordan, PLO, and Israel.
28 Sept. 1995	Israeli–Palestinian Interim Agreement on the West Bank and the Gaza Strip (Oslo II).
4 Nov. 1995	Yitzhak Rabin is assassinated and Shimon Peres succeeds him.
11 Apr. 1996	Israel launches Operation Grapes of Wrath in south Lebanon.
29 May 1996	Likud defeats Labour in Israeli elections.

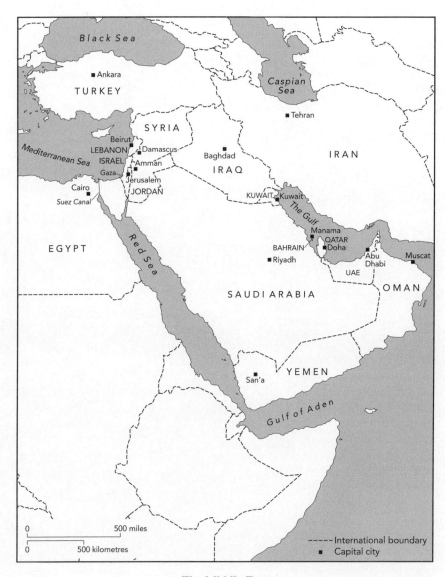

The Middle East

Introduction

YEZID SAYIGH AND AVI SHLAIM

The Cold War lasted from the end of the Second World War in 1945 to the collapse of the Soviet Union in 1991. During these four and a half decades, the Cold War dominated world politics; but despite intensive research and a voluminous literature, it remains one of the most enigmatic and elusive conflicts of modern times.

Three features of the Cold War are essential for understanding its nature and consequences: bipolarity, nuclear weapons, and ideology. First, the post-1945 international system was described as bipolar because of the enormous disparity in power between the two new superpowers, the United States and the Soviet Union, and the rest. This bipolar structure of the international system had a profound effect on postwar politics, for example, in engendering mutual suspicion and antagonism and in dividing Europe and much of the rest of the world into rival spheres of influence. Second, the rise of bipolarity coincided with the emergence of nuclear weapons. This new military technology influenced international politics in several ways: it greatly increased the danger of war while at the same time inducing the superpowers to go to great lengths to avoid being dragged by their allies into a nuclear confrontation. However, the Cold War was more than traditional Great Power geopolitical rivalry with nuclear weapons thrown in. A third feature which further complicated and exacerbated the Cold War was the ideological confrontation between East and West, between communism and capitalism. Since both superpowers sought not only to extend their power but to export their social and economic systems, the geopolitical rivalry between them assumed the character of a sweeping struggle between two ways of life.

The ideological clash was reflected not only in the relations between the superpowers but also in the debate among historians about the origins and character of the Cold War. While the Cold War was in full swing, scholarly detachment and objectivity were not easy to maintain. On the American side, in particular, a fierce battle among the historians accompanied the actual political battle between the superpowers. During the 1950s the traditionalist view held sway. According to this view, Soviet expansionism was responsible for the outbreak of the Cold War, while American policy was essentially reactive and defensive. In the 1960s, in the context of the Vietnam war and the crisis of American self-confidence that accompanied it, a new school of thought emerged, a revisionist school of mostly younger, left-wing scholars. According to this school, American capitalism was the main cause of the conflict and it was the Soviet Union that reacted defensively. In the 1970s, following the opening up of the archives, a third school of thought emerged, the post-revisionist school. A re-examination of the assumptions and arguments of both traditionalists and revisionists in the light of new evidence gradually yielded a post-revisionist synthesis. The aim of the post-revisionists was not to allocate blame to this party or that but to try to understand the complex dynamics of the conflict that we call the Cold War.

The most significant landmark in the evolution of Cold War historiography, however, was the end of the Cold War itself. With the disintegration of the Soviet empire in Eastern Europe in the late 1980s and the formal dissolution of the USSR itself in 1991, the Cold War came to an end. Today we are much better placed to assess the Cold War and its consequences than all the earlier generations of scholars, including the post-revisionists. In the first place, we have a great deal more documentary material available to us and this material is being constantly augmented by the opening up of the Soviet archives. Secondly, the discussion of the Cold War can proceed in a much more relaxed atmosphere, largely free from partisanship and political pressures. Third, and most importantly, we have a much broader perspective than earlier historians because we know the outcome of the contest. In short, now that the Cold War is over, we can treat it as history.

This book is concerned not with the Cold War in general but with the Cold War and the Middle East. It covers the period from the end of the Second World War to the Gulf War of 1991. The case of the Middle East is particularly instructive because it has always been closely linked with Great Power politics in modern times. In the aftermath of the Second World War the Middle East remained deeply and ceaselessly caught up in Great Power rivalries because of its strategic importance and because of its oil resources. All regions of the world were affected, in varying degrees, by Cold War rivalries, but the impact of these rivalries in the Middle East appeared to be particularly pervasive and profound.

The key to the international politics of the Middle East during the

Cold War era, or any other era for that matter, is the relationship between outside powers and local states. From this perspective, the history of the Middle East in the twentieth century may be divided into four phases: the Ottoman, the European, the superpower, and the American. The Ottoman phase lasted four centuries and ended with the collapse of the Ottoman empire in 1918. The European phase, during which Britain and France played the leading roles, lasted from 1918 roughly until the Suez War of 1956. The superpower phase began in the mid-1950s and ended with the Gulf War and the disintegration of the Soviet Union in 1991. These two events also marked the beginning of the American phase in the history of the Middle East.

On the relative weight of external and regional forces in shaping the development of the contemporary Middle East, however, there is no consensus among scholars. The conventional view, shared by many in the region, is that external forces have played a decisive role. In keeping with this view, the international history of the region is sometimes written as if local powers had no will of their own, no freedom of action, virtually no influence over the Great Powers, and no control over their own destiny. In the more simplistic versions of the conventional view, the local powers are portrayed as mere pawns in a game played by the Great Powers.

Middle East specialists, on the other hand, whether or not they directly challenge the conventional view, tend to assign much greater weight to local forces in shaping the development of the region. The local states, they point out, have much more leverage in dealing with outside powers than is generally recognized. They also have a narrower range of interests and much more at stake and may therefore be expected to work more energetically and single-mindedly to protect these interests. Moreover, the greater the competition between the external powers, the greater the scope for local initiative and direction. For all these reasons, local powers are at least as likely to manipulate outside powers as they are to be manipulated by them.

These two competing approaches to the study of Middle East history may be termed the systemic and the regionalist. Plainly, neither approach is adequate on its own. Any serious account of this international history of the Middle East must take into account the part played by all the major actors, both inside and outside the region. That much can be said without fear of being contradicted.

A great deal has been written on the international politics of the Middle East during the Cold War era, but most of this literature has tended to focus on the policies and impact of the superpowers. To say this is not to accuse the authors of a partial or distorted vision but simply to point out that much of this literature has as its subject the policy of the United States or that of the Soviet Union towards the Middle East, or the rivalry between them in this region.

The purpose of the present book is to fill something of a gap in the literature by examining the Cold War era in the Middle East from the perspective of the local powers. All the contributors to this book are international relations generalists who are also Middle East area specialists. The chapters in this book represent a combination of detailed research, analysis, and reflection. Our aim is to add to the existing literature by explaining the impact of the Cold War on different countries by looking at them not merely from the 'outside in' but mainly from the 'inside out'. For this reason we have not included in the book chapters on the United States or Soviet Union and the Middle East during the Cold War. Our intention is to examine the politics of the region during the Cold War era rather than the policies of the superpowers towards the region. The first chapter, by Fred Halliday, does deal with the superpowers but only in the context of an introduction to the debate about the Cold War in general. All the other chapters in the book, except for the Conclusion, deal with individual countries from the region. Separate chapters are devoted to Egypt, Syria, Lebanon, Jordan, the Palestinians, Israel, Iraq, Iran, and Turkey.

The inclusion of some states in this book and the exclusion of others requires explanation. In theory, a book on the Cold War and the Middle East could cover all the Arab states from the Maghreb to the Persian Gulf. But for practical reasons we decided to leave out the Maghreb countries and the countries of the Arabian peninsula and to concentrate on the core area of the Middle East round the Eastern Mediterranean. This is also the main area of the Arab–Israeli conflict which intersected in so many different ways with the East–West conflict. Accordingly, there is a chapter on each of the confrontation states: Egypt, Syria, Lebanon, Jordan, Israel, and the Palestinians, who were a significant non-state actor. Iraq, although not strictly speaking a confrontation state, was included because of the important part it played in regional and international politics during the Cold War, not least in provoking two Gulf Wars. Iran and Turkey are a special case, both being Islamic but non-Arab states. The reason for their inclusion in this book is that they constituted the 'northern tier' of the Middle East during the Cold War and featured prominently in Western plans for the defence of the region. A second reason for their inclusion is that they affected significantly the security and economic policies of the Arab states of the region.

To give the book a clear structure, to make the analysis more systematic, and to facilitate comparison, we suggested a set of general guidelines to be followed by all the contributors. The obvious, central question to be addressed in each chapter was: how did the Cold War affect the strategic perceptions and political behaviour of the actor under discussion? This question could be explored at three levels: relations with the superpowers, relations with other regional powers, and domestic politics.

The first level focuses on general foreign policy orientations, such as membership of alliances or non-alignment, as well as specific aspects of the relationship with the superpowers such as economic aid and the supply of arms. The second level focuses on the impact of the Cold War on the behaviour of the actor in regional politics. For the Arab actors the two principal arenas to be discussed were inter-Arab politics, or the Arab Cold War, and the Arab–Israeli conflict. Although the book is not specifically about the Cold War and the Arab–Israeli conflict, this conflict predictably received considerable attention in the chapters on Israel and the Arab states. The third level focuses on the impact of the Cold War on domestic politics. Among the factors to be explored here are the quest for legitimacy, the relationship between government and opposition, the role of nationalist, communist, and 'Islamist' parties, trends towards democracy or authoritarianism, and strategies of economic development. In short, the third level focuses on the interplay between external relations and domestic politics during the Cold War.

The end of the Cold War has fundamentally altered the overarching international framework within which regional politics were conducted. To assess this impact on the region at the strategic, political, economic, and ideological levels is beyond the scope of this book. But the various analyses it presents of the patterns established during more than forty years of superpower rivalry help to explain the manner in which local actors have adjusted to the sweeping changes since the fall of the Berlin Wall. Indeed, one of the striking observations to be drawn from the following chapters is that the Cold War had already lost some of its significance in the preceding decade as a primary context for the formulation of policies in both foreign and domestic spheres. This fact, as much as the constant striving of local actors for strategic autonomy and the assertion of their own political agendas, suggests that, far from being only the passive 'receivers' of superpower dictates, the local actors also exerted an active influence on the course of the Cold War and contributed materially to its ultimate demise.

1

The Middle East, the Great Powers, and the Cold War

FRED HALLIDAY

THE COLD WAR AND THE THIRD WORLD

The international conflict known as the Cold War was the dominant issue in world politics from the late 1940s until the late 1980s. It involved competition, on a number of levels, between two rival blocs: if it was often focused on military rivalry, nuclear and conventional, it also involved rivalry for political influence, for diplomatic advantage, and for economic goals. To a considerable extent it was a conflict between two ways of life, two variant, competitive, and incompatible definitions of modernity. For many commentators, during and after the Cold War, the conflict was little different from other periods of rivalry between Great Powers and was, in essence, another chapter in the competition of such powers for domination on the international scene. There were certainly strong elements of such traditional Great Power rivalry in the Cold War, replete as it was with spheres of influence, the quest for junior allies, and issues of prestige and credibility. But the Cold War was more than just a traditional rivalry between Great Powers, since it also had a strong ideological element, both in terms of the appeals made by both sides to potential allies and in terms of the kind of model each offered to such allies. The Cold War was a competition between two rival social and political systems, each of which sought to present itself as the solution to the problems of the world and each of which believed it could prevail over the other, in a long-term competition: outright nuclear conflict could be avoided, but a range of military, political, economic, and cultural pressures would be brought to bear to prevail over the other.[1] This was the logic both of Western strategy, summarized in Kennan's 1946 doctrine of containment, according to which the West would win provided it hung on and gave of its best,

[1] I have gone into the issue of what the Cold War was in greater detail in *Rethinking International Relations* (London: Macmillan, 1994), chs. 8–10.

and of Soviet policy, epitomized in Brezhnev's theory of the 'corre-lation of forces', according to which the global balance of forces, sig-nificantly but not exclusively military, would shift in favour of the Soviet bloc. If many doubted the reality of this inter-systemic con-flict during the Cold War itself, it was a little harder to do so once the Cold War was over and one side had, however reluctantly, found itself the victor. The Cold War may not have been meant to have an end, but it did: the Western bloc prevailed over the communist system.[2]

The Cold War was a global conflict, in the sense that it involved the aspiration of each bloc to prevail on a worldwide level, and in the sense that each sought to muster as many states as it could to support its position in that rivalry. All regions of the world, includ-ing the Middle East, were affected by it and had, in turn, an impact on the evolution of the conflict. Yet this global character did not pre-vent different regions of the world from assuming distinct roles in the conflict. The front line, in the sense of the area where military pre-paredness was the greatest, was from the start in the 1940s to the end in the late 1980s in central Europe. If the crisis of Berlin in 1948–9 marked the high point of the early Cold War, the fall of the Berlin Wall, in November 1989, signalled its demise. Europe was also cen-tral for another reason: it was the record in Europe of the two rival systems that as much as anything led to the final verdict. The com-parative economic and social records of, respectively, the EEC and the Soviet bloc states was perhaps *the* most decisive factor in com-munism's loss of confidence and collapse.

Such, indeed, was the importance of Europe in the conflict that some, notably Kennan himself, regarded the rest of the world as largely irrelevant, and responded to Soviet gains there with indiffer-ence. In the late 1940s and early 1950s this was also the view of Joseph Stalin.[3] Yet the other arena of rivalry, that of the states of Asia, Africa, and Latin America, was important: in contradistinc-tion, real or supposed, to the two blocs, this area came by the early 1960s to be known first in French and then in English as *le tiers*

---

[2] A point little noted during the Cold War was that the term, normally ascribed to the phil-anthropist Bernard Baruch and popularized by Walter Lippman in a series of essays later pub-lished as a book (*The Cold War*, 1947), had been used centuries earlier by the Spanish writer Don Juan Mañuel, to describe the Spanish conflict with the Arabs. 'War that is very strong and very hot ends either with death or peace, whereas cold war neither brings peace nor gives honour to the one who makes it'(*Escritores in Prosa Anteriores al Siglo XV*, Madrid: Biblioteca de Autores Españoles de Rivadeneira, 1952, 362). The resurgence of speculation about an atavistic conflict between 'Islam' and the 'West' after the end of the Cold War suggests—wrongly—a return to this earlier meaning of Cold War.

[3] A later variant of this thesis, according to which the Cold War was confined to Europe, can be found in Allen Lynch, *The Cold War is Over—Again* (Oxford: Westview Press, 1992).

monde, 'the Third World'. Throughout the Cold War it played a major part in inter-bloc competition. Here the majority of the world's population lived and here, from the early 1920s onwards, Soviet strategists had seen the greatest likelihood of revolutionary advances against Western power and 'imperialism': with the rise of the nationalist and anti-colonial movements of the 1940s and 1950s, in part stimulated by World War II, it appeared that this perspective would be vindicated. It was here too that boundaries between the spheres of influence of each bloc were most insecure and the dangers of miscalculation the greatest: in Europe, with the partial exception of Greece, the lines had been drawn with the end of the Second World War, and military dispositions made accordingly; in the Third World, a much greater fluidity of spheres and indeed of frontiers opened the way for four decades of rivalry. Most important of all, perhaps, it was in the Third World that the issue of greatest importance for the Cold War, the choice of political and economic system, was in many countries unclear as the more unsettled and acute social conditions generated rivalries for power between pro-communist and pro-Western tendencies, of a kind and intensity largely absent in Europe itself.

It was not surprising, therefore, not only that the Third World was drawn into the Cold War but that for much of the forty-year conflict it appeared as if that conflict was not just mainly concerned with the Third World but was above all a rivalry for influence in this as yet undecided zone: certainly this was how many in Moscow, Washington, and related capitals saw it. Indeed, this shared perspective led to the emergence of two contrasted but reinforcing strategic ideologies. For the Soviet Union, the movements of the Third World were part of a worldwide upsurge of oppressed peoples against capitalism and imperialism, part of the correlation of forces shifting in Moscow's favour. For the USA, the challenges of the Third World necessitated the enunciation of security doctrines to which every US president, except Gerald Ford, put his name: there could be no better token of how the Third World was seen as a threat to US interests than this listing of 'doctrines', from Truman and Eisenhower, through Kennedy, Johnson, Nixon, Carter, and Reagan, under which Washington justified its Third World roles and mobilized domestic support for such commitments.[4]

At the level of military conflict this distinctiveness of the Third World was evident: if, apart from Greece and, later, Cyprus and Ireland, Europe was without overt and significant armed conflict

---

[4] I have gone into this in greater detail in *Cold War, Third World* (London: Radius/Hutchinson, 1989), ch. 3.

during the Cold War, the Third World was the site of dozens of conflicts, inter-state and intra-state, in which an estimated 20 million people lost their lives.[5] While it was simplistic to claim that these wars were simply caused by the Cold War, most were, if not caused, then exacerbated by it, through arms sales, diplomatic rivalry, and ideological association. Such indeed was the contrast between a central, European front at peace and a Third World at war that many took the mistaken view that in some way the Cold War had been 'displaced' or transferred by the Great Powers onto the poorer countries of the world. Equally, the Third World provided the site for most of the most dangerous moments of the Cold War, those points at which Great Power rivalry, usually mediated through some local conflict, led to a nuclear alert and, with it, the risk of an all-out exchange of nuclear weapons: of the twenty cases in which US forces were put onto nuclear alert, and in the one known case when Soviet forces were, sixteen, i.e. over three-quarters, were a result of developments in the Third World.[6] Of these sixteen, seven involved the Middle East.[7] Yet this picture of overall confrontation in the Third World and the Middle East needs to be balanced by a recognition of the degree to which the two blocs managed, if not restrained, their rivalry in the Third World: at no point did the forces of the core states clash directly, and they showed, from the very earliest crises of the 1940s, an ability, not to prevent conflict, but to manage crises when they occurred. These restraints were, as elsewhere, evident in the Middle East: with the brief exception of the US intermediate-range missiles stationed in Turkey between 1961 and 1963, neither the USA nor the USSR is known to have stationed nuclear weapons on the territory of a Middle Eastern ally; at moments of greatest crises, namely in the three Arab–Israeli wars of 1956, 1967, and 1973, they worked through the UN Security Council to limit the conflict, in 1956 supporting broadly the same policy. The Third World in general, and the Middle East in particular, therefore illustrated both the extent and the limits of the Cold War's influence on the Third World.[8]

[5] No exact measure of the cost of these conflicts exists. For two calculations, see Andrew Wilson, *The Disarmer's Handbook* (London: Penguin, 1983), and Evan Luard *The Blunted Sword: The Erosion of Military Power in Modern World Politics* (London: I. B. Tauris, 1988).

[6] See my *The Making of the Second Cold War* (London: Verso, 1983), 50.

[7] Suez 1956 (Russian and American alerts), Lebanon (1958), Jordan (1958), Turkey (1963), Jordan (1970), Arab–Israeli war (1973). On at least three other occasions the two blocs found themselves in potentially dangerous confrontations, even though there is no record of nuclear forces being mobilized, or their use threatened, on either side: Azerbaijan 1946, Turkey–Syria 1957, Afghanistan 1979.

[8] Steven Spiegel (ed.), *Conflict Management in the Middle East* (London: Pinter, 1992).

THE MIDDLE EAST AND THE COLD WAR

Turning to the Middle East, it is not difficult to write a history of that region during the Cold War in such a way as to highlight the interaction of regional conflict and global Cold War. First, it is often forgotten that in two important respects the Cold War began in the Middle East or, more particularly, in what to the West is known as the 'northern tier' and the Russians as the 'Central East', or *Sryedni Vostok*: the crisis over the Soviet refusal to withdraw forces from Azerbaijan in March 1946 was the first major crisis of the Soviet–American alliance after the end of the Second World War. Although there is no record of Truman explicitly threatening the use of nuclear weapons, Stalin was well aware, a few months after Hiroshima and Nagasaki, of American capabilities. The Azerbaijan crisis was followed a year later by the proclamation of the first of the US security doctrines, in this case the 'Truman Doctrine', with specific application to Greece and to Turkey: if the former was seen as threatened by the communist guerrilla movement, the latter had been the subject of apparent Soviet military pressure after the end of the war.[9] The 'Truman Doctrine' also encompassed Iran, which was, some years later, to become the site of a major conflict during the premiership of Mohamad Mosadeq (1951–3). Following the Egyptian revolution of 1952, the Soviet Union began to acquire a strong following amongst Arab nationalists, and for two decades this was to be the main axis of Soviet influence in the Middle East: the establishment of an alliance with Egypt, in 1955–6, greatly helped by the Suez crisis, was followed by the development of ties with nationalist military regimes in Syria, Iraq, Algeria, Sudan, North Yemen, and, later, South Yemen and Libya. The USA for its part developed closer ties to Israel, Iran, Turkey, and Saudi Arabia.

For these two decades, between the mid-1950s and mid-1970s, the Arab world appeared to be one of the areas of the Third World where the conflict of East and West was at its sharpest, a perception that received its sharpest confirmation in October 1973 when, in the midst of the fourth Arab–Israeli war, Washington for the last time in the history of the Cold War declared a nuclear alert.[10] From the

---

[9] Louise Fawcett, *Iran and the Cold War* (Cambridge: Cambridge University Press, 1992); Bruce Kuniholm, *The Origins of the Cold War in the Middle East* (Princeton: Princeton University Press, 1980); Alvin Rubinstein, *Soviet Policy Toward Turkey, Iran, and Afghanistan* (New York: Praeger, 1982).

[10] See Raymond Garthoff, *Detente and Confrontation* (Washington, DC: Brookings Institution, 1983); LeBow and Stein, *We All Lost the Cold War* (London: Princeton University Press, 1993).

mid-1970s, even as Soviet influence declined, the Middle East came to play an important part in the broader worsening of East–West relations that was known as 'the second Cold War': for influential elements in the US Congress, Soviet policy towards Israel, linked to its supposed instigation of the Arab attack in October 1973, support for Arab terrorism, and blocking of Jewish emigration from the USSR itself, constituted an important part of a new Soviet aggressiveness. In the late 1970s a series of further events in what Zbigniew Brzezinski called 'the Arc of Crisis'—the crisis of 1978–9 in the two Yemens, the Soviet airlift to Ethiopia, the Iranian revolution, and, most importantly, the dispatch of combat forces to Afghanistan in December 1979—were proof of this communist danger.[11]

Moreover, if the external perception was often one that saw the Middle East as central to the rivalry of the blocs, actors—states, popular movements, commentators of all hues—were not slow to analyse the developments of their own region in terms of this global conflict. Here the exogenous rhetoric of the Cold War was superimposed upon a political culture, and in particular an approach to international issues, that easily—far too easily—cast events in terms of external conspiracies, and denied agency, influence, or power to political forces within the region. The posing of the valid question of how much and in what ways the global conflict could explain events in the Middle East was displaced by the assumption of an all-pervasive conspiracy: thus not only events with a clear Cold War dimension—the Suez crisis, the 1967 and 1973 Arab–Israeli wars, or the US supply of arms to the Shah of Iran in the 1970s—but also events that had little to do with the Cold War—the assassination of King Faisal of Saudi Arabia in 1975, the Iranian revolution of 1979—were seen in a Cold War light. And this over-globalization of Middle Eastern politics was replayed in another form, namely the perception by many in the Middle East of the Cold War as in some way wholly or largely about the Middle East itself: thus the Arab world saw US–Soviet relations predominantly through the lens of their particular preoccupations—US presidential elections and congresses of the Communist Party of the Soviet Union were analysed almost wholly in terms of what they meant for the Middle East. On its side Israel came, after an initial period of sensible evaluation, to see the USSR's hostility to the West as an expression of anti-Semitism, and Khomeini ended up by attributing the crisis of the Soviet Union to

---

[11] 'An Arc of crisis stretches along the shores of the Indian Ocean, with fragile social and political structures in a region of vital importance to us threatened with fragmentation. The resulting political chaos could well be filled by elements hostile to our values and sympathetic to our adversaries'(*Time*, 15 Jan. 1979).

Gorbachev's rejection of Islam. Thus the twin delusions of facile globalization and regional narcissism produced a situation in which the differential, partial interrelationship of the Cold War with the Middle East was obscured by belief in a single, all-encompassing logic.[12]

GLOBAL TRENDS, REGIONAL VARIATIONS

With this caution in mind, it may be possible to see how, beyond the course of events itself, the Cold War shaped the Middle East in the latter part of the twentieth century. The impact of the Cold War on the Third World and on the Middle East in particular was pervasive and fundamental, as can be seen by identifying at least four major areas in which this occurred:[13] such an identification of general Third World trends may help to establish how each affected the Middle East.

The first was decolonization, meaning both the ending of formal colonial control and the more diffuse lessening of informal influence on Third World states: no single cause can explain the sudden, unexpected abandonment by the European colonial powers of their colonial possessions in Asia and Africa, but the Cold War, following the Second World War, had a major part in it. On the one hand the Soviet Union provided encouragement, military and political, to nationalist movements and regimes across the Third World. On the other, the fear of communist exploitation of colonial regimes, and US encouragement of decolonization as a means of forestalling revolutionary advance, combined to drive the British, French, Belgians, and Dutch out of the Third World and to allow over 100 states to attain independence. If decolonization had begun before the Cold War, in Iraq, Egypt, Syria, and elsewhere, the advent of Cold War stimulated nationalist movements and made it more difficult for the traditionally dominant states to hold onto their positions, be it the informal systems of influence enjoyed by the British in Iran and Egypt or the formal systems of control retained by Britain along the

---

[12] One striking instance of regional narcissism was the Middle Eastern reaction to the Soviet invasion of Afghanistan in Dec. 1979: this caused panic in several Middle Eastern capitals—Ankara, Damascus, Baghdad, and Saudi Arabia among them—on the grounds that if the Red Army had been able to attack Afghanistan it would also be able to invade these countries. Any sober evaluation of the geographical, logistical, political, and international character of the Afghan case, whatever its rights and wrongs, would have shown this to be nonsense.

[13] This draws on the analytic framework developed in my 'Assessing the Consequences: The Third World and the End of the Cold War', in Barbara Stallings and Eric Hirschberg (eds.), *Global Change, Regional Response: The New International Context of Development* (New York: Cambridge University Press, 1996).

coastlines of the Arabian peninsula, from Kuwait to Aden, or by the French in the Maghreb.

It was in the context of this gradual retreat of the colonial powers that the second dimension of the Cold War became evident, namely the evolution of new ideological commitments by Third World states to, respectively, the Soviet and Western models. In the case of the USSR, this ranged from the full-scale adoption of the communist model, found in a minority of only eight Third World countries (two of them, China and North Korea, independent of the USSR),[14] to the more negotiated forms of identification found in regimes of 'African' or 'Arab' socialism, or in what the Russians, in a variety of delicate formulations, termed 'non-capitalist', 'national democratic', or 'socialist-oriented' states.[15] This bloc of pro-Soviet states was, however, always a minority, two dozen at most, compared to the majority who remained, to varying degrees, part of the Western camp: the latter sought not a 'third' way but integration on better terms with the developed capitalist countries. Indeed, for all the talk of Soviet influence in the Third World, the striking thing about the impact of the Cold War on the Third World is how it accompanied, and in some cases stimulated, the development not of socialism but of a Third World capitalism: nowhere was this more true than in the East Asian region, where the response to the very real communist threat was to stimulate a unique burst of capitalist development. The overall historical judgement on communism, that its greatest historical achievement was the reform of capitalism, was nowhere more vindicated than in this context.[16]

For the Middle East, the verdict was less clear, but ultimately the same: if a range of states espoused various forms of 'Arab socialism' and 'socialist orientation', the majority of their trade remained with the capitalist world, and their overall economic records were unimpressive. By contrast, in the core of pro-Western states—the Arabian peninsula oil-producers, Turkey, Israel—a combination of factors (oil, Western official, and private financial assistance) led to substantial increases in living standards.

The longer-term outcome of this rivalry of political and economic systems was, however, masked by a further broad consequence of the Cold War, namely the strategic rivalry between the two blocs: as

---

[14] In addition to China and Korea, the other 6 communist regimes were Mongolia, Vietnam, Laos, Cambodia, Afghanistan, and Cuba. These six were the recipients of over 80% of all Soviet economic aid to the Third World.

[15] For further discussion see *Cold War, Third World*, ch. 4; Margot Light, *Troubled Friendships, Moscow's Third World Ventures* (London: British Academic Press, 1993).

[16] Eric Hobsbawm, *Age of Extremes* (London: Michael Joseph, 1994).

already suggested, this was a major but not the sole factor in incidence of wars in the Third World. Even where the causes had little
to do with the rivalry of the two blocs—as was the case in the Indo-
Pakistani and Arab–Israeli arenas—these acquired a Cold War character as each side sought to ensure strategic backing from one side
or the other, and fuelled a regional arms race.[17] This was perhaps the
most striking contribution of the Middle East to the Cold War, for
the conflict was accompanied here, more than in any other part of
the Third World, by dangerous inter-state conflicts, most notably in
the five Arab–Israeli wars, which carried with them a risk, never realized, of Great Power nuclear confrontation.[18] Inter-state rivalry
almost necessarily acquired a Cold War dimension, not only in the
Arab–Israeli context but also in the rivalries of Iran and Iraq, of
Egypt and Saudi Arabia, of Turkey and Syria, and of North and
South Yemen. The one striking exception was the rivalry between
Greece and Turkey: here the regional rivals, each of which faced a
challenge from communism in the immediate post-1945 period,
sought to prosecute their individual interests by *both* joining NATO.
They thereby acquired diplomatic, and military, support that would
otherwise not have been available, and were able to use the superfi-
cial unity of NATO to continue their rivalry by other means. Such
was Turkish support for NATO that even after 1974, when the USA
cut off arms supplies and Moscow, backing Turkey's stance on
Cyprus, openly hoped for a 'national democratic' faction to emerge
within the Turkish military, the strains within NATO were contained.[19]

This strategic rivalry led to a fourth aspect of the Cold War's
impact on the Third World: namely the formation of competitive
alliance systems, in which military, political, and diplomatic considerations combined to align states with one or other bloc: this was

[17] The appearance of symmetry in the policies of the two blocs does not hold in one crucial
respect: the West—France and the USA—allowed one of their allies, Israel, to acquire nuclear
weapons, while the Soviets kept complete control over their allies' access to this technology.

[18] 'I don't think we came close to nuclear war. Even in the circumstances in which we went
on alert, in October 1973, I, as the principal adviser and as the operator, the co-ordinator of
the system, did not think so. We went on alert twice. Once was in September 1970, when the
Syrians invaded Jordan, and the second was in October 1973. You have to understand, though,
what is meant by going on alert. We have five stages of readiness. Our forces are generally in,
or most frequently in, the stage of readiness four. What we did was to go from four to three,
except for nuclear forces when we went to two. We never went to readiness stage one. In neither case did we think we were anywhere close to nuclear war, but we wanted to send a signal
to the Soviets that we were prepared to go to war'. Henry Kissinger in conversation with Fred
Halliday in *From Potsdam to Perestroika: Conversations with Cold Warriors* (London: BBC
News and Current Affairs Publications, 1995), 25–6.

[19] This did not prevent the widespread belief within NATO that were a world war to become
imminent Turkey would leave the Western alliance and reassert its neutrality.

rarely a matter of coercion alone, but involved the ideological affinity already mentioned and calculations of interest in which the junior partner was able to manoeuvre, often by exploiting the very commitment which the Great Power had made to supporting it. Thus, in the Middle East, Israel and the conservative Arab states came to align with the USA, while a number of revolutionary and nationalist states were, at various points in the Cold War, aligned with the USSR: Egypt, Algeria, Libya, Iraq, Syria, and South Yemen. At various points these all signed treaties of friendship with the USSR. The support they received went beyond the provision of arms, important as this was, and included some economic and political assistance.

Yet, as so many incidents were to bear out, this alliance with the USSR did not guarantee Soviet control over either the domestic or the foreign policies of these states. Indeed, what the history of these states' relations with Moscow was to show was how much leeway the local states had to take initiatives: Nasser in 1967 and Sadat in 1973 were perhaps the most striking examples, but there was much in the conduct of Libya, Iraq, and South Yemen to exemplify this too.[20] Even such a weak negotiating partner as the PLO was able to defy Soviet pressure on the issue most central to it, namely willingness to recognize the right of an Israeli state to exist. Elsewhere in the Third World the same flexibility could be noticed: from Kim Il-sung in North Korea to Fidel Castro in Cuba, it was often the junior allies which took the initiatives to which the Great Power found itself subsequently committed. In one specific and important way, this Soviet experience with the Middle East was to play a role in the end of the Cold War itself; for if one were to chart the gradual Soviet disillusionment with Third World socialism, and with the regimes supposedly championing it, this would probably begin with the deterioration of the Soviet relationship with Egypt. Indeed, it has been said that if the Americans suffered from a 'Vietnam Syndrome', the Russians were affected by an 'Egyptian Syndrome', a reluctance to trust and subsidize supposedly loyal and militant Third World regimes that could, all too easily, turn their backs on the USSR.[21]

On the US side comparable difficulties continued: the Arab world, with the exception after 1977 of Egypt, refused to reach a political settlement with Israel, or accept the legitimacy of an Israeli state at all; the Shah of Iran, once he had found his feet again after the 1953

---

[20] In regard to South Yemen, see my *Revolution and Foreign Policy: The Case of South Yemen, 1967–1987* (Cambridge: Cambridge University Press, 1990), ch. 6.

[21] For one, disabused, Russian account see Alexei Vassiliev, *Russian Policy in the Middle East: From Messianism to Pragmatism* (Reading, Berks.: Ithaca Press, 1993).

coup, became more and more independent of US policy; the Turks, as already noted, paid little attention to Washington when it came to perceptions of national interest in Cyprus.

A QUALIFIED IMPACT

The preceding general analysis provides a basis for situating some of the consequences of the Cold War on the Middle East region and locating what may appear to be specific, regional developments in a global context. It may be important here to avoid excess generalization—applying without qualification worldwide trends to an area that, while not immune to general historical trends, has its own redoubtable specificity.

For all its participation in a global process, and the inflaming of inter-state conflict, the Cold War itself had a limited impact on the Middle East: in many ways, and despite its proximity to the USSR, the Middle East was less affected than other parts of the Third World. Compared to the Far East, or southern Africa, it did not produce a pro-Soviet revolutionary movement: there were strong communist parties in a number of Arab states—Iraq and Sudan notably—but they never had the character of mass communist movements of the kind seen in China, Korea, and Vietnam, or in Angola, Mozambique, or South Africa. Of the Arab regimes allied to the USSR, only one, the People's Democratic Republic of Yemen, had an orthodox 'socialist-oriented' ruling party, and that was riven by bloody internal divisions that Soviet pressure was unable to resolve. The strongest mass communist party ever seen in the region was the Tudeh party of Iran; but despite its great influence in the late 1940s and 1950s, it failed to capitalize on its advantages and fell victim, probably inevitably, to the coup of August 1953.[22] Ironically, the only country in the region where a *communist* party ever came to power was in Afghanistan, where the militant but small, divided, and beleaguered People's Democratic Party of Afghanistan took power in April 1978, with disastrous consequences. Removed by culture and geography from the conventional map of the Middle East, Afghanistan none the less exhibited, in extreme form, many of the political trends, and much of the political culture, of the Iranian and Arab world to its west: the ultimate destiny of that regime—a coup

---

[22] For general background on the Tudeh party, see Ervand Abrahamian, *Iran Between Two Revolutions* (Princeton: Princeton University Press, 1982), chs. 6 and 7. For a cogent dismissal of the argument that the Tudeh Party could have prevented the 1953 coup in Iran, see Ervand Abrahamian, *Khomeinism* (London: I. B. Tauris, 1993), 166 n. 67.

by frustrated middle-class army officers and intellectuals, out of which emerged an intolerant Jacobin regime, replete with murderous factionalism and cults of the personality—was one which would be immediately comprehensible to anyone in the region as a whole.[23]

The history of the Middle East and the Cold War reveals another striking limitation. Prior to the end of World War II the Russian revolution had had, despite hopes and fears on both sides, remarkably little impact on the region: from 1921 the treaties signed by Turkey, Iran, and Afghanistan with Moscow had effectively insulated those countries from Bolshevism, and the Arab world was almost totally unaffected. After 1945 the direct strategic impact of the USSR in the postwar period came, not at the height of the Cold War, but preceding it, in the clashes over Turkey and Iran up to 1946 and then, after the height of the Cold War, from the 1950s onwards, in the growing relationship to Arab nationalist states. For Stalin the Arab world itself was of little importance. The conflicts of the Middle East acquired an East–West dynamic, but this had less to do with the impact on the region of the Cold War than with the way in which inter-state conflicts (Arab–Israeli, Iran–Iraq) in the region, and endogenous revolutionary and nationalist forces, provided the context for greater East–West competition. The most important conflict in the region, between Israel and the Arab world, owed nothing in its origins to the Cold War: Stalin supported the establishment of the state of Israel as much as the West did, and it was only later that this inter-state and inter-ethnic conflict was fitted into the Cold War system.

A further corrective to any simple, 'globalist' view of the Cold War in the Middle East is the recognition of how far, even during the Cold War, the rivalries *within* each of the major blocs were played out in the Middle East. On the Western side, no other region of the world, developed or developing, comes close to the Middle East as the one in which the policies of the USA on the one hand and its European allies on the other diverged. The Middle East was, of course, the site of the greatest crisis of the Atlantic alliance in the whole Cold War period, Suez, but to this can be added divergences over Israel in 1948, Anglo-US rivalry in Iran in 1951 and 1952, competition and border clashes between respective British and American clients in the Arabian peninsula in the late 1950s (Buraimi, Saudi–South Arabian frontier), and the refusal of any NATO ally bar Portugal to allow US overflights to Israel during the 1973 Arab–Israeli war. One obvious explanation for this may be historical: the Middle East was always, prior to the Cold War, the

---

[23] See esp. Raja Anwar, *The Tragedy of Afghanistan* (London: Verso, 1988).

site of such rivalries, and continued to be so, not least because of competition over oil. Another explanation may, however, be that it was *precisely because of the relatively mild impact of the Cold War, and the comparative weakness of pro-Soviet mass movements*, that the Western powers could allow themselves the luxury of such intra-alliance competition. Since the end of the Cold War these divergences—on Israel, or Iran—have become even more evident.

On the communist side, a parallel and later more acrimonious process of inter-bloc conflict occurred: from the mid-1950s onwards, the Chinese saw the Middle East as providing occasions to denounce Soviet policy, first in a 'left' mode, according to which Moscow was selling out the struggling peoples of the region, 'contending' but also 'colluding' with the USA, and then, from the early 1970s onwards, in a 'right' mode, according to which the expansionist USSR was responsible for all the ills of the region.[24] Thus Peking, which in 1958 had attacked Moscow for inaction over Lebanon and Jordan and in 1967 denounced the 'revisionist' capitulation in the face of Israeli aggression, was by the mid-1970s congratulating Sadat on his expulsion of Soviet troops, and welcoming Princess Ashraf Pahlavi with invocations of the Great Silk Road. While in retrospect Chinese influence in the region was slight (China only became a significant actor in the Middle East when it began exporting intermediate-range missiles in the late 1980s), it did not always appear so, and part of the explanation for Soviet policy lay in its fear of a Chinese flanking movement along its southern frontier.

In this concern, Moscow was joined by some of the nationalist leaders of the Middle East, not least Nasser, who conceived a deep suspicion of China after its support for anti-Nasserist forces in Iraq in 1959. Indeed, this fear of China, rather than espousal of any neutral position between the blocs, may go a long way to explaining Egypt's enthusiasm for the founding of the Non-Aligned Movement in 1961. All three of the Third World leaders—Nasser, Tito, Nehru—who met at Brioni in Yugoslavia to set up the Non-Aligned Movement were at that time the objects of Chinese and allied radical hostility: Washington was suspicious of Soviet influence in the Non-Aligned Movement, but the hidden agenda of the NAM, then and for many years to come, was as much to preclude Chinese influence as to establish any genuinely independent bloc within Third World countries.[25]

---

[24] Fred Halliday, 'China and the Middle East', *Arab Affairs* (autumn 1990); Lillian Craig Harris, *China Considers the Middle East* (London: I. B. Tauris, 1993).

[25] This question is often obscured by inaccurate claims that the Non-Aligned Movement was founded at Bandung in 1955. Bandung was a conference not of 'non-aligned' but of 'Afro-

One can also correct, in the light of history, the belief prevalent in much of the Middle East that this was the region of the world which was above all affected by the Cold War. Two forms of corrective may be pertinent here, one that of comparison, the other that of evaluation. On the comparative side, one can argue that, compared not only to Europe but also to the Far East and, in many respects, to Southern Africa, the Middle East was *less* affected by the Cold War. It had a high incidence of inter-state conflict, notably in the Arab–Israeli context, and was the region into which the Great Powers poured much of their weapons exports to Third World countries; it was most certainly a region of heightened rhetorical and ideological confrontation. But the actual level of fighting, and of real ideological opposition, was in some respects less than in these other regions: the casualties of the Arab–Israeli dispute, extended over four decades, pale before those of Korea or Vietnam, Mozambique or Angola.[26] The level of direct Western military intervention was also far lower than in the Far East, southern Africa, or Central America. Equally, it can be argued that much of what happened in the Middle East was largely or wholly independent of the Cold War: where theorists of systemic domination, Cold War strategists, and alarmists of both blocs, or, more vulgarly, conspiracy theorists, saw everything as the outcome of decisions taken in Washington or Moscow, the reality was rather different. A dynamic of regional politics was often more important than any global process: an abstract contraposition of two positions, *either* 'system'-dominant, i.e. determined by the Cold War, *or* 'sub-system'-dominant, i.e. determined by regional politics, is an unsound way in which to grasp what is often a shifting determination. The least one can say is that, while the Cold War acted as a global context and as a contributor to many local processes, the imagery and analysis of the period based on exogenous determination could do with some retrospective correction.[27]

Asian' states and hence with Chinese participation (as well as that of Israel and Japan). It founded a separate Afro-Asian People's Solidarity Organization, which remained under Chinese influence until the latter part of the 1960s: the rivalry between the two groupings was most evident in 1965–6 when AAPSO tried, with Chinese support, to hold a conference in Algiers, at which the USSR was to be denounced by Third World participants. A combination of Soviet pressure and the Boumedienne coup that ousted Ben Bella prevented the conference from taking place. AAPSO was subsequently drawn into the Soviet orbit, with headquarters in Cairo.

[26] Total dead in the entire Arab–Israeli conflict, including related fighting in Lebanon, for the period 1947–89 is estimated to total 100,000–200,000, the great majority of them Arabs (total Israeli dead in this period were 9,600 military and around 2,200 civilians; Wilson, *The Disarmer's Handbook*, 38). Casualties in the Korean war were estimated at near 4 million, in Vietnam 2–3 million.

[27] Among many discussions see Bassam Tibi, *Conflict and War in the Middle East, 1967–91: Regional Dynamic and the Superpowers* (London: Macmillan, 1993), and Fawaz Gerges, *The*

THE END OF COLD WAR

The end of the Cold War in the region also had a particular character: indeed, it could be argued that if the Cold War is defined above all as the dominance of international politics by the Soviet–US competition, then it ended not in the late 1980s but a decade earlier, with the Iranian revolution in 1979 and the onset of the Iran–Iraq war in 1980. Whilst Moscow and Washington were in continued rivalry in the area, the main line of division and conflict was not that of the Cold War, but that between the Islamic revolutionary movement in Iran and the states opposed to it. Indeed, throughout the eight years of the Iran–Iraq war, the USSR and USA were supporting the same side, Baghdad, against Khomeini's revolutionary programme.

This said, it is possible to identify several important dimensions of the end of the Cold War that certainly had their impact on the Third World in general and on the Middle East in particular.

The end of strategic rivalry

The pragmatic cooperation of Moscow and Washington in the region, evident from 1980 *vis-à-vis* Iraq, became more comprehensive during the latter half of the 1980s, including above all the moves towards a joint international initiative on the Palestine question. With the end of significant Soviet arms deliveries to the region, and with Moscow in effect acting as a secondary supporter of US policy, the attempt to find a diplomatic solution to the most explosive regional issue was initiated. Yet the impact of the end of the Cold War was not limited to the Arab–Israeli region, since it had important consequences for Soviet and US policy in relation to other areas of conflict, among them the Iran–Iraq war, the Iraq–Kuwait crisis, and the unification of Yemen.[28]

Beyond these immediate policy adjustments, a broader change could be noted: the consequent strategic retreat of Russia not only visible in its reduced international, particularly military, role, but above all because of its geographical retrenchment, with the abandonment of Transcaucasia and Central Asia. At the end of 1991, and for the first time in two centuries, Russia did not have a common border with the Middle East. It therefore became a country with a

Superpowers and the Middle East: Regional and International Politics 1955–1967 (London: Westview, 1994).

[28] Galia Golan, *Moscow and the Middle East: New Thinking on Regional Conflict* (London: Pinter, 1992).

policy relationship more like that of Western European countries—Britain, France, Germany—and more dependent on whatever economic links it could build from afar. In the aftermath of the Soviet collapse military links continued, via arms sales, but the potential for Russian–Middle Eastern economic relations appeared to be limited.

For the US, the ending of the rivalry with the USSR, and the apparent lack of major challenges from other states, meant in the first instance that it could devote more attention to its core interest, the reliable flow of oil, to its own and allied economies, and at what were judged to be 'reasonable' prices. However, despite the fact that this involved above all a continuation of policies already established, some major changes could be observed: first, as a direct result of the 1990–1 Gulf War and of alarm about the long-run instability of the region, Bush and Baker took the decision to advance the Arab–Israeli peace process, breaking with the static support for Israel that had prevailed until then; secondly, as a result of the end of the Cold War, and the ending of the rivalry with the Soviet Union, US policy in the region became more selective as to which countries it chose to deal with—a process of 'marginalization' of countries deemed not to be intrinsically important, and to have lost whatever strategic position the Cold War invested them with. The question being increasingly asked, in Washington, as in Western European countries, was why a particular country 'mattered'—i.e. why the West should spend time cultivating it diplomatically or providing it with military or economic assistance. The assumption of regional states that they could attract the attention of the West, and particularly of the USA, because of strategic importance (often, even in the midst of the Cold War, exaggerated) was less valid than ever: some smaller countries were already in this category (e.g. Sudan), but so too were some larger ones (Israel, Iraq, Iran, Pakistan).

New regional configurations

The disappearance of Russia as a state adjacent to the Middle East was an event of major importance, particularly for the states of the norther tier—Turkey, Iran, Afghanistan. Where Russia would retain a vital interest, and where, if anything, the end of the Cold War created even greater uncertainty, was with regard to the new patterns of inter-state relationship emerging in the region. Three in particular merit attention: the relationship between Iran, Turkey, and Russia in central Asia, and Transcaucasia; the relations between Iran, Iraq, and the Gulf Cooperation Council (GCC); and those between Egypt, Syria, and Israel. The end of the Cold War meant that the old controls by the Great Powers, such as they were, and the element of predictability involved, had gone. Russia was particularly alarmed about the revival of Turkish power, something it had fought from the mid-eighteenth century until 1918 to reduce and oppose; and it was tempted to develop a pragmatic relationship with Iran, and even Saudi Arabia, to counter it. There was no reason to suppose that strategic relations between Russia and Turkey, or between Turkey and Iran, would necessarily become antagonistic, let alone lead to war. But these developments required considerable diplomatic management, not least because third parties—other states, or groups within states—tried to draw external powers in on their side. The pattern already discernible between the 1940s and the 1980s, whereby the regional and internal conflicts of the Middle East attracted international intervention, beyond that which external forces may initially have intended, were to some degree reproduced in this new, post-Cold War situation.

For the USA, the challenge was not so much a new strategic presence in the region, even after the war with Iraq, as that of developing policy to reconcile and work with the new strategic situation amongst Middle Eastern states. In some areas, Washington made progress—above all, in advancing the Arab–Israeli peace process, although at the time of writing it is too early to say what will come of this. More problematic was its relationship to the situation in the Gulf region, where no progress was made on finding a working solution to the problem of integrating the three major states into a new security system.[29] Iran was excluded from the post-Gulf War system being evolved by Washington and the GCC, and signalled its refusal to accept it: Washington still did not accept that there could be no security system in the Gulf without Iranian involvement. The Iranian leadership, meanwhile, unable to take serious political or economic initiatives within the country, resorted to demagogic initiatives in foreign policy that would only serve to isolate the country further. Iraq, too, remained outside the regional security system, contained by the Gulf War and its aftermath: yet while the US and its allies were able to isolate it, they developed no answer to the central question that predated the war, namely what relationship Iraq was to have with the other states in the region. Saudi Arabia had been the beneficiary of the war, but had squandered the advantage which this gave it, engaging in vindictive settling of accounts with Arab forces that disagreed with it (Yemen, Jordan, the Palestinians) and pursuing an oil

---

[29] A graphic picture of the longer-run military capabilities of two Gulf states in the 1990s is given in Anthony Cordesman, *Iran and Iraq: The Threat from the Northern Gulf* (London: Westview Press, 1994).

policy that pleased the West while failing to recognize how the root cause of Iraq's hostility to Kuwait was the low-price policy being pursued before August 1990. In other words, in the aftermath of the Cold War and with the disappearance of the Soviet challenge, neither the USA nor its main ally in the Gulf/peninsula region addressed the underlying causes of instability in the area.

Crisis of the development model

The discrediting of the Soviet model, in the Arab world as elsewhere in the Third World, did not have to await the final throes of *perestroika* and the crisis of August 1991. If in the 1950s and 1960s the Soviet model, adjusted to the particularities of 'Arab socialism', enjoyed immense prestige in the Arab world, it began to lose its preeminence from the late 1960s onwards, in the often-discussed 'crisis of the petty bourgeois regimes' that led not, as left analysis hoped, to a more radicalized Arab world but rather to the right-wing developments within Egypt under Sadat.[30] If in the Arab world state control of the economy has endured to an extent greater than elsewhere in the Third World, this is due above all to the combination of repressive state apparatuses with oil money, and to a combination of political pressures, rather than to any strictly economic rationale (Iraq, Syria, Libya, Algeria). In the People's Democratic Republic of Yemen, the most ambitious Arab experiment in socialism, it was evident from the late 1970s onwards that the path of socialist orientation did not run smoothly.

In this ideological vacuum, the Arab world and the region as a whole now find themselves in a contradictory situation. On the one hand, the old 'socialist' variant state-centred model may be discredited, and there are powerful forces, situated in the oil-producing states, favouring increased opening to the market. Yet in many states—Egypt is a prime example—strong popular and bureaucratic pressures prevent any abandonment of the state's role in the economy. Moreover, although the region has considerable oil reserves and income derived from this, it has, over the past decades, fallen comparatively behind in the international process of development. Agricultural self-sufficiency is down, and changes are limited by the great restrictions on water; Iran's repeated attempts, under Shah and Imam alike, to boost agricultural output and non-oil exports show how difficult these goals are to achieve. In a few, small-population Gulf states, per capita incomes may be high or at medium

---

[30] This story is well told in Mohamed Heikal, *Sphinx and Commissar: The Rise and Fall of Soviet Influence in the Middle East* (London: Collins, 1978).

levels, but this is largely due to oil revenues, directly earned or real-located by inter-state flows: if the most demanding contemporary index of development is taken, namely levels of exports of manufactured goods to OECD states, then no Middle East states, except Israel, Turkey, and Tunisia, are at all significant. Even the most prominent of other Middle East states—Egypt, Iran, Syria,—are at the same level as Mauritius, or in the Syrian case, Mali, and far behind such Third World states as Malaysia, the Philippines, and the majority of Latin American states.[31] Compare the record of a country like Singapore, thirty years ago poorer than most Middle Eastern states, which now produces half the computer hard discs in the world. State-centred development has failed, but in the race for competitive capitalist development the Middle East as a whole, apart from its oil revenues, has stagnated or receded, and is on most development criteria more comparable to Africa than to either Asia or Latin America.[32] Private foreign direct investment avoids the region. This may be the most dramatic of all the conclusions to be drawn from the Middle East's encounter with the Cold War: that the forty-year obsession with the East–West conflict has obscured the degree to which, in another, comparative and developmental, perspective the region has failed to take advantage of the opportunities presented to it and has fallen behind other areas of the Third World.

Democratization

The collapse of the Soviet system was accompanied by much speculation about the global triumph, actual or inevitable, of the Western conception of democracy and free market. At the ideological level there is much truth in the claim, articulated by Francis Fukuyama, that there is no global challenge, no internationally accepted alternative, to this model. But as a description of reality, or of the plausible future, it is mistaken and simplistic. First, few societies in the world even approximate to the free-market model of liberal theory—the development of Japan, Singapore, Korea, and before that of Germany and Britain, relied centrally on state intervention. Secondly, democratization is not a sudden, all or nothing, event but a gradual process, over decades and centuries: it took Britain and the

[31] Figures for manufactured exports to OECD states in 1991 were: Egypt ($793 m.), Iran ($676 m.), Syria ($53 m.). Malaysia, by contrast, exported goods worth $12,857 m. and the Philippines $5,637 m. (World Bank, *World Development Report*, Oxford: OUP, 1993, 270–1).
[32] For a dramatic analysis of this situation, see Thomas Naff, 'Hazards to Middle East Stability in the 1990s: Economics, Population and Water', in Phebe Marr and William Lewis (eds.), *Riding the Tiger: The Middle East Challenge After the Cold War* (Oxford: Westview Press, 1993).

USA 300 years and three internal wars between them to go from tyranny to the kind of qualified democracy they now have. Thirdly, no one can be certain that a democracy is reasonably stable unless it has been installed for at least a generation—many have appeared, only to disappear (Lebanon, Sri Lanka, Liberia, to name but three). Moreover, democracy can only function if certain preconditions exist: a reasonably functioning economy, a degree of tolerance, the prevalence of secular law, and, most importantly, a guarantee for different sectors in society that their interests will not be overridden.

In the Middle East context this process has begun but faces many obstacles: intolerance within societies, on ethnic, tribal, religious, and class grounds; profound economic difficulties; virulent anti-democratic ideologies, masquerading as religion; entrenched élites who, by taking control of economic resources, manipulate political and social processes; tensions between regional states that strengthen the repressive and military apparatuses in societies and prevent democratic evolution. The use made of regionalist and religious particularism by regional élites, such as those of GCC states, to deny the possibility of democratization is simply a means of justifying continued monopoly of power.[33] The revolutionary rhetoric of some other states— including Iran—serves similar purposes. At the same time, democratization will be a slow, sometimes contested, process, and it will take decades before it can be consolidated on a region-wide basis. In the past, regional dictatorships were invested with a spurious legitimacy by external powers—be it in myths of a particular 'Arab' democracy propagated in the West or in those of 'socialist democracy' propounded in Brezhnevite Russia. Now, a range of myths are being generated in the region, either to describe as 'democratic' processes that are still in their early stages, or to erect bogus objections to liberalization on the grounds that such a process is part of an 'imperialist' intervention.

CONCLUSION

The Cold War was important for the Middle East, as for other areas of the Third World, for a combination of military, diplomatic, and ideological reasons. If neither the 'systemic' nor the 'regional' approaches are, in their simpler forms, adequate explanations of this forty-year period, the foregoing argument, and the case studies that follow, should at least indicate the degree to which regional actors—

[33] On the human rights debate, see my *Islam and the Myth of Confrontation* (London: I. B. Tauris, 1996), ch. 5.

states, popular movements, military élites—could think and act independently of the two Great Powers. One can moreover argue that most of what occurred in the Middle East during this period could have taken place without the Cold War at all: the Arab–Israeli dispute, the rise of Arab nationalism, the emergence of the oil-producing states, the Islamist challenge to the Shah and other regimes—none of these was centrally reliant on the Cold War for its emergence and development. Yet the Cold War, like its precursors, the ages of liberalism and colonialism, provided an international context—a global military one, but also a global political and ideological one—that affected these processes in a variety of ways.

Perhaps the greatest function of the Cold War in the Middle East, as in Europe, was that it served as a distraction: it diverted attention from other, pressing problems within the societies concerned, and froze developments that might otherwise have accelerated. In this sense, the end of the Cold War becomes not an end of change but the beginning of a period in which the underlying realities can more clearly be grasped. Here two questions would appear to be central. The first, already mentioned, is that of the political character of the regimes present in the region, and their ability to meet some at least of the aspirations of their peoples: the crisis of the first generation of post-independence regimes, be this in Iran, Algeria, or Egypt, offers little encouragement on that score.

The other central issue facing the Middle East, as with other areas of the Third World, is that of economic and political development and of the opportunities presented by the new international economic and strategic climate. In a longer perspective, this has been the major question confronting the region for the past two or three centuries. In the past century, two major attempts to resolve the question of development, one from the right and one from the left, have been generated from within more developed states—colonialism (1870–1960) and communism (1917–91). Both would now appear to have failed. The question now posed is how far, freed of these two kinds of false answer, the countries of the Third World can make best use of the advantages presented to them, resolve their own internal differences, and make economic and political progress in the years ahead.

2

Egypt

ADEED DAWISHA

That the Cold War had an impact on Egypt's domestic and international behaviour is without doubt. After all, no behaviour occurs in isolation, and Egyptian leaders could hardly pursue their policies without being influenced consciously or subconsciously by the world beyond their borders. Thus, Egypt's policies, like the policies of any other state, are determined at least as much by its own needs and the opportunities it is able to grasp as by the constraints imposed on it by the international system, the main feature of which was the Cold War.

Egypt is a state whose centrality in the Arab world is unquestioned. A number of objective and permanent factors underpin this leadership role. But, as this chapter will show, Egypt's leadership was enhanced by the state's intense activism in the region, especially during the Nasserist era. And there can be little doubt that, at least in the regional context, the country would not have played such an important role had it not been for the politics of the Cold War.

EGYPT'S CENTRALITY

Egypt has been, and continues to be, the most important Arab country. Egypt lies between the Eastern and Western parts of the Arab world, and for centuries has constituted the bridge between the two sectors. Egypt has, in Cairo and Alexandria, the largest city and the largest seaport in the Arab world; and because of its strategic location it has developed extensive contacts with the three continents of Africa, Asia, and Europe. Unlike other Arab states, whose legal status rested on artificial boundaries drawn up by old colonial powers, Egypt has been a distinct geographical unit for over 4,000 years.

These objective facts of Egypt's geography were firmly implanted in the perceptions of all of Egypt's leaders. But these perceptions found vigorous expression particularly during the Nasserist era (1952–70), resulting in a highly activist posture regionally and globally. Mohamed Heikal, President Nasser's eloquent spokesman, once wrote: 'Because of its location . . . Egypt has a special position. This position constantly links it with the surrounding region, and brings it into the arena of world conflict.'[1]

Supplementing its geographical location, Egypt has the largest population in the Arab world, which elevates her to the forefront of military potential. It was accepted throughout the Arab world that no Arab country, nor any constellation of Arab countries, could wage war against Israel without Egypt. The Israelis agreed with this assessment. Short of a comprehensive peace with all the Arabs, neutralizing Egypt was the next best thing for the Israelis.

Egypt's population also provides her with a huge middle class that has helped her cultural domination of her region. Throughout the 1950s, 1960s, and 1970s, but admittedly less so in the 1980s, Egyptian books, journals, magazines, and newspapers flooded Arab cities. Egyptian teachers were conspicuous in every part of the Arab world, and tens of thousands of Arab students studied in Egyptian academic institutions. And when it came to art and leisure in the Arab world, only the films, music, and television productions of Egypt could compete with Western offerings.

Because of all of this, Egypt has traditionally *behaved* as the leader of the Arab world. As has been argued, this role was articulated, and acted upon, most vigorously during the Nasserist era. But even when Egypt withdrew from Arab politics after the signing of the peace treaty with Israel in 1979, it did not consciously relinquish its leadership role. Nasser's successor, Anwar Sadat, saw this leadership as a structural 'property that could not be challenged or taken away. Consequently, he did not feel the need to pursue an activist Arab policy to maintain this leadership.'[2] Indeed, Egypt's signing of the treaty itself testified to its centrality. No other Arab country could dare do such a thing. And under the contemporary presidency of Hosni Mubarak, Egypt, with less bravado than in the Nasserist era, again acts as, and is perceived as being, the leading country in the region.

Perhaps Egypt's role is best encapsulated in a comment once made by Saudi Arabia's late King Faisal to President Nasser. The king told Egypt's leader that his father, King Abdul Aziz, had given his children one piece of advice: 'He told us to pay attention to Egypt's role, for without Egypt the Arabs throughout history would have been without value.'[3]

[1] *Al-Ahram* (Cairo), 11 Feb. 1966.

[2] Ali E. Hillal Dessouki, 'The Primacy of Economics: The Foreign Policy of Egypt', in Bahgat Korany and Ali E. Hillal Dessouki, *The Foreign Policy of Arab States* (Boulder, Colo.: Westview Press, 1984), 130.

[3] *Al-Ahram*, 10 Jan. 1970.

THE EGYPTIAN REVOLUTION AND
DOMESTIC POLITICS

There can be no doubt that Egypt's centrality in the region received a major boost with the Nasserist revolution of 1952. If, prior to the revolution, Egypt's leadership was assumed, it became a pronounced goal as well as a vital capability of Egypt's foreign policy in the post-revolutionary period. The orientation of Egypt's foreign policy under Nasser was regionally interventionist and globally activist. As we shall see later, the Cold War had much to do with that. It is also true, however, that some of the major changes that occurred in Egypt as a result of the Nasserist revolution had little, if anything, to do with the Cold War.

Take the abolition of parliament and political parties. This happened as a result of a number of factors, almost none of which had anything to do with the Cold War. First, the army officers were utterly disillusioned with the political institutions of the monarchical regime, which they perceived as having been utterly corrupt, geared to serve the interests of a small and privileged section of society. Second, Nasser and the army believed that the monarchical regime had so debilitated the country that to resurrect it they needed a centralized, mobilizational regime that would not be hindered by a time-consuming and obstructionist opposition. Thirdly, and related to the above, the officers worried that the enemies of the revolution, feudalists and the moneyed classes, would use the parliament and political parties to undermine and destabilize the revolutionary regime.

The Cold War, therefore, had little to do with the creation of Egypt's authoritarian system under Nasser. What it did do, however, was to become an element of that system's legitimation. Nasser constantly used the Cold War and the ambitions of its various antagonists as a reason for not allowing a multi-party system or a truly functioning parliament. Thus, he saw 'no advantage for Egypt in the establishment of a parliament in which men serving the interests of . . . London, Washington, or Moscow would sit masquerading as Egyptians'.[4] Similarly, he observed that if a multi-party system were to be allowed, there would be 'a party acting as an agent to the American CIA, another upholding British interests, and a third working for the Soviets.'[5]

The same kind of argument could be applied to the adoption of a socialist economic system, which was a function of power

[4] *New York Times*, 5 May 1955.   [5] *Egyptian Gazette*, 9 May 1966.

considerations rather than of infatuation with the Soviet model. It is instructive to remember that, while the revolutionary officers immediately enacted the agrarian reform law in which large tracts of lands were divided into smaller lots and given to tenant farmers and landless peasants, the same officers undertook the far from socialist policy of offering liberal incentives for business and industry, enacting laws that encouraged foreign capital, allowed tax exemptions for investments, lowered custom dues on imports, etc.[6]

While on the surface this may seem contradictory, in fact it was not. The feudalists were perceived as the backbone of support for the ancien regime. They epitomized the very essence of the term 'reactionary', a label that the officers would slap on all alleged enemies of the revolution. Businessmen and industrialists, on the other hand, were seen as modernizers. They were generally urban and mostly Westernized, supposedly on the same wavelength as the 'modernizing military'. If Egypt were to catch up with the advanced industrial world, it would do it on the backs not of the reactionary feudalists but of the modernizing business and industrial class in alliance with the military officers.

Initially, therefore, the Cold War had little impact on the economic policies of the revolutionary regime. But in the following decade or so, the Cold War was indeed a factor in the rapid growth of socialism in Egypt. The process was gradual, beginning in 1955 after the pro-Western Iraqi and Turkish regimes signed the Baghdad Pact, continued through the Suez crisis and the gathering estrangement of Egypt from the Western powers, and reached its zenith in 1961 after the break-up of the United Arab Republic (UAR). Nasser was convinced that the Syrian secession from the UAR was engineered by business and industrial interests hostile to socialism and aided by external pro-Western forces alarmed by Egypt's improving relations with, and increasing dependence on, the Soviet Union.

So in a broad sweep against the enemies of the revolution and their 'imperialist' Western backers, the Nasserist regime nationalized all financial institutions and industrial concerns, and assumed partownership and/or direct control over external trade and large-scale corporate industry. These measures were a culmination of a nationalization process that contributed to a fundamental socio-economic transformation of the country.

---

[6] P. J. Vatikiotis, *The History of Modern Egypt: From Muhammad Ali to Mubarak* (Baltimore: Johns Hopkins University Press, 1991), 394.

THE REVOLUTIONARY REGIME AND REGIONAL POLITICS

As we have seen, Egypt is the dominant country in the Arab world. Its attributes are many, its capabilities immense. But by their very nature, these remain the elements for *potential* power. In the first two years of the revolution, the regime focused so much of its attention on its domestic environment that it showed little interest in the Arab world, except for Sudan and the question of the 'unity of the Nile valley'. Yet from 1955 Egypt turned its attention to the Arab world, adopting a vigorously activist stance, fully utilizing its capabilities, and thus transforming its potential power into real power. The catalyst for this dramatic change in posture and policy was the Baghdad Pact, one of the links in the anti-Soviet chain of alliances that the West was endeavouring to build.

As early as May 1953 the American secretary of state, John Foster Dulles, realizing the centrality and weight of Egypt in the Middle East, visited Cairo to muster support for a Western defence alliance to counter communist threats to the region. Egypt's response was at best lukewarm. Nasser and other members of the leadership could not take seriously the alleged threat from a power that was over 5,000 miles away, a power that, unlike Western states, traditionally had not been politically or militarily involved in the region. On the contrary, they perceived the American plan as a new effort to continue in a different form the colonialism under which the region had languished. Dulles thus was told that Egypt had no desire to take sides in the Cold War or to join any alliance.

Rebuffed by the Egyptians, Dulles focused his attention on the pro-Western government of Nuri al-Said in Baghdad, bringing the endeavour to fruition with the signing of the Baghdad Pact in January 1955. The Baghdad Pact had the immediate effect of detonating latent regional rivalries, and putting a Cold War label on inter-Arab politics. The Baghdad Pact also allowed for the entry of the Soviet Union into Middle Eastern politics. Dismayed by Nasser's opposition to the Baghdad Pact, Dulles refused an Egyptian arms request, a response that prompted the Egyptian leader to take his request to the Soviet Union. This led to the Czech arms deal of September 1955.

Western obsession with the Soviet Union and 'international communism' blinded Western leaders to the complexity of local conditions. Nationalist and anti-colonialist sentiments were interpreted as manifestations of communist leanings. Particularly galling to Dulles was Nasser's proclaimed neutrality in the conflict between the super-powers. Dulles considered neutrality between good and evil as inherently evil.

So when Nasser asked for financial help to build the Aswan Dam, the United States, Britain, and the World Bank offered to help, but attached to the offer several conditions which Nasser considered to be tantamount to foreign control of Egypt's economy. Nasser's hesitation was interpreted by Dulles and Britain's prime minister, Sir Anthony Eden, as a surreptitious effort to negotiate a separate deal with the Soviet Union. In July 1956 Dulles announced that the US would withdraw its offer of assistance. Nasser retaliated quickly and decisively. He declared that since the Western powers refused to finance the dam, Egypt was compelled to raise her own money. This it could only achieve by nationalizing the Suez Canal Company.

One thing evident from the unfolding of these events is the inter-active relationship between the Cold War on the one hand and Egypt's regional policies on the other. For the US and the West, dealing with the region through an essentially Cold War prism brought about two unexpected results that would prove highly detrimental to Western interests.

First, as the West's relationship with Nasser grew worse, Egypt turned increasingly to the Soviet Union, an opportunity that Moscow heartily welcomed. By 1954 the West had succeeded in constructing two alliances against the Soviet Union and 'international communism', the North Atlantic Treaty Organization (NATO) and the Southeast Asian Treaty Organization (SEATO). The Baghdad Pact, later to be expanded and renamed the Central Treaty Organization (CENTO), was the central link in the chain that would complete the effort to contain the global communist forces. For Moscow, the best way to undermine the Baghdad Pact was to create a presence for itself in the area. And to do this in Egypt, the most prestigious and dominant state, was especially fortuitous. The Baghdad Pact not only was denied Egypt, the undisputed jewel in the crown, but, because of Egypt's weight, was denied other countries as well. Jordan and Lebanon, for example, were considered certain to join the Western-sponsored alliance until Egypt stepped in with a propaganda barrage that forced the two countries to shy away from the pact, never to contemplate joining it again.[7] And indeed, shortly after the Iraqi revolution of July 1958, Iraq itself withdrew from the pact, making it little more than a meaningless entity.

[7] The events are described in A. I. Dawisha, *Egypt in the Arab World: The Elements of Foreign Policy* (London: Macmillan, 1976), 11–14.

The irony for the West was that this undoubted Soviet success came about not so much because of Moscow's intense activism in the region but more through the West's persistence in viewing regional politics from a global, essentially Cold War, perspective. One aspect of this view was the notion that the 'vacuum' left by the withdrawal of the old colonial powers, Britain and France, from the area could not be filled by a local actor, or a combination of local actors, but only by a global power, namely the Soviet Union or the United States. This was the reasoning behind the Eisenhower Doctrine, articulated by the US president in January 1957. The doctrine proclaimed the readiness of the US to extend assistance, including the dispatch of military forces, to any country requesting aid 'against overt armed aggression from any nation controlled by International Communism'.[8] The doctrine was a less than veiled threat against Egypt and Syria, two countries which the people of the area considered to be nationalist, independently minded—certainly not communist—states. The Eisenhower Doctrine, therefore, served only to heighten local suspicions of Washington's determination to supplant Britain and France as the new imperial power in the Middle East. The net result was to accelerate the drive to attain Soviet assistance, and to encourage a Soviet presence, in order to stop this 'new imperialism'.

The second result of the Western effort to bring Cold War politics into the Middle East was the rise of Nasser as the foremost political leader in the area. The West's decision to 'punish' and undermine Nasser for his reluctance to join Western alliances proved utterly counterproductive. Contrary to Western expectations, which were nourished by local allies such as Iraq's Nuri al-Said, Nasser moved from one great success to another. The effective assault on the Baghdad Pact, the Czech arms deal, the nationalization of the Suez Canal Company, his perceived 'victory' over Britain, France, and Israel in the Suez war, the creation of the United Arab Republic, and the Iraqi revolution were all manifestations not only of Nasser's increased power and reach in the area but also of the diminishing influence of the West.

The point here is that all this might not have happened had it not been for the Cold War. The Cold War resurrected and nourished latent local rivalries, thus creating the conditions for the political dominance of Nasser and Egypt. Perhaps more importantly, Nasser might not have been able to achieve this dominance had he not had access to the other pole in the Cold War relationship. For a while

---

[8] P. E. Zinner (ed.), *Documents on American Foreign Relations, 1957* (New York: Harper & Brothers, 1958), 201.

there was almost total convergence of Egyptian and Soviet interests. The Soviet wanted a presence in the Middle East; the Egyptians pursued a goal of political dominance; and both goals were served by the onslaught against the West and its allies in the area.

During the 1960s, until June 1967, this state of affairs remained more or less constant. The Soviet Union and its allies, Egypt, Iraq, and Syria, kept the pro-Western states on the defensive. Republicanism, nationalism, and socialism had become the dominant ideological symbols, commanding wide popular support among the Arab masses. And Nasser, though his aura had lost a little of its earlier lustre, was still the only Arab leader whose appeal extended far beyond the borders of his country. There were, of course, setbacks. The collapse of the UAR was one such failure. Yet another was Egypt's long and debilitating military intervention in the Yemen. But the one major foreign policy disaster that would fundamentally alter the regional power configurations, as well as the region's interactive relationship with the politics of the Cold War, was Israel's extraordinary victory over Egypt and other Arab states in the Six-Day War of June 1967.

THE 1967 WAR

The superpowers had little to do with the immediate causes of the crisis that led to the 1967 war. The immediate origins of the crisis were regionally generated. It probably could be traced to the accession to power in 1966 of a Marxist-oriented, neo-Ba'athist leadership in Syria committed to the liberation of Palestine through a revolutionary struggle on the Vietnam model. Consequently, the new Syrian leaders extended their wholehearted support to the infant Palestinian guerrilla groups. As a result of increasing guerrilla activity, the level of violence on the Syrian–Israeli border steadily rose throughout 1966 and the early part of 1967. Israeli retaliation gained in intensity: in April 1967 Israeli pilots shot down six Syrian MIGs, and Damascus was subjected to the indignity of an air parade staged by the victorious Israelis. The temperature continued to rise throughout May, as the Israelis and Syrians hurled recriminations, accusations, and threats at each other.

Nasser's entry into the fray was a foregone conclusion. Egypt was the senior partner among the revolutionary and socialist states. Egypt was the leader of radical Arab nationalism, and Nasser was the keeper of its conscience. If Syria were to be crushed by the Israelis, as it certainly would have been, it would be Egypt's ignominy as much as Syria's. Consequently, at the end of May, Egyptian troops reoccupied positions hitherto held by UN forces, including Sharm al-Sheikh, and closed the Straits of Tiran to Israeli shipping. This show of force was designed to bolster the Syrians and to warn the Israelis that Syria did not stand alone. It is also possible that Nasser saw political benefits for Egypt in the unfolding events. If the crisis were to peter out with his troops in control of all of Sinai, he would score an impressive political victory that would balance the failures of the UAR and the Yemen war.

What is certain is that Nasser did not contemplate war. He certainly was warned against it in no uncertain terms by his Soviet allies, who were unwilling to be dragged into an inadvertent nuclear confrontation with the US, and who spent the last week of May and early June trying to avert war through intense diplomacy with Egypt and Syria on the one hand and the US on the other.[9] But the Israelis had irrevocably made up their minds.

The immediate aftermath of the war found Egypt in an almost hopeless position. Apart from the nearly total decimation of her armed forces, her economy was in desperate condition. The Suez Canal was closed, the oil fields in Sinai were under Israeli control, and a massive migration to an already overpopulated Cairo from the canal cities of Suez, Ismailia, Port Said, and elsewhere was beginning to gather momentum. These domestic liabilities, plus the humiliating presence of Israeli troops on Egyptian soil, necessitated a change in Nasser's regional and global policies.

Regionally, Egypt gradually abandoned its revolutionary posture and its intrusive behaviour. This occurred because the country's economic well-being became dependent on the financial assistance of oil-rich but conservative and pro-Western Arab states; the very states against which Nasser's radical policies had been directed.

Globally, while Egypt continued to pay lip-service to the concept and policy of 'non-alignment', in reality the country was compelled to finally abandon neutrality, turning exclusively to the Soviet Union for military support and protection. In fact, Egypt's need for security was so urgent that Nasser was prepared to sacrifice the hitherto sacrosanct ideal of Egyptian sovereignty by deciding to offer the Soviet Union a substantial physical presence in Egypt.[10]

[9] See Karen Dawisha, *Soviet Foreign Policy Toward Egypt* (London: Macmillan, 1979), 40–1.

[10] *The USSR and the Third World* (London: Central Asian Research Centre, 1972), 31.

THE PINNACLE OF SOVIET INFLUENCE

The process began immediately after the end of the war, when all of Egypt literally lay undefended against, and open to, Israel's victorious army. By November 1967 the Egyptian armed forces had been completely reorganized by the Soviets, with over 1,500 Soviet military advisers attached to all Egyptian military units above brigade level. All Egyptian combat aircraft, almost totally decimated by the Israelis during the war, were replaced by the Soviets. Soviet warships arrived in Alexandria and Port Said, with the Egyptian authorities granting them extensive autonomous facilities. This coincided with Soviet strategic objectives, which increasingly considered the Mediterranean to be a legitimate sphere for Soviet activity. Moscow justified its policy in the following terms:

Our state, which is, as is known, a Black Sea and consequently also a Mediterranean power, could not remain indifferent to the intrigues organized directly adjacent to the borders of the USSR and other socialist countries. No one can be allowed to turn the Mediterranean into a breeding ground for a war that could plunge mankind into the abyss of a world-wide nuclear missile catastrophe. The presence of Soviet vessels in the Mediterranean serves this lofty ideal.[11]

A year after the war, the Soviets had rebuilt Egypt's armed forces sufficiently to allow Nasser to engage in a limited military action against the Israelis, which took the form of intermittent artillery duels across the canal. By March 1969, however, the Egyptians felt confident enough to escalate the bombardment dramatically. The Egyptian leaders labelled this their 'war of attrition'. The Israeli air force answered by repeated bombing of Egyptian positions, but when after nine months this policy did not stop the Egyptian bombardment, the Israelis decided to attack targets deep inside Egypt. Egypt's military response to Israel's 'deep penetration bombing' depended heavily on, and was led by, the Soviets. Soviet technicians manned SAM-3 missiles, and Soviet pilots began to fly operationally against the Israeli air force.

Nor did the Russians make much of an effort to hide their engagement in active operations. On their arrival in Egypt, the SAM-3 missiles were driven openly through city streets, with their Russian crews waving openly to people, and Soviet pilots, patrolling the Egyptian skies, communicated openly on their intercoms in Russian. Indeed, it was this new, perilous possibility of a clash with the Russians that

---

[11] Quoted in Dawisha, *Soviet Foreign Policy Toward Egypt*, 45–6.

forced Israeli leaders in the spring of 1970 to halt all aerial operations over Egypt. This moved Nasser publicly to thank the Soviet Union for 'helping us safeguard our skies against the American-made phantom planes'.[12]

By the summer of 1970 it had become evident that nowhere outside the socialist bloc was the Soviet Union so actively and massively engaged as it was in Egypt; an engagement that, in the Cold War configuration, placed Egypt firmly in the Soviet camp, making the country a client of the communist superpower. Indeed, from then on and right until the end of the Cold War in the late 1980s, Egypt would lose its 'neutralist and non-aligned' stance. It would ally itself closely to one or the other of the two superpowers, first to the Soviet Union, then, under the presidency of Anwar Sadat, to the United States.

EGYPT UNDER ANWAR SADAT

Egypt's policy change toward reliance on the US did not come abruptly with the ascendancy of Sadat to the presidency. Initially Sadat seemed to follow in his predecessor's footsteps. Indeed, in May 1971 he went further than Nasser by signing the Soviet–Egyptian Treaty of Friendship and Cooperation. Moscow benefited by gaining Egypt's contractual commitment not to veer from the path of socialism, and not to enter into any alliance or take part in any grouping of states directed against the Soviet Union. For the Soviet leaders this was an insurance policy against any possible *rapprochement* between Egypt and the US.

To Sadat it was not ideology, nor notions of global Cold War strategy, that impelled him to sign the treaty; it was more a matter of his own political survival. Sadat, initially considered weak and indecisive, known as *Bikbashi Aywa* (Colonel Yes-Man), and seemingly lacking in charisma, could not embark on a major shift in Egypt's economic and foreign policies without establishing a legitimacy that was independent of Nasser's. For him to survive and take control of Egypt, he needed to emerge from under the towering shadow of his charismatic predecessor. This he could do only if he were to prove to his population that he was a successful and meritorious leader, a man worthy of their support. Sadat soon realized that such an image transformation would occur only if he were to reverse the disastrous consequences of the Six-Day War by engaging the

---

[12] American University of Beirut, *Arab Political Documents, 1970* [in Arabic], 270.

Israelis in a new conflict from which he would emerge victorious, even if in a limited way. Without this, his political survival would be in doubt. Sadat, therefore, needed to guarantee the continuation of Soviet economic and military support in his stand against Israel. He thought he received this guarantee by signing the treaty.

But doubts soon emerged. During 1972 there were frequent and intensive negotiations between the two superpowers over limiting strategic arms (soon to come to fruition in the SALT-1 and ABM treaties). Sadat became concerned that the Soviet preoccupation with *détente* might lead to a Soviet–American condominium designed to maintain the status quo and prevent the outbreak of war in the region. And this concern did not lack reason, for while the Soviets naturally wanted to maintain their presence and influence in Egypt, they continued to be reluctant to be drawn into a possible nuclear confrontation with the US as a result of some rash military action by Sadat or another Arab leader. But what was beneficial for Moscow happened to be highly detrimental to the political interests of the Egyptian leader. And when Sadat's fears seemed confirmed by Brezhnev's prevarication over the supply of long-awaited offensive weapons, he decided in July 1972 to expel Soviet personnel from Egypt.

Within less than two weeks, the Soviet presence in Egypt was reduced from 15,000 to under 1,000. Most of the advanced weaponry under Soviet control was also withdrawn. A month later both countries recalled their ambassadors, and relations reached a low ebb. While Sadat talked about self-reliance, he also made initial enquiries in Western Europe and the US for purchasing arms. He also appeared to move closer to Saudi Arabia, and began to talk about encouraging the private sector and attracting foreign capital.

Sadat knew that his chances of getting arms from the West to fight Israel were minimal. He also knew that this was not the time for a fundamental restructuring of the economy. But these were never his goals. What he had achieved was to serve notice on Moscow not to take him for granted; not to assume that he was bereft of options, that because he was so closely allied to the Soviets, he had lost all freedom to exploit and manipulate the competitive elements of the Cold War equation. The Soviets were impressed. In October, in a meeting in Moscow with the Egyptian prime minister, Soviet Premier Aleksei Kosygin proclaimed that the opponents of Soviet–Egyptian friendship

are circulating the invention that the Soviet Union had allegedly reached some 'collusion' with the imperialists concerning a Middle East settlement to the detriment of the interests of the Arab countries. We emphatically reject such inventions. The Soviet Union has one foreign policy, one political line in Middle Eastern affairs. This is a line of all-out support for the Arab peoples and progressive regimes in the Arab countries in their struggle against Israel's aggression.[13]

Relations soon improved, and arms began to flow into Egypt once again, allowing the Egyptian high command to prepare for war.

THE 1973 OCTOBER WAR

The Egyptian–Syrian attack began on 6 October 1973. Very quickly both armies made significant gains, with the Syrians pushing back the Israelis on the Golan and the Egyptians crossing the Suez Canal and breaking through Israeli positions at the Bar Lev line on the canal's east bank. The two superpowers endeavoured to tread a thin line of actively propping up their respective allies while avoiding any damage to *détente*.

This situation changed during the second week of the war. The Syrian offensive had been successfully stopped and repulsed, allowing the Israelis to shift their troops and put their full military weight on to the Egyptian front. By 16 October Israeli forces were beginning to cross to the west bank of the Canal in an effort to cut off the Egyptian forces on the east bank. It was then that the Soviet union acted to save its client.

Kosygin asked Henry Kissinger to come to Moscow for urgent consultations. The negotiations resulted in an agreement for a 'cease-fire in place', which Kissinger pressured the Israelis to accept. But when the Israelis broke the ceasefire and continued their advance, encircling Egypt's Third Army and putting the whole Egyptian military effort into great jeopardy, Brezhnev, in a note to Nixon, threatened to take 'the appropriate steps unilaterally'[14] if the US did not stop its client from further committing violations. This threat was accompanied by troop movements, deemed serious enough for the Americans to put their forces on a nuclear alert, and to make certain that their Israeli clients complied with the ceasefire.

Thus ended an episode of Cold War diplomacy in which the superpowers were almost pushed to the brink by a local conflict, but had enough diplomatic wherewithal, and just about enough control over their clients, to draw away from the brink, leaving both clients in reasonably advantageous bargaining positions.

---

[13] *The USSR and the Third World*, 514.
[14] Quoted in Dawisha, *Soviet Foreign Policy Toward Egypt*, 68.

The Soviets essentially saved Egypt. But if they thought they would be rewarded by increased Egyptian dependence, they were hugely mistaken. What the 1973 October war did was to give Sadat the legitimacy he had sought since coming to power three years earlier. Egyptian military successes (particularly in relation to the disaster of 1967), magnified many times over, sometimes to ludicrous levels, by Egypt's propaganda machine, propelled Sadat into the position of undisputed leader. He was now *batal al-ubur*, the hero of the crossing, a man who had exploded the myth of Israeli invincibility and who now could steer the ship of state in any direction he saw fit.

This was bad news for the Soviets. Sadat had become convinced that Egypt could not sustain an ongoing conflict with Israel, and that the only way to achieve equitable peace with the Jewish state was through the Americans, who after all were rich enough to reward Egypt handsomely for its labour. Moreover, unlike Nasser, Sadat never cared for the frugal life, and was therefore not psychologically attuned to the austere puritanism of the socialist way of life. The 1973 October war gave Sadat the chance to take Egypt and defect to the other side of the Cold War configuration, a decision that did not lack support among Egyptians, resentful of the long years of perceived Soviet dominance of their economy and society.

THE AMERICAN ERA

Egypt's political, economic, and ideological transformation began immediately after the conclusion of the October 1973 war. When external diplomatic intercession was needed to diffuse the potentially explosive situation on the war front, it was not to the Russians, but to America and its secretary of state, Henry Kissinger, that Sadat would turn. Kissinger embarked on his famed 'shuttle diplomacy', producing the first disengagement agreement between Israel and Egypt in January 1974. The Soviets and Syrians, who preferred a comprehensive agreement and who were suspicious of Kissinger's step-by-step approach, were dismayed. But there was little they could do. Sadat's commitment to the total transformation of Egypt coincided with Kissinger's determination to score a famous Cold War victory by wresting the most important Arab country away from the socialist camp.

Egyptian–American relations improved rapidly and substantially. In March 1974 diplomatic relations were resumed, and American businessmen began to explore business opportunities in Egypt. A year later, through Kissinger's labour, the Suez Canal was reopened and Egypt and Israel signed a three-year disengagement agreement, in which the Israelis agreed to withdraw from the Sinai passes. Needless to say, the Soviets, who continued to insist on multilateral negotiations, were being gradually marginalized by the new Sadat–Kissinger condominium.

Simultaneously, Sadat proceeded to dismantle Egypt's socialist monolith by inaugurating his *Al-Infitah*, the open-door economic policy, whose main goal was to attract foreign investment into Egypt under very favourable conditions. America was bound to be pleased, not only because of the new investment opportunities but also because of the resultant growth of the private sector in Egypt's economy.

The dramatic improvement in American–Egyptian relations was accompanied by an equally dramatic worsening of Egyptian–Soviet relations. Sadat complained bitterly about Moscow's prevarication in supplying arms to Egypt. In this he had the support of his army officers, not only because of their urgent need for arms but also because of their dislike of the Soviets, who were characterized as 'brusque, harsh, frequently arrogant and usually unwilling to believe that anyone has anything to teach them'.[15] Sadat also bitterly criticized the Soviets for their refusal to reschedule Egyptian debts, which by 1976 amounted to over $11,000 million. On both counts, it seems that Moscow saw no reason to accommodate Egypt, while its leader was dismantling socialism and vigorously courting the United States.

The inevitable conclusion occurred on 14 March 1976, when Sadat in a speech to the parliament unilaterally abrogated the Soviet–Egyptian treaty of 1971. In addition to the Soviets' refusal to supply arms and reschedule debts, Sadat also accused Moscow of opposing his peace initiative and his new economic policy. Moreover, it was a matter of Egyptian honour and prestige:

The Soviets thought at one time that they had Egypt in their pocket, and the world has come to think of the Soviet Union as our guardian. I wanted to tell the Russians that the will of Egypt was entirely Egyptian; I wanted to tell the whole world that we are always our own master. Whoever wished to talk to us would come over and do it, rather than approach the Soviet Union.[16]

The abrogation of the treaty was followed in December 1977, after Sadat's visit to Israel, by the closure of Soviet consulates in Alexandria, Port Said, and Aswan. And the process culminated in September 1981 with the closure of the Soviet embassy in Cairo.

---

[15] Quoted in Dessouki, 'The Primacy of Economics', 137.   [16] Quoted ibid. 136.

By this time, not only was Egypt a full client of the United States, but it also had signed, in March 1979, a separate peace treaty with Israel that isolated it from the Arab world, its natural political environment which it had led for so long. Moreover, the introduction of free-market economic policies had not alleviated Egypt's economic woes. Instead, it succeeded only in considerably widening the gulf between the rich and poor. Sadat's policies may have made him the darling of the Western media, but domestically they contributed to the simmering discontent that was to eventually lead to his assassination on 6 October 1981.

THE MUBARAK ERA

Whether able to play one superpower against the other, or wholly allied to one or the other of the superpowers, Egypt was always a coveted prize because of its central and dominant position in the Arab world. As long as it was involved in Arab politics, its global patron could hope to exert influence beyond the borders of Egypt. And in a relationship that was mutually advantageous, Egypt itself would hope to reap some of the fruit of its patron's increased influence in the region. Essentially, that had been the essence of the interactive process between Egypt and the politics of the Cold War.

By the time Mubarak ascended to the presidency, Egypt no longer possessed this kind of leverage. This was the legacy his predecessor had left him. In response to Egypt's peace treaty with Israel, the Arab states broke off diplomatic relations with Cairo, suspended Egypt's membership of the Arab League, and transferred the League's headquarters from Cairo to Tunis.

The one valuable card which Mubarak possessed was Egypt's peace with Israel. That netted him over $2.5 billion of American military and economic aid. But unlike past aid patterns, this money was relatively independent of the Cold War relationship. It was given, not to seduce Egypt away from the Soviet Union, but purely to encourage it to maintain peaceful relations with Israel. Even so, it tied Mubarak inexorably to the source of the money, namely Washington. This was because of his urgent need for massive injections of capital.

By the mid-1980s Egypt's population was just under 50 million, its external debt was nearly $40 billion, and its budget deficit had gone beyond $6 billion. These economic woes contributed to widespread social discontent, which was exploited by Islamic militants. During the second half of the 1980s (i.e. the last years of the Cold War) the Islamists mounted a semi-insurrection in Egypt.

Consequently, Mubarak made few moves in the issue-area of the Cold War and superpower rivalry. He had become totally dependent on the US and the West, and did not even have diplomatic relations with the other superpower. He had been generally excluded from the Arab world, leaving him with little leverage over it. And he was burdened by mammoth economic problems that led to the kind of violent social discontent to which he had to concentrate much of his attention.

This highly constraining state of affairs persisted until the late 1980s, when a number of significant changes occurred. In 1987 normal bilateral relations between Cairo and Moscow were re-established, and in December the first trade agreement in ten years between the two countries was signed. In November of the same year six Arab states, including Iraq, resumed diplomatic relations with Egypt, with others following suit in 1988 and 1989. The last to hold out, Syria, re-established relations in the spring of 1990. For Egypt it was a triumphant return to the Arab fold, an avowal of its enduring centrality even when Arabs believed they had excluded it, for Mubarak made no compromises on his country's relations with Israel. The other Arabs even succumbed to Egypt's demand to relocate the headquarters of the Arab League from Tunis back to Cairo, the city in whose skies fluttered the Israeli flag.

But these changes occurred in a global environment that was vastly different from that of the earlier eras. By the late 1980s the Cold War had lost much of its past venom, due primarily to Gorbachev's desire to decrease military spending, increase trade with the West, and encourage Western investment in the Soviet Union. The Intermediate-range Nuclear Forces Treaty (INF), the first superpower agreement to *reduce* strategic weapons, had been signed in 1987, and negotiations were well under way for the Conventional Forces in Europe Treaty (CFE, signed in 1990) and the Strategic Arms Reduction Treaty (START, signed in 1991). In short, the Soviet Union no longer saw itself in a necessarily competitive position with the US.

At the very time that Egypt made its triumphant return to the Arab world, establishing yet again its centrality in its natural environs, the choices at the global level diminished with the rapid thawing of the Cold War. No other period could illustrate this better than the first half of the 1990s.

When the Bush administration decided to confront Saddam Hussein immediately after Iraq's invasion of Kuwait in August 1990, its first priority was to enlist Arab support, lest the operation be seen as no more than an illustration of American imperial reach. Indeed, one can go as far as to say that without Arab support the legitimacy of the Desert Shield/Storm operation would have been severely compromised. In this, Egypt played a key role. President Mubarak, utilizing his country's weight and centrality, called for an Arab summit, and announced that Egypt would be willing to participate in a joint Arab force that would help in removing Iraqi forces from Kuwait. The public declaration of Egypt's stance in regard to the Gulf crisis helped muster a majority among the Arab leaders in favour of a resolution to oppose Iraq and send military forces to Saudi Arabia. Mubarak had played a key role in legitimizing the essentially Western operation, and for that his country was rewarded with generous debt write-offs.

Did the Egyptian leadership's role in the Gulf crisis help the country improve its bargaining position at the global level? Subsequent developments show that this was not so. As the US extended military protection to the Gulf, and as other Arab countries began to carve out their own political and economic relations with Israel, the importance of Egypt to the US declined. By 1993–4, members of the US Congress, for the first time since the late 1970s, began to question the aid package to Egypt of over $2 billion. By 1995, Egypt seemed to have little to argue in its favour for maintaining the aid package except to scare the Americans with the prospect of an Islamist takeover.

The embarrassing wrangle that preceded the indefinite extension of the nuclear non-proliferation treaty (NPT) was yet another illustration of Egypt's increasing marginality at the global level. In February 1995 Egypt's foreign minister, Amre Mahmoud Moussa, warned that Egypt would refuse to sign the NPT pact, scheduled to be renewed in April, unless Israel committed itself in principle to abide by the terms of the treaty.[17] The following month, President Mubarak endorsed his foreign minister's position by insisting that either Israel sign the accord, or at a minimum offer a timetable for eventually meeting the treaty's terms.[18] Indeed, at the conference on 10 May Egypt, backed by thirteen Arab countries, introduced a proposal that called for Israel to be singled out for mention in the final document. The Egyptians were soon to discover that they had exaggerated their country's international weight. The Americans, freed from concern over Soviet interference, did not budge from their position that references to Israel should be removed. And the Egyptians were finally

---

[17] *Facts on File* (New York: Facts on File, 1995), 99.   [18] Ibid. 222.

made to accept what was essentially a humiliating compromise that referred vaguely to 'unsafeguarded nuclear facilities in the Middle East'.[19]

It is clear that radical changes in the international environment, particularly the demise of the Soviet empire, contributed significantly to a perceptible decrease in Egypt's options and opportunities at the global level. Even had Mubarak wanted to—and there is no evidence that he did—he would not have been able to interact with the superpowers in the way his two predecessors did in an earlier, and altogether different, era.

CONCLUSION

Without the analytical certainty of causal relationship, we can still reasonably conclude not only that the Cold War had an impact on a variety of Egyptian policies but that on many occasions Egypt itself was able to exploit the Cold War for its own purposes and to serve its perceived interests. Indeed, one can go so far as to say that, had the global system in the 1950s and 1960s, approximated to the post-1991 system, with its unipolar tendencies, the contemporary history of the Middle East would have had to be rewritten.

Bearing this in mind, it is useful to conclude with a brief overview of the impact of the Cold War on Egypt's domestic, regional, and international environments.

The domestic environment

As we have seen, the initial political and economic changes that occurred in the wake of the Nasserist revolution had little to do with the Cold War. Thus, for example, Egypt's authoritarian system was created in response to purely domestic impulses: the disillusionment of the Free Officers with the political institutions of the monarchical regime, their perceived need to resurrect the failing economy quickly and decisively, and their fear that the enemies of the revolution would exploit democratic institutions to destabilize the new political order.

What the Cold War did, however, was to aid in the legitimation of the authoritarian system. Nasser would constantly use the alleged greed and ambitions of the two superpowers as an excuse for not allowing a multi-party system or a truly functioning parliament.

---

[19] Ibid. 354–5.

Later on, when Sadat proceeded to reverse the Nasserist model, his motivation was again primarily domestic, even personal. In addition to his own distaste for the frugality of socialist life, Sadat calculated that his own political legitimation in Egypt was predicated on a wholesale change of the Nasserist political and economic order.

We might thus conclude that, in domestic politics, the Egyptian leaders have tended to respond directly to internally generated factors of political power, even political survival. Here, the Cold War became relevant in an indirect way—only when in the calculations of the leaders it could be used to aid their political control.

The regional environment

In contrast to the domestic scene, Egypt's activity in the regional environment, especially during the Nasserist period, had much to do with the Cold War. The intense involvement of Nasser's Egypt in the region, which propelled it to its position of regional leader, occurred almost as a direct response to the Baghdad Pact.

A creation of the Cold War, the Baghdad Pact was the supposed central link in the anti-Soviet chain of alliances that the West had endeavoured to build. Egypt's response to the Baghdad Pact highlights the intensely interactive relationship between the Cold War on the one hand and Egypt's regional policies on the other. In the wake of his effective assault on the Baghdad Pact, Nasser moved on to other great regional successes, such as the Czech arms deal, the nationalization of the Suez Canal Company, his perceived victory over Britain, France, and Israel in the Suez War, and the Iraqi revolution.

The point here, as explained earlier, is that all this might not have happened had it not been for the Cold War. It was not only the creation of the Baghdad Pact: the Cold War resurrected and nourished latent local rivalries, thus creating the conditions for the dominance of Nasser and Egypt.

The global environment

The first manifestation of the impact of the Cold War on Egypt's global activity was Nasser's decision in 1955 to keep Egypt out of superpower rivalry by adopting the policy of 'positive neutralism'. Along with countries such as India, Ghana, and Yugoslavia, Egypt spearheaded an international neutralist orientation that was later to develop into the non-aligned movement.

However, because of the global rules of the game which were

dictated primarily by the Cold War (especially in terms of economic and military aid), it was difficult for any country to remain truly unaffected by superpower rivalry. The result was that, while continuing to pay lip-service to the concept of neutrality and non-alignment, Nasser's Egypt by the 1960s had turned exclusively to the Soviet Union for support and protection. And when Sadat decided to move Egypt out of Soviet control, the nature of the Cold War situation restricted him to one realistic alternative: the United States. If the history of Egypt's global policies from 1952 to 1990 emphasizes anything, it is the resilience and global dominance of the Cold War bipolar system.

It is not that Egypt did not follow policies that ran against the wishes of its superpower patron at the time. As this chapter shows, all of Egypt's presidents were able to do that. The point here is that Egypt, like most other countries, found that it could not achieve its regional and global goals, and on occasions even its domestic goals (for instance, restructuring its economy), without the active support of one or the other of the superpowers. It is perhaps this relationship of objective dependency, of the absolute need for the support of one or the other of the superpowers, of the utter inability to go it alone, that ultimately tells us most about the nature of the relationship between the Cold War and regional actors, even influential ones such as Egypt.

3

Syria

PATRICK SEALE

INTRODUCTION

In the last three and a half decades of the Cold War—say, from 1954 to the late 1980s—Syria and the Soviet Union were intimately involved with each other. So close did their relations seem that outsiders often portrayed Damascus as Moscow's principal Arab ally, even as its main Cold War partner in the region, more steadfast than Egypt, less fickle than Libya, less marginal than Algeria, more predictable than South Yemen. Syria had become, it was thought, a Soviet forward base in the very heart of the region. At moments of regional crisis, in 1956–7 for example, and again in 1966–7, there was anxious talk in the Western camp that Syria had made the dangerous leap from being a client of the Soviet Union to becoming a 'satellite'. Syria, it was said, was 'going communist'.

This was a classic Cold War misunderstanding. Obsessed with each other, Great Powers tended at the time to exaggerate what they observed of local Arab politics, often reading into them sinister machinations by their rivals. With hindsight, a very different picture emerges. The evidence now suggests that, after a brief honeymoon period, the relationship between Syria and the Soviet Union was marked less by complicity, cooperation, and strategic dependence than by false expectations, contradictory ambitions, mutual suspicion, and plain muddle. Their dialogue it would seem, was largely a dialogue of the deaf. At the end of the day, they were both disappointed.

This is not to say that Syrian politicians were not deeply concerned about what the two superpowers and, indeed, other lesser powers like Britain and France were up to in the region. Syrian politicians—whether Khalid al-'Azm, the so-called 'red millionaire' who, at various times in the 1940s and 1950s, served as prime minister, finance minister, foreign minister, and defence minister, or Hafiz al-Asad, Syria's long-serving leader from 1970 to the present day—followed Cold War politics closely, and were well aware of the immense influence of the Great Powers on their strategic environment.

But there was little sign that the foreign-policy orientations of such leaders dictated their behaviour on the domestic or the regional stage. Although Damascus edged closer to Moscow and kept a beady eye on Washington, seen as Israel's mainstay, Cold War considerations seemed *relatively* unimportant in shaping the policies of the key players. It was usually the other way round: foreign political alignments were put to work in the service of local needs and ambitions. One might go further still and say that developments on the internal Syrian scene, or on the inter-Arab level, sometimes had a determining influence on the fate of Great Power schemes in the region. The tail sometimes wagged the dog.

Nevertheless, Syria's thirty-year relationship with the Soviet Union left a profound imprint on several aspects of Syrian life, and the legacy was by no means all negative, as may be judged by major projects like the Euphrates dam, built with Soviet help, or the technical training given in the Soviet Union to tens of thousands of young Syrians, whether in the armed services or in civilian life.

Three fairly distinct periods may be identified in the relationship— a 'honeymoon' period from 1954 to 1958; a roller-coaster 'marriage', marked by numerous ups and downs, from the mid-1960s to the mid-1980s; followed by 'divorce' and disillusion, when the earlier intimacy, and the great cooperative ventures, whether political, military, or economic, came to seem like a distant memory.

THE 'HONEYMOON'

The turbulent years in Syria from 1954 to the union with Egypt in 1958 saw the spectacular launch of the Syrian–Soviet relationship. It was an age of high excitement but also of innocence, characterized by what seemed like a real concordance between Syrian needs and Soviet objectives. The alarms of that decade—the battle over the Baghdad Pact in 1955, the Suez War of 1956, the Syrian crisis of 1957, the creation of the United Arab Republic in 1958—all these events threw the West onto the defensive in the Middle East and gave the Soviet Union a chance to break into what had hitherto been a jealously protected Western domain. In terms of Cold War competition, Moscow emerged as a champion of the Arabs, and little Syria, a victim of vast regional and international pressures, felt it had found a Great Power protector.

Both partners were seeking security: the Syrians wanted security against predatory Arab neighbours, against their former colonizers, and especially against Israel, while the Soviets, always sensitive to a

potential strategic threat from the south, sought a forward presence
in the Eastern Mediterranean, the better to protect themselves and
their vulnerable Black Sea ports from the regional build-up of
American power. Although their standpoints, motivations, and
expectations were very different, they agreed on goals: Syria and the
Soviet Union were at one in wanting to remove Western influence
and Western military pressure from the Middle East. But a closer
look at events serves to correct this largely Cold War analysis: even
in this honeymoon period, stresses and strains on the domestic and
regional levels were at least as important as superpower rivalries in
shaping the course of Syrian history.

To understand Syria at that time, it is perhaps necessary to recall
its anxieties in the chaotic years which followed the Second World
War. French troops had left Syria in 1946, but Syrian independence
was still imperfect. Decolonization was far from complete. The
Middle East was still very much in the West's sphere of influence,
and Britain—present in Iraq, in Egypt's Canal Zone, in Transjordan,
the Gulf, and Aden—was still the dominant external power.

Defeat in Palestine in 1948 brought home to the Arabs the reality
of their own impotence and disarray. The Arabs had been wholly
unprepared for the trial of strength with the new Jewish state. Their
regimes were shaky and their armies ramshackle. The region was
awash with refugees. In Syria, the notables who had inherited power
from the French were largely discredited, and came under fierce
attack from outraged nationalist opinion, from a rebellious street,
and especially from students whom the emerging Ba'th party had
mobilized into a strident extraparliamentary pressure group. In the
countryside, too, were rumblings of revolt, especially on the great
estates of central Syria, where men like the populist firebrand Akram
al-Hawrani were beginning to rouse the oppressed peasantry against
their masters.

Such was the background to the three military coups of 1949—the
first in the Arab world—bringing to the fore military governments
which lasted until 1954, when Colonel Adib al-Shishakli, the last of
the putschists, was overthrown, earning Syria a reputation for instability and ungovernability (which persists in people's minds to this
day despite the unchanging political landscape of the past quarter of
a century dominated by Hafiz al-Asad). Contributing greatly to the
alarm and instability of the 1950s were a number of external conflicts
which were grafted on to the disorderly domestic scene, illustrating
the dense interconnection of the different levels of internal, regional,
and Great Power politics.

The first of these external conflicts was the battle for Arab leadership between the Hashemites in Amman and Baghdad on the one hand and Egypt, backed by Saudi Arabia, on the other. The Hashemites were anxious to bring about a 'Greater Syria' or 'Fertile Crescent' unity—that is to say, a union of Transjordan and Syria, or even of Transjordan, Iraq, and Syria—while Egypt was determined to uphold the Arab League formula of a family of independent and separate Arab states loosely grouped around the Egyptian 'elder sister'—a formula which guaranteed Egyptian predominance. Syria was the prize in this contest for regional hegemony. In the first postwar decade it had not yet emerged as a major actor in its own right, in charge of its own destinies, as it was later to become under Hafiz al-Asad. Instead, it was something of a political football, kicked back and forth between rival Arab and international players.

A maxim of the period was that whoever wished to control the Middle East had to control Syria. This was a back-handed tribute to Syria's centrality in Arab affairs, due to the resonance of its Umayyad past, to its renowned Arab nationalist temper, and to its geopolitical situation controlling the north-eastern approaches to Egypt, the northern approaches to the Arabian peninsula, and the land bridge between Iraq and the Mediterranean. For an Arab state to have an Arab policy at that time was to have a policy regarding Syria. As a result, Syria was on the receiving end of numerous external pressures as well as large sums in bribe money, while the differing sympathies of Syrian politicians, often depending on whether they came from Aleppo or Damascus, swung the country back and forth between the different Arab contestants for regional leadership, and dictated the external alignments of the military putschists. The internal Syrian political scene, with its hectic ebb and flow, often seemed to hold the key to the outcome of these wider inter-Arab contests.[1]

Most Syrians distrusted the Hashemites' British connection and had no wish to be ruled from Baghdad. They were attached to their republican regime. Above all, they were soon swept off their feet by the charismatic Egyptian leader, Gamal Abdel Nasser, who came to power in 1952 and who, within a couple of years, had captured a vast audience across the Arab world with his message of 'neutralism', of freedom from Western guiding strings, of standing up to Israel, and *of total Arab independence.* This struck a profound chord—and nowhere more than in Syria. Syrian opinion had been deeply affected by the bitter experience of the French mandate, by the defeat in Palestine, by the West's part in the creation of Israel, and by the

[1] Patrick Seale, *The Struggle for Syria* (Oxford: Oxford University Press for RIIA, 1965; new edn., London: I. B. Tauris and Yale University Press, 1986).

widespread view that Syrian independence was a fiction and that the country was at the mercy of the Great Powers. Nasser seemed to offer a cure for past wounds and present ailments.

If inter-Arab conflicts were one hugely disruptive factor on the Syrian scene, another was the Cold War rivalry of the Powers which started to affect Syria as early as 1950–1. It was at that time that Western planners, especially in the US and Britain, started to worry about how to contain the Soviet Union, and more particularly about how best to resist Soviet incursions along the whole periphery of the communist bloc. Anxious to secure oil supplies for European reconstruction, the West's immediate concern was to erect a military barrier against what it feared might be communist penetration and subversion of the vulnerable Middle East.

The West's view of this alleged communist threat was shaped by events outside the Middle East: by the communist coup in Czechoslovakia, the Berlin blockade, the collapse of Chiang Kai-shek, the Korean War. A single quotation from the *New York Times* of 30 November 1951 may serve to illustrate the black-and-white, apocalyptic, even hysterical view of the threat at the time: 'In the whole Middle East the ultimate dilemma is Communism or Western democracy. We say that the answer must be Western democracy because if it isn't the West probably cannot survive . . .'

But the more the West worried about defending the Middle East against communism, the more nationalists in the region resented Western defence plans, seeing in them no more than a new phase of colonialism. For its part, Western opinion felt nothing but impatience with Arab frustrations and with the angry mood of the Arab street, if it bothered to consider such things at all. So began a grave estrangement, a profound misunderstanding between the West and the emerging forces of Arab nationalism, which was to shape Syria's internal and external policies and leave its mark on the next several decades.

The whole Western debate about how to resist the encroachment of communism in the Middle East largely passed the Arabs by. Their anxieties were parochial: they were more concerned about containing Israel than international communism, of which they had little experience and which they did not see as a threat. Their gaze was fixed on internal conflicts inside their countries and on contests between Arab states. Their leaders—with rare exceptions like the pro-British Iraqi statesman Nuri al-Said—had no interest in cooperating with Western defence plans. Quite the contrary: they wanted to eject the West— militarily and politically—from their region, seeing it as the main obstacle to their independence, their unity, and the reform of their backward societies. In their struggle for such local objectives, some began in the early 1950s to see in the Soviet Union a source of support, a very daring thought at the time.

The dispute over Western defence plans for the region came to a head with the Baghdad Pact of February 1955, of which the kernel was a British–Iraqi–Turkish understanding on regional defence. In assessing the impact of the Cold War on Syrian and regional politics, the point needs to be underlined that, although the pact was billed as an attempt to erect a military barrier against possible Soviet encroachment, it had another local and less publicized function. It was a political device, cooked up by the Iraqi statesman Nuri al-Said and his British friends in order, first, to wrest Arab leadership away from Nasser's Egypt and give it to Iraq and, secondly, to salvage something of Britain's regional influence which the loss of the Suez Canal Zone base in 1954 had much diminished. Nasser's message of complete Arab independence was a threat to Britain's remaining strong-points in the region. The battle over the Baghdad Pact, therefore, presented a classic case of the intermingling of Arab domestic and regional concerns with Great Power ambitions, and as such provided fertile ground for misunderstanding.

Syria's central and much-courted position gave it what amounted to a casting vote on the pact's future: had it applied for membership, other Arab states would have followed and Nuri al-Said's ambitions for regional leadership might have been fulfilled. But Syria had already opted for a different course. At elections in 1954, following the fall of the Syrian dictator Adib al-Shishakli, the radical pan-Arab Ba'th party had emerged as a powerful force, and a communist, Khalid Baqdash, was for the first time elected to the Syrian parliament. On the very day that Nuri signed the Baghdad Pact with Turkey's prime minister Adnan Menderes—24 February 1955—a change of government was engineered in Damascus which brought a 'neutralist' team to power. Syria came out against the pact. As a result, the pact was 'frozen' and Iraq, its only Arab member, was isolated. Nasser's Egypt had scored a notable victory.

A few days later, on 28 February, Israel mounted a large-scale raid on Gaza, killing scores of Egyptians—a crude demonstration of force which, instead of causing the Syrians to distance themselves from Egypt, as was no doubt intended, had the contrary effect of rallying Syrian opinion still further to Nasser's banner. The outcome was the conclusion of a Syrian–Egyptian military alliance in the spring of 1955. Alarmed by this expansion of Nasser's influence, Britain and the US encouraged Turkey to concentrate troops and armour on Syria's frontier. But once again, far from intimidating the Syrians,

such heavy-handed threats only drove Syria still closer to Egypt—
and, inevitably, to the Soviet Union.

Syria had already been singled out for special Soviet attention as
early as Shishakli's overthrow in 1954. Even before Nasser's 'Czech'
arms deal of 1955—the first major transfer of Soviet arms to the
Arabs for which the groundwork was laid at a meeting between
Nasser and Zhou Enlai at Bandung—Syria had concluded an arms
deal with Czechoslovakia in 1954 (when it bought a small consignment of second-hand tanks). But now, responding to Turkey's armed
posturing, the Soviet Union publicly took Syria under its protection.

Moscow was beginning to feel confident. The Soviet economy,
shattered by the Second World War, had been rebuilt and a first test
of a hydrogen bomb had been carried out in 1953, only a year after
the US. Moreover, even before Stalin died that year, Moscow had
developed a strategy more in tune with Arab sentiment than that of
its Western rivals: it set about mobilizing support in the developing
countries, not by trying to turn them into communists, but by har-
nessing for its own purposes their neutralist, nationalist, and anti-
Western feelings. In all this Moscow was understandably anxious to
undermine the anti-Soviet alliances which the West was trying to
erect. It saw the Baghdad Pact as a particular threat, and it chose
to neutralize it by leapfrogging the 'northern tier' of Turkey, Iraq,
Iran, and Pakistan, and establishing close relations with Syria as well
as with Egypt.

Syria's dominant emotions at that time were solidarity with Egypt,
hatred for Nuri al-Said's Iraq, fear of Turkey, suspicion of the West,
and—a new sentiment this—gratitude towards the Soviet Union.
Moscow's pledge to build Egypt's high dam at Aswan, after the withdrawal of Western aid offers, made a tremendous impact on Syrian
opinion. The Suez crisis of 1956 carried this sentiment further. Once
Nasser had survived the 'tripartite aggression' of Britain, France,
and Israel, he was more than ever the darling of the Syrian masses,
while admiration for the Soviet Union seemed to know no bounds.
Alarmed by these developments, and convinced that Syria was 'going
communist', Britain, the US, and Iraq mounted a conspiracy to overthrow the Syrian government in 1956, timed to coincide with the
Suez campaign against Egypt—but the plot was uncovered, and only
served to inflame Syrian opinion further.

Such was the background to the ground-breaking journey to
Moscow in July–August 1957 of Syria's defence minister Khalid
al-'Azm. As he recounts in his memoirs,[2] he went to Moscow to

---

[2] Khalid al-'Azm, *Mudhakarat Khalid al-'Azm* (Beirut, 1973), 1. iii. 5–31.

negotiate a major economic agreement which was to lay the foundations for economic cooperation with the Soviet Union. 'Azm knew
that Syria needed to create new industries, prospect for oil, build
dams to free its agriculture from dependence on uncertain seasonal
rains, and develop a modern transport system to move export crops
to the sea—but it had no money to do any of these things. World
Bank and US government loans came with political strings attached.
On his way to Moscow, 'Azm stopped off in Bonn where, instead of
offers of aid, he was shocked to learn that the West German government proposed cutting imports of Syrian grain from 150,000 tons
to 30,000 tons—a punitive measure which he interpreted as pressure
to force Syria to join a Western defence pact.

In agreeable contrast, Moscow offered him long-term loans at 2.5
per cent, low-cost arms on easy terms, and technical assistance—'a
far cry,' he commented, 'from the conditions the World Bank wanted
to impose . . . What did we give in return? Nothing! . . . We did not
attach ourselves to them politically or militarily . . . The Soviets
understood our firm commitment to our independence.'

Soon Syrian contacts with the Soviet bloc were so numerous as to
make enumeration tedious: trade, aid, exchange visits, scholarships,
low-interest loans for development projects abounded, but it was
arms transfers above all which eventually cemented the relationship.

In the summer of 1957, Western hysteria about a communist
takeover in Syria reached new heights, and London and Washington
hatched new plots against Damascus with Turkish help. Invoking the
Eisenhower Doctrine, the US became convinced that Syria was
about to become a Soviet satellite. Although the plots were once
again uncovered, they contributed to a sense of panic and national
emergency which thoroughly rattled Syria's senior officers, most of
them of Ba'thist persuasion, causing them to think that their country might fall either to a Western conspiracy or to their communist
rivals. Turning to Nasser for salvation, they pitched their country
into an ill-considered union with Egypt in February 1958.

Western fears notwithstanding, in the years before the brief
unhappy experiment of the United Arab Republic (1958–61) Syria
never came close to becoming a Soviet satellite. No institutional link
was forged between Moscow and Damascus. Even at the peak of the
Syrian–Soviet honeymoon in 1956–7, Syria's Ba'thist leaders
remained wary of communism at home. They knew that Marxist
internationalism was the enemy of Arab nationalism and they
had little interest in a 'world proletarian revolution'. Ba'thists
had on occasions allied themselves tactically with the communists
in battles against 'reactionary' enemies, but they never forgot that

the communists were dangerous rivals, competing for the same clientele.

Some Syrian intellectuals had been influenced by Marxism in their student days, Michel 'Aflaq, the Ba'th founder and a Sorbonne graduate, among them. And some, holding the view that capitalism and imperialism had deliberately stifled economic development in the Third World, believed that salvation lay in central planning on the socialist model. But Syrian radicalism was by and large home-grown, owing little or nothing to communist indoctrination, although this was not always understood by Western observers. At a popular level, or even among the more sophisticated student population, communism made few inroads, and the Syrian Communist Party never became a mass movement. Although pressured and propositioned by Cold War rivals, Syrians, and Arabs generally, remained extraordinarily parochial in their interests. Among all classes there was a limited understanding of what the superpowers could do, and of what each really hoped to gain from the Middle East. (Unlike Israel, where there are numerous research institutes, neither Syria nor any other Arab country to my knowledge established specialized research centres or departments devoted to the systematic study of either the Soviet Union or the United States—or indeed of Israel.) Syria may have flirted with the Soviet Union, and may, with considerable naïvety, have pinned great hopes on it, but the relationship was at best one of convenience, with little depth or conviction to it. At no point was Syria a Soviet Cold War pawn.

THE ROLLER-COASTER 'MARRIAGE'

Several of the trends observed in the honeymoon period—notably the quest for security by both Syria and the Soviet Union—were carried through into a more formal and institutionalized relationship in the 1960s, 1970s, and beyond. But there were significant differences. As the two countries grew to know each other better, the earlier innocence and optimism gave way on both sides to a certain measure of cynicism, opportunism, and mutual disregard. The gloss wore off the relationship. Each sought to benefit as it could, but without much warmth or trust. Although Soviet military and economic aid grew considerably in volume, there were rows, recriminations, and long moments of coldness.

The main reason for the change of climate was undoubtedly the impact of the two wars of 1967 and 1973—defeats for the Arabs and also for Soviet arms. They highlighted the ambivalence at the heart of the Soviet–Arab relationship. After the 1967 war, the Arabs wanted to reverse the verdict of the defeat and regain their lost territories, by force of arms if necessary. But this programme came up against Soviet reservations, as Professor Alexei Vassiliev, a candid and perceptive Russian analyst, explains:

While arming Egypt and Syria, the Soviet Union neither desired nor planned a military solution to the problem, a decisive preponderance of Arabs, or a change in the status quo. First, the leaders were afraid of a new Arab defeat. Secondly, in the event of such a defeat the USSR would have had to raise the level of its involvement in the conflict in order to save its friends and its investments. Thirdly, actions of this kind might provoke a US reaction and lead to a confrontation. Fourthly, a settlement would decrease the dependence of the Arab countries on Soviet support.[3]

While formally working for a peace settlement, the USSR was in fact interested in maintaining a 'no peace, no war' situation. It wanted to secure the Arabs' friendship by improving their military capability, but it did not dare arm them to the point where they might seriously threaten Israel. The Soviet leaders viewed Israel as an 'imperialist base', but they also recognized its right to exist. It was legitimate to help the Arabs defend themselves against an eventual Israeli attack—so long as this stopped short of providing them with the means to win an all-out war. Thus, what Moscow was prepared to deliver fell a good deal short of what the Arabs demanded. This was to result in much acrimonious bargaining of little benefit to the overall relationship. On the domestic scene it was to make Syria's leaders even more wary of the local communists than they were already inclined to be. They wanted Soviet arms but no Soviet interference in their regional strategies, in their decision to wage war or to make peace, still less in their domestic affairs.

Before reviewing the post-1967 situation, two prewar developments deserve a mention, as they helped prepare the ground for war. The first was the Soviet Union's perceived need in the mid-1960s to cultivate Arab friends so as to safeguard its own security; the second was the coming to power in Syria in 1966 of the Salah Jadid regime, the most left-wing and doctrinaire Syria had ever known.

A consistent Soviet goal was to remove or reduce any potential strategic threat to itself from the south, represented in the early 1960s by a more visible US presence. Soviet fears grew more acute, and its interest in the Arabs correspondingly more intense, when in 1963 submarines of the US 6th Fleet acquired Polaris nuclear missiles able

[3] Alexei Vassiliev, *Russian Policy in the Middle East: From Messianism to Pragmatism* (Reading, Berks.: Ithaca Press, 1993), 75.

to target major Soviet cities from the Mediterranean.[4] The Soviet response was first to deploy and then reinforce a naval squadron in the Mediterranean, its so-called 5th Eskadra. In due course this fleet needed friendly ports at which to call—ports such as Port Said, Alexandria, Mersah Matruh, Lattakia, Tartus—and friendly airfields in both Egypt and Syria from which land-based aircraft could defend the ships and carry out reconnaissance missions against the US 6th Fleet.[5] The strategic position of both Egypt and Syria in the Eastern Mediterranean made them important partners for the Soviet Union. Their cooperation was the price Moscow wanted them to pay for its help in building up their armed forces and developing their economies. But, needless to say, the closer the Soviet ties with Egypt and Syria, the greater the American and Israeli interest in changing the regimes in Cairo and Damascus. This explained American tolerance, indeed its quiet approval, of Israel's pre-emptive strike in 1967.

The coup in Damascus of 23 February 1966, which brought Salah Jadid's left-wing Ba'thist faction to power, created the conditions for even closer relations with Moscow. For perhaps the first time since the start of the Syrian–Soviet relationship, reliance on and admiration for the Soviet Union seemed to shape the nature of domestic Syrian politics, or so it seemed to outside observers. Salah Jadid, the 'strong man' of the regime, professed to believe in 'scientific socialism' and set about a brutal refashioning of Syrian society. His closest associates were three radical medical doctors, Dr Nur al-Din Attasi who became head of state, Dr Yusuf Zu'ayyin, prime minister, and Dr Ibrahim Makhus, foreign minister. However, they were perhaps less influenced by Soviet dogma than by a spell serving as volunteer medics with Houari Boumedienne's forces during Algeria's war against France (1954–62). As chief of staff of the Syrian armed forces, Salah Jadid brought in Ahmad al-Suwaydani, who had served as military attaché in Beijing where he had absorbed a strong dose of Maoism.

After a brief initial hesitation (perhaps because of the Chinese connection—this was at the height of the Sino-Soviet dispute), Moscow gave the regime its support. Arms supplies were increased and a start was made on several major projects such as the road and rail networks, the great dam on the Euphrates, and the opening up of newly discovered oil-fields in the north-west.

---

[4] Alexei Vassiliev, *Russian Policy in the Middle East: From Messianism to Pragmatism*, 79–80, 268, 360.
[5] Amnon Sella, *Soviet Political and Military Conduct in the Middle East* (London: Macmillan, 1981), 42 ff.

Once again, Western observers were frightened Syria would fall to the communists—especially when, for the first time in Syrian history, a communist entered the government (as minister of communications). But for all their radicalism, Salah Jadid's Ba'thists did not lose their suspicion of communism, nor their resolve to rule alone. As was the case with their milder Ba'thist predecessors, the 'leftism' of Jadid's team was essentially home-grown and had not really much to do with Algerian, Chinese, or Soviet inspiration. It was the result of local conditions, not of global or even regional politics. Nevertheless, Syria under Salah Jadid did adopt some of the worst features of a Leninist state, such as the stifling of free expression, the emergence of all-powerful security services, the abandonment of political pluralism, and the adoption of a one-party regime; and some of this at least was perhaps attributable to the Soviet model.

Ideologically, the Jadid team's vision of socialism and Arab nationalism seemed to offer several points of contact with Soviet policy. But, if Professor Vassiliev is to be believed, the Soviets were not wholly convinced of the soundness of their Syrian partners. Moscow hoped they would evolve in the 'correct' direction, but 'their socialist verbiage was regarded as no more than a dispensable tool in the struggle for power and for personal enrichment . . . the affiliation of many Baathist-minded officers with the clandestine Alawiyya sect aroused suspicion that their real motives had nothing to do with nationalism or socialism.'[6]

Syria wanted Soviet protection against Israel, but it wanted no interference by Moscow in its internal or its regional policies. This was to be a constant of Syrian policy—and indeed a constant of all Arab dealings with the Soviet Union: in essence, the Arabs wanted Moscow's help against their regional enemies, while holding the Soviets at arm's length.

In 1967 Salah Jadid's regime stumbled, wholly unprepared, into war. It helped trigger the conflict by encouraging Palestinian guerrillas to mount raids into Israel, once it felt it had no other way to contest Israel's forceful take-over of three demilitarized zones on the Israeli–Syrian border, sovereignty over which had been left undefined by the 1949 armistice agreement. As Vassiliev comments, these guerrilla forays against Israel from Syrian territory were conducted in a 'sometimes hysterical' atmosphere, 'often sustained by the Soviet media'. The brief but devastating war, which was to change the Middle East political landscape, illustrated some of the fundamental contradictions in Syrian–Soviet relations, notably a lack of

[6] Vassiliev, *Russian Policy in the Middle East*, 63–4.

coordination before the outbreak of hostilities and a lack of agreement on aims once the war was fought and lost.

What was the superpower input to the 1967 conflict? On the US–Israeli side of the equation, William Quandt concludes, after a careful examination of the evidence, that there was no *active* US–Israeli collusion to weaken or even topple Nasser (or, one must presume, the Jadid regime in Syria), but that 'there was [American] acquiescence in what [President] Johnson had come to believe was an inevitable Israeli resort to force to solve a problem for which the United States could offer no solution on its own'.[7] There was no clear American green light for Israel to attack, but nor was there a red light. A yellow light was all the Israelis needed—and that they certainly got.

On the Arab side, there was little or no prewar coordination of strategy with the Soviet Union, in spite of their many contacts. The Soviets had been concerned about the immense distrust between Egypt and Syria—stemming from Syria's secession from the United Arab Republic in 1961 and from the fierce repression of the Nasserists in Syria once the Ba'th had regained power in 1963. In December 1966 Kosygin managed to bring about some sort of a reconciliation between Cairo and Damascus, but mutual suspicion remained. Each imagined that the other would not be unhappy to see it toppled by Israeli action.

Moscow did not welcome having to mediate in inter-Arab quarrels. The more it became involved in regional affairs, the more often it found itself in awkward situations. In Vassiliev's words, 'More influence—more involvement—more headaches!'[8]

As the crisis approached its climax, Syria's head of state, Dr Nur al-Din Atassi, accompanied by Foreign Minister Makhus, went to Moscow on 30 May 1967, a few days before the outbreak of war, in a last-minute bid to seek Soviet protection—but by all accounts he got nothing, which may have encouraged the Israelis (who read Syrian communications) to believe that they would face no Soviet interference in the *blitzkreig* they were planning.

The Soviets may have been a touch complacent. Between 1956 and 1967 they had strengthened the Arabs' military capability and seemed to believe that, in any clash with Israel, their friends would give a good account of themselves. There was, however, no joint preparation for war, as Nasser admitted when, on 22 June 1967, two

---

[7] William B. Quandt, *Peace Process: American Diplomacy and the Arab–Israeli Conflict Since 1967* (Washington, DC: Brookings Institution and University of California Press, 1993), 52–4.

[8] Vassiliev, *Russian Policy in the Middle East*, 64.

weeks after the defeat, he had a meeting in Cairo with the Soviet president, N. V. Podgorny. As the record shows, early in their discussions Nasser declared

As far as our relations with you are concerned, they have lacked one thing, which is military cooperation. During the fighting our people kept asking: 'Where are the Russians, our friends?' I know of course that you couldn't have had a military presence because *no previous agreement* had been made with you about such an arrangement.[9]

Soon after the war, at a meeting in Moscow on 18 July between senior members of the Central Committee of the CPSU and an Arab delegation consisting of President Arif of Iraq and President Boumedienne of Algeria, Brezhnev commented on the prewar situation:

We had 400 military experts in the United Arab Republic and we had instructed them not to interfere in anything unless they were specifically asked. Our officers put in a request to the Egyptian military command to go and see Sinai to acquaint themselves with the deployment plan for the forces, but their request was turned down.[10]

Yet there was a distinct Soviet input to the crisis—although, in the event, not a helpful one. It will be recalled that, in the tense weeks leading up to war, the Russians warned Egypt that Israel was preparing to attack Syria, and that this warning was a major factor in Nasser's decision to move troops into Sinai and to ask the UN forces to move out. Nasser feared that an Israeli attack on Syria would inevitably suck him in. Anxious to avoid war, yet not trusting the Syrians to handle the explosive situation on their own, Nasser moved to take the management of the crisis into his own hands. He sent Egyptian troops into Sinai to shift the epicentre of the crisis away from the Syrian border with Israel, which he could not control, to the Egyptian border, which he thought he could. But his move into Sinai, followed by his closure of the Straits of Tiran, was the pretext Israel seized upon to attack him.[11] Far from helping its Arab friends, Moscow's warning to Nasser actually helped precipitate the Arab catastrophe.

However, on 10 June 1967, once Israel, having defeated Egypt and Jordan, captured the Golan plateau and seemed about to march on Damascus, Moscow made clear to Washington that it would not

[9] Abdel Magid Farid, *Nasser: The Final Years* (Reading: Ithaca Press, 1994), 4 (emphasis added).

[10] Ibid. 39.

[11] See Patrick Seale, *Asad: The Struggle for the Middle East* (London: I. B. Tauris, 1988), for the run-up to the 1967 war and subsequent developments in Syrian politics.

tolerate the destruction of a friendly regime. Prompted by Yugoslavia—no doubt Tito's friendship with Nasser played a role— the Soviet Union broke off relations with Israel as a means of inducing it to halt its advance and accept a cease-fire.

So, while there was muddle rather than coordination between Damascus and Moscow before the war, by its end the Russians were invoking a 'red line' on the Arabs' behalf. They made it clear that there was a limit beyond which Israel could not move against Syria without risking Soviet intervention. This no doubt gave the Syrians some small comfort in their disastrous situation, yet there was much hollow and unrealistic crowing in the Syrian and Soviet media at the time that Israel had really lost the war because it had failed to destroy Syria's 'progressive' regime.

In reality, the Soviet leaders were frightened that Israel would strike again and finish the job. As Brezhnev told Arif and Boumedienne on their visit to Moscow, there could be more large-scale Israeli military operations against Syria and Egypt which could lead to the downfall of the regimes. No Arab country was in a position to put up serious resistance: officers and men were untrained, the populations were politically unprepared for a struggle, and Arab economies were unsound. Two or three years would be needed before the Arabs could contemplate military action. The best way to safe-guard the 'progressive regimes', Brezhnev argued, was to agree to end the state of war with Israel. What did it matter if they were to accept a piece of paper with the words 'ending the state of war' written on it, in return for the survival of their regimes and continuing the struggle? What did it matter if ships flying the Israeli flag went through the Suez Canal?[12] Moscow was impatient with the Arab position, as confirmed by the Khartoum summit of 29 August–1 September 1967, that any policy leading to the recognition of Israel or to the (even momentary) acceptance of its conquests was unacceptable.

Hafiz al-Asad, the Syrian defence minister who had lost the war on the Syrian front and the Golan, went to Moscow in August 1967 for talks with his Soviet opposite number, Marshal Andrei Grechko. It was Asad's first real contact with the Soviet leadership, and there is some suggestion that he and the Russians were in rueful agreement about the dangers posed by the hot-heads in the Syrian regime who had given free rein to the Palestinian guerrillas. The Soviets made it clear that they could no longer bear to hear the slogans of 'armed struggle' or 'people's war'. They suspected that the Chinese were

---

[12] Farid, *Nasser*, 36–7.

egging the Syrians on to rash adventures as part of their worldwide campaign against the Soviet Union. As Podgorny explained to Nasser in June 1967, the Chinese 'are now trying to make us lose Syria by pushing the Syrians into an unequal fight regardless of the entirely predictable outcome of such an encounter'.[13]

In any event, Asad persuaded the Russians to re-equip and re-train the much-battered Syrian armed forces, including Asad's beloved air force, which had been destroyed in the conflict. His aim was to put relations with the Soviets on a calm, businesslike basis in which mutual interests would be addressed. Thus the 1967 war ushered in a period of close Syrian–Soviet relations—but the very closeness of the relations highlighted a number of problems. The Syrians became heavily dependent on the Russians and this gave Moscow the opportunity to consolidate its position. American influence was correspondingly reduced, almost eliminated. Syria had no diplomatic relations with Washington for more than seven years, from 1967 to 1974.

But rebuilding the Syrian armed forces after the 1967 defeat and training them in the use of Soviet weapons were no easy tasks. There were many technical and cultural barriers to overcome, of which the Russian language and the relatively low educational level of Syrian troops were only the most obvious.

There were also, as has been suggested, contradictions on the level of aims. The Soviets wanted more of what they had already begun to get: they wanted to consolidate their position in the region, acquire a stable presence and listening-post at the heart of the Middle East, reduce American influence, be given access to friendly facilities for their fleet and their aircraft, bind key Arab countries to them by means of trade, aid, and arms transfers, and encourage them along the 'non-capitalist path' of development. Above all, they wished to achieve strategic parity with the US in the whole region from their southern borders to the Indian Ocean. But, in pursuing these aims, they did not want to take any serious risks. They knew that to raise Arab military preparedness to the point that the Arabs could defeat Israel in war was a Herculean task, as well as a high-risk one. The danger of a US–Soviet confrontation was very real. The US would always make sure that Israel had the military edge.

In the circumstances, Arab objectives were virtually impossible to attain. The overriding Arab aims were to recover the territories lost in 1967, push back the powerful Israeli enemy to behind its pre-June 1967 frontiers, and attempt to contain it there—but even to approach

[13] Ibid. 8.

these goals would require wholehearted Soviet support, and that was not forthcoming. The Soviets found themselves in the position of arming Arab clients whose aims they considered unrealistic and over whose policies they had no real control. It was not a comfortable situation, and a certain duplicity entered into the relationship.

The simple concordance of aims which had obtained in the 1950s was supplanted by a more complex and less candid relationship. There was still some overlap between Syrian and Soviet aims, but by this time they were far from identical. Whatever the Arabs may have hoped, there was no way in which the Soviet Union was going to give them the means to wage a *total war* against Israel which would inevitably have brought it face to face with the United States and risked triggering a nuclear exchange. Only a limited war would be tolerated, and one which the superpowers could control before it got out of hand. Like the US, the Soviet Union had a strong interest in preventing regional explosions of unpredictable consequences. This was to be the source of much Arab frustration and disappointment.

The Arabs found they had to bargain hard to overcome Soviet inhibitions and secure from Moscow the advanced weapons they wanted. In Egypt's case, it was to lead to the breach of 1972 and the expulsion of Soviet experts. Syria took no such dramatic action, but its relationship with the Soviets was also plagued by tensions and disagreements as the Syrians eventually grasped that the Russians were more interested in building influence in the Arab world than in building effective Arab military power. It was only later, following the collapse of communism, that Russian sources admitted that the Soviet policy of compelling the Arabs 'to squeeze weapons out of us, consignment by consignment, irritated them, and that irritation accumulated and poisoned the atmosphere of personal relations. It would have been more correct to show our cards to our partners and explain our strategy on arms supplies to them.'[14] It was only later, too, that Moscow realized that the use of arms supplies as a means of political pressure was a sign of weakness rather than of strength, and that the resulting influence they secured was both temporary and questionable.[15]

The 'Black September' crisis in Jordan in 1970 was another landmark in the region's unwitting involvement in Cold War politics. On the regional level, the crisis marked the bloody dénouement of a long-smouldering contest between King Hussein and radical Palestinians who hoped to overthrow him—but whom he routed instead. On the level of domestic Syrian politics, it provided the

---

[14] Vassiliev, *Russian Policy in the Middle East*, 284, quoting an unnamed Soviet diplomat.
[15] Ibid. 269.

opportunity for Hafiz al-Asad to oust his rival, Salah Jadid, and seize power. But on the superpower level, the US—in the person of Henry Kissinger—chose to view the crisis through the binoculars of the East–West contest, so providing another classic example of the intermingling of actors and motivations on different levels—with each participant or observer choosing to interpret the sequence of events from his own standpoint.

When, in September 1970, King Hussein had had enough of Palestinian provocations and ordered his army into action, Asad, then Syria's defence minister, sent Syrian armour across the border to relieve Hussein's pressure on the guerrillas. He chose to do so although he had no particular liking for irregular forces and no sympathy for the Palestinians' aim of toppling the King. Apparently blind to the local components of the conflict, Kissinger in Washington convinced himself that Moscow was using the *fidayin* and its Syrian client to bring down Jordan's pro-Western government and expand its own influence in the region. So when King Hussein, uncertain of Syrian intentions, called on the US for help, Kissinger asked the Israelis to mount a show of force in Jordan's support. Accordingly, Israel staged some well-publicized military manoeuvres, which emboldened Hussein to send in his armour and air force against the Syrian tanks. After taking some casualties, the Syrians prudently withdrew behind their border.

There is no evidence that the Russians, wary of involvement in local Arab affairs, had encouraged the Palestinians to rebel against King Hussein or Asad to intervene in Jordan. They had no interest in any such adventure. In 1969–70 they had been sucked in to Nasser's 'War of Attrition' against Israel across the Suez Canal, and had found that propping up the Egyptian leader in the face of Israel's evident attempts to bring him down, with its deep penetration raids into the Egyptian heartland, was a costly and thankless task. Moscow had sent Egypt military advisers, combat aircraft, and pilots—and had lost a few in dogfights with the Israeli air force, before bringing hostilities to a close. Having, with some difficulty, extinguished the fires on the Suez Canal, it is highly unlikely that the Soviet Union wished to set the Jordanian front alight. As a GRU officer interviewed by Professor Vassiliev remarked, the Soviet military were very cautious about Syria: 'All the time we were expecting that the Syrians would entangle us in some unforeseen complication for which the military alone would end up paying.'[16]

The Syrian intervention in Jordan was not a Soviet plot, nor was

[16] Ibid. 220.

the Palestinian assault on Hussein. 'Black September' was an inter-Arab and an Arab–Israeli struggle—a result of the fraught triangular relationship between the Arab states, Israel, and the dispossessed Palestinians. But, seen from Washington's Cold War perspective, Israel had faced down not just the Syrians, but the Russians as well. To reward Israel, Kissinger promoted it to a privileged place on the US side of the superpower struggle, thereby launching the US–Israeli 'strategic relationship' which was to prove so beneficial for Israel and so damaging to the Arab cause. Washington's misreading of events, or Kissinger's deliberate design, had caused a local inter-Arab struggle, and an episode in the Arab–Israeli conflict, to acquire a Cold War complexion which was to be of huge advantage to Israel but adversely to affect the destinies of other local players.

When people think of modern Syria they inevitably think of Hafiz al-Asad, and rightly so, because he has dominated the scene for a quarter of a century. Most Syrians—and it is a young population—have known no other rule but his. He came to supreme power in 1970, shortly after the 'Black September' crisis, but he has been close to the top since the Ba'th coup of 1963. As a result, almost every aspect of Syria, every move it has made or policy it has adopted, tends to be attributed to him. It is often forgotten that Asad inherited a considerable legacy, and that many of his moves within the Cold War context were a continuation of earlier trends. The closer the US–Israeli relationship became, the more Asad, much like his predecessors, was driven to depend on the Soviets. When he made his first trip to Moscow as ruler of Syria in February 1971, the Syrian–Soviet relationship was already fifteen years old and was, for good or ill, well established.

Soon after taking power, Asad conceived the plan of wresting back the occupied territories from Israel by force. This meant forging a military alliance with Egypt but, for the alliance to be credible, it also meant securing the wholehearted supported of the Soviets. From 1971 to 1973 Asad paid at least half a dozen visits to Moscow for talks with Brezhnev and his generals, and it must be assumed that there was a good deal of tough haggling over the aircraft, tanks, and air defence batteries he needed for his enterprise. Asad knew that in preparing for war he was taking enormous military and political risks, so he was determined to secure from the Soviets all the aid he could. Moscow supported the Arab case for a full Israeli withdrawal to the pre-1967 lines and self-determination for the Palestinians, but it was not too happy with the notion, to which Asad was totally committed, that only war would make Israel disgorge. The central Soviet dilemma in those years was the one already mentioned: to retain influence with Syria and Egypt, Moscow had to give them the weapons which they thought might enable them to recover their lost territory. This was their most urgent national priority. But Moscow, frightened of a confrontation with the US, wanted to head off a war.

In June 1973, less than four months before the October war, the Soviet leadership grasped that the Arabs had run out of patience and were seriously preparing for war. To appeal for further restraint risked undermining Soviet influence with them. Instead, Brezhnev and Foreign Minister Gromyko appealed to the Americans. At a meeting with Nixon and Kissinger at San Clemente, California, they proposed that Israel withdraw to its pre-1967 borders in return for an end to the state of belligerency, with final peace to follow after negotiations with the Palestinians. But Kissinger rejected terms which he considered pro-Arab and likely to consolidate Soviet influence.

In 1973, as in 1967, the Soviets and the Arabs did very little joint strategic planning. The Soviets helped the Arabs prepare for war without being told the secrets of Arab war planning. As E. D. Pyrlin, former deputy chief of the Middle East department of the Soviet foreign ministry, explained, 'to prepare for war and to start a war are two different things'.[17] A GRU officer denied that the Soviet leadership had participated in the decision to go to war: 'It was all done without our approval. I can say so categorically. We had reports that certain preparations were under way, but we weren't going to put our foot down about that. We hinted to them, "It's up to you to decide, it's you own business." ' He added that it had been assumed in Moscow that the Arabs would be beaten pretty quickly, so the Soviets had rather distanced themselves from them beforehand. 'We didn't need war, we were afraid of it. The situation of "no peace, no war" suited us. We didn't want a collision with the Americans. But of course we couldn't hold back the Arabs.'[18] One or two episodes from the October War may serve to illustrate the poor coordination between the Arabs and Moscow and the large element of misunderstanding and incomprehension in their relations.

In 1972, more than a year before the war, a violent row broke out between Egypt and the Soviet Union, which came to a head when Sadat abruptly expelled several thousand Soviet military advisers and weapons experts. He claimed that Moscow had been starving Egypt of weapons because it did not want it to fight, and that he had no alternative but to make the disagreement public. Arab interests, he declared, were being sacrificed on the alter of *détente*. Asad happened

[17] Vassiliev, *Russian Policy in the Middle East*, 97.   [18] Ibid. 99–100, 102.

to be in Moscow at the time, and was aghast at the recklessness of an act which endangered a relationship absolutely vital to the Arab war effort. On Brezhnev's prompting, he agreed to fly at once to Cairo to try and patch things up. However, the real motive for Sadat's move, as it later emerged, was his attempt to attract Kissinger's attention to Egypt's predicament, and its inability to tolerate for very much longer the strains of 'no peace, no war'. The paradox was that the expulsions reinforced Israel's complacent conviction, shared by its American ally, that the Arabs were neither able nor willing to fight. No one took seriously Sadat's trumpetings about 'the year of decision'. His war preparations were dismissed as bluff. Without his having planned it, his dramatic gesture in kicking out the Soviet experts helped catch Israel napping when the Arabs attacked, and contributed to the initial success the Arabs were able to achieve.

An incident during the war highlighted the breakdown of Soviet–Arab relations. On the evening of 6 October, when the Syrian and Egyptian armies were bursting across Israel's defence lines, the Soviet ambassador in Cairo told Sadat that Asad had asked Moscow to work for a cease-fire. Sadat was astounded and rang Asad for confirmation. Asad vehemently denied the report. A cease-fire at this point would have made nonsense of his whole war strategy. The initiative came from the Russians, who, fearing that their Arab friends might not be able to keep up the momentum of war and anxious to avoid a confrontation with the US, favoured an early cease-fire. The Soviets guessed that a moderate blow to Israel might suit the Americans if it brought the Israeli leadership to the conference table. But the Arab blow to Israel was greater than had been anticipated, forcing it to fight back with all the means in its power. The US then had no alternative but to support its ally with a massive airlift, and the Soviets were in turn also sucked in, mounting one of their largest air-supply operations in support of their Arab friends.

As the incident shows, there was little coordination or even plain speaking between Arabs and Russians, whereas Kissinger's cooperation with Tel Aviv was total, embracing tactics as well as goals. Both he and the Israelis wanted to rub the Arabs' noses in the folly of attempting to impose a military solution, and the equal folly of depending on Moscow. In contrast to the Soviet's botched attempts at an early cease-fire, Kissinger used cease-fire diplomacy to give Israel the time and the means to turn the tables on its opponents, and inflict another defeat on Soviet arms. As Kissinger was later to write derisively, 'The Soviets' passionate Middle Eastern clients involved Moscow in risks which were out of proportion to any conceivable Soviet gain.'[19]

At the end of the war, however, the Soviets did help save Egypt's 3rd Army from total destruction, much as they had helped prevent Israel from marching on Damascus in 1967. When Israel broke the cease-fire and, ignoring Security Council Resolutions, pressed home its attack against the besieged Egyptians and menaced Suez and even Cairo, the Kremlin threatened to send troops to the battlefield. Seven Soviet paratroop divisions were put on the alert. Kissinger responded with a US nuclear alert. But by this time Sadat had, in any event, convinced himself that only the US could help him. To the great alarm of his Syrian ally and his Soviet protectors, he abandoned himself to the tender mercies of his 'dear friend, Henry'.

Soon the Soviets found themselves ousted both from their Egyptian base facilities and from the Middle East peace process. The Geneva conference, in which they hoped to play a role, was convened for little more than a day, and soon gave way to an American-brokered search for a bilateral Egyptian–Israeli agreement. Gromyko hurried to Damascus—in fact he came four times between March and May 1974, and Asad went to Moscow in April—to share with the Syrians his alarm that Kissinger was not only dividing the Arabs but was also undercutting the Soviets. Sadat, they both agreed, was a traitor. Relations between Damascus and Moscow were upgraded and cooperation in all fields expanded. This, however, did not prevent Asad from sensing which way the wind was blowing. He set about restoring his relations with Washington, which was accomplished when President Nixon visited Damascus in June 1974.

But by this time Kissinger had established a commanding diplomatic lead, and there was nothing that Asad or the Soviets could do to stop him. His real triumph was the signing in September 1975 of the second Sinai disengagement agreement, which removed Egypt from any further military confrontation with Israel. Twenty years after Egypt and Syria had first joined forces to fight the Baghdad Pact, a great chasm now opened up between them. The Syrian–Egyptian alliance, the backbone of Arab strength, was broken.

The conclusion one might draw was that poor coordination of both military tactics and political strategy caused the defeat of Moscow and its Syrian friends. Neither Syria nor Egypt gave the Soviets any control over their decision-making, either in war or in peace. They took Soviet arms but, their initial military successes

[19] Henry Kissinger, *Diplomacy* (New York: Simon & Schuster, 1994), 526.

notwithstanding, they did not successfully apply Soviet military doctrine during the campaign. One way and another, there was a good deal of room for mutual embarrassment and discomfiture.

What Asad saw as Kissinger's duplicity and gross partiality in favour of Israel caused him to tilt strongly once more towards the Russians in the mid-1970s, without, however, ever becoming a Soviet satellite. Syria was no Cuba, Mozambique, or Angola, even though Asad might have been tempted to develop closer ties, seeing that the Soviets under Brezhnev were in the 1970s at the height of their power and prestige. For a moment, Asad enjoyed the privilege of being Moscow's most favoured Arab partner—but not for long. The civil war in Lebanon was soon to disturb the Syrian–Soviet *entente* and demonstrate yet again that, on the regional scene, Asad made his own calculations and plotted his own course.

In 1976, Asad sent his army into Lebanon to prevent the Palestinians and their left-wing allies from defeating the Christians, who had been driven up into their mountain heartlands. His fear was that the beleaguered Christians might turn to Israel for help, or that Palestinian and other radicals might manage to set up a sort of mini-People's Republic in southern Lebanon, which might also provoke an Israeli intervention. So, braving Soviet displeasure, Asad marched in to tame the Palestinians and keep the Christians out of Israel's arms. Asad's move forced the Russians to make an unwelcome choice. They did not like having to choose between Asad and Yasser Arafat's PLO, or between Asad and the Lebanese Druze leader, Kamal Junblat, holder of a Lenin Peace Prize, and as a result their diplomacy was in disarray. Their Palestinian and Lebanese friends were bitter that Moscow failed to intervene to save them from the Syrians, while Asad was angry that Moscow failed to grasp why his intervention in Lebanon was both timely and necessary. It was not until the late 1970s that he managed to persuade the Soviets to resume arms deliveries on the scale and of the quality he felt he needed.

The late 1970s and early 1980s were the most trying years of Asad's presidency. At home he faced a ferocious terrorist onslaught from Islamic militants, while in the region, the signature of Egypt's separate peace with Israel in 1979 left other Arab countries—Syria and Lebanon prominent among them—exposed to Menachem Begin's belligerence. Feeling friendless and uniquely vulnerable, Asad turned to Moscow for protection, this time as a petitioner. In October 1980 he signed a Treaty of Friendship and Cooperation with the Soviet Union—a formal tie he had previously resisted. 'Friendship needs no treaty,' he used to say.

With Egypt out of the Arab line-up and Israel's ultra-nationalists brimming with menacing self-confidence, he needed help. The outbreak of the Iraq–Iran war added to his sense of danger. In Moscow he fought hard not only for Soviet arms but also for a firm Soviet commitment to come to Syria's defence if it were attacked. The Russians responded that, in that case, they would need military bases in Syria. They had had air and sea facilities in Syria since the 1960s, but never bases as such, manned by their own troops and under their full control. Asad demurred. According to a source close to him, he explained to the Soviet leaders that Syrian independence was precious, and that no external threat, however grave, could justify compromising it.

Once again Asad had demonstrated that, although he needed a Soviet counterweight to the grave pressures he was facing, he was not Moscow's man. As a Soviet diplomat commented, 'We weren't allies of Syria in the true sense, we were partners in a concrete political game.'[20] Whenever possible, Asad was still at pains to establish some sort of balance between the superpowers. Just as he had welcomed Nixon to Damascus after the October War, although in that war he had been heavily dependent on the Soviets, so after holding a summit meeting with Brezhnev in Moscow in 1977, he contrived a month or two later to hold a summit with Jimmy Carter in Geneva.

Asad, however, never visited the US, and his knowledge of that country was largely gleaned from the many American envoys who came to see him over the years and with whom he enjoyed jousting. Whatever he might have intended or hoped for, he never achieved any sort of real equilibrium between the Soviet Union and the United States. Moscow remained his chief support, while Washington was that of his Israeli enemy.

But one might also argue that the Arabs in general and Syria in particular did not put the Soviet link to full use. They got the weapons, but could not use them effectively. There was reticence, a lack of candour, and political and military ineptness on both sides, and above all a failure to agree on realistic goals. At no time could the Soviets deliver what the Arabs most wanted—the defeat of Israel.

There was, however, one important occasion when, after a slow start, the Soviet connection eventually proved greatly and unambiguously to Syria's advantage. When Israel invaded Lebanon in 1982 and destroyed Syria's missile defences in the Biqa as well as much of the Syrian air force, the Soviets reacted cautiously.[21] They

---

[20] Vassiliev, *Russian Policy in the Middle East*, 284.

[21] Dennis B. Ross, 'Soviet Behavior Towards the Lebanon War, 1982–84', in George Breslauer (ed.), *Soviet Strategy in the Middle East* (Boston: Unwin Hyman, 1990), 105–7.

remained passive during the war, and throughout the merciless
Israeli shelling of Beirut. Syrian officers blamed their defeat in the
Biqa air battles on Soviet equipment—a view the Soviet military did
not share. Impatient with what they saw as Arab unreliability and
incompetence, they had little sympathy with Syria's problems.
Politically, the Soviet leadership was not inclined to take decisive
action. Brezhnev was distracted by the crises in Afghanistan and in
Poland. He was anxious as ever to avoid a superpower confronta-
tion. He was also ill, and manoeuvring for the succession in the
Kremlin had already begun. Angry and puzzled at Soviet inaction,
Asad flew secretly to Moscow to find out for himself what the Soviets
could do for him. He knew that if Israel succeeded in bringing
Lebanon into its orbit, it would be like a gun at Syria's head. His
regime would truly be in danger.

The Lebanese war highlighted yet again the inherent contradiction
in Syrian–Soviet relations. Asad wanted weapons and protection, but
he also insisted on autonomy. On that visit to Moscow in 1982 he
met Yuri Andropov, who was to take power when Brezhnev died
that November, and at Brezhnev's funeral he renewed the acquain-
tance. The relationship was to prove crucial, for it was Andropov,
overruling the views of Gromyko and Defence Minister Ustinov,
who decided to rearm and re-equip Syria in late 1982 and early 1983.
There was a personal element in it as well. Asad, a rather shy man,
was not much at ease with Soviet leaders. Andropov was an exception. His KGB background had given him a detailed knowledge of
Arab politics—of the stresses and strains at ground level—which
Asad may have found reassuring. (When Andropov fell ill, Asad paid
a secret visit to Moscow to see him—and it was on that occasion that
he met Gorbachev for the first time. But that was still some years in
the future.)

In a move reminiscent of their support for Nasser during the War
of Attrition of 1970, the Soviets in late 1982 and early 1983 took over
responsibility for Syrian air defence, sending some 5,000 military
advisers to Syria together with SAM-5s, the first time this ground-
to-air missile was supplied outside the Soviet bloc. The Soviet
Union's swift and massive help at that critical time gave Asad the
strength and confidence to confront and destroy the 17 May 1983
accord between Israel and Lebanon—an accord which would have
drawn Lebanon into Israel's sphere of influence, reduced that of
Syria, and even, as has been suggested above, endangered the regime.

As occurred so rarely during their uneasy 'marriage', Syria and the
Soviet Union now had clear common aims, which they pursued with
energy and efficiency. They were both determined to destroy the

Israel–Lebanon accord which the US had brokered, because they feared it would herald an era of US–Israeli hegemony. The destruction of the accord, which was finally accomplished with the aid of Syria's local Shia and Druze allies, marked a dramatic reversal of fortune which, from Syria's point of view, must be counted one of the great successes of Asad's presidency.

'DIVORCE' AND DISILLUSION

Asad's disenchantment with Moscow began several years before the Soviet Union's final disintegration. It seems likely that he was one of the first leaders of the Third World to realize that the reformist Soviet leader, Mikhail Gorbachev, was bad news so far as he was concerned. He paid a secret visit to Moscow in 1986 when his fears were first aroused. According to a member of the Syrian delegation on that occasion, Gorbachev, full of energy and confidence, explained to Asad at length how he intended to democratize the Communist Party and allow the emergence of an internal opposition. Asad asked him one question—although a prescient one: 'Do you intend to destroy the Communist Party of the Soviet Union?' Gorbachev was taken aback, and protested that that was not at all his intention, but Asad's sense that Gorbachev would not be a steadfast ally took shape at that meeting. Leaving Gorbachev's office but while he was still in the Kremlin, Asad gathered his advisers around him and, in sombre tones, enjoined them, 'We must look for other options!'

The irony was that Asad's growing disillusion with the Russians from 1986 onwards could not immediately be compensated for by any improvement in his relations with the West. The Hindawi affair of April 1986—when Syria was accused of being implicated in a plot to blow up an Israeli airliner at London's Heathrow airport—resulted in Britain breaking off diplomatic relations with Syria and a general worsening of Syrian relations with a number of Western countries. The US put Syria on the State Department list of countries lending support to international terrorism. It was not until 1988, with the arrival of Edward Djerejian in Damascus as US ambassador, that Asad was able to begin to effect that improvement in his relations with the US which was made necessary by the dramatic changes taking place within the Soviet bloc.

When Asad returned to Moscow in April 1987, the practical consequences of Moscow's 'new thinking' became plain. Ideology was to be eliminated from Soviet foreign policy. The competitive zero-sum game with the West—in effect the Cold War—was to be brought to an end.[22] It was then that Asad learned what he had already begun to suspect, notably that he could no longer count on Soviet military or political support in his conflict with Israel. The Soviet Union was retreating to a position of neutrality in the Arab–Israeli conflict. It was during that visit to Moscow that Gorbachev unveiled his new policy of 'normalization' of relations with Israel—which, by 1989–90, to the alarm of Syria and the Arab world as a whole, was to be followed by the massive emigration of Soviet Jews to Israel.

The Soviets now spoke of resolving the Arab–Israeli conflict on the basis of a 'balance of interests'. On the question of arms transfers, they said that Syria should be content with 'reasonable defensive sufficiency', arguing that if they supplied Syria with advanced weapons, the US would simply go one better with Israel, adding a further twist to the spiral of the arms race, so there was no point to it. Asad's ambition to achieve 'strategic parity' with Israel—which, to his way of thinking, was a necessary precondition for a durable peace—had to be scaled down, if not abandoned altogether. It was a bitter awakening.

Asad adapted as best he could to the new international environment, but there is little doubt that the end of the Cold War and the loss of Soviet support were serious blows to his long-term strategy of holding Israel in check. However, he escaped comparatively lightly. Had he moved still closer into the Soviet camp, as he might have been tempted to do in the 1970s and early 1980s, he might have suffered more than he did when the Soviet system collapsed. He was not swept away in the maelstrom as were other leaders, in Eastern Europe and elsewhere, who had been more closely bound to Moscow. In retrospect, his caution and prickly nationalism served him well.

The Gulf Crisis of 1990–1, and the war against Iraq waged by a coalition of 37 nations, were further setbacks to Asad's hopes of containing Israel and protecting what he saw as the Arab heartlands. When Saddam Hussein invaded Kuwait on 2 August 1990, Asad recognized at once that Saddam's aggression was a deadly threat to Syria's interests—as it was to the interests of every other major player in the region. All realized that the combination of Iraq and Kuwait together would dominate the whole Middle East system. Had Saddam not been challenged, he would have been in a position to dictate the oil, foreign, and defence policies of his neighbours. Asad had long detested Saddam. Although the Ba'th was the ruling

---

[22] Galia Golan, *Moscow and the Middle East: New Thinking on Regional Conflict* (London, 1992).

party in both Syria and Iraq, its Syrian and Iraqi branches had been locked in a bitter war to the death since 1966. Moreover, when Saddam attacked Iran in 1980, Asad had condemned him and sided with Iran—thereby earning Saddam's vengeful enmity. Asad knew that if Saddam got away with his seizure of Kuwait, Syria would be his next target.

So it was inevitable that Asad should join the American-led coalition and send troops to help defend Saudi Arabia. He could follow no other course. He then participated (cautiously) in the war to kick Saddam out of Kuwait and restore the political status quo in the Arab Gulf.

But, in spite of the mutual hostility between Asad and Saddam, Asad did not welcome the Gulf War. He deplored the destruction of Iraq and the depletion of Arab financial reserves. The war split and impoverished the Arab world as never before, and brought it more than ever under American influence. After the devastation of the Gulf War, and its bitter legacy of inter-Arab hatred, there was no longer any realistic possibility of Syria and Iraq combining in an 'Eastern front' against Israel, which had always been Asad's hope and Israel's nightmare.

These developments, therefore, were very much to Israel's profit and Syria's loss. After the Gulf War, it was clear that Israel no longer faced any serious military threat from its Arab neighbours. Its position was unassailable—although the Scud missiles which Iraq launched at it during the war raised the spectre of a possible future threat if a hostile state in the region were ever to acquire nuclear, chemical, or biological warheads for its missiles.

Such was the background to the Middle East peace initiative launched shortly after the Gulf War by President George Bush and his secretary of state, James Baker, and which Asad joined after some considerable hesitation. He had now to come to terms with a world dominated by a single superpower, moreover one wholly committed to Israel's cause, as he was to discover to his bitter disappointment during the Clinton presidency. But Asad was an old warrior, as determined to defend his independence under American hegemony as he had been under Soviet patronage.

The Cold War was a mixed blessing for the Arabs, and for the Syrians in particular. Their relations with Moscow—characterized more by muddle and mutual frustration than by real friendship and cooperation—were never able to match Israel's intimate relations with Washington. Israel was an 'insider' in Washington, able to a remarkable degree and with the aid of its American friends to shape America's Middle East policy to its own advantage. But in Moscow, for all their frequent visits, the Arabs remained 'outsiders'. They had been useful to Moscow in the 1950s and 1960s when the Soviets were concerned to protect their own security in the face of American power, but thereafter they had become something of a burden

On the big issues—containing Israel, recovering the Occupied Territories, avoiding humiliating defeat in peace as in war—the Soviet Union had aroused expectations in its Arab allies which it was never in a position to fulfil. But just who was most to blame for the unsatisfactory outcome of the relationship must remain a subject of conjecture and debate. In conclusion, one should perhaps spare a sympathetic thought for the new post-communist Russia: it emerged to nationhood in a world in which the US–Israeli strategic alliance was more intimate and active than ever before in shaping the region to its designs, while Russia's own relations with the Arab countries, on whom the Soviets had lavished so much treasure, had now been reduced to dust and ashes.[23]

[23] Vassiliev, *Russian Policy in the Middle East*, 358.

4

Lebanon

FAWAZ A. GERGES

In divided societies, it is difficult to distinguish or to separate foreign policy from domestic politics. This is nowhere truer than in the case of Lebanon during the Cold War era. Of all the Middle Eastern countries, Lebanon has one of the most complex and fragmented sociopolitical structures. This diversity does not translate into political pluralism, however. Lebanon's various constituencies are deeply divided along sectarian, religious, and ideological lines, behaving more like tribes than a civil society. Each community has its own conception of Lebanon's role in the regional and international environment.

Given the fragmentation of the internal scene, strong state control has been difficult to develop: the Lebanese state is one among many players; it could only function as a 'democratic management of a perennial conflict situation'.[1] The symptomatic weakness of the state apparatus led two astute observers to wonder whether Lebanon actually pursues any foreign policy, since sects and political parties have different foreign policies.[2] Hence any systematic study of Lebanon's foreign policy must focus on the organic interplay between the internal mosaic and the external balance of power. Most of the controversial issues that have erupted into crises belong to the realm of both internal and external politics.[3] Lebanon's constituencies have

I want to thank Professor William Quandt, Professor Richard Augustus Norton, Professor Paul Salem, Professor Michael Suleiman, and Dr Jocelyn De Jong for reading and commenting on this chapter.

[1] Kamal Salibi 'Lebanon and the Middle Eastern Question', *Papers on Lebanon* 8 (Oxford: Centre for Lebanese Studies, May 1988), 7.

[2] Ghassan Salame, 'Is a Lebanese Foreign Policy Possible?', in Halim Barakat (ed.), *Toward a Viable Lebanon* (London: Croom Helm and the Centre for Contemporary Arab Studies, Georgetown University, 1988), 347–8; Paul Salem, 'Reflections on Lebanon's Foreign Policy', in Deirdre Collings (ed.), *Peace for Lebanon? From War to Reconstruction* (Boulder, Colo.: Lynne Rienner, 1994), 72.

[3] In an otherwise superb essay, Nassif Hitti makes the unconvincing claim that the controversial issues that erupted into political crises and armed violence belong to the realm of foreign policy rather than domestic politics. Yet his analysis indicates the close linkage between the two realms. See Nassif Hitti, 'The Foreign Policy of Lebanon: Lessons and Prospects for the Forgotten Dimension', *Papers on Lebanon* 9 (Oxford: Centre for Lebanese Studies, Apr. 1989), 3.

allied themselves with regional and Great Powers to strengthen their positions *vis-à-vis* the state or their adversaries, compromising the independence of their country and jeopardizing its national unity. As a result, Lebanon became an arena for regional and international rivalries.

Lebanon thus provides an ideal case study through which to examine the impact of the Cold War on domestic politics, relations with other regional powers, and the superpowers. Although the three levels are closely interconnected, what happened at the regional level—the inter-Arab scene and the Arab–Israeli theatre—often had a much more determining influence on Lebanon than that of the superpower struggle.

Sandwiched strategically between Israel and Syria, Lebanon became a political football, kicked by Arabs and Israelis alike. The Israeli issue was a divisive and destabilizing factor in internal Lebanese politics due to the lack of consensus among Lebanon's various communities *vis-à-vis* Israel. Furthermore, by relinquishing its main responsibility—protecting the national territories—the ability of the state apparatus was further undermined, creating a power vacuum which was exploited and filled by rival groups. The Egyptians, Syrians, Palestinians, Israelis, Iranians, and others turned Lebanon into an arena for surrogate conflict.

This bloody circus was accepted and even encouraged by the superpowers as long as it did not spill over into the Israeli–Syrian or into the Israeli–Egyptian front. This was particularly the case after the 1967 Arab–Israeli war, when US–Soviet regional competition and Arab–Israeli tensions made Lebanon a victim of the Cold War regime. Little wonder that when the war broke out in Lebanon in 1975, neither Washington nor Moscow felt the need to engage diplomatically there as long as the conflict did not affect their vital interests. In fact, Henry Kissinger's disengagement diplomacy toward Lebanon was informed not only by his perception of the inherent precariousness of the country but also by the strategic need for a safety valve where Arab–Israeli tensions would be released without the threat of a major Arab–Israeli confrontation.

The above reading, however, does not imply that the Lebanese accepted their humble status and weak position in international relations. On the contrary, they suffered from an opposite tendency: an overestimation of their own and of Lebanon's importance in the world. In the heyday of the Cold War, some Lebanese leaders, being on the defensive internally and regionally, tried to compensate for their weakness by going on the offensive and by exploiting the superpower rivalry. In 1958 and 1982–3, respectively, Presidents Camille

Chamoun and Amin Gemayel relied on US military and diplomatic weight to try to win the fight against Egypt and Syria and their supporters inside Lebanon. In both instances, the opposition won the contest. Chamoun and Gemayel discovered that pursuing an active foreign policy to counterbalance their domestic and regional opponents not only was costly but also endangered the very survival of the country.

This chapter will present the two case studies—that of Chamoun and Gemayel—as examples of the Lebanonist miscalculation and of the inability of the state effectively to use the Cold War card and pursue an independent foreign policy. It will also examine the post-1967 period—a third case study—to show the opposite: how Lebanon became an unwilling pawn in Cold War politics. The three case studies shed much light on the primacy of domestic and regional dynamics in shaping the politics of Lebanon. What took place at the local level was much more decisive and had a more determining influence on the destiny of the region than any diversionary actions by external forces.

The chapter advances a double thesis: first, external powers, particularly regional powers, used Lebanon as an arena where regional and international conflicts were played out, directly as well as through proxies. Second, some Lebanese leaders—Chamoun and Gemayel—attempted to exploit the polarized regional and international system and drag the Great Powers in on their side. Chamoun and Gemayel's gamble was a dismal failure, however. The result is that Lebanon ended up being a casualty of Cold War politics, thus compromising its sovereignty and endangering its independence.

LEBANON IN INTER-ARAB AND SUPERPOWER RIVALRIES

Although the international system polarized along East–West lines by the late 1940s, the Cold War waves did not reach the Lebanese shore until the mid-1950s. Before the mid-1950s Lebanon, like all Arab countries, had a pro-Western orientation; it also was not threatened by either local or international communism. Although the Lebanese Communist Party had been operating for a long time in Lebanon, it failed to attract a large membership. In 1957 not even Chamoun, the staunchly pro-Western president, was worried about the potential threat of domestic communism: 'No doubt communism has made some progress here. But with appropriate measures its advance can be halted.'⁴

Culturally, economically, and politically, Lebanon remained well within the orbit of the Western sphere of influence. The impact of the Cold War on internal Lebanese politics was minimal as long as relations between the Arab world and the Western powers were not hostile and the Arab–Israeli conflict did not escalate out of control. Again, this is another indication of how developments on the regional, rather than the global, level affected the ebb and flow of political forces on the domestic Lebanese scene.

By the second half of the 1950s, however, Lebanon's ability to insulate itself against the polarizing and disintegrating effects of the global and Arab Cold War was considerably restricted. This new situation was due to the changing regional context and the deterioration of relations between the Arab nationalist movement and the Western powers. In the 1950s the Arab world witnessed the emergence of a nationalist, anti-imperialist movement under the leadership of Egyptian President Gamal Abdel Nasser. While Nasser led the pan-Arab nationalist forces, Iraq, representing the pro-Western Arab states, spearheaded the opposition to Egypt in a quest for regional dominance. As a result, no Arab state was able to escape from the flames of the Arab Cold War, especially Lebanon.

THE 1958 CRISIS: CHAMOUN AND THE COLD WAR CARD

The crisis which broke out in the spring of 1958 is a classic case of how the Cold War affected Lebanon's foreign policy orientations, its relations with other regional players, and the ebb and flow of its domestic politics. Ultimately, however, the complexity and fragility of the Lebanese internal structure and inter-Arab dynamics had a determining influence on the state apparatus's international relations and on how external powers acted towards it. The genesis of the crisis lay in its domestic, regional, and international dimensions, all closely related to one another.⁵ It is only by examining these three dimensions that the 1958 Lebanese war can be understood.

On the domestic front, a struggle for power between the opposition and Chamoun was polarizing Lebanese society. The opposition

⁴ Tom Streithorst, 'Face to Face with Camille Chamoun', *Middle East Forum* (Apr. 1957), 7; Leila M. T. Meo, *Lebanon, Improbable Nation: A Study in Political Development* (Westport, Conn.: Greenwood Press, 1965), 123.
⁵ Fahim Qubain, *Crisis in Lebanon* (Washington, DC: Middle East Institute, 1961), 30.

accused Chamoun of attempting to internationalize the internal power struggle by inviting US military intervention. That was precisely the overall strategy of the tenacious president and his combative foreign minister, Charles Malik. Chamoun and Malik were determined to win the battle of wills against the opposition by portraying the problems in Lebanon as an extension of superpower rivalry. During the heyday of the Cold War, small actors, like Lebanon, were able to obtain economic aid and military supplies from the superpowers by exploiting the polarized international system. Washington and Moscow played into the hands of their clients by viewing local disputes in Cold War terms. In 1957–8, by overemphasizing the threat of international communism and flirting with Lebanon, the Eisenhower administration led Chamoun and Malik to believe that they could count on Washington for support. Both the Chamoun government and the Eisenhower administration tried to use each other. However, Chamoun's bargaining position was limited, given Lebanon's inconsequential political weight and its meagre resources.

The main CIA contact with Chamoun, Wilbur Eveland, claimed that the CIA provided 'massive' funding for the pro-government deputies during the 1957 parliamentary elections. According to Eveland, the US did so in the knowledge that the new parliament would elect a new president in 1958. He portrayed the elections as a CIA-run operation.[6] Although no specific US documents relating to Washington's input in the elections have been released yet, recently declassified sources hint that the US 'played an active role'. They also show that Malik sought US assistance to influence the elections.[7]

Chamoun's refusal to deny these allegations publicly convinced his opponents and supporters alike of his intention to seek a second term. Both the CIA and the US embassy in Beirut concluded that Chamoun fixed the elections in such a way as to ensure his re-election.[8] It would be misleading, however, to think of the Lebanese

[6] Wilbur Crane Eveland, *Ropes of Sand: America's Failure in the Middle East* (London: W. W. Norton, 1980), 248–58, 266.

[7] The Officer in Charge of Lebanon–Syria Affairs to the Director of the Office of Near Eastern Affairs, 17 Jan. 1958, in *Foreign Relations of the United States, 1958–1960: Lebanon and Jordan*, xi (Washington, DC: US Govt. Printing Office, 1992), 4. [Henceforth this series will be referred to as *FRUS, 1958–60*, xi.] The Lebanese Foreign Minister's Call on the President, 6 Feb. 1957, 3. For the 1958 crisis, I rely heavily on recently declassified US documents obtained, by the Centre for Lebanese Studies, Oxford, from the Dwight Eisenhower Library, Abilene, Kansas; Marine and Naval Corps Historical Centers; Central Intelligence Agency; and National Archives and Records Administration, Washington, DC, and Suitland, MD.

[8] The Lebanese constitution does not permit two consecutive terms. Current Intelligence Weekly Summary, CIA, Office of Current Intelligence, 1, 15, 29 May 1957, 10 of 20; Dept. of State, Bureau of Public Affairs, Office of the Historian, Historical Studies, The United States and Lebanon, 1958, No. 6, 2; and US Embassy, Beirut, 25 June 1958 [no identification].

crisis as a purely internal affair or as a clash of temperaments and personalities. Internal dissatisfaction with Chamoun was fuelled mainly by the government's pursuit of regional and international policies which were seen to be provocative and divisive.

The birth of the Arab Cold War was closely related to the superpower Cold War. Anglo-American efforts to bolster Western security in the Middle East by creating defence pacts served not only to accentuate anti-Western sentiments in the Arab lands but also to polarize the latter between two positions—those Arabs who saw the region's progress and destiny closely allied to the West, and those Arabs who preferred to follow an independent policy between the Western and Eastern blocs. As a result, the flames of the Arab Cold War engulfed the whole Arab order, including Lebanon.[9] Chamoun and Malik's decision to align Lebanon with the pro-Western forces burdened the Lebanese political system as well as sucking the country deeper into the quagmire of inter-Arab rivalries.

Chamoun's pro-Western orientation led him to entertain the idea of joining the 1955 Baghdad Pact—a military alliance among Iraq, Turkey, Pakistan, and Britain—thus antagonizing Egypt and later Syria, which allied itself with Cairo. An exchange of visits in 1955 between the Lebanese and Turkish presidents indicated Chamoun's interest in aligning Lebanon with Iraq and Turkey. This policy did not contradict the terms of the 1943 National Pact, which called on Lebanon to pursue some form of non-alignment or neutrality and cooperate with its Arab sisters.[10] The question was whether Lebanon could afford to side with the pro-Western Iraqi camp against the Arab nationalist, non-aligned position of Egypt and Syria. This question takes for granted the existence in Beirut of a sovereign and strong state apparatus with few domestic constraints on its ability to undertake initiatives in the region and beyond. This was not the case, however, by the second half of the 1950s.

The Egyptian–Iraqi rivalry over the Baghdad Pact not only poisoned inter-Arab relations but also was the first spark to ignite the fire of new mass politics in the Arab world. Lebanon was no exception in that regard. At this stage, two political constituencies could be discerned. The first—the Asile du Liban school, with its emphasis on the Phoenician origin and special historical character of the Lebanese—was closely allied with the state and reflected a conservative Christian (Maronite) vision of Lebanon. This particularist,

    [9] Fawaz A. Gerges, *The Superpowers and the Middle East: Regional and International Politics, 1955–1967* (Boulder, Colo.: Westview Press, 1994), ch. 2.
    [10] Salem, 'Reflections on Lebanon's Foreign Policy', 70; Meo, *Lebanon, Improbable Nation*, 96.

Lebanonist community identified itself culturally and politically with the West rather than with *dar al-Islam*; it called for a more active Lebanese foreign policy and for a direct strategic alliance with the Western powers rather than indirectly with Iraq and Turkey. Their idealized view of the West fostered exaggerated expectations: it was assumed that the West would fight to protect the 'only Western model' in the Arab area.[11]

Another diametrically opposing view was that of the Arab nationalist constituency. The latter saw the political destiny and future of Lebanon within an Arab/Islamic framework. The Arab nationalists were adamantly opposed to any Lebanese membership in the Baghdad Pact lest it undermine Lebanon's neutrality in inter-Arab affairs and tie Lebanon to the West further. They also felt an ideological affinity with Nasser's budding ideas of Arab independence, unity, and non-alignment.

Bowing to domestic and local constraints, the Lebanese government decided against joining the Baghdad Pact. In this context, the retreat of the Chamoun administration signalled the state apparatus's inability to prosecute its own regional and foreign policy in the face of strong opposition by the Arab nationalist constituency. From now on, Lebanon's various communities would clash over the direction of foreign policy, thus restricting the state's freedom of action.

The deliberations to join the Baghdad Pact highlighted two unpleasant realities of the Lebanese scene:

1. The existence of serious disagreements between the two main constituencies over Lebanon's place in the region and the world. This gap was bound to widen due to the heightening tensions in inter-Arab and superpower rivalries.
2. Many at home and abroad perceived Chamoun as supporting the Hashemites in Baghdad and Amman in their struggle against Nasser, thus violating the principle of neutrality that had served Lebanon well in its relations with its Arab neighbours.[12] As a result, Lebanon was sucked deeper and deeper into the Arab Cold War and, consequently, into the East–West struggle.

Whatever one's assessment of Chamoun's tenure, one thing is clear: he tried to avoid marginalization by actively engaging in regional politics and by asserting the state apparatus's fundamental role in the formulation and execution of foreign policy. He was determined to preserve and further Lebanon's pro-Western orientation, uninhibited either by the internal constraints or by inter-Arab

---

[11] Ibid. 97; Hitti, 'The Foreign Policy of Lebanon', 13–14.
[12] Meo, *Lebanon, Improbable Nation*, 97.

imperatives. Chamoun's, along with that of the Lebanonist constituency which he represented, inflated image of Lebanon's civiliza-
tional and political weight distorted his world view, leading to an
overestimation of the country's importance to the West. The failure
to maintain a balance between goals and means (resources) produced
reckless policies based on miscalculation and improvisation.

Given Chamoun's own position and the close linkage between
internal and external politics, the further deterioration of relations
between the Western powers and Arab nationalists was bound to
strain relations between Egypt and Syria on the one hand and
Lebanon on the other, and to deepen internal divisions inside
Lebanon. The 1956 nationalization of the Suez Canal Company and
the consequent Anglo-French–Israeli attack on Egypt was a case in
point. By shaking the Arab East with a storm of populist protests,
the Anglo-French–Israeli invasion put Egypt's Arab opponents on
the defensive and forced some of its arch-enemies, such as the Iraqi
prime minister, Nuri al-Said, to pay lip-service to Arab solidarity and
close ranks with Nasser. Not so with Chamoun. Disregarding the
force of Lebanese public opinion and the request of his premier,
Abdallah al-Yafi, Chamoun refused to sever diplomatic relations
with Britain and France, precipitating the resignation of the government and provoking accusations by the nationalist/Islamist constituency that he betrayed the Arab cause.

Far from being deterred, however, Chamoun appointed a new
conservative government headed by Sami es-Solh, with Malik as foreign minister. The choice of Malik, an outspoken admirer of the
West and a ruthless critic of communism, signalled Chamoun's commitment to drawing closer to the American alliance even at the cost
of a confrontation with his domestic and regional opponents.
Furthermore, Malik, being a committed ideologue, argued that
Lebanon should play a critical role in the Cold War by 'holding the
dike' and ensuring that the West will not 'go down'.[13] Rhetoric
apart, Chamoun and Malik hoped to receive not only generous US
economic and military assistance to strengthen their authority but
also protection under the US umbrella against the rising forces of
Arab nationalism.

Here was an example of a small state trying to manipulate superpower rivalry to score financial and political gains and pre-empt its
enemies at home. For neither the president nor his foreign minister
believed that there existed any serious communist threat—whether
domestic or international—to Lebanon. Chamoun and Malik's posi-

[13] Memorandum of a Conversation, Dept. of State, Washington, 30 June 1958, in *FRUS,
1958–60*, xi. 161, 186. xi. 4, 161, 168.

tion raises a few disturbing questions: could Lebanon, with its fragile political process, afford the high costs of its entanglements in the Cold War? To what extent did Chamoun and Malik overvalue Lebanon's place on the Western strategic chessboard and set goals beyond their capabilities? Did they dupe themselves into believing that 'tiny' Lebanon was high on Washington's complex global agenda and that their alliance with the West was mutual? Or did they really think that in case of conflict with Egypt and Syria, the US would be more sensitive to Lebanon's interests than to the former's security concerns?

Like their Asile du Liban compatriots, the Arab nationalist/Islamist adherents in Lebanon fell victim to the same misconceptions, and suffered from a similar 'geostrategic myopia'. They digested uncritically the slogans of radical Arab nationalism emanating from Cairo and Damascus. To them, Lebanon had to march with the pan-Arab caravan whatever the consequences and costs. As Nadim al-Jisr, a leading Lebanese opposition figure, put it, by standing up to the West and by defending the Arab cause, Nasser 'became, to all Arabs and Moslems, an object of worship next to God'.[14] In a sense, the Arab nationalist proponents in Lebanon were pawns in the Egyptian game of regional and international politics. The interests of Lebanon were subordinated to those of its immediate environment.

Chamoun's anti-Egyptian stand did not help either. Neither the president nor his foreign minister seemed to take much account of the domestic implications inherent in pursuing an anti-Egyptian policy. Instead, they swam against the current of public opinion, thus undermining the bases of their political legitimacy.[15] For example, during the US–Syrian crisis of 1957, Chamoun and Malik received the US envoy, Loy Henderson, without consulting Syria. Malik exhorted the Eisenhower administration to topple the Syrian regime, informing Henderson that pro-Western Lebanon could not coexist with neutralist or communist-oriented Syria: 'Sooner or later one or the other must disappear.'[16] When in February 1958 Egypt and Syria

---

[14] Beirut to Dept. of State, The Roots of the Lebanese Revolution, 14 Oct. 1958, 10–11.

[15] Nadim Dimechkie, 'The United States Intervened Militarily by Sending the Marines to Lebanon in 1958: Why Did This Happen?', paper given at the University of Texas Conference on Lebanon in the 1950s, 10–13 Sept. 1992, 10–13, 19; Agnes G. Korbani, *US Intervention in Lebanon, 1958 and 1982: Presidential Decisionmaking* (New York: Praeger, 1991), 34; Qubain, *Crisis in Lebanon*, 36–7; Meo, *Lebanon, Improbable Nation*, 104.

[16] Beirut to Secretary of State, 28 Aug. 1957; quoted in David W. Lesch, 'Prelude to American Intervention in Lebanon: The 1957 American–Syrian Crisis', paper given at the University of Texas Conference on Lebanon in the 1950s, 10–13 Sept. 1992, 18.

formed their union, Chamoun initially refused to recognize the new entity—the United Arab Republic (UAR).[17]

Chamoun's pronounced pro-Western policy only compounded his internal and regional difficulties. He, Malik, and the new premier, Sami es-Solh, were staunch supporters of the West. They tied Lebanon's fortunes to US policy in the Middle East. Their strategy could have been beneficial but for the steady deterioration of relations between the West and the Arab nationalist movement beginning in the mid-1950s. This development confronted the Chamoun government with problematic choices.[18] The state apparatus had to choose between either a close association with Washington, thus risking domestic instability and regional isolation, or an appeasement approach toward Nasser's nationalist forces that would ensure domestic peace. Chamoun chose the former for political, ideological, and practical reasons. He saw in the Cold War a golden opportunity to put Lebanon on the map and avoid marginalization; he also hoped to pre-empt the opposition by closely aligning Lebanese foreign policy with the US.

Most of all, however, the East–West struggle provided Chamoun with an ideology of progress that promised Lebanon abundant resources to make its capitalist model of development effective and successful. Little wonder that Chamoun and Malik quickly seized on the 1957 Eisenhower Doctrine, an initiative designed to arrest revolutionary change in the region, to request US economic aid and military assistance. During the debate in the Lebanese parliament on the doctrine, Malik tried to impress on his colleagues the financial and military benefits which would accrue to Lebanon by accepting the doctrine; he painted a rosy picture of a potentially strong army and flourishing economy.

Even before the US Congress approved the Doctrine in March 1957, Malik informed Eisenhower that Lebanon welcomed his initiative and was ready to combat communist subversion in the region. He also asserted that Egypt and Syria were falling under Soviet domination. 'It was essential', added Malik, 'that political change take place in Syria and Egypt.'[19] With the exception of Libya, Lebanon

[17] US Ambassador to Dept. of State, 14 Feb. 1958, 2 of 6; M. S. Agwani, *The Lebanese Crisis, 1958: A Documentary Study* (London: Asia Publishing House, 1965), 3–4.

[18] Dept. of State, Office of the Historian, 1; and Joint Chiefs of Staff [JCS] and National Policy, 1956–8, 420.

[19] The Lebanese Foreign Minister's Call on the President, 6 Feb. 1957, 2–3; JCS and National Policy, 1956–8, 420; and Richards to Secretary of State, Beirut, 16 Mar. 1957. As early as 1955, Lebanon's ambassador to the US requested US economic and military aid, proposing, in return, that the US consider the participation of Lebanon in a regional defence organization. Dept. of State Memorandum of Conversation, subject: The 'Northern Tier' Defense Organization and the Relations to It of the Arab States; Arab–Israeli Relations,

was the only Arab country to endorse the Doctrine officially. The other pro-Western Arab governments recognized the inherent danger in such a move.

The opposition resented Chamoun's lukewarm attitude toward the UAR and his pro-Western foreign policy. They believed that, by aligning Lebanon with the West against Egypt and Syria, he not only violated Beirut's traditional neutrality but also threatened the delicate balance among the various Lebanese factions. As two of the opposition leaders, Kamal Jumblat and Nadim al-Jisr, put it, the 1958 uprising was a direct response to foreign influence and to Lebanon's dependence on the West.[20] After the conclusion of the Egyptian–Syrian union, Damascus virtually became the site of pilgrimage for Lebanese politicians and citizens, who poured there to pay homage (*mubaya'a*) to the pan-Arab Egyptian leader. In their zeal for Arab unity under Nasser, demonstrators trampled the Lebanese flag in the streets of Tyre.[21]

Given the diametrically opposed views of the Lebanonist and Arab nationalist/Islamist constituencies, the stage was set for a confrontation in which each side sought external support to consolidate its position. While Chamoun and Malik courted Washington, the opposition welcomed with open arms Egyptian and Syrian political and material assistance. Both sides played a dangerous game: they mortgaged the future of their country to foreign creditors.

As tensions increased in the early months of 1958, the Chamoun administration tried to emphasize the external nature of the crisis and to impress on Washington the need for decisive action. Beleaguered at home, Chamoun and Malik looked for outside support. From the onset they had portrayed the conflict as a struggle between pro-Western Lebanon and radical Arab nationalism, which was allied with international communism.[22] The cause of the crisis, contended Chamoun, was not his ambitions but Lebanon's

February 9, 1955. Declassified Documents Quarterly Catalog 8(1) (Jan.–Mar. 1982), No. 00309, 24; cited in Irene L. Gendzier, 'The Declassified Lebanon 1948–1958: Elements of Continuity and Contrast in US Policy Toward Lebanon', in Barakat (ed.), *Toward a Viable Lebanon*, 197.

[20] Beirut to Dept. of State, The Roots of the Lebanese Revolution, 14 Oct. 1958, 2, 10; Dept. of State, Office of the Historian, 2; and JCS and National Policy, 1956–8, 420. Kamal Jumblat, *Fi Majra al-siyasa al-Lubnaniya* [In the Course of Lebanese Politics] (Beirut: Dar al-tali'a, n.d.); 57. B. J. Odeh, *Lebanon: Dynamics of Conflict, a Modern Political History* (London: Zed Books, 1985), 100.

[21] Kamal Salibi, 'Recollections of the 1940s and 1950s', paper given at the University of Texas Conference on Lebanon in the 1950s, 10–13 Sept. 1992, 26; *Egyptian Gazette*, 5 Mar. 1958.

[22] McClintock to Secretary of State, Beirut, Nos. 4115, 4272, 5108, 22, 27 May and 25 June 1958; and Beirut to Dept. of State, the Roots of the Lebanese Revolution, 14 Oct. 1958, 4. Agwani, *The Lebanese Crisis*, 58, 85.

adherence to the Eisenhower Doctrine. By emphasizing the external menace and by playing the Cold War card, Chamoun and Malik's strategy was designed to internationalize the dispute and precipitate US military intervention. In contrast, the opposition were adamantly against the internationalization of the crisis because the configuration of forces was in their favour. They asserted that the roots of the conflict were internal and had nothing to do with the UAR. Nevertheless, they relied heavily on the moral and material support of the UAR.[23]

Contrary to popular perceptions, the reason for the US military intervention in Beirut in July 1958 was not because US officials believed that Lebanon's independence and sovereignty were threatened by international communism or that Lebanon in itself represented an important link in the Western chain of anti-communist posts in the Third World; the weight of evidence suggests, rather, that the Eisenhower administration probably would not have sent troops to Lebanon if the July 1958 Iraqi *coup d'état*, which destroyed the royal regime in Baghdad, had not occurred. Before the Iraqi coup, and notwithstanding the repeated requests for US intervention by Chamoun and Malik, Eisenhower was reluctant to send US forces to Lebanon. The consensus in Washington was that armed intervention could have regional repercussions that would be inimical to Western interests. Neither Eisenhower nor Dulles was prepared to risk a confrontation with Egypt–Syria over Lebanon.

But in US eyes, the dramatic events in Iraq introduced a dangerous element and threatened to destroy the whole Western security structure in the Middle East. Shocked by the success of the 1958 Iraqi revolution and concluding that it was a *fait accompli*, US officials changed their minds, and suddenly Lebanon acquired a temporary special status in the East–West struggle. In this sense, US intervention should be viewed within a broader context than the frontiers of Lebanon. Far from being seen as a proof of Western commitment to the security of Lebanon, US intervention was part of the tug-of-war between the West and Nasser's brand of Arab nationalism. The Lebanonist constituency did not appreciate Lebanon's inconsequential role on the Western strategic chessboard. As Dulles bluntly put it, Lebanon was 'not very important in itself'.[24] Despite

[23] Chamoun, *Crise au Moyen Orient*, 11; Beirut to Dept. of State, 9 Jan. 1958, in *FRUS, 1958–60*, xi. 1–2; Dept. of State, Office of the Historian, 2; Charles W. Thayer, *Diplomat* (New York: Harper & Brothers, 1959), 24–5; Eveland, *Ropes of Sand*, 256, 276; *New York Times*, 17 July 1958.

[24] Memorandum of a Conversation between the Secretary of State and the British Embassy (Lord Hood), Washington, 14 July 1958; and Conference with the President, 14 July, in *FRUS, 1958–60*, xi. 212–13, 238.

its military intervention, the US sacrificed Chamoun at the altar of its wider regional interests by concluding a deal with Nasser to replace Chamoun with his military chief, Fouad Chehab.

I have devoted a great deal of space to the 1958 crisis to highlight some enduring themes and conclusions.

1. Far from being influenced by Soviet communism, the opposition in Lebanon was basically inspired by Nasser's brand of Arab nationalism. The major opposition figures were mainstream Arab nationalists rather than communists. The opposition's major demand was that Lebanon should follow a neutral policy in inter-Arab affairs and a non-aligned course in international relations. Although initially Eisenhower and Dulles believed that the problem in Lebanon was 'Communistic in origin', senior US officials publicly acknowledged the fact that communism played 'no direct or substantial part in the insurrection. The outside influences came mostly from Syria and Egypt.'[25] In fact, the Soviet Union emerged as a passive player throughout the Lebanese crisis. It had neither the military capabilities nor the desire to confront the US. Unlike their threats and posturing during the Suez crisis, the Soviets' response to the events in Lebanon was very restrained, limited to rhetoric. This fact reflected the marginal place which Lebanon occupied in Soviet strategy. The events in Lebanon proved beyond any doubt that Washington was the dominant actor there. The main challenge to the Western powers emanated from the region itself: Moscow's role was secondary.

2. US military intervention in Lebanon did not reflect any strategic commitment to the Lebanonist or to the state apparatus's agenda. The US used Lebanon as an arena to project its military power and demonstrate its will to protect other vital regional interests, mainly oil supplies. US officials wanted to signal to their adversaries their readiness to use force, if necessary, to arrest the further crumbling of the Arab conservative order. As one US policy-maker put it, 'Lebanon was a test case in eyes of the others.'[26]

While Chamoun and his adversaries enticed external actors to intervene on their behalf, they lost sight of the fact that the latter used them as proxies to fight their own wars. The result was to transform Lebanon into a surrogate for the Cold War, thus inflaming and exacerbating domestic problems. This is another example of the

---

[25] Dept. of State, Office of the Historian, 5; Diary, 14 July 1958; Memorandum for Record, 15 May 1958, 2; Memorandum of Conversation with the President, Dept. of State, Lebanon, 15 June 1958, 4; and Eisenhower to Paul Hoffman, 23 June 1958, 2. *Department of State Bulletin*, 27 Oct. 1958, 650–1.

[26] Minutes of Cabinet Meeting, 18 July 1958, 4; JCS and National Policy, 1956–8, JCS History, ch. 9, 'The Lebanon Crisis and After', 469.

linkage between internal wars and external interventions which have helped to shape the course of Lebanon's troubled history.[27]

The Lebanonist constituency did not fully appreciate Lebanon's limited influence in relation to that of Egypt and Syria. In reality, the US saw Cairo, not Beirut, as the nerve centre of the Arab world. Here lies the explanation behind Washington's abandonment of Chamoun and its secret agreement with Nasser to resolve the Lebanese crisis. This modality—negotiating with Lebanon's neighbours rather than with the state apparatus to contain upheavals inside Lebanon—would become a pattern of US behaviour toward Lebanon.

3. Chamoun's attempt to play an active part in the Cold War was bound to have major repercussions for several reasons: (*a*) the division within the ruling élite; (*b*) the weakness of the state apparatus; (*c*) deep cleavages between the two main political constituencies—the Lebanonist and the Arab/Islamist. But what provided the first spark was Chamoun's position on inter-Arab issues, particularly his challenge of the dominant current—Nasserism—in Arab politics in the second half of the 1950s. Given the trans-national nature of Lebanese politics, the state apparatus could not afford the heavy political costs of taking sides in the Arab Cold War, let alone to align itself with an external power against an Arab state. In this context, the 1958 crisis should be seen as an extension of inter-Arab rivalries and as a clear example of how developments on the regional level affected superpower behaviour, such as US military intervention.

LEBANON AFTER 1967: UNWILLING PAWN IN COLD WAR POLITICS

In his first major foreign policy initiative after the 1958 crisis, President Fouad Chehab repudiated the Eisenhower Doctrine and adopted non-alignment. Furthermore, he took serious steps to repair Lebanon's connections with Egypt's Nasser. The new administration appreciated the saliency of regional politics and the need to navigate carefully in its rough waters. Interestingly, the Chehab–Nasser *rapprochement* did not come at the expense of Lebanon's pro-Western orientation. Lebanon remained within the Western economic and cultural orbit, maintaining its free market and Western-oriented educational system. No expansion of Soviet influence occurred in Beirut, and Soviet–Lebanese relations remained lukewarm. The only major

---

[27] Marwan R. Buheiry, 'External Interventions and Internal Wars in Lebanon: 1770–1982', in Lawrence I. Conrad (ed.), *The Formation and Perception of the Modern Arab World: Studies by Marwan Buheiry* (Princeton, NJ: Darwin Press, 1989), 129, 137–8.

change undertaken in foreign policy was that Lebanon would follow the UAR's lead in the region and would not join in any Western alliances against Egypt and Syria. Little wonder that the brief period between 1958 and 1967 ushered in relative stability and harmony.

However, the brief period, 1958–67, of tranquillity was not only short-lived but also deceptive. The Chehab–Nasser pact ensured social peace by tying Lebanon to Egypt's Arab policy. This strategy worked as long as Egypt maintained its predominance in inter-Arab affairs and inter-Arab relations did not escalate beyond a dangerous ceiling, and as long as other local and international developments did not disturb the internal balance of power. Again, Lebanon's political fortunes were closely tied to the precarious regional order, which underwent a radical change in the late 1960s.

The 1960s witnessed a steady deterioration of both inter-Arab and Arab–Israeli relations. The resurfacing of the Arab–Israeli question was very much related to the escalation of Israel's Arab policy and the intensification of inter-Arab tensions—the breakup of the UAR and the serious challenge to Egypt's dominance of the Arab world by both conservatives and revolutionaries. Little wonder that Israel played a divisive role in inter-Arab politics, putting enormous strains on the inter-Arab state system.

The result was the 1967 Arab–Israeli, war whose devastating effects overburdened the fragile political system in Lebanon. First, the war accelerated the mobilization of the Palestinian community and the success of the Palestine Liberation Organization (PLO) in turning Lebanon into a theatre of military operation against Israel. Second, the occupation of the Golan Heights enhanced the strategic value of Lebanon in Syrian and Israeli calculations.[28] In this context, Lebanon became a battlefield on which the Palestinians, Israelis, and Syrians fought each other. Third, one of the most important consequences of the war was the rekindling of internal tensions over Lebanon's role in the Arab–Israeli theatre.

While the Lebanonist constituency called for neutrality in the Arab–Israeli context, the Arab nationalist community expected Lebanon to engage fully against Israel by granting maximal freedom of operation to the PLO and severing Lebanon's links with the US. Unlike the 1958 crisis, the 1967 war radicalized the Arab nationalist adherents, who blamed the Western powers for the shattering Arab defeat and who came to equate Israel with the West.[29]

[28] Walid Khalidi, 'State and Society in Lebanon', in Fawaz (ed.), *State and Society In Lebanon*, 39.

[29] Hitti, 'The Foreign Policy of Lebanon', 14–15; Ghassan Salame, 'Lebanon: How "National" Is Independence?', *Beirut Review* 6 (fall 1994), 2.

The increase of US intelligence, business, and political presence in Beirut after 1967—after the breaking of diplomatic relations between several Arab states and the US—added to the anti-American feeling among the Arab nationalist/Islamist proponents. The latter's resentment was directed against the state apparatus for allowing Lebanon to become an outpost of 'American imperialism'.[30] A host of leftist Lebanese parties and emergent Palestinian guerrilla movements looked toward Moscow for arms and military training. The upshot was to turn Lebanon into an arena for regional and superpower conflict.

On the one hand, by trying to be neutral in the Arab–Israeli conflict, the Lebanonist view denied the peculiarities and specificities of inter-Arab relations and its geographical importance to the other regional actors; it also opened up the Pandora's box of the identity issue. This policy prescription lacked consensus at home and proved to be divisive and impossible to implement. On the other hand, the nationalist/Islamist perspective not only suffered from unrealistic assessment between goals and capabilities but also served, consciously or unconsciously, as a conduit and mirror for the PLO's and Syria's policies: Lebanon's national interests took a back seat.[31]

Here is another example of how developments on the regional level had a direct impact on Lebanese domestic politics. In the contemporary history of Lebanon, the most controversial issues dividing its citizens have centred mainly around two principal arenas: inter-Arab politics and the Arab–Israeli conflict. The Cold War was relevant because it fuelled and inflamed these two loci of conflict and because local powers exploited superpower rivalries to gain support. In the 1950s Chamoun tried, with no success, to play an active role in regional politics by aligning Lebanon with the US. In the late 1960s and 1970s, however, the state apparatus was unwilling and incapable of performing one of its basic functions—protecting its citizens and territory.

The escalation of the Arab–Israeli conflict introduced a very destabilizing element into regional politics and, as a consequence, into the Lebanese domestic scene. The state apparatus failed to adjust to this stage of Arab–Israeli hostilities created by the influx of the PLO's military machine into Lebanon by formulating a politico-security policy to tackle the new situation. The notion that 'Lebanon's strength lies in its weakness' meant that the state surrendered its main role—ensuring the security of the country.[32] After the destruc-

---

[30] Paul Salem, 'Superpowers and Small States: An Overview of American–Lebanese Relations', *Beirut Review* 5 (spring 1993), 57.
[31] Hitti, 'The Foreign Policy of Lebanon', 14–18.   [32] Ibid. 17.

tion of the PLO's military infrastructure in Jordan, Lebanon became the PLO's major theatre of operations against Israel.

The Palestinian–Israeli confrontation in Lebanon proved to be costly for several reasons: making Lebanon an operational arena for inter-Arab and Arab–Israeli hostilities; undermining Lebanon's political integrity as a sovereign state; and exacerbating internal tensions. One wonders, for example, if the 1975 upheaval and the consequent collapse of the state apparatus could have been avoided had the Lebanese state not relinquished its security responsibly to other players. What if the state had stood up to Israel in order to protect its fragile communal balance and defend the Palestinians in Lebanon, thus obviating the need for the PLO's War of National Liberation from Lebanon? Would not the loss of south Lebanon to Israel have been less costly than the state of anarchy and chaos which prevailed in the country from 1968 until 1975, leading to the destruction of state and society? Although he had appreciated the likelihood of a military defeat, King Hussein of Jordan decided to participate in the 1967 war. Hussein realized that Jordan could not remain aloof, for this would have resulted in a civil war in Jordan.[33]

The above scenario presupposes that Lebanese leaders had the vision, the inclination, and the freedom to adopt such a radical course of action. First, the state apparatus could not break ranks and divorce itself from its strategic partner—the Asile du Liban constituency. Since the establishment of Greater Lebanon, the state allied itself with this Lebanonist segment. The latter was adamantly opposed to Lebanon's engagement in the Arab–Israeli conflict; they also took up arms in the early 1970s against the Palestinians and their leftist and Muslim Lebanese allies, whom they perceived as usurping the state's power.

Second, Presidents Charles Hilu (1964–70) and Sulayman Franjiyya (1970–6) could not adopt a hostile posture against Israel—even if the domestic barriers were absent—lest they antagonize their superpower patron, the US. As mentioned previously, in the context of the Cold War, official Lebanon remained within the Western economic and political orbit. The Soviet Union was unable to establish a strong foothold in Lebanon, except within the ranks of the Palestinian–leftist coalition. Hilu and Franjiyya were well attuned to the US position, which called on Lebanon to refrain from antagonizing the Israelis by curtailing Palestinian activities inside the country.

In fact, in the early 1970s the US became so alarmed at the rapid advances made by the Palestinian–leftist coalition that it lent its

---

[33] Gerges, *The Superpowers and the Middle East*, 215–16.

political support to a tougher Lebanese stance against the Palestinians. In 1973, in a test of wills, Franjiyya sent the army against a Palestinian refugee camp, only to retreat in the face of stiff Syrian and internal opposition.[34] The state was too constrained by domestic and regional considerations to act decisively. This example shows how the superpower rivalry played itself out on the regional and Lebanese domestic scene. Moscow and Washington, however, were responding to local developments over which they had no control and which they hoped, at most, to influence in order to preserve and maximize their interests.

When the 1975 war broke out in Lebanon, neither of the superpowers seemed very concerned about the unravelling of the Lebanese polity. Moscow did not have much of a stake in a traditionally pro-Western country. Although the war afforded the Soviets a golden opportunity to establish a presence on the ground through their support to the Palestinian–leftist coalition, they did not have an ambitious agenda in Lebanon. In a similar vein, the US resigned itself to the fact that nothing could be done to save Lebanon.

Through the 1970s, up until about 1980, US officials looked at Lebanon as a 'dangerous sideshow' in the broader Arab–Israeli conflict; they did not engage diplomatically in Lebanon as long as the war there did not spill over into the other Arab–Israeli fronts. In 1976, for example, when the escalation of the Lebanese conflict threatened to drag Israel and Syria into a confrontation, US Secretary of State Henry Kissinger brokered an informal understanding between Israel and Syria whereby the two sides agreed to respect each other's security interests in the country.

In a deal similar to the one struck by the Eisenhower administration with Nasser over Lebanon in 1958, Kissinger and the State Department sanctioned a larger Syrian role in the country. The US went further by blessing the entry of Syrian troops, who were armed and trained by the Soviets, into Lebanon in June 1976: it sacrificed Lebanon's independence on the altar of regional stability. US officials were preoccupied with the Egyptian–Israeli negotiations which were the centrepiece of American strategy at that time; the Lebanese drama was a distraction and nuisance that should not be allowed to derail the potential for Arab–Israeli peace.[35]

Ironically, Cold War considerations did not figure highly in US calculations. The early 1970s saw the emergence of *détente* between the superpowers. The 1975 war in Lebanon was viewed in local terms

---

[34] Salem, 'Superpowers and Small States', 57.

[35] William Quandt, 'American Policy Toward Lebanon', in Fawaz (ed.), *State and Society in Lebanon*, 77; Salem, 'Superpowers and Small States', 59.

rather than as an extension of the East–West struggle. Little wonder then that the near-collapse of the state apparatus, a pro-Western entity, and the success of the Palestinian–leftist coalition, which was closely allied with Moscow, in the first year of the war did not elicit any serious response by the US. Washington's inaction raises a few critical questions about Lebanon and the Cold War. Despite its inconsequential role in regional and international politics, Lebanon acquired a special importance during the heyday of the Cold War. In contrast, *détente* had the effect of marginalizing Lebanon further in US and Soviet eyes.

One wonders then whether the Cold War was not a blessing in disguise for Lebanon, notwithstanding the fact that it sometimes overburdened the fragile Lebanese political system. For example, would the superpowers have tolerated the disintegration of the country in the 1970s had not the Cold War been replaced by *détente*? To what extent did the Cold War regime serve as an effective regulating mechanism in local conflicts? Would the US have given Syria—a pro-Soviet state—a yellow or green light to intervene militarily in Lebanon had the Cold War been at its height? Although it concluded a secret agreement with Nasser in 1958, the US did not sanction Egyptian physical presence in Lebanon, attempting instead to rejuvenate Lebanese institutions. This lesson was not lost on some Lebanese politicians: they impatiently awaited the coming of the second Cold War in the early 1980s, hoping to use it in order to change the internal and regional balance of forces in their favour.

GEMAYEL AND THE COLD WAR CARD: 1982–1983

Détente was short-lived, however. The 1979 Soviet invasion of Afghanistan and the consequent coming to power of President Ronald Reagan, a conservative, marked the end of *détente* and the beginning of the second Cold War. As usual the Third World, including the Middle East, became the arena for superpower rivalry and surrogate conflict. Israel and its Lebanese allies saw in the new situation an opportunity to roll back the Syrian–Palestinian advances in Lebanon and create an Israeli-dominated order; both sides—realizing the predisposition of the Reagan administration to see problems in the Third World as extensions of the Cold War—pleaded their own causes in terms of the US–Soviet struggle.[36]

[36] Karim Pakradouni, *Al-salam al-mafqoud: Ahd Elias Sarkis, 1967–1982* [The Lost Peace: The Elias Sarkis Administration, 1967–1982] (Beirut: al-Shark Lilmanshurat, 1984), 249–50, 233–4.

The result was the 1982 Israeli invasion of Lebanon. Here was a classic example of how the Cold War affected the behaviour of Israel and its Lebanese allies. Having failed to achieve their objectives during their 1978 limited invasion of Lebanon, Israeli leaders found in the Cold War atmosphere of the 1980s a golden opportunity to create a new order in Lebanon, hoping that the US would acquiesce and that their Lebanese proxies would attack the Palestinian–leftist coalition. That would have meant political suicide for the newly elected president, Bashir Gemayel, the head of the Christian militia. Although he relied on Israel for arms, training, and assistance and although he hoped that Israel would defeat his erstwhile enemies, Gemayel could not, given the fragile domestic balance, fight alongside the Israelis. He was fully aware of certain internal and inter-Arab constraints that he could ignore only at his peril.[37]

The Israeli option was soon to evaporate with the assassination of Gemayel in September 1982. The Reagan administration discovered sooner rather than later the high costs of its viewing the Arab–Israeli conflict in a Cold War context. Likewise, the Lebanonist constituency learned the hard way the pitfalls of relying on the US or on Israel to change the balance of forces domestically and regionally. However, the polarized atmosphere of the early 1980s was too inviting and promising for official Lebanon. After all, certain elements within the Reagan administration did see Lebanon, between 1981 and 1984, in rather exaggerated terms as a 'major theatre of surrogate Cold war confrontation'.[38]

Indeed, a procession of Lebanese leaders visited Washington and tried to court the new administration, promising US officials that Lebanon could become, with US support, a strategic base for the West at peace with Israel and a bridge to the Arab world. Here was another example of how the Cold War fed the illusions of Lebanese politicians. They hoped to manipulate the polarized international system and rearrange the political map in Lebanon. Such was the thinking that led Bashir Gemayel to conclude a tactical pact with Israel, and then turn towards the Americans proposing to them a strategic alliance in isolation from the Israelis.[39] His death and the consequent massacres of Palestinian civilians in the Sabra and

---

[37] Karim Pakradouni, *Al-salam al-mafqoud: Ahd Elias Sarkis, 1967–1982,* 251; Elie A. Salem, *Violence and Diplomacy in Lebanon: The Troubled Years, 1982–1988* (London: I. B. Tauris, 1995), 6–7, 10; Ze'ev Schiff and Ehud Ya'ari, *Israel's Lebanon War* (London: Unwin Paperbacks, 1985), 17–44, 230–6; Ariel Sharon with David Chanoff, *Warrior: An Autobiography* (London: Macdonald, 1989), 427, 441–3, 497–8.

[38] Quandt, 'American Policy Toward Lebanon', in Fawaz (ed.), *State and Society in Lebanon*, 78; Salem, *Violence and Diplomacy in Lebanon*, p. vi.

[39] Pakradouni, *Al-salam al-mafqoud*, 275; Salem, *Violence and Diplomacy in Lebanon*, 6.

Shatila refugee camps brought the US marines back into Lebanon for the second time in a month without the US having a clear and defined vision and without an appreciation of the complexity of Lebanese domestic and regional settings.

President Reagan made it clear to Lebanese officials that 'the United States is willing to help Lebanon end the war and regain its stability'. When Lebanese leaders asked Reagan whether the US would persevere in spite of the difficulties, he retorted: 'I have no reverse gear.'[40] Encouraged by US support and pleased to have a friend in a superpower which would help him defeat his enemies, Amin Gemayel's confidence in the US commitment was 'boundless'. Accordingly, Gemayel became less motivated to undertake serious reforms and was emboldened to negotiate with Israel, ignoring the Syrians and their Lebanese proxies. Like Chamoun in 1958, Gemayel was asserting the state apparatus's prerogative to pursue an independent foreign policy.[41] As Foreign Minister Elie Salem put it: 'The decision to negotiate was ours; we were dealing with Lebanese territory only, and we felt that it was not necessary to involve the Syrians fully before progress was made in the discussions with the Americans and the Israelis.'[42]

Gemayel's US policy bore fruit with the signing of the agreement of 17 May 1983 between Israel and Lebanon. The Israelis sent a casual side-letter to the US government stating that they would not withdraw unless the Syrians and the PLO withdrew first. Little wonder that Syria saw the 17 May agreement as a direct threat to its security interests, and warned Gemayel against signing the Israeli–Lebanese agreement. Lebanon was stuck between a rock and a hard place: While the Israelis wanted the Lebanese to act as if they were signing a peace treaty with them, the Syrians were adamantly opposed to any ties between Lebanon and Israel. Gemayel was not deterred, however. He continued to rely on the Reagan administration to support Lebanon's efforts to get rid of all foreign forces from its territory.[43]

Gemayel had a short memory: he failed to remember what happened to Chamoun in 1958 after his challenge of Egypt and his attempt to align Lebanon with the Eisenhower Doctrine. Neither leader considered Lebanon's peculiar position in inter-Arab politics and its fragile political system: Lebanon could not cut itself off from

[40] Ibid. 23–5, 70.
[41] Amin Gemayel, *Al-Rihan al-Kabir* [The Big Gamble] (Beirut: Dar al-Nahar lilnashr, 1988), 81, 210.
[42] Salem, *Violence and Diplomacy in Lebanon*, 55.
[43] Gemayel, *Al-Rihan al-Kabir*, 114.

its surroundings. Chamoun and Gemayel suffered from a 'geostrategic myopia' caused by their misreading of the US commitment to their policies. What they failed to see is that

Egypt's Nasser and Syria's Asad, even as adversaries, were by far more important to appease because of their capabilities and regional status than a vulnerable, divided, unconditionally pro-American Lebanon. Both leaders learned the hard way a very basic lesson of realpolitik: a detente with a regional superpower is more rewarding than an entente with an underdog.[44]

The Syrians and their Lebanese proxies undertook a major offensive to destabilize the pro-Western regime in Lebanon. Gemayel called on the US to help him stop the Syrian offensive. He discovered belatedly that the US was unwilling to over-invest in Lebanon, and it could not afford the high costs involved: Lebanon was not worth it. Lebanon's prime minister, Shafiq al-Wazzan, was shocked to learn that 'the greatest power on earth does not seem able to help us'. He and the foreign minister concluded that 'the Americans talked big, but delivered little'.[45] When the US government withdrew its marines from Beirut in early 1984, Gemayel conceded defeat by scrapping the moribund 17 May agreement and appointing a new cabinet, including pro-Syrian ministers.

Gemayel's defeat, coupled with the withdrawal of US forces, marked the beginning of Syria's era in Lebanon. The Reagan administration washed its hands of Lebanon and concluded that Syria had the means to maintain order in the country. Syria's 1990 attack on the Christian heartland and its occupation of the Lebanese presidential palace could not have taken place without implicit US consent. US officials became tired of the Lebanese headache, finding in Syria a strong and effective panacea for the Lebanese problem. Contrary to President Reagan's promises, the US did reverse gear in Lebanon. Salem was told bluntly that 'Lebanon was no longer important to the United States, and no one in Washington believed that Lebanon was pivotal to the success or failure of American policy in the Middle East'.[46] Little wonder that Asad was given a free hand over Lebanon's domestic and foreign policy. US officials rewarded Asad in Lebanon as a means to open a dialogue with Damascus on broader regional issues, such as Iran and the Middle East peace process.

The events of the 1980s proved beyond any doubt the saliency of the local level. It appears that both superpowers were caught off guard by Israel's invasion of Lebanon; they were forced to act to pre-

[44] Hitti, 'The Foreign Policy of Lebanon', 16.
[45] Salem, *Violence and Diplomacy in Lebanon*, 110, 113–14, 172.   [46] Ibid. 187, 258.

vent the escalation of the Syrian–Israeli confrontation and reassure their allies. Gemayel's problem was that of miscalculation and over-estimating Lebanon's value on the Western strategic chessboard. He believed he could play the Cold War card and create a new order in Beirut informed by the Lebanonist vision. The upshot was to make Lebanon an arena for surrogate conflict and play into the hands of Syria and its Lebanese allies. Gemayel's action had the opposite effect. Here is yet another example of how the Cold War affected the behaviour of Lebanon. In this context, superpower rivalries had a disastrous impact on the country.

CONCLUSION

On the whole, the Cold War had a negative and destabilizing effect on Lebanon. The polarization that preceded the 1958 crisis, the 1982 Israeli invasion of Lebanon, and the consequent US military inter-ventions had their roots in Cold War dynamics. To say this, how-ever, is not to imply that the internal struggle in Lebanon reflected the East–West confrontation. The first conceptual point to stress is that regional dynamics—inter-Arab rivalries and the Arab–Israeli conflict—have affected Lebanon's behaviour much more strongly than have developments on the global stage. It was the Arab Cold War rather than the East–West Cold War that ultimately influenced the foreign policy agenda of Lebanon, though the two Cold Wars were closely interconnected. The superpower competition was a minor affair in comparison to the local disputes that split and frag-mented the Lebanese body politic.

Given its complex socio-political structure, Lebanon has been exceptionally vulnerable to the convulsions which have shaken the region since the mid-1950s. For example, the 1958 crisis, the pro-tracted conflict with Palestinian guerrillas from 1969, and the all-out war that erupted in 1975 had their roots in the main communities' differing perceptions of Lebanon's relations with its regional envir-onment. Similarly, the only periods of relative political stability in Lebanon coincided with the convergence between internal and regional politics rather than internal and international politics. The 1958 crisis was finally resolved when Chehab realigned Lebanon's foreign policy with that of the UAR. Chehab's policy of accommo-dation with Nasser ensured social peace until 1967. Likewise, the 1975 war came to a halt in 1990 after Lebanese politicians were forced to accept Syria's unconditional hegemony.

The Great Powers themselves recognized the primacy of the local level. After its 1958 intervention in Beirut, the US government acknowledged publicly that the genesis of the crisis lay in the tensions and strains within the Lebanese socio-political structure and the inter-Arab state system rather than in the Cold War. Little wonder that in the 1970s neither the US nor the Soviet Union was willing to intervene to stop the bloody cycle of destruction which devastated state and society in Lebanon.

In this context, a second conceptual point should be highlighted: Lebanon was a marginal player in regional and foreign affairs. On the whole, inaction and passivity characterized Lebanon's external relations with the outside world during the Cold War era. Since the mid-1970s, the state apparatus had been no longer capable of formulating foreign policy autonomously. Tiny Lebanon was seen as the sick man of the Middle East, as a non-viable political entity, and as a dangerous sideshow in the Arab–Israeli drama. In the overall context of the Arab and superpower Cold Wars, Lebanon was a casualty of the system. The seeds of impotence were planted ever since the French created Greater Lebanon in 1920: Lebanese politicians have failed to develop a positive, national ideology that transcends the provincial concerns and fears of their particular constituencies.

This leads me to my third conceptual point: the inability of the state apparatus to formulate and follow an active and independent foreign policy lies in the fact that the state is one among many constituencies on the Lebanese scene. Each constituency has a different vision about Lebanon's place in the world. Lebanon's various factions served, consciously or unconsciously, as a conduit for and mirror to other policies, such as those of Nasserism, the PLO, Syria, Israel, and the Islamic Republic of Iran.[47] Thus the 'Wars of Others' in Lebanon have been fought by willing Lebanese accomplices. As the weakest link in the Arab chain, Lebanon became a safety-valve arena where regional and international conflicts were played out, directly as well as through proxies.

A final point needs to be reiterated: the failure of the Lebanonist constituency to actively align Lebanon with the Western powers did not result in the replacement of Lebanon's pro-Western stand with a pro-Soviet position. Since it achieved independence in the 1940s, Lebanon has had a pro-Western orientation, espousing a capitalist system and free-market economy and maintaining extensive political, diplomatic, and military relations with the West. Neither the 1958

---

[47] Salem, *Violence and Diplomacy in Lebanon*, 14–15.

crisis nor the 1975 war has had a major impact on Lebanon's pro-Western outlook.

Apart from their influence on a small communist party, the Soviets never succeeded in establishing close links with Lebanon. Ironically, official Lebanon—be it under Egyptian or Syrian tutelage—remained well within the Western economic and political orbit. In this context, the impact of the Cold War on Lebanon's international orientation was minimal. In contrast, the Arab Cold War and the Arab–Israeli wars have affected Lebanon's domestic politics and its local alignment as well. This fact testifies to the primacy of regional politics. Lebanon's destiny wll continue to be shaped and conditioned by its hegemonic neighbours rather than by Great Power rivalries.

5

Jordan

LAWRENCE TAL

Much scholarship on the Cold War and the Hashemite Kingdom of Jordan has focused on the role of external powers. Jordan has been viewed as merely responding to pressures emanating from Washington and Moscow, rather than shaping its own destiny. Most observers consider Jordan an 'artificial' entity lacking policy options.[1] Another characteristic of the literature is its emphasis on King Hussein and neglect of other actors in the policy-making system.[2] The image of a brave king pitted against diabolic foes is enthralling, but does not explain the Jordanian encounter with the Cold War. The fact is that, rather than being manipulated by the superpowers, the Jordanian regime used external support to construct a durable polity capable of withstanding the challenges of radical pan-Arabism, the Arab–Israeli conflict, and internal opposition. By portraying local and regional crises as Soviet-backed attempts to destabilize the Middle East, Jordan garnered generous Western backing for regime consolidation and state-building.

This chapter analyses how Jordan entered the Cold War a precarious, 'unviable' entity and emerged as a reasonably robust state capable of liberalizing its political system more quickly than other Arab states and signing a peace treaty with Israel. The first section of the chapter examines the constraints on Jordanian foreign policy and the operational environment—including the nature of the Jordanian political system, the composition of the internal opposition, and the role of the political élite and the military in policy-making—in which

[1] Naseer H. Aruri, for example, calls Jordan 'an artificial creation', *Jordan: A Study in Political Development (1921–1965)* (The Hague: Martin Nijhoff, 1972), 3. J. C. Hurewitz writes that Jordan is both 'unviable' and 'artificial', *Middle East Politics: The Military Dimension* (Boulder, Colo.: Westview Press, 1982), 308.

[2] Some of the more prominent works emphasizing the role of the king include: Hussein bin Talal, *Mahnati ka-malak* [My Job as King] (Amman: National Press, 1986); Munib al-Madi and Suleiman Musa, *Tarikh al-urdunn fi al-qarn al-'ashreen* [The History of Jordan in the Twentieth Century] (Amman, n.p., 1959); Hussein bin Talal, *Uneasy Lies the Head* (London: Heinemann, 1962); James Lunt, *Hussein of Jordan: A Political Biography* (London: Macmillan, 1989); Kamal Salibi, *A Modern History of Jordan* (London: I. B. Tauris, 1993); and Peter Snow, *Hussein* (London: Barrie & Jenkins, 1972).

decision-makers function. Four brief case studies comprise the second section. History never comes in tidy bundles, and the studies presented here are no exception. They do, however, represent the best examples of 'Cold War crises' in Jordanian history. The chapter concludes with an analysis of the Gulf War and an assessment of Jordan after the Cold War. How the regime will cope with the challenges of peace, political Islam, political liberalization, and economic decline are discussed.

CONSTRAINTS ON JORDAN

Despite its perceived weaknesses, Jordan is no more 'artificial' than any other state, in so far as states are 'artifices', or artificial creations of individuals or groups pursuing political ends. What makes Jordan unique are the constraints on its freedom of action. The first is structural and derives from Jordan's requirement for external sources of support.

When Jordan (or Transjordan) was created by British Colonial Secretary Winston Churchill 'on a Sunday afternoon' in 1921, its chances of survival appeared slim.[3] Jordan had a total area of 91,880 square kilometres, of which 72,000 were desert, and lacked natural resources. Today, after decades of exploration by Western companies, the country has only five million barrels of proven oil reserves.[4] Jordan also lacked vast water supplies. The only resources the country possessed were potash and phosphates. Another impediment to state-building was Jordan's tiny, heterogeneous population which owed no allegiance to the Meccan Hashemites. Fewer than 350,000 people, including a Sunni Muslim majority and Christian, Circassian, and Chechen minorities, inhabited the territory. Some urban and tribal leaders resisted the centralizing impetus of the fledgling Hashemite entity.

Prince Abdullah overcame these handicaps by creating a 'neo-patrimonial', *rentier* state. The theory of 'rentierism' is quite simple.[5] External sources of revenue are utilized to 'buy' support from the governed. As Rex Brynen writes, 'coercion becomes less important as political legitimacy is, in a very real sense, "purchased" through

---

[3] Benjamin Shwadran, *Jordan: A State of Tension* (New York: Council for Middle Eastern Affairs Press, 1959), 134.

[4] Anthony H. Cordesman, *After the Storm: The Changing Military Balance in the Middle East* (Boulder, Colo.: Westview Press, 1993), 285.

[5] See Hazem Beblawi and Giacomo Luciani, *The Rentier State* (London: Croom Helm, 1987), and Giacomo Luciani, *The Arab State* (London: Routledge, 1990).

economic rewards.'[6] From 1921 to 1957 Jordan's chief patron was Britain, which initially paid Abdullah a monthly subsidy of £5,000. Annual British aid reached £100,000 by the mid-1920s, £2 million by the mid-1940s, and £12.5 million by 1957.[7] Abdullah, in effect, 'occupied a median position between a European power, that held ultimate control, and a local social structure'.[8] The palace became the locus of political interaction as notables competed for access to the potentate, who controlled the purse-strings. Unlike democratic systems, where political actors—at least ostensibly—succeed on merit, Jordanian politicians knew their fortunes depended on access to, and the continued success of, the monarchy.

The first shift in the pattern of Jordan's external dependence came in 1957. Under the terms of the Eisenhower Doctrine—which promised American aid to any Middle Eastern state threatened by 'International Communism'—the US replaced Britain as Jordan's principal foreign sponsor. Annual American aid to Jordan rose from $1.4 million in 1951 to $34 million in 1958.[9] By 1970, Jordan had received over $700 million in US assistance. Jordan ranked second only to Israel in terms of per capita American aid.[10]

The second shift in Jordanian dependency came after the 1967 war, when Jordan began receiving increased Arab assistance. Israel's capture of the West Bank cost Jordan about 40 per cent of its Gross National Product (GNP). The Khartoum Arab summit of August–September 1967 pledged Jordan $55 million in emergency grants and $112 million per annum (Libya and Kuwait ceased paying Jordan after the 1970 civil war, but Saudi Arabia continued its subsidy of $41 million).[11] At the Baghdad summit in 1978, the Arab League promised Jordan another $1.25 billion per year for rejecting the Camp David Accords. Jordan received only part of this aid, but 'it still dwarfed the other external aid Jordan then received'.[12] By the 1980s, Jordan began diversifying its sources of aid, 'replacing the old special link with America—or with any single Great Power—by a more balanced relationship between the main international power

---

[6] Rex Brynen, 'Economic Crisis and Post-Rentier Democratization in the Arab World: The Case of Jordan', *Canadian Journal of Political Science* 25(1) (Mar. 1992), 74.

[7] Ibid. 78.

[8] Mary C. Wilson, 'King Abdullah and Palestine', *Brismes Bulletin* 14 (1987), 37.

[9] Aruri, *Jordan*, 63. Details on the Eisenhower Doctrine can be found in Paul E. Zinner, *Documents on American Foreign Relations, 1958* (New York: Council on Foreign Relations Press, 1959), and US Dept. of State, Historical Office, *American Foreign Policy, Current Documents, 1958* (Washington, DC: US Govt. Printing Office, 1962).

[10] Harry N. Howard, 'Jordan in Turmoil', *Current History* (Jan. 1972), 16.

[11] Ibid. 17.

[12] Adam M. Garfinkle, 'Negotiating by Proxy: Jordanian Foreign Policy and US Options in the Middle East', *Orbis* (winter 1981), 875.

blocs: the United States, the Soviet Union and the European Community'.[13] Jordan also received remittances from its expatriate workers in the Gulf. In 1985, for instance, such payments totalled $846 million.[14]

To put the impact of external funding on Jordan's economy in perspective, aid accounted for up to one-third of Gross Domestic Product (GDP) between 1952 and 1966. Aid contributed 58 per cent of government revenues between 1967 and 1972, and 55 per cent from 1973 to 1980.[15] Annual economic growth rates of nearly 10 per cent during the 1960s and 1970s were, in large part, the result of external aid.[16] Despite the peace treaty Jordan signed with Israel in October 1994, and prospects for joint development projects, Jordan remains dependent on external powers.

The second constraint on Jordan stems from the kingdom's precarious geopolitical position in a hostile environment.[17] Consequently, Jordan's foreign relations seldom remained static during the Cold War. Alliances were formed, readjusted, and broken as Amman jockeyed to secure a firm footing during crises. Israel, for instance, allowed overflights of British troops dispatched to Jordan in 1958. Israel also aided Jordan during the civil war in September 1970. Israel was not always so amicable, though. In October 1953, for example, a force led by Ariel Sharon decimated the village of Qibya, killing 66 villagers, most of them women and children.[18] After the 1967 war, too, Jordanian–Israeli relations went into a tailspin with Israel's capture of the West Bank.

Syria and Egypt backed anti-Hashemite coup attempts and riots in the 1950s, but mended fences with Hussein before the 1967 war. Despite this *rapprochement*, Syria launched an invasion of Jordan in 1970. By 1988, Jordan possessed only 25 per cent of Syria's tank strength, 23 per cent of Syria's aircraft strength, and 5 per cent of Syria's mobilizable manpower strength.[19] Depending on who presided in Baghdad, Iraq could be a menace. Jordan had plans to

---

[13] Robert Stephens, 'Jordan and the Powers', in Patrick Seale (ed.), *The Shaping of an Arab Statesman: Abd al-Hamid Sharaf and the Modern Arab World* (London: Quartet Books, 1983), 41.

[14] Brynen, 'Economic Crisis', 73.   [15] Ibid. 78.

[16] See E. Kanovsky, *The Economy of Jordan: The Implications of Peace in the Middle East* (Tel Aviv: University Publishing Projects, 1976); Bichara Khader and Adnan Badran, *The Economic Development of Jordan* (London: Croom Helm, 1987).

[17] As Bichara Khader writes, Jordan 'is a hostage of its geography'. See 'Jordan's Economy, 1952–1989: Past Achievements and Future Challenges', *Journal of Arab Affairs* 9(2) (1990), 103.

[18] See Benny Morris, *Israel's Border Wars, 1949–1956: Arab Infiltration, Israeli Retaliation, and the Countdown to the Suez War* (New York: Oxford University Press, 1993).

[19] Cordesman, *After the Storm*, 287.

topple the Iraqi republican regime in 1958. Relations between the two sides remained frosty during the 1960s and 1970s. Yet Amman and Baghdad were close allies during the Iran–Iraq war. By 1990, Iraq supplied 95 per cent of Jordan's petroleum. Jordan rarely enjoyed warm relations with Saudi Arabia, its long-time dynastic rival. Riyadh supported Hussein's clampdown on his opponents in 1957, but in 1958 opposed overflights of American aircraft delivering emergency supplies to Jordan.

The Cold War witnessed both the crystallization and extinction of four broad strands of opposition within Jordan. The first comprised groups opposed to the state, including the Islamic Liberation Party, 'Islamic Trotskyists' calling for the establishment of a Caliphate, and radical Arab nationalists.[20] The second encompassed those who accepted the state but opposed the monarchy. Examples included members of the National Socialist Party (NSP) and the Jordanian Communist Party (JCP). The third included the 'constitutional opposition', such as the Muslim Brotherhood, which accepted the legitimacy of state and regime under the terms of the 1952 Constitution.

The fourth source of opposition came from the Palestinians. The Palestinians, however, were not a monolithic community with unified aims. King Abdullah co-opted West Bank notables into his governments, tying them to the state with economic and political rewards.[21] Refugees were more concerned with their economic position than with opposing the Hashemite regime.[22] Others, however, denounced the regime and tried to topple the Hashemites: Abdullah was assassinated by a disgruntled Palestinian, and Hussein was nearly overthrown by Palestinian guerrillas. Nevertheless, the integration of Palestinians into East Bank social structures and political institutions continued apace even after the 1970 civil war. Indeed, Palestinians became 'indispensable to the functioning of the monarchy'.[23]

THE NATIONAL SECURITY ESTABLISHMENT

During the Cold War, King Hussein relied on a coterie of tribal and urban notables, military commanders, family members, and foreign

[20] See 'Awni Jadu'a al-'Abidi, *Hizb al-tahrir al-islami* [Islamic Liberation Party] (Amman: Dar al-Liwa' Press, 1993). Also Lawrence Tal, 'Dealing with Radical Islam: The Case of Jordan', *Survival* (autumn 1995), 139–56.

[21] Joel S. Migdal, 'Dispersal and Annexation: Jordanian Rule', and Shaul Mishal, 'Conflictual Pressures and Cooperative Interests: Observations on West Bank–Amman Political Relations, 1949–1967', in Joel S. Migdal (ed.), *Palestinian Society and Politics* (Princeton, NJ: Princeton Univ. Press, 1979).

[22] Avi Plascov, *The Palestinian Refugees in Jordan, 1948–1957* (London: Frank Cass, 1981).

[23] Adam M. Garfinkle, 'Jordan and Arab Polarization', *Current History* (Jan. 1982), 24.

diplomats to aid him in the policy-making process. Despite its authoritarian exterior, the Jordanian system of rule incorporated various opinions and political shades. When a prime minister with pro-Egyptian sympathies came to office (Bahjat al-Talhuni, for instance), a *rapprochement* with Cairo was at hand. When a politician with good relations with Syria served (such as Zaid al-Rifa'i), Jordanian foreign policy tilted toward Damascus. This is not to argue that there were alternate centres of political gravity in Jordan. King Hussein, to be sure, was the ultimate arbiter between various factions, mediating conflicts. But strong personalities—such as Wasfi al-Tell, Sharif Nasser, and Queen Mother Zein—had no qualms about confronting Hussein on policy issues. In the end, though, rivalries within the political élite were 'all horizontal; they [did] not interfere with the politicians' basic understanding that the prime consideration [was] the welfare of the regime'.[24]

There are few studies of the military in Jordan, although it occupies a prominent place in the country's history.[25] Many rely on outdated data and stereotypes ascribing the military's fidelity to some sort of 'Bedouin ethos'. The fact is that the loyalty of the military can be accounted for in terms of vested interests. Soldiers are well paid, receive excellent benefits, and occupy prestigious positions in society. 'Economic dependence', in particular, bound the military to the state.[26] By 1965, Jordan had the highest force levels in the Arab world. About 23 of every 1,000 Jordanians served in the military, while only 14 were employed in manufacturing.[27] By the late 1980s, the military formed about 18 per cent of the labour force.[28] The military is more than a fighting force; it is also a welfare system providing economic advantage to those from impoverished rural and urban areas.

King Hussein realized the military was the ultimate protector of his regime. As one American diplomat stated bluntly during the turbulent 1950s: 'No government is likely to remain in power without army support. The allegiance of the army to the Throne is the major source of royal power in the real sense.'[29] Accordingly, Hussein used

[24] Clinton Bailey, 'Cabinet Formation in Jordan', in Anne Sinai and Allen Pollack (eds.), *The Hashemite Kingdom of Jordan and the West Bank: A Handbook* (New York: American Academic Association for Peace in the Middle East, 1977), 107.
[25] The only full-length studies available in English are Syed Ali el-Edroos, *The Hashemite Arab Army: An Appreciation and Analysis of Military Operations* (Amman: Publishing Committee, 1980), and P. J. Vatikiotis, *Politics and the Military in Jordan: A Study of the Arab Legion, 1921–1957* (London: Frank Cass, 1967).
[26] Tariq Tell, 'The Social Origins of Jordanian Glasnost', unpublished paper, 6.
[27] Hurewitz, *Middle East Politics*, table 18.   [28] Brynen, 'Economic Crisis', 82.
[29] Merriam to DOS, 18 Nov. 1957, DOS 785.00/11-1857, National Archives (NA), Washington.

the Cold War to attract Western support to transform the army from a Praetorian guard into a national establishment.[30] From a force of 5 officers, 75 riflemen, and 25 machine gunners in 1920, the Arab Legion, as it was known in British times, reached a strength of 25,000 by 1956, 50,000 by 1965, and 100,000 in 1991. Hussein also built a modern air force, which reached a peak strength of 11,000 men, 114 combat aircraft, and 24 armed helicopters in 1988.[31] Annual defence expenditures jumped from $29.4 million in 1955 to $58.8 million in 1965. Defence spending accounted for nearly 17 per cent of GDP during the 1980s.

The military used its position as paramount guardian of the monarchy to increase its influence in Jordan. Officers interacted with notables, opposition groups, foreign agents, and the palace, and constantly sought to secure increased budgetary support for the military. Army commanders intervened directly in politics, either by conspiratorial means or by seeking to sway the king. There were coup attempts by army factions in 1951, 1957, 1958, and 1959. The plotters, however, failed to secure the backing of pivotal sectors of the enlisted ranks. Further, rebel officers—many without tribal, urban, or rural bases of support—did not form solid alliances with civilian politicians who possessed popular legitimacy. Other examples of military intercession in politics included army plans for offensive action against Syria in 1960 and Iraq in 1958 and 1959; the unseating of a prime minister in 1959; and the clashes with the Palestine Liberation Organization (PLO) in 1970 and 1971.

JORDAN AND THE SUPERPOWERS

The Soviet Union was not a significant feature of the Jordanian encounter with the Cold War. Moscow never enjoyed decisive influence among Jordan's political élite.[32] Although Russia was popular among leftist circles in the kingdom, Moscow never controlled the Jordanian Communist Party (JCP), the Ba'th Socialist Party, or the National Socialist Party (NSP). Nor did it exercise anything other than ideological leverage over indigenous leaders. One reason was, quite simply, that Moscow never had substantial interests in the Hashemite Kingdom. Unlike Egypt, Syria, or Iraq—the ideological poles of the Arab world—Jordan was viewed by the Russians as a

[30] Vatikiotis, *Politics and the Military in Jordan.*
[31] Cordesman, *After the Storm*, 296.
[32] Interview with Dr Abdel Rahman Shuqair (former leader of the *Jubhat al-watiniyya*, or National Front), Amman, Jordan, 20 Apr. 1993.

bastion of Western imperialism, a reactionary state.[33] The Soviets claimed that Hussein's 'throne rests on foreign bayonets'.[34]

Another reason for the lack of Soviet influence in Jordan sprang from the philosophy and ambitions of the Hashemite dynasty. As descendants of the Prophet Muhammad, neither Abdullah nor Hussein would have any truck with communism. They believed, as did many Muslims, that communism was an anti-Islamic creed. Hussein's address before the United Nations in 1960 is an example of his unequivocal rejection of communism: 'I wanted to be sure that there is no mistake about where Jordan stands in the conflict of ideologies that is endangering the peace of the world. . . . In the great struggle between Communism and freedom, there can be no neutrality.'[35]

In addition to ideology, international, regional, and domestic political variables contributed to Jordan's anti-communist stance. The Soviet Union was arrayed against the West, the benefactor of the Hashemites. Soviet Prime Minister Khrushchev, for example, compared Western intervention in the Middle East to Hitler's invasion of Poland.[36] Egypt's Gamal Abdel Nasser, although hardly a dedicated Marxist or Leninist, opposed Jordan's pro-Western proclivities. Jordanian leftists sought to unseat Hussein. Hussein had everything to lose, and nothing to gain, by embracing the Soviets, Nasser, or Jordanian radicals.

Jordan, however, occasionally made overtures toward Moscow to counterbalance American support for Israel. This was possible because Jordan—despite its antipathy toward communism—never considered the Soviet Union a direct threat. It was Israel and the radical Arabs who imperilled Hussein, not Russia. Although Amman established diplomatic ties with Moscow in 1963, Hussein only turned to the Soviets for arms when he discerned the depth of the American commitment to Israel.[37] In October 1967 the king made his first trip to Moscow, where the Soviets offered him military assistance and condemned Israeli 'aggression'.[38] Similarly, after the Carter and Reagan administrations refused to sell arms to Jordan after it rejected the Camp David Accords, Hussein arranged a Soviet arms

---

[33] See Galia Golan, *Soviet Policies in the Middle East: From World War II to Gorbachev* (Cambridge: Cambridge University Press, 1990).

[34] Moscow to FO, 4 Sept. 1958, FO 371.133797, Public Record Office (PRO), London.

[35] Lunt, *Hussein of Jordan*, 65–6. Other examples of Hussein's philosophy can be found in *Al-Majmu'a al-kamila li-khutub jalalat al-malak al-Hussein bin-Talal al-mu'adhim, 1952–1985* [Complete Collection of the Speeches of His Majesty King Hussein bin Talal the Great, 1952–1985] (Amman: Ministry of Information, Directorate of Press and Publications, n.d.).

[36] Letter from De Gaulle to Khrushchev, 23 July 1958, FO 371.133796/V 10338/32, PRO.

[37] Parkes to FO, 21 Aug. 1963, FO 371.170277/EJ 103138/8, PRO.

[38] Howard, 'Jordan in Turmoil', 16.

deal.[39] In the late 1980s the USSR replaced the US as Jordan's largest arms supplier; Jordan received $875 million in weapons during 1984–8.[40] Such steps were taken to fortify Jordan, not to express any new-found affinity for the Soviet credo.

Jordan relied upon Britain and America for external support during the Cold War. As the case studies will indicate, it was Western aid, not Soviet, which allowed Hussein to consolidate his regime and build a sturdy state. However much Jordan paid lip-service to Western ideals, though, it never put them fully into practice. Jordan never had an unfettered market economy. The state was always the predominant actor in the economy. Parliament was dissolved on a number of occasions by royal decree. Neither the lower nor the upper houses ever successfully challenged the palace. Martial law was declared during 1957–8 and again between 1967 and 1992. Defence regulations granted wide powers to the security apparatus (the army, the 6,000-strong *Amn al-'Amm*, or Public Security Directorate, and the *Mukhabarat*, or General Intelligence Directorate). Communism was restricted by a 1953 law. Other legislation circumscribed public assemblies, trade unionism, political pluralism, and press freedoms.

Despite Jordan's failure to install a Western system of liberal government, Britain and the US felt the country was worth supporting. First, policy-makers believed that 'the Middle East is a battle ground in the Cold War between Soviet Russia and the West'.[41] Jordan was an ally in the struggle against Arab radicalism and, by implication, the USSR. Jordan was 'insignificant with respect to trade and commercial interests', but was important 'to achieve stability and head off "extremist action" '.[42] Second, policy-makers thought that 'the continued existence of Jordan was necessary to maintain the status quo in the Middle East and to prevent a renewal of the Arab–Israeli conflict'.[43] British Foreign Secretary Selwyn Lloyd put it succinctly: 'Israeli interest in the West Bank alone justified a policy of maintaining Jordan's independence.'[44] Finally, Jordan represented a solution to the Palestinian refugee problem. Policy-makers felt that Jordan could provide a permanent home to displaced Palestinians.[45]

---

[39] Lunt, *Hussein of Jordan*, 201.   [40] Cordesman, *After the Storm*, 291.
[41] 'A Policy for the Middle East', report by the Chiefs of Staff Committee, 11 Aug. 1958, DEFE 5.84, PRO.
[42] Amman to DOS, 25 July 1957, 885.00-TA/7-2557, National Archives, Washington, DC (NA).
[43] New York to FO, 15 Aug. 1958, PREM 11.2381, PRO.
[44] Lloyd to Steel, 23 July 1958, FO 371.133786/V 1014/82, PRO.
[45] See e.g. Hood to FO, 5 Aug. 1958, PREM 11.2381, PRO, and Johnston to FO, 18 Aug. 1958, PREM 11.2381, PRO.

Western support for Jordan, however, was not unstinting. There were times, particularly during the early years of the Cold War, when American and British policy-makers appeared willing to leave Hussein to his own devices. During the 1958 crisis, for instance, some American officials felt that continued support for Jordan was fruitless given the intensity of local and regional opposition to Hussein.[46] It was through skilful salesmanship and brinkmanship that Hussein managed to win accolades as a staunch ally of the West. The 1950s–1970s were replete with examples of the Jordanian regime's determination to market itself as a 'strategic asset' for Washington.

Using conflicts for regime consolidation and state-building is not exclusive to the Middle East. As Charles Tilly writes, 'governments themselves commonly simulate, stimulate, or even fabricate threats of external war' for their own ends.[47] The following studies sketch briefly how the Jordanian regime exploited the Cold War to consolidate its power and create vested interests in the state by portraying local and regional hazards as Soviet-sanctioned bids to acquire influence in the Middle East.

THE BAGHDAD PACT CRISIS, DECEMBER 1955–MARCH 1956

The Baghdad Pact was a Western defence scheme designed to protect the Northern Tier—Turkey, Iraq, Iran, and Pakistan—against Soviet encroachment. The Pact 'internationalized the local struggle for power in the Middle East' by polarizing the Arab world into pro-Western and pro-Soviet camps.[48] Egypt's Abdel Nasser vehemently opposed the agreement, viewing it as a Western tool to divide the Arabs. In September 1955 Nasser had shocked the international community with his 'Czech arms deal'. He now set about scuttling the Baghdad Pact.

Jordan was initially in favour of the Pact, but later rejected the agreement after weeks of anti-Pact rioting throughout the kingdom. Perceptions of the crisis differed among members of the policy-making establishment. Some (such as Hazza' al-Majali and Wasfi al-Tell) favoured the Pact; they believed that it would strengthen Jordan against the forces of radical pan-Arabism and deflect internal

---

[46] Hood to FO, 5 Aug. 1958, PREM 11.2381, PRO.

[47] Charles Tilly, 'War Making and State Making as Organized Crime', in Peter B. Evans, Dietrich Rueschemeyer, and Theda Skocpol (eds.), *Bringing the State Back In* (Cambridge: Cambridge University Press, 1985) 171.

[48] Stephens, 'Jordan and the Powers', 48.

pressures to embrace the Soviet Union. Others (notably Na'im Abdel Hadi and 'Azmi al-Nashashibi) opposed the agreement. These policy-makers viewed the Pact as a Western defence scheme designed to protect Western interests. To this camp, Soviet support was preferable to Western domination of the Arab world.

Nasser torpedoed Jordan's accession to the Pact by, first, unleashing his propaganda machine and, second, funding opposition circles in Jordan. Cairo ordered General 'Abdel Hakim 'Amr and Colonel Anwar al-Sadat to Jordan to fan the flames of resistance. Sadat reportedly offered three politicians £9,000 each for their resignations.[49] Egypt was successful in fomenting opposition. On 17 December 1955, 'the worst riots the kingdom had ever witnessed' broke out.

Normally quiet towns like Hebron, Jericho, Bethlehem, and Aqaba erupted for the first time in memory; traditional hotbeds of opposition like Amman, Nablus, Irbid, and Salt shook as never before; refugee camps, usually docile and well controlled, exploded, too.[50]

Hussein snatched victory from the jaws of defeat by joining Nasser instead of opposing him. The regime used the Cold War context of the crisis to shore up domestic stability by appearing to tilt away from the West. Jordan had gone through four prime ministers in 26 days, as successive governments were toppled by the opposition.[51] Hussein sensed the gravity of public resentment to the Pact and co-opted the forces of pan-Arabism to bolster his rule by rejecting the agreement. His actions strengthened the regime by quelling the riots and establishing his credentials as a nationalist leader. He further undercut his opponents by dismissing the British commander of the Arab Legion, General John Glubb, in March 1956. Uriel Dann assessed the king's handling of the crisis as follows:

Hussein managed, with a dexterity remarkable for a person of his age and experience, to garner credit with the British for his determination in having the riots suppressed, foist public opprobrium for the bloodshed on General Glubb and gain popular applause for not joining the Pact.[52]

[49] Robert B. Satloff, *From Abdullah to Hussein: Jordan in Transition* (Oxford: Oxford University Press, 1994), 123.

[50] Ibid. 121. As diplomat Richard Parker reported, 'Any dreams the British or we may have had regarding eventual Jordan accession to the Baghdad Pact have been rudely interrupted' (Parker to DOS, 31 Dec. 1955, DOS 785.00/12.3155, NA).

[51] For detailed lists of the composition of the various governments, see *al-Watha'iq al-urdunniyya: al-wazarat al-urdunniyya, 1921–1984* [Jordanian Documents: Jordanian Ministries, 1921–1984] (Amman: Ministry of Information, Directorate of Press and Publications, 1984), and Hani Salim Khayr, *al-Sajl al-tarikhi al-musawwar, 1920–1990* [The Illustrated Historical Record, 1920–1990] (Amman: Al-Ayman Printing Press, 1990).

[52] Uriel Dann, *King Hussein's Strategy of Survival* (Washington, DC: Washington Institute for Near East Policy, Policy Paper No. 29, 1992), 11.

The regime, however, was careful to maintain its economic lifeline to the West. Diplomatic communications between Amman and London emphasized the point that Jordan had appeased Nasser and, by extension, the Soviets, because it had no other choice. Whitehall continued to pay its subsidy to Hussein, although Britain began seeking ways to extricate itself from Jordan.

THE ABU NUWAR PLOT, APRIL 1957

The 1957 crisis was the quintessential Cold War drama, replete with communist provocateurs, seditious politicians, a thwarted coup, riots, and military rule. The origins of the imbroglio can be traced to the *ta'rib*, or Arabization, of the army which occurred after Glubb's expulsion. Hussein filled the positions vacated by the British with Jordanian officers, and young officers, many with little military experience were promoted almost overnight. Major 'Ali Abu Nuwar, for example, was elevated to major-general and soon became chief of staff of the army. Abu Nuwar reorganized the army's structure, abolishing division headquarters and forming separate brigade headquarters. He also placed his followers in positions of authority.[53] One diplomat reported: 'Hussein [is] no longer [the] master of his own fate and will retain [the] throne only if he accommodates himself to the views and plans of Nuwar.'[54]

The second act in the drama came with the parliamentary elections of October 1956, when Suleiman al-Nabulsi became prime minister and set about aligning Jordan's foreign policy with those of Egypt and Syria. Although Nabulsi was no committed communist, he believed that 'Jordan cannot live forever as Jordan', and pressed for the establishment of ties with the Soviet Union and the People's Republic of China. Buoyed by anti-Western sentiments generated by the Suez fiasco, Nabulsi demanded the abrogation of the Anglo-Jordanian treaty—the kingdom's economic lifeline—and its replacement with Arab aid. In January 1957 Jordan signed the Arab Solidarity Agreement, whereby Egypt, Syria, and Saudi Arabia agreed to replace the British subsidy; in March, Jordan abrogated its treaty with Britain.

By February, Hussein was 'looking for a pretext to dismiss Nabulsi'.[55] The king sent a forthright message to his prime minister:

---

[53] Vatikiotis, *Politics and the Military in Jordan*, 128–9; interview with Hikmat Mihayr (former Chief of Police and Public Security Dept. officer) Amman, Jordan, 13 Apr. 1993.

[54] Tel Aviv to SOS, 22 May 1956, DOS 785.00/5-2156, NA.

[55] Johnston to FO, 1 Feb. 1957, FO 371.127878/VJ 1015/6, PRO.

'We want this country to be inaccessible to Communist propaganda and Bolshevik theories.'[56] He ordered the press to cease its attacks on the Eisenhower Doctrine, the anti-communist assistance programme promulgated by the US in January 1957. In April Nabulsi resigned at the king's behest, and a military conspiracy was uncovered by the regime.

The official version of this plot was that Abu Nuwar and others planned a coup against the monarchy, but that Hussein was tipped off by loyalists and executed a counter-coup against the rebels. Another interpretation, which has yet to gain academic credibility, is that the coup was engineered by King Hussein and the Americans, who agreed to replace the British subsidy to Jordan after the crisis.[57] On a number of occasions, Hussein had emphasized to Western diplomats his intent to stem the tide of communism in Jordan.[58] In effect, the regime played the US off the USSR by telling American officials that Jordan would be forced to accept Russian aid unless Washington made a commitment to the kingdom. Hussein passed a message through 'intelligence channels' to the US, outlining his plans to crush his opposition and impose martial law. He asked for American assistance in the event of Soviet or Israeli intervention.[59] Eisenhower and Dulles agreed that Jordan merited support, and on 24 April America announced that 'the independence and integrity of Jordan was vital' to US interests. Washington demonstrated its seriousness by dispatching the 6th Fleet to the Eastern Mediterranean in a show of force for Hussein; granting $10 million in emergency aid to Jordan (the 'most quickly negotiated in US history', according to Satloff);[60] and giving Jordan highly favourable press coverage.[61] The CIA reportedly began paying Hussein 'millions of dollars' under a covert programme named 'No Beef'.[62]

Whatever version of events one chooses to believe, Hussein's actions allowed him to regain control of a rapidly deteriorating situ-

---

[56] Satloff, *From Abdullah to Hussein*, 162. Also, Tehran to DOS, 4 Feb. 1957, DOS 785.11/2-457, NA.

[57] Erskine B. Childers discusses a version of this plot in Appendix B of his *The Road to Suez: A Study of Western–Arab Relations* (London: MacGibbon & Kee, 1962). Also, interview with Mahmud al-Mu'ayta (former Free Officer and Ba'thist) Amman, Jordan, 15 Apr. 1993.

[58] See e.g. Johnston to FO, 5 Mar. 1957, FO 371.127878/VJ 1015/10, PRO; Uriel Dann, *King Hussein and the Challenge of Arab Radicalism* (New York: Oxford University Press, 1989), 13.

[59] Satloff, *From Abdullah to Hussein*, 171.

[60] Dulles to Amman, 24 June 1957, DOS 785.5-MSP/6-2457, NA. See also Richard M. Saunders, 'Military Force in the Foreign Policy of the Eisenhower Presidency', *Political Science Quarterly* 100 (1) (spring 1985), 97–116.

[61] See e.g. *Time*, 29 Apr. 1957.

[62] Bob Woodward, 'CIA Paid Millions to Jordan's King Hussein', *Washington Post*, 18 Feb. 1977.

ation. The most important result of the crisis was the replacement of one external actor, Britain, with another, the US. With American backing, Hussein managed to foil a coup, ban all political parties (which remained illegal until the November 1993 elections), and place Jordan under military rule. Martial law strengthened the role of the army *vis-à-vis* society, granting commanders virtually unlimited authority.[63] Although Jordan became a police state by the end of 1957, another crisis loomed on the horizon.

THE JULY 1958 EMERGENCY

The roots of the 1958 crisis were planted with Hussein's firm handling of the April 1957 intrigues. In one fell swoop, Hussein lost the nationalist image he had acquired by forswearing the Baghdad Pact and sacking Glubb. When Egypt and Syria formed the United Arab Republic (UAR) in February 1958, Jordan was regarded as a pariah by the 'progressive' Arab camp. To counter Nasser, Hussein turned to his cousins in Iraq and formed the Arab Union (AU). Hussein, moreover, hoped that Jordan would benefit from close economic and military cooperation with Baghdad. Iraq could help settle Jordan's 500,000 disenfranchised Palestinians; Iraqi trade could develop the Jordanian port of Aqaba; Iraqi petroleum would allow Jordan to cancel plans to build a refinery; and Iraq offered a potentially lucrative market for Jordanian agricultural products. The Iraqi military could deter the Israelis or the Syrians from attacking Jordan.[64] Nasser reacted to the AU with fury, proclaiming that 'the collaborators of imperialism are even more dangerous than imperialism'. Jordan responded by charging Nasser with 'secretly carrying on negotiations with the Jews in the corridors of the UN'.[65]

Months of jousting between the UAR and the AU resulted in the discovery of another plot against Hussein.[66] The details of this conspiracy remain hazy. It seems, though, that a cabal of ambitious

[63] Details of the 1957 conspiracy can be found in *Qarar al-mahkama al-'urfiyya al-'askariyya al-khassa* [Decision of the Special Military Court Martial] (Amman: n.p., 1957). I wish to thank Mike Duran for showing me his copy of this document.

[64] Mason to Hadow, 26 Feb. 1958, FO 371.134026/VJ 10393/69, PRO, and Johnston to FO, 20 Feb. 1958, FO 371.134025/VJ 10393/47, PRO. An official account of the negotiations leading to the formation of the AU can be found in Iskander M'arouf, *al-Urdunn al-jadid wa al-ittihad al-'arabi* [New Jordan and the Arab Union] (Baghdad: New Iraq Press, 1958).

[65] Minute on 'Nasser's open declaration of war against the Arab Union', 27 Feb. 1958, FO 371.134026/VJ 10393/71; also Tel Aviv to FO, 12 Mar. 1958, FO 371.133876/V 1431/4 (B) [confidential].

[66] See Lawrence Tal, 'Britain and the Jordan Crisis of 1958', *Middle Eastern Studies* (Jan. 1995).

officers felt that Jordan should become a republic and join the
UAR.[67] On 16 July Hussein made a formal request for Western
troops. He emphasized that, with the demise of the Iraqi Hashemites,
Jordan remained the last outpost of anti-communism in the Levant.
If Jordan were not supported, the Soviets would consolidate their
hold on the region and Nasser would score an important victory.
After a lengthy cabinet debate Britain sent forces to Jordan, while
the US deployed troops to Lebanon.[68] Throughout the summer
British troops remained on alert in Amman, while American
Globemaster aircraft delivered emergency fuel supplies to Jordan.
The Ben-Gurion government signalled its commitment to the
Hashemite regime by permitting overflights of British aircraft
throughout the summer.

The presence of the British Parachute Brigade provided Hussein
with the breathing space he required to shore up his rule. He 'began
a round of successful visits to Army units, showing characteristic
courage in moving without an escort through crowded gatherings of
troops drawn from units of doubtful allegiance'.[69] The king
appointed regime stalwart Habis al-Majali head of the army and the
reliable Sharif Nasser military commander of Amman. Guards were
posted outside all Western diplomatic compounds, potential hot-
spots such as Nablus were sealed off by the army, and orders were
given 'to suppress any hostile demonstrations ruthlessly'.[70] In July
alone, over 150 officers and NCOs of dubious loyalty were arrested
by the security services.[71]

At the international level, the crisis assumed Cold War significance
as the superpowers confronted each other at the UN. Some US policy-
makers believed Hussein was in a position whereby 90 per cent of his
country opposed his leadership. But Eisenhower and Dulles decided
it was better to have an unpopular, but strong, regime in power than
face the possible disintegration of Jordan. Soviet attempts to censure
the Anglo-American interventions in the Middle East failed. The crisis ended when the UN adopted a resolution calling for all Arab

---

[67] Interview with Sadiq al-Sher'a (former Deputy Chief of Staff) Amman, Jordan, 12 Apr.
1993.

[68] 'Rescue and Evacuation of British and Friendly Nationals from Amman', memorandum
from COS Committee, 13 June 1958, DEFE 5.84 [top secret]. A discussion of the crisis can be
found in Sa'ad Aboudia, *'Amaliyat itakhadh al-qarar fi-siyasat al-urdunn al-kharijiyya* [The
Foreign Policy Decision-making Process in Jordan] (Amman: n.p., 1983), 213–30.

[69] Charles Johnston, *The Brink of Jordan* (London: Hamish Hamilton, 1972), 107.

[70] Mason to FO, 16 July 1958, FO 371.134008/VJ 1015/35 (C), PRO.

[71] One of those arrested was Hamad al-Farhan (former Economic Under-Secretary). Farhan
believes he was unjustly arrested, and says his only crime was being an Arab nationalist.
Interview, Amman, Jordan, 20 Apr. 1993.

states to observe 'strict non-interference in each other's internal affairs'.[72] Secretary General Dag Hammarskjöld sent a UN observer mission to Amman (the mission left Jordan in 1962). America rewarded Hussein's 'courageous and praiseworthy' handling of the crisis with closer ties and increased levels of aid. In 1959, Hussein made his first trip to Washington. Britain left a military training mission in Jordan, where it remained until 1963.

Hussein consolidated his rule by placing his ties with the West on a firmer footing. With the help of the UN, he succeeded in gaining a place for Jordan on the international agenda. The American and British press were filled with stories about the 'plucky young king' defending the Middle East against 'the communist menace'. For the first time since he inherited the throne in 1953, Hussein could devote his energies to state-building. Martial law was lifted in December 1958, and economic development became the regime's priority. By the early 1960s, prime ministers such as Hazza' al-Majali and Wasfi al-Tell began reforming the inefficient government machinery. Steps were taken to place the military under civilian control, eliminate corruption and nepotism, and reduce Jordanian dependence on foreign aid. Dann contends that Tell's first government (January 1962) represented, in some respects, 'the birth of modern Jordan'.[73]

BLACK SEPTEMBER, 1970

The Jordanian–Palestinian civil war of 1970 has often been treated as a superpower confrontation. President Richard Nixon and National Security Advisor Henry Kissinger considered the crisis 'a superpower psychodrama', a Cold War showdown writ large.[74] The literature upholds this interpretation. Nowhere does there exist a published account dealing with the internal dynamics of the crisis. Although 'the Nixon White House viewed the Middle East situation

---

[72] Dixon to FO, 22 Aug. 1958, PREM 11.2381, PRO; also, *Middle Eastern Affairs* (Oct. 1958).

[73] Dann, *Radicalism*, 120. Also, Asher Susser, *On Both Banks of the Jordan: A Political Biography of Wasfi al-Tall* (London: Frank Cass, 1994), and Suleiman Musa, *'Alam min al-urdunn: Safhat min tarikh al-'arab al-hadith* [Prominent Personalities from Jordan: Pages from Modern Arab History] (Amman: Dar al-Sha'ab, 1986).

[74] Adam M. Garfinkle, 'US Decisionmaking in the Jordan Crisis: Correcting the Record', *Political Science Quarterly* 100(1) (spring 1985), 118. Also Alan Dowty, *Middle East Crisis: US Decisionmaking in 1958, 1970, and 1973* (Berkeley: University of California Press, 1984); and William B. Quandt, *Peace Process: American Diplomacy and the Arab–Israeli Conflict since 1967* (Washington, DC: Brookings Institution and University of California Press, 1993), 94–115.

in geopolitical terms that far transcended the region',[75] Black September was a civil war, a home-grown crisis which pitted two mutually exclusive political forces against each other. Once again, however, the Jordanian regime played the Cold War card by 'marketing' the crisis as a Soviet-supported attempt to destabilize the Middle East.

The genesis of Black September came after 1967, when guerrilla factions seized the helm of the Palestinian liberation movement. The PLO began capturing the hearts and minds of Arabs after its participation in the battle of Karameh in 1968, when Palestinian commandos joined the Jordanian army in repelling an Israeli armoured incursion into the Jordan valley. The Arabs fought well, and were aided in their task by a low cloud cover which hampered Israel's use of fast ground-attack aircraft.[76] Jordan hailed the battle as a great victory, but the PLO also took credit, giving the Palestinian movement a great boost.

By the summer of 1970 the PLO had created a 'state within a state' in Jordan. After radical Palestinians hijacked several aircraft to Jordan, the international community began doubting Hussein's ability to govern his kingdom. Intense pressure from military commanders (Habis al-Majali, Sharif Zaid bin Shakir, Mazin 'Ajluni, and Qassim Ma'ayta) and other members of the political élite (Wasfi al-Tell, Moraiwid al-Tell, and Zaid al-Rifa'i) forced Hussein to establish a military government on 16 September. Hussein unleashed his army on the guerrillas, and Jordan was plunged into civil war. Hussein's problems were exacerbated by the presence of 20,000 Iraqi troops in Jordan and the threat of a Syrian intervention on behalf of the PLO.

On 19 September a Syrian force of nearly 300 tanks began attacking Jordanian positions in the Irbid region. At this juncture, external support for Hussein became critical. Nixon had already ordered the aircraft carriers *Saratoga, Independence,* and *John F. Kennedy* on alert in the Mediterranean, and US marine units had been placed on standby. On 20 September Hussein requested American assistance against the Syrians. Nixon and Kissinger decided that, if ground action were required, Israel should aid Hussein. The Israelis planned to send 200 tanks—backed by air power—toward Irbid. With American and Israeli backing secured, Hussein ordered his tiny air

[75] Garfinkle, 'U.S. Decisionmaking', 121.

[76] Interview with Zaid al-Rifa'i (former Prime Minister), Amman, Jordan, 19 Apr. 1993. For an account of the battle of Karameh, see Lawrence Tal, 'Karameh', in Richard W. Bulliet, Philip Mattar, and Reeva S. Simon (eds.), *Encyclopedia of the Middle East* (Basingstoke, Macmillan, forthcoming).

force to attack the Syrian armoured positions. The Syrians quickly withdrew across the border.[77]

External backing helped Hussein consolidate his regime and crush his opponents. The Nixon administration took credit for successfully resolving the crisis. America, however, 'exaggerated the global US–Soviet dimension of the crisis'.[78] The importance of US and Israeli support for Hussein was that it gave him the reassurance he needed fully to engage his own military forces. It also allowed Hussein to expel the last PLO guerrillas from Jordan during the summer of 1971. Nixon authorized $10 million in aid to Jordan, later requesting an additional $30 million to reinforce the regime against forces which 'threaten to weaken the stability of that country'.[79]

NEW CHALLENGES FOR JORDAN

After the 1967 war and the 1970 civil war, Jordan became increasingly dependent on Arab aid, although the US continued to fund the kingdom. The chief factors driving Jordan's turn toward the Arab world were: the end of the Arab Cold War and demise of radical pan-Arabism; the oil boom and its economic effects in the Arab world; and Jordan's realization that the US was unwilling to pressure Israel to disgorge the territories it captured in 1967.

Signs of divergence between Jordan and the US surfaced with the Camp David Accords in 1978. Jordan rejected the American-brokered agreement between Egypt and Israel for two reasons. First, the Accords assigned a role to Jordan in resolving the Palestinian problem, yet King Hussein had not been consulted by the US, Israel, or Egypt. Jordan resented the assumption that it would go along with what others had negotiated. Second, Jordan rejected the Accords for dealing with the Palestinian problem as a refugee issue, rather than one of national self-determination. The US responded to Jordan's rejection by reducing American aid to the kingdom.[80]

Jordan, however, remained in the Western camp and sought to expand its leverage in regional politics. When the second Cold War

---

[77] Hafez al-Assad decided against committing his air force to aid the Syrian armoured force. See Patrick Seale, *Asad of Syria: The Struggle for the Middle East* (Berkeley: University of California Press, 1988). Also, interview with Field Marshal Habis al-Majali (former Commander in Chief of the Jordanian army), Amman, Jordan, 12 Apr. 1993; interview with General Fahd Jureidat (Finance Minister in military government of Sept. 1970), Amman, Jordan, 12 Apr. 1993.

[78] Quandt, *Peace Process*, 112.   [79] Howard, 'Jordan in Turmoil', 18.

[80] For details, see Madiha Rashid al-Madfai, *Jordan, the United States and the Middle East Peace Process, 1974–1991* (Cambridge: Cambridge University Press, 1993).

began with the Soviet invasion of Afghanistan in 1979, the Jordanian regime launched a campaign designed to present Jordan as a bastion of moderation and stability in a turbulent region. In speeches and in diplomatic overtures to the US, King Hussein, Crown Prince Hassan, and other decision-makers emphasized Jordan's rejection of extremism, be it communist or Islamist in nature. Jordan's wariness of the Soviets and of Iran's brand of radical political Islam struck a responsive chord in Washington. In 1983, for instance, the Pentagon—as part of its RDF/CENTCOM strategy—proposed that Jordanian special forces be used as a rapid deployment force for the Persian Gulf.

Jordan's policies during the Iran–Iraq War also met with favour in the US. When Iraq invaded Iran in 1980, Jordan was at the forefront of those supporting Baghdad. First, Hussein and other policy-makers believed Iran was intent on exporting its revolution. Iraq served as a counterweight to a hegemonic Iran. Second, Iraq was an ally against Syria. Jordan always sought the support of at least one major Arab power. After Egypt's removal from the confrontation line in 1978, and Syria's continuing hostility, Iraq became a natural ally. Finally, Jordan had much to gain economically from ties with Iraq. Because Iraq was essentially landlocked, the Jordanian port of Aqaba served as the key transit point for Iraqi trade. Throughout the 1980s, the Jordanian economy was boosted by a vast expansion in Iraqi trucking and shipping from Aqaba.

When Iraq invaded Kuwait in August 1990, Jordan tried to straddle the fence by condemning both the invasion and Western military intervention in the Gulf. Given Jordan's reputation as a friend of the West, why was Hussein reticent about supporting the American-led military coalition arrayed against Saddam Hussein's Iraq? First, as argued above, Jordan had become extremely dependent on Iraq for its economic well-being: Iraq supplied 95 per cent of Jordan's petroleum and purchased a large portion of Jordan's exports. Moreover, over 70 per cent of Jordan's industrial capability was geared toward Iraq.[81] Severing links with Iraq was not in Jordan's economic interest.

Another factor behind Jordan's policy was its fear of Israel. With the advent of hard-line Likud governments in the late 1970s and 1980s, Jordan had increasingly looked to Baghdad to offset the threat of an expansionist Israel. Many Likud supporters believed that 'Jordan is Palestine' and advocated 'transferring' thousands of

[81] Mustafa B. Hamarneh, 'Jordan Responds to the Gulf Crisis', in Phyllis Bennis and Michel Moushabeck (eds.), *Beyond the Storm: A Gulf Crisis Reader* (New York: Olive Branch Press, 1991), 236.

Palestinians to Jordan. Under the Shamir government, Soviet Jewish immigration to Israel increased, fuelling fears in Amman that Israel was poised to expel droves of Palestinians to Jordan.

A third factor driving Jordan's anti-Western stance stemmed from domestic calculations on the part of King Hussein and others in the political élite. In 1989 a spate of anti-regime riots had erupted in traditional areas of Hashemite support. Hussein responded by holding Jordan's first parliamentary elections in twenty-two years. The Muslim Brotherhood and other Islamists swept the polls and spearheaded a campaign advocating economic and political reforms. Accusations of corruption and fiscal mismanagement were levelled at officials close to the palace. When the Gulf crisis erupted, Hussein and his advisers were presented with an excellent opportunity to bolster their flagging legitimacy. For the first time in Jordanian history, the regime allowed, and even encouraged, anti-Western demonstrations to occur in public places. The Muslim Brotherhood was given a fairly free hand to channel popular dissent toward 'constructive' ends; that is, toward backing the king's policy of opposition to Western military intervention in the Gulf. Consequently, Hussein emerged from the crisis enjoying unprecedented popularity. He appeared to have responded to the wishes of his people and simultaneously forestalled calls for further liberalization.

Finally, Jordan was able to oppose Washington because Hussein realized that the end of the Cold War had diminished his country's geo-strategic importance to the West. The Soviet Union was on the verge of collapse; hence Jordan had no Soviet card to play with the Americans. Further, America's unwavering support for Israel, its refusal to modernize the Jordanian military, and the fairly paltry aid package Jordan received from America convinced Hussein that he owed little to Washington. Whereas securing US support in 1957, 1958, and 1970 was crucial for Jordan, Washington's backing in 1990 meant far less.

There were two significant ramifications of the Gulf crisis for Jordan. The first was that the crisis allowed Hussein—as other crises had in Jordanian history—to consolidate his reign. He emerged from the Gulf War enjoying massive approval among both Transjordanians and Palestinians. He was one of the few Arab leaders who could claim to have taken an Arab 'nationalist' stance against the West. Egypt and Syria, supposedly the heartlands of pan-Arabism, had 'capitulated' to Washington, while tiny Jordan took a stand. Moreover, with the post-crisis economic downturn in Jordan, the regime managed to stall the impetus for substantive political and economic reforms by calling for a period of 'national unity' in the face of Western, Israeli, and Arab condemnation. The second significant result of the crisis was that Jordan lost its aid from the Gulf states. In this respect, Hussein's Gulf War policy was far less successful than it had been on the domestic front. Although Hussein managed to rehabilitate himself in Washington, forgiveness from the Gulf states was less forthcoming. Recent Jordanian policy, however, indicates that the kingdom plans to distance itself from Iraq and cement its alliance with the West.

JORDAN AFTER THE COLD WAR

What does the demise of superpower rivalry herald for Jordan?[82] The first product, albeit indirect, of the end of the Cold War is peace. Hussein had long sought accommodation with Israel, but was made a series of unrealistic peace offers by successive Israeli and American governments. Jordan's loss of Arab aid and American support in 1990, however, meant that Hussein had little choice but to sue for peace. Jordan participated in the Madrid peace conference in October 1991 and the bilateral talks which followed. Jordan was careful not to become the first Arab state (after Egypt) to sign a treaty with Israel. However, when the PLO signed its peace agreement in September 1993, Jordan was free to pursue its own agenda, which culminated in a treaty signed with Israel in October 1994. International aid, American debt forgiveness, and the economic benefits of tourism and joint ventures with Israel were among the chief reasons Hussein made peace. While Islamist and some secular groups have been active in their opposition to the peace process, the regime has thus far deflected criticisms and is currently stable.

Other post-Cold War developments are potentially destabilizing. The first is the growing strength of the Islamist movement in Jordan, the West Bank, and Gaza. In the past, the Hashemites adeptly co-opted Islamists in the struggle against communism. Now that the communist 'menace' has receded, the Islamists remain a thorn in the side of the regime.

A second challenge is the issue of Palestinian identity in Jordan. During the Cold War, the Hashemites took pains to underscore the cohesiveness of the Jordanian–Palestinian relationship. However, the prospect of an independent Palestinian state raises questions—dormant since 1970—about the political allegiance of Jordan's

---

[82] See Lawrence Tal, 'Peace for Jordan?', *The World Today* 49(8–9) (Aug.–Sept. 1993), 168–71; 'Is Jordan Doomed?', *Foreign Affairs* 72(5) (Nov.–Dec. 1993), 45–58; and 'New Challenges for Jordan', *The World and I* (Apr. 1994), 80–5.

Palestinian community. Jordanian nationalists, although not a homogeneous coalition, want Jordan's Palestinians to choose affiliations. This group—composed of Transjordanian families, tribes, and Palestinian luminaries who migrated to Jordan before 1948—has traditionally depended on access to the security and civil services.[83] Most wish to reduce the role Palestinians play in governing Jordan.

A third challenge to the regime is political liberalization. During the 1950s and 1960s, the regime blamed the lack of political pluralism on the Cold War. How, it asked, could Jordan be expected to liberalize when leftist radicals wanted to subvert the country? After 1967, the main justification for the absence of political accountability and democracy was the Israeli occupation of the West Bank. 'Aid and remittances', moreover, 'financed a massive expansion of higher education, allowing even poor households access to lucrative employment abroad.'[84] Economic prosperity stifled the impetus for reforms as Jordanians and Palestinians prospered from the oil boom. But the petro-dollar era has waned. The chief problem for the regime is that further liberalization could undermine the structures which have underpinned the Jordanian state since its inception, and which were reinforced by the Cold War. Political transparency and accountability could weaken the patronage system which benefits the regime's main backers.

THE COLD WAR, REGIME CONSOLIDATION, AND STATE-BUILDING

The Cold War provided King Hussein with opportunities for laying a firmer foundation for the system of rule Abdullah had created. Superpower rivalry allowed Hussein to shore up his regime against radical pan-Arabism, Israel, and internal opponents by portraying local and regional crises as Soviet-backed attempts to gain ground in the Middle East. Because Hussein had proved his mettle in successive 'trials by fire', the Western powers, particularly the US, generally turned a blind eye to the lack of political freedoms in Jordan. As long as Jordan remained moderate and anti-communist in its orientation, it would be backed by Washington.

---

[83] For more on the 'Jordan first' or 'East Bank first' school of thought, see Valerie Yorke, *Domestic Politics and Regional Security, Jordan, Syria, and Israel: The End of an Era?* (Aldershot: Gower for International Institute for Strategic Studies, 1988); Yossi Nevo, 'Is There a Jordanian Entity?', *Jerusalem Quarterly* 16 (summer 1980); and Jamal al-Sha'ir, *Siyassi yatadhakkir* [A Politician Remembers] (London: Riyad al-Rayyes Publishers, 1987).

[84] Tell, 'Social Origins of Jordanian Glasnost', 12.

Regime consolidation, in turn, led to state-building by, first, providing the requisite stability for economic and political development and, second, creating a political field in which irreconcilable differences could be reconciled. As external aid increased during the 1960s and 1970s, the regime built a resource pool to co-opt opponents and create vested interests in the state. Old foes were rehabilitated and placated with ambassadorial and ministerial appointments. Supporters of the regime were rewarded with cabinet and senate posts. The military was allocated substantial portions of national budgets. The Cold War, in short, transformed the Hashemite polity from a precarious entity into a durable state. Despite the trials Jordan will face in the twenty-first century, its survival is no longer in doubt.

6

The Palestinians

YEZID SAYIGH

The Palestinians offer a unique case study of the impact of the Cold War on Middle East politics. Stateless, and suffering exile and dispersal after 1948, they came to enjoy a presence in regional and international fora that was wholly out of proportion to the physical capabilities of the body that represented them, the Palestine Liberation Organization (PLO). The diplomatic status of the PLO and the markedly statist character of its institutions and internal politics set it apart from virtually all its Third World contemporaries. Yet, as the course of both its armed struggle against Israel and its diplomacy showed, external (or systemic) constraints severely limited Palestinian means and ends alike. Indeed this was virtually inevitable, since the PLO sought to alter the regional status quo. The fact that it was a non-state actor further reduced the 'domestic' sources of its political autonomy—social, economic, and institutional—and accentuated the impact of the global ideological contest on the evolution of its internal politics.

The core argument of this chapter is that the Cold War was a principal factor, if not the single most important one, determining the outcome of the Palestinian national struggle at every stage, and that PLO politics and policies were affected by it at every level. The impact was not always direct—the Cold War often operated through the intervening role of the Arab states—but it remained pervasive throughout. At the same time the PLO was hardly a passive actor. It worked purposefully to assert the Palestinians as a distinct regional player, devise autonomous strategies, and utilize the Cold War to its own diplomatic advantage. This was particularly true in 1973–82, during which period the PLO sought actively to manipulate US–Soviet relations. There were structural limits to what it could achieve, but the PLO's ability to embody and institutionalize Palestinian nationalism and to survive as a political organization demonstrated that the local actor (or agent) was not wholly subject to systemic constraints at every level. In order to assess the impact of superpower rivalry on the perceptions and policy responses of the

PLO, the following sections examine its foreign policy orientation (including a case study), regional relations, 'domestic' politics, and the end of the Cold War.

FOREIGN POLICY ORIENTATION

Following 1948, the Palestinians lacked a government or a similar, para-statal body that could define national interests and pursue them in relation to regional and global powers. There could not be a foreign policy orientation in such circumstances, properly speaking, and the impact of the Cold War could only be felt to the extent that it affected the political behaviour of the Arab states that hosted and controlled the disparate Palestinian communities in the West Bank and Gaza Strip and in exile. US–Soviet rivalry was initially experienced secondhand, and was not directly relevant to the evolution of Palestinian nationalism. Only with the establishment of the PLO with the approval of the Arab states in 1964 and, more importantly, following its transformation into a politically autonomous organization under the command of the independent guerrilla groups after June 1967 could there be a meaningful Palestinian foreign policy. The previous absence of an institutional framework meant, first, that there was an inevitable 'learning' process as the PLO leadership acquired, tested, and evolved a foreign policy orientation. It also meant that the personal perceptions and formative experiences of the individuals who composed that leadership were of particular importance, especially as the requirements of armed struggle encouraged authoritarian political structures.

PLO foreign policy after 1967 was at first driven to a considerable degree by ideology and polemics, as a result of the heady atmosphere of revolutionary expansion and the accompanying contest between the various guerrilla groups (and within some of them) for organizational supremacy and political legitimacy. It was not until the defeat in Jordan in 1970–1 and the subsequent decline of the armed struggle that the PLO came to recognize clearly the extent to which the Cold War constrained its options. The turning-point in this learning process came with the October 1973 war, as a result of which the manipulation of international politics in general and of superpower rivalry in particular became central to PLO strategy, above all in the period until 1982. The Cold War may always have 'set the ceiling', but the PLO chose one manner of response over another of its own volition, especially after 1973. The choices it made constituted its foreign policy orientation, and as such reflected the world-view of its principal leaders, the order of importance they attributed to various external actors, and their search for a viable strategy.

The making of a foreign policy orientation

The foreign-policy orientation of the PLO and its main constituent guerrilla groups in the main period of Cold War relevance, 1973–82, was shaped by a number of factors. One was the world-view of the men who assumed leadership of the PLO in the late 1960s—their assumptions about the nature and utility of power, the exercise of influence, and the conduct of international politics. This was shaped by the events they had witnessed between 1948 and 1967, and affected the orientation of the two principal nationalist groups: the Arab Nationalists' Movement (ANM), founded in 1951–2, and Fateh, founded in 1958–9.

The ANM drew on the writings of nineteenth-century European nationalism—romantic and absolutist—and contemporary Arab thinkers to formulate a pan-Arab nationalism with fascist undertones.[1] It held a strictly normative view of politics, and strove to build its domestic and regional relations within a well-defined ideological framework. It condemned the West for its colonial past and perceived role in the Palestinian 'catastrophe' of 1948, but also distrusted the USSR for recognizing Israel and castigated the Arab communists for echoing Soviet calls for coexistence with the Jewish state. The ANM saw Arab unity as the prerequisite for the destruction of Israel and the liberation of Palestine, and idolized Egyptian President Gamal Abdel Nasser, whom it adopted as its pan-Arab hero after 1956.[2] The formal doctrine and pantheon of external allies were to change after 1967—to Marxist-Leninism in the former case and to international working-class solidarity, headed variously by Third World communist countries, China, and the USSR, in the latter—but the patterns of ideologically and strategically determined political alignment did not.

Fateh was to take control of the PLO in alliance with other guerrilla groups in February 1969, a position it had not relinquished by the end of the Cold War, many years later. A majority of its founders started their political careers in the ranks of the Muslim Brotherhood Society and reflected much of its outlook, not least the antipathy to

---

[1] For a detailed account of the ideological origins of the ANM, see Basil al-Kubaysi, *Harakat al-Qawmiyyin al-'Arab* [The Arab Nationalists' Movement] (Beirut: Institute for Arab Studies, 1985), ch. 2.

[2] Walid Kazziha, *Revolutionary Transformation in the Arab World: Habash and His Comrades from Nationalism to Marxism* (London: Charles Knight, 1975), 51–2, 53.

both colonialism and communism. Yet the attachment to Islam was not dogmatic: it was a means to national salvation, much as pan-Arabism or socialism were for other Palestinians. Fateh's ideology, if any, was Palestinian nationalism, and national unity its main priority. Like the ANM, Fateh considered the role of external powers to be of primary importance, but its perception of political causality differed markedly. It argued that there were three concentric circles of action and reaction affecting the national cause: Palestinian, Arab, and international.[3] Palestinian action would lead to mobilization of Arab military, economic, and political resources, and in turn exert an appreciable influence on the international community. International reactions would support the Arab and Palestinian position and isolate Israel, or so Fateh hoped. The synergy assumed in the 'three circles' view was simplistic, but it revealed the assumption that the strategic balance could be shifted through manipulative politics. Just as importantly, it showed the importance attached by Fateh to the attainment of regional status and international recognition. This, coupled with the willingness to utilize all means available and secure any gains possible, indicated a pragmatic approach to national goals and to the conflict with Israel that was ultimately to dominate PLO strategy after 1974.

The foundations of PLO foreign policy orientation were laid during the tenure of its founder and first chairman of its executive committee in 1964–7, Ahmad al-Shuqayri. The USSR was at best indifferent to the establishment of the PLO, but in June 1965 the PLO's parliament-in-exile, the Palestine National Council (PNC), noted 'with appreciation the glorious recent stands taken by the socialist countries, and the USSR at their forefront, in support of the Arab position on the Palestine cause at the [United Nations]'.[4] China allowed the PLO to open an office in Beijing and provided light weapons and modest financial assistance, and was rewarded in May 1966 with a special tribute from the PNC, which also urged the Arab states to recognize the People's Republic.[5] The PNC still noted Soviet policy in positive vein, and extolled the role of the non-aligned countries, the (Soviet-backed) Tri-Continental Movement, and other national liberation movements.[6] This balanced emphasis—on China,

[3] This view is echoed by the Palestinian Islamists, who define three circles—Palestinian, Arab, and Islamic—drawn around Palestine, the 'navel of the earth'.

[4] Rashid Hamid, *Muqarrarat al-Majlis al-Watani al-Filastinim, 1964–1974* [Resolutions of the Palestine National Council, 1964–1974] (Beirut: PLO Research Center, 1975), 75.

[5] e.g. letter of thanks from Shuqayri to Chinese Premier Zhou Enlai, 9/65/15, 7 Oct. 1965; and letter discussing arms requests from PLA commander Wajih al-Madani to Shuqayri, Q'A/9/1/330/, 3 May 1967. PLA HQ Archives.

[6] Hamid, *Muqarrarat*, 94–5.

the USSR, and the Third World—was maintained after Fateh took control of the PLO with the election of Yasir Arafat as chairman in February 1969. Having omitted to salute the USSR during the brief tenure of left-leaning lawyer Yahya Hammuda in 1968, the PNC now thanked the USSR for supporting the Arab states and urged it to increase its assistance, while thanking China, North Korea, Cuba, and Vietnam for their solidarity and again identifying the US as 'part of the enemy camp'.[7]

The ascendance of the mainstream nationalist Fateh had a decisive impact on PLO foreign policy. Its pragmatism was reflected in particular in growing PLO acknowledgement of the central role of the superpowers in the Arab–Israeli conflict. This was in contrast to the initial radicalism of the Palestinian left, which went through a stridently Maoist phase in 1968–70. However, the defeat of the Palestinian guerrillas in Jordan in 1970–1 discredited the political slogans of the left and weakened it physically. Consequently, Fateh was able to assert its political and organizational predominance and to confirm the PLO as the principal decision-making body in Palestinian national politics. It also developed the modest contact established with the USSR during an unofficial visit in July 1968 by Arafat, who secretly travelled as a member of the entourage of Egyptian President Nasser. Fateh appreciated the strategic influence that the USSR could bring to bear as the world's second superpower and leader of a sizeable bloc of socialist countries—especially in contrast to China, with which Fateh had enjoyed warm relations since 1964, and continued to enjoy for many more years—and its ability to counterbalance what it perceived as hostile US policy in the Middle East. The first PLO delegation to make an official visit to Moscow did so in February 1970 at the invitation of the Afro-Asian Solidarity Committee, and Soviet embassy officials in Amman commenced regular contacts with the PLO leadership in the following period.

The Fateh-led PLO was increasingly aware of superpower influence in regional affairs and alert to the implications for its own strategy. However, the loss of its principal base in Jordan and its inability to revive the armed struggle against Israel after 1970 made it doubly wary: of US and Soviet intentions generally, and of seeming to align itself too closely with one against the other. The attitude of the Fateh-dominated PLO towards the Palestinian communists (then a branch of the Jordanian Communist Party) offered an example of its caution: the communist Ansar guerrilla group was allowed to join

---

[7] Ibid. 153.

low-level PLO military committees in 1970, but denied formal representation in its policy-making bodies, and a senior communist was granted a seat in the PNC in February 1971, but only in his individual capacity as an 'independent'.

One reason for Palestinian caution was the hesitation of the Soviet leadership, which still doubted the significance of the PLO.[8] Another was the launch of *détente*, which convinced the PLO leadership, along with the heads of the key Arab states, that the superpowers had privately agreed on the terms of an Arab–Israeli settlement without referring to the views and interests of the core protagonists.[9] This uncertainty explains the omission of any mention of the superpowers in the formal political statements issued by the PNC at its sessions of April 1972 and January 1973. Besides, the immediate concern of the PLO in the wake of its expulsion from Jordan was to preserve its autonomy and the legitimacy of its claim to represent the Palestinians. It was convinced that Israeli and Jordanian attempts to undermine its political appeal in the Occupied Territories in spring 1972 had US backing, and Fateh demonstrated its ire with a series of terrorist acts over the next year, including the murder of the US ambassador to Khartoum in February 1973.[10] Yet Arafat, in particular, grasped that superpower *détente* also offered an opportunity. Following publication of a joint US–Soviet statement in June 1973 that spoke for the first time of 'the legitimate interests of the Palestinian people', he sent several secret messages to the US administration expressing willingness to coexist with Israel.[11]

It was against this background that the Arab–Israeli war in October suddenly offered the PLO the chance to devise an activist diplomatic strategy. US Secretary of State Henry Kissinger now concluded that American interests would be better served by holding a

---

[8] This Soviet view was expressed by, or on behalf of, Mikhail Suslov and Boris Ponomarev to a Syrian Communist Party delegation in May 1971. Leaked minutes published in *Qadaya al-Khilaf fi al-Hizb al-Shuyu'i al-Suri* [Issues of the Dispute in the Syrian Communist Party], Report of the 3rd Congress of the SCP (Beirut: Dar Ibn Khaldun, 1972), 153. A fuller account of the development of Soviet–PLO relations in this period is in Nabil Haydari, 'al-Ittihad al-Suvyati wa Munazzamat al-Tahrir al-Filastiniyya, 1970–197' [The USSR and the PLO, 1970–1973], *Shu'un Filastiniyya* 217–18 (Apr.–May 1991), 22–53.

[9] This view was also shared by the pro-Soviet DFLP and the Syrian-backed Sa'iqa; see e.g. the statement by Sa'iqa leader Zuhayr Muhsin cited in *al-Kitab al-Sanawi li al-Qadiyya al-Filastiniyya 1973* [The Yearbook of the Palestine Cause 1973] (Beirut: Institute for Palestine Studies, 1976), 30.

[10] King Hussein proposed reuniting the West Bank with Jordan in a United Arab Kingdom in March 1972, while Israel conducted municipal elections in the West Bank in April. The PLO condemned the former as 'a treasonous pact with Israel and the Americans', and deemed the latter to be 'part of the colonialist plot'. Text of statement in Hamid, *Muqarrarat*, 209, 222.

[11] William Quandt, *Decade of Decisions: American Policy Towards the Arab–Israeli Conflict, 1967–1976* (Berkeley: University of California Press, 1977), 160; Henry Kissinger, *Years of Upheaval* (London: Weidenfeld & Nicolson, 1982), 626–7.

direct dialogue with the PLO, and authorized two rounds of secret exploratory talks in November 1973 and March 1974.[12] The results were inconclusive and Kissinger discontinued the effort, but it convinced Arafat of two things. First was the utility of the combined effect of the October war, Arab oil embargo and diplomatic solidarity, and Soviet support in prompting a shift in US policy. Second was that the convergence in US and Soviet policies in the Middle East was sufficient to allow the superpowers to impose a settlement on the Arabs and Israel. Repositioning the PLO, he won the PNC's approval in June 1974 for a new political programme that defined the establishment of a 'national authority' on any territory evacuated by Israel as the foremost objective of the PLO, at least in the current historical phase.[13] The PLO stopped short of accepting direct negotiations with Israel, let alone recognizing it, but diplomacy now occupied a central position in its strategy. Over the next year it was rewarded for the relative moderation of its goals by receiving confirmation of its status as the sole legitimate representative of the Palestinians from the Arab states and varying degrees of recognition from the countries of the Non-Aligned Movement and the Soviet bloc.[14]

The elements of a Cold War strategy

From 1973 onwards the principal PLO goal was to achieve Palestinian self-determination in the form of a state in the West Bank (including east Jerusalem) and Gaza Strip, although it was not to refer to statehood explicitly until 1977, in order to avoid accusations from its internal opposition that it envisaged coexistence with Israel.[15] Arafat and his allies within the Fateh and PLO leadership were convinced that 'the US holds the key to Israel', and so the ultimate purpose of their diplomacy was to prompt the US, through one means or another, to accept two principal provisions: to involve the PLO as a direct party to negotiations, and to place Palestinian statehood on the negotiating agenda.[16] Indeed, these tenets were to remain constant until the end of the Cold War and beyond.

[12] The talks were conducted by General Vernon Walters, then Deputy Director of the CIA. Andrew Gowers and Tony Walker, *Behind the Myth: Yasser Arafat and the Palestinian Revolution* (London: Corgi Books, 1991), 141–3, 157–8.

[13] Text of programme in the PLO official weekly, *Filastin al-Thawra*, 12 June 1974.

[14] A careful discussion of Soviet-bloc attitudes is Galia Golan, *The Soviet Union and the Palestine Liberation Organization: An Uneasy Alliance* (New York: Praeger, 1980), ch. 7. On international recognition, see also Kemal Kirisci, *The PLO and World Politics: A Study of the Mobilization of Support for the Palestinian Cause* (London: Frances Pinter, 1986).

[15] An excellent survey of the internal political debate is in Alain Gresh, *The PLO: The Struggle Within* (London: Zed Books, 1985).

[16] From an interview with Arafat in *Time*, 11 Nov. 1974, cited in Gowers and Walker, *Behind the Myth*, 213.

The PLO also expected the USSR to play a critical, if supporting, part in its strategy. In the first place, the Soviet leadership had consistently pressed the PLO since the start of bilateral contacts to accept UN Security Council Resolution 242 of November 1967, which called for the return of occupied Arab territories and the right of all states in the region, implicitly including Israel, to peaceful and secure borders.[17] After the October 1973 war the USSR urged the PLO to join the peace process and extract concrete gains, and promised to adopt Palestinian proposals 'as relates to the West Bank and Gaza Strip and Palestinian rights'.[18] The PLO viewed the Soviet relationship as a means both of impressing the US with its importance in regional affairs and of gaining diplomatic leverage. This was equally applicable in the event both of bilateral Palestinian–Israeli negotiations and of an international peace conference at which a unified Arab delegation and the USSR would form a common front against Israel and the US. The latter option was most favoured by the USSR and Syria, the former seeing a means of securing its role and the latter seeking to maximize the bargaining power of each Arab party through a joint Arab diplomatic effort in pursuit of a comprehensive peace settlement; but the PLO tended to a more tactical view.

The PLO entertained certain misconceptions, not least of which was the assumption that the US could 'deliver' an unwilling Israel. The PLO moreover failed to enunciate a coherent policy towards the US, let alone grasp the relationship between the domestic and foreign spheres of US policy-making. Instead, it assumed that both the American public and government could be swayed by appeals to US economic interests in the Middle East. Arafat reflected this outlook in his speech to the UN General Assembly in November 1974, when he reminded the 'American people that their friendship with our Arab nation is more important, lasting, and *beneficial* [than the alliance with Israel]'.[19] The fact that neither the PLO chairman nor any of the key members of the Palestinian leadership had direct experience of Western society and politics was not insignificant in this context, and led to simplistic and vague assumptions about the means of influencing US foreign policy.

[17] Khalil al-Wazir, *Harakat Fath: al-Nushu', al-Irtiqa', al-Tatawwur, al-Mumaththil al-Shar'i: al-Bidayat 1* [Fateh: Genesis, Rise, Evolution, Legitimate Representative: Beginnings Part 1] (n.p.: Research and Mobilization Center, 1986), 83.

[18] According to Zahayr Muhsin, head of the Sa'iqa guerrilla group and of the PLO military department, interviewed in *al-Muharrir*, 5 Nov. 1973. Additional detail on PLO–Soviet relations in this period in Nabil al-Haydari, 'al-Ittihad al-Suvyati wa Munazzamat al-Tahrir al-Filastiniyya, 1973–1974' [The USSR and the PLO, 1973–1974], *Shu'un Filastiniyya* 223–4 (Oct.–Nov. 1991), 21–57.

[19] Text in *Shu-un Filastiniyya* 40 (Dec. 1974); quotation from p. 8. Emphasis added.

These flaws were matched by an inflated assessment by the PLO of its own importance to the USSR, which tended, conversely, to view the relationship as tactical rather than strategic, to be subordinated to wider Soviet–Arab and Soviet–US ties.[20] The USSR was particularly reluctant to overplay its backing for the PLO in the mid-1970s lest it jeopardize *détente* with the US, and moreover withheld full recognition of the PLO as *sole* Palestinian representative until late 1978. Last but not least, the PLO sought contradictory operational goals that affected its standing with both superpowers: at one level its commitment to an international peace conference was merely nominal, with its pragmatic preference being to strive for bilateral dialogue with the US, but at another level it hoped to protect its interests and improve its bargaining position by involving the other Arab parties and the USSR directly in the negotiations once it had made the concessions necessary to reach the negotiating table.

None the less, PLO strategy and operational objectives after 1973 were reasonably clear: to construct regional and international coalitions that would bring material and political pressure to bear on the US. To this would be added PLO diplomatic overtures, reinforced, when necessary, by demonstrative military action against Israel.[21] The first component of this strategy was to mobilize Arab solidarity. The PLO expected the Arab states to undertake concerned diplomatic action on its behalf and to employ the recycling of petrodollars and the ability to offer (or deny) oil supplies and financial aid to gain leverage with the US, Western Europe, and the Third World.[22] To that end, it was determined to maintain close ties with key pro-Western Arab states such as Saudi Arabia and Egypt, while preserving steady working relations with Syria, which had offered crucial support for the adoption by the PLO of the moderate political programme of June 1974, and even with militant states such as Iraq and Libya if possible. The anticipated synergy between the various diplomatic tracks—including relations with the USSR and its bloc—was entirely in keeping with the Fateh notion of the three

[20] Galia Golan, *Soviet Policy in the Middle East: From World War II to Gorbachev* (Cambridge: Cambridge University Press, 1990), ch. 8.

[21] PLO strategy and its implications for military activity discussed in Yezid Sayigh, 'Palestinian Armed Struggle: Means and Ends', *Journal of Palestine Studies* 16(1)(61) (autumn 1986) 95–112.

[22] Employment of the Arab oil weapon was first urged by the PNC in 1965; text of statement in Hamid, *Muqarrarat*, 75. A more articulate example of this thinking is the article by the then PLO executive committee member Yusif Sayigh, 'al-Naft al-'Arabi fi Istratijiyyat al-Mujabaha al-'Arabiyya al-Isra'iliyya' [Arab Oil in the Strategy of the Arab–Israeli Confrontation], *Shu'un Filastiniyya* 16 (Dec. 1972), 34–62.

concentric circles of strategic interaction, and formed the core dynamic of PLO foreign policy.

The development of PLO relations with the Third World offers additional insight to the above framework. The PLO did not regard itself as part of either superpower camp, but neither was its involvement with the Non-Aligned Movement (NAM) an assertion of neutrality or an ideological statement of Third Worldism. It became a full member of the movement and joined its secretariat, but NAM, like the Islamic Conference Organization, the Organization of African Unity, and others, which the PLO also joined in various capacities, was simply another major bloc of states in the international community to be mobilized in support of the Palestinian cause. To reinforce this track of its diplomatic strategy over the next decade, the PLO provided military assistance (including arms shipments and combat pilots) to various Third World states, pressured others to abandon relations with Israel by arming and training their opposition groups, and arranged cheap oil supplies or loans from Arab states in return for diplomatic support at the UN. The PLO made no attempt, otherwise, to develop shared doctrines or policy platforms on social issues or the international economic order with Third World counterparts, nor to institutionalize its bilateral relations with developing countries for long-term influence.

PLO diplomatic strategy was wholly pragmatic, therefore. The PLO maintained ties with China, developed close working relations with key Third World countries and multilateral groupings, and increasingly courted Western Europe, but its diplomatic strategy now relied primarily on building a partnership of convenience with the USSR while seeking a substantive dialogue with the US. The conduct of the latter exercise in following years gave rise to four main lessons. First was that PLO strategy was most effective during superpower *détente*, but severely constrained during periods of intense superpower rivalry. This seems paradoxical in light of the tendency of state actors to feel constrained by *détente* and to prefer to play the superpowers off against each other; but the PLO had come to the realization that its hopes of statehood depended primarily on US willingness and secondarily on the diplomatic influence that the USSR could wield if it had good working relations with the US. Yet ironically, the second lesson was that even under conditions of *détente* there was a point beyond which the PLO could not develop its dialogue with the US, indirect as it was, without arousing the suspicions of the USSR, Syria and the militant Arab states, and the Palestinian opposition. Their counter-moves could, and did, prevent the PLO from seizing the most likely opportunities for a formal dialogue and participation in the peace process that presented themselves in 1973–82. Conversely, third, the PLO could resort to playing the 'Soviet card' when superpower relations deteriorated, as a means both of defusing combined Soviet, Arab, and Palestinian pressure and of signalling its ability to affect US regional and global interests, and, by that token, the need to draw it into the US-led peace process. Fourth, the PLO strove to use the Soviet card sparingly lest it alienate the US altogether, but its balancing act was difficult to maintain in the face of constant pressure from internal and external actors to force it into a frank alliance with the USSR.

Playing the Cold War: a case study

These lessons were graphically displayed in the main period of Cold War relevance to the PLO, 1973–82. A major 'window of opportunity' opened for the PLO following the inauguration of the Carter administration in January 1977, coinciding as this did with a passing revival of Arab solidarity and US–Soviet consultation. As a substantive, if indirect, dialogue got under way through Egypt, Carter called for the creation of a Palestinian 'homeland' within the framework of Jordan 'or by other means', while the US State Department later acknowledged 'the need for a homeland for the Palestinians whose exact nature should be negotiated between the parties'.[23] The US required the PLO to recognize Israel and accept UNSC Resolutions 242 and 338 as the basis for negotiations, and the PLO indicated its willingness to move some way towards satisfying these terms.[24]

However, the dialogue faced obstacles. One was Israeli insistence that there would be no Palestinian 'mini-state' and no talks 'with the terror organization called the PLO'.[25] The election of a right-wing nationalist government under Likud Party leader Menachem Begin in May made progress even less likely; it also altered Egyptian and Syrian calculations fundamentally and set the two Arab states on a divergent course once more, with negative consequences for PLO diplomacy. The PLO already faced bitter opposition from the

[23] Carter statement on 16 Mar. 1977, cited in William Quandt, *Peace Process: American Diplomacy and the Arab–Israeli Conflict since 1967* (Washington, DC: Brookings Institution, 1993), 260. Text of State Dept. statement reproduced in William Quandt, *Camp David: Peacemaking and Politics* (Washington, DC: Brookings Institution, 1986), 73.

[24] e.g. statement by US Secretary of State Cyrus Vance on 17 Feb. 1977, *Arab Report and Record* (15–28 Feb. 1977); report on discussions between Arafat and Egyptian Foreign Minister Isma'il Fahmi, *Egyptian Gazette*, 18 Feb. 1977; and interviews with PLO 'Foreign Minister' Faruq al-Qaddumi, *al-Ahram*, 26 Feb. and 28 Mar. 1977.

[25] Prime Minister Yitzhak Rabin, *New York Times*, 20 Jan. 1977; cited in *Arab Report and Record*, 16–31 Jan. 1977.

'rejectionist' guerrilla groups and their Iraqi and Libyan backers, but just as worrying was growing Soviet pressure. This was signalled by criticism from Soviet-backed leftists of PLO contacts with the US and 'reactionary' Arab states, an invitation to rejectionist leader Ahmad Jibril to visit Moscow in July, and an unprecedented four messages from the Soviet leadership to Arafat in the space of only ten days in August. The US State Department reiterated on 13 September that 'the Palestinians must be involved in the peace-making process. Their representatives will have to be at Geneva for the Palestinian question to be solved', but Arafat was unable to accept US terms.[26] Any hopes raised by the joint US–Soviet statement issued on 1 October were dashed when Israeli pressure forced Carter to retract, and Sadat overturned all calculations several weeks later by announcing his intention to visit Jerusalem to make peace with Israel.

The conduct of the separate Egyptian–Israeli peace talks over the next sixteen months demonstrated the remaining lessons, revealing as it did so the symbiotic relationship between the political influence of the Palestinian left, the polarization of inter-Arab relations, and Soviet priorities in the slide towards the second Cold War. Arafat and his closest colleagues were loath to lose the Egyptian channel, and did not cease efforts to resuscitate the dialogue with the US throughout this phrase and beyond.[27] However, the Palestinian left had already accused the 'centrist right-wing' PLO leadership of 'kowtowing to Egyptian–Saudi–US plans' in September, and Fateh now resorted to the Soviet card.[28] 'We consider the USSR to be one of our biggest friends in the world,' Fateh central committee member Salah Khalaf stated in late January 1978, and in March Arafat visited Moscow to meet Brezhnev and Gromyko and request increased military assistance.[29]

However, Soviet displeasure with Arafat for maintaining a discreet dialogue in this period with Egypt, and implicitly with the US, was revealed in May, when the USSR's Palestinian allies joined the rejectionist groups for the first time in a joint memorandum accusing the PLO leadership of trying to 'obtain a seat on the American train'.[30]

---

[26] Quandt, *Camp David*, 102.

[27] The Fateh central committee made clear its reluctance to break with Sadat in a moderately worded statement; *WAFA News Agency*, 17 Nov. 1977.

[28] Quote from Hawatma interview held in private papers of the Institute for Palestine Studies, Beirut, and reproduced in *al-Watha'iq al-Filastiniyya al-'Arabiyya li-'Am 1977* [Palestinian Arab Documents for the Year 1977] (Beirut: Institute for Palestine Studies, 1978), 311.

[29] Quote from *WAFA News Agency*, special supplement, 22 Jan. 1978.

[30] *Al-Safir*, 25 May 1978.

Soviet-backed groups, including recognized communist parties, also issued unprecedented public criticism of the Fateh leadership in following weeks after a crackdown on dissident leftists. The conclusion of the Camp David accords in September deepened the PLO's predicament. Arafat secretly enquired of the US administration if the outline for Palestinian autonomy in the West Bank and Gaza Strip in the accords offered scope for further discussion, but any hope of salvaging a diplomatic option had to be abandoned.[31] On 4 October the Fateh central committee took the unprecedented step of advocating a closer alliance with the socialist countries 'headed by the USSR', and the PLO joined Syria, Libya, Algeria, and South Yemen in a statement describing the US as an enemy and calling for deeper ties with the USSR and the socialist countries.[32] Arafat turned the situation to advantage by winning full Soviet recognition of the PLO as the sole legitimate representative of the Palestinians during a meeting with Brezhnev at the end of the month.

This was as far as the PLO wished to go in relations with the USSR and its Arab allies, but the Palestinian opposition asserted firmly that 'the [Arab] confrontation states have effectively split into two camps: one is the camp of surrender represented by Egypt and one is the camp of steadfastness represented by Syria, Iraq, and the PLO.'[33] Syria and Iraq now shelved their bitter feud to declare a joint National Charter, and coordinated policy with their allies and Soviet-backed groups in the PLO, as did Libya. Having succeeded previously in confining the PNC to expression of solidarity with the socialist camp and praise for Soviet–Palestinian friendship and cooperation, the mainstream PLO leadership could no longer prevent a frank declaration of alliance with the socialist countries, led by the USSR, in January 1979.[34] On 23 March Carter made a last attempt to draw the PLO into the peace process by repeating his offer to start an official dialogue if it accepted UNSCR 242, even with reservations, but this Arafat could not do.[35] Three days later Carter presided as Sadat and Begin signed the final peace treaty between their two countries in Washington. Arafat uncharacteristically threatened to 'cut off the hands' of the US, reiterated the

[31] Quandt, *Camp David*, 265.

[32] Fateh statement in *WAFA News Agency*, 4 Oct. 1978. Joint Arab statement in *al-Ba'th* (Damascus), 24 Sept. 1978 (reproduced in *Palestinian Arab Documents 1978* (1980), 452–4).

[33] Text of interview with Hawatma held in private papers of the Institute of Palestine Studies, Beirut, and reproduced in *Palestinian Arab Documents 1977*, 311; interview with Sa'iqa leader Zuhayr Muhsin in *al-Safir*, 15 Dec. 1978.

[34] Text in *Shu'un Filastiniyya* 65 (Apr. 1977), 6; and *Journal of Palestine Studies* 8(3)(31) (spring 1979), 168.

[35] Cited in *Arab Report and Record*, 11 Apr. 1979.

importance of special relations with the USSR, and made veiled threats, as did his political adviser Hani al-Hasan, against US interests in the region, including oil supplies from the Gulf.[36] The window of opportunity had closed, but the mainstream PLO leadership continued to hope for a revival of the dialogue and indeed pursued a minor channel of contact with the Reagan administration in 1981–2.[37] As it did so, it retracted the frank alignment with the USSR, limiting the PNC in February 1981 to calls for 'friendship and cooperation' with the USSR and 'democratic and progressive forces' everywhere.[38]

The course of events up to 1982 revealed major stumbling-blocks in the way of PLO diplomatic strategy. First was that its manipulation of relations with the superpowers had to be based on a balancing act in which it kept a certain distance from each. The PLO could not play Cold War politics in the manner of Jordanian King Hussein or Egyptian President Sadat, who presented themselves as anti-communist allies of the US, nor in the manner of Syrian president Asad, who utilized relations with the USSR ultimately to win leverage with the US. Second was that although the PLO was agreed with the US and USSR on the desirability of a negotiated settlement with Israel, it could not resolve the conundrum posed by the conflicting political requirements that each party demanded. The US insisted that the PLO accept UNSCR 242 as the basis for negotiations and recognize Israel, but the Fateh-led mainstream insisted equally on retaining what it regarded as major bargaining cards until it reached the negotiating table.[39] It may have been willing to relinquish these cards in return for a firm commitment to place Palestinian statehood on the negotiating agenda, but in the absence of such a commitment the costs of 'crossing the floor' in terms of Palestinian, Arab, and Soviet reactions were too high. The window of opportunity was not to open again until the convening of the Madrid peace conference in October 1991, on the eve of the formal dissolution of the USSR.

[36] Arafat interviewed in *al-Mustaqbal*, 22 Apr. 1979, and cited in *Arab Report and Record*, 11 Apr. 1979; Hasan cited ibid. 25 Apr. 1979.

[37] On US–PLO contacts, see Gowers and Walker, *Behind the Myth*, 252–4.

[38] Text of PNC statement in *Journal of Palestine Studies* 10(4)(40) (summer 1981), 186–7. On the PLO leadership's attitude, see Khalid al-Hasan, *Qira'a Naqdiyya li-Thalath Mubadarat* [A Critical Reading of Three Initiatives] [Amman: Dar al-Karmil for Samid, Samid al-Iqtisadi series 16, Political Papers 3, 1986), 20–1. On the opposition attitude, see Bilal al-Hasan, 'Dawrat al-Tadqiq fi al-Qarar al-Siyasi' [The Session of Examination of the Political Decision], *Shu'un Filastiniyya* 115 (Apr. 1981), 9.

[39] US conditions were formalized in a secret protocol with Israel in Sept. 1975; text in *International Herald Tribune*, 11 Sept. 1975; confirmed in Quandt, *Decade of Decisions*, 275.

REGIONAL POLITICS

Much as was the case with the foreign policy orientation of the PLO, the Cold War did not have a direct impact on Palestinian regional relations until after October 1973. In the following period the state of US–Soviet relations had a considerable effect on PLO policy towards other regional actors, although the key factor determining the extent of that influence and the mechanisms through which it operated was the parallel state of inter-Arab relations. Briefly, the PLO gained the most room for diplomatic manoeuvre and maximized its strategic advantage when Arab solidarity and superpower *détente* coincided, as in 1973–4 and 1977, and suffered the most when the polarization of the Arab state system converged with the deterioration of US–Soviet ties, as in 1975–6 and in the slide to the 'second' Cold War from 1978 onwards. In the former case, the PLO was freer to conduct the regional relations it chose and to pursue its preferred diplomatic course, and in that sense was not significantly affected by Cold War politics, but in the latter case the Arab 'Cold War' subjected the PLO to severe constraints that were reinforced by the additional restraining influence of the USSR.

The dynamic of 'negative reinforcement' was clearly discernible during the Lebanese conflict in 1975–6. Both Syria and the USSR initially backed military escalation against the Lebanese Maronite militias as a means of countering the separate Egyptian–Israeli military disengagement talks brokered by Kissinger, whereas the Fateh-led PLO anxiously sought a cease-fire. The roles were reversed in spring 1976, when PLO belief that the USSR wished to see a radical nationalist government established in Lebanon encouraged it first to challenge *pax Syriana* and then to expect forceful Soviet action to reverse the Syrian military intervention of June.[40] This erroneous belief was to cost the PLO dear. The USSR did in fact exert diplomatic pressure and slowed arms deliveries to Syria, but was ultimately unwilling to threaten relations with its strategic ally, Syria, on behalf of a tactical one, the PLO.[41] Soviet caution was in sharp contrast to the behaviour of Iraq and Egypt, which eagerly extended military aid to the PLO as a means of furthering their feuds with Syria.

[40] Fateh central committee member Salah Khalaf confided to a senior PLO official that his repeated insistence that 'the road to Palestine passes through Junia', the Maronite stronghold, was intended for Soviet ears. Author's interview with Mahjub 'Umar, then Deputy Director of the PLO Planning Center.

[41] For a detailed discussion of Soviet–PLO relations in this period, see Nabil Haydari, 'al-Ittihad al-Suvyati wa Munazzamat al-Tahrir al-Filastiniyya, 1975–1976' [The USSR and the PLO, 1975–1976], *Shu'un Filastiniyya* 240–1 (Mar.–Apr. 1993), 9–40.

Indeed, the PLO's relationship with Egypt was another issue of contention with the USSR after 1974. The deterioration of Soviet–Egyptian relations and the new orientation of Egyptian foreign policy towards the US made the USSR especially suspicious of Arafat's insistence on maintaining contacts with President Sadat, and subsequently with his successor after 1981, Husni Mubarak. The USSR refrained from imposing direct sanctions, but its stance deprived the PLO of a means of countering pressure from Soviet-backed Arab states. By the same token, this episode also revealed that the USSR could only exert an effective 'spoiling' influence on PLO diplomacy when the latter was already subject to severe Arab constraints. In contrast, the USSR proved unable to influence Arab regional policies in favour of the PLO. This was starkly shown by Soviet inability to energize the anti-Sadat Steadfastness and Confrontation Front formed in December 1977 by Syria, Libya, Algeria, South Yemen, and the PLO. This front offered the PLO little succour during the protected Israeli onslaught on south Lebanon in 1978–81, and remained largely inactive during the siege of the PLO in Beirut in summer 1982. The USSR was moreover unable to persuade Syria to permit delivery to the PLO of weapons worth $20 million paid for by Algeria.[42] Similarly, it could neither dissuade Syria from backing the Fateh officers who rebelled against Arafat in 1983 nor secure Syrian support for the reunification of the PLO in 1987.[43]

Just as serious was the impact of Cold War politics on the extensive, non-bipolar network of regional and international relations that the PLO worked so hard to construct. From 1978 onwards, the PLO came under especially strong pressure to adopt Soviet causes around the world. The USSR, Palestinian opposition, and above all Syria saw this as a litmus test of its resolve to break with Egypt and the US following the start of the separate Egyptian–Israeli peace talks. In certain cases the PLO was quite willing to align itself with the USSR and oppose US policy where this served its own interest—for instance in Nicaragua—but tried to avoid a pro-Soviet stance when Arab states were directly involved. Thus the PLO offered to mediate in the border war between North and South Yemen in 1978, whereas the Palestinian left sided frankly with Marxist Aden. It had also tactfully avoided taking sides over ownership of the Western Sahara

---

[42] Mahmud 'Abbas (Abu Mazin), *Awraq Siyasiyya: Ma Ashbah al-Ams bi al-Yawm . . . Wa Lakin?* [Political Papers: How Similar Yesterday Is to Today . . . But?], pt. 2 (n.d., approx. 1985), 260; and Algerian Foreign Minister Talib Ibrahim, *Middle East Economic Digest*, 21 Jan. 1983.

[43] Tamar Weinstein (with Adam Jones), 'Soviet Union', in Rex Brynen (ed.), *Echoes of the Intifada: Regional Repercussions of the Palestinian–Israeli Conflict* (Boulder, Colo.: Westview Press, 1991), p. 252.

since 1974 and failed to develop significant ties with the Soviet-backed Polisario front, but PLO insistence on neutrality in the dispute between Algeria and Morocco became impossible in 1979–80 and damaged its relations with both. The greatest challenge was posed by the Soviet invasion of Afghanistan, which exposed the PLO to unprecedented pressure from its various constituents, allies, and partners. The USSR needed as much support as it could muster in the Middle East precisely because its action threatened the Arab and Islamic states so directly. Yet for the PLO to back it would endanger the political goodwill and financial assistance offered by Saudi Arabia and the other Gulf states—besides the support of Muslim countries such as Pakistan, which provided military and diplomatic support, and Indonesia which wielded considerable influence in NAM—and could fracture its block vote at the UN. The PLO found itself in an intolerable position, with Arafat and 'foreign minister' Qaddumi taking divergent stands at the Islamic Conference Organization and other fora.

The case of Afghanistan also revealed that it was the Syrian attitude, rather than the Soviet, that most affected PLO ties in the region. Syria, which faced insurrectionary violence at home from the Muslim Brotherhood and a hostile Iraqi–Jordanian axis abroad, signed a mutual defence treaty with the USSR in August 1980 and compelled the PLO to boycott the Arab summit conference held in Amman in November. The Syrian role again became evident in August 1981, when the then Crown Prince Fahd of Saudi Arabia published a proposal for Arab–Israeli peace. Syrian and opposition pressure compelled the PLO to distance itself, although Arafat had helped Fahd in drafting the text, causing a chill in Saudi–PLO relations. By the same token, anything that weakened or neutralized Syrian influence also tended to reduce Soviet leverage, to the extent that it existed, over the PLO. This was demonstrated when Syrian-backed Palestinian forces forced Arafat and his loyalist followers to evacuate the northern Lebanese city of Tripoli in December 1983. Yet, freed from the threat of military retaliation, the PLO chairman's first act was to visit Cairo, breaking the six-year-old boycott of Egypt. The USSR openly opposed this and the consolidation over the next year of the PLO–Jordanian partnership, which was formed in order to bridge differences between the PLO and US over the terms of Palestinian participation in the peace process, but could do little. For its part the PNC signalled PLO dissatisfaction with Soviet policy by describing China as an ally in 1984, after years of neglect, and by placing the USSR and China on equal footing in its pantheon of international friends in 1987.

However, the PLO still needed Soviet diplomatic and strategic support to mitigate the effects of its isolation among Soviet-backed Arab states. This was especially important during the difficult mid-1980s, when the PLO fell out of favour not only with Syria and Libya, which sought Arafat's downfall, but also with Algeria and South Yemen, which made normalization of ties conditional on intra-Palestinian reconciliation. The USSR adopted a similar attitude after the conclusion of the Jordanian–PLO Amman accord of February 1985, downgrading political ties, ceasing direct military aid, and refusing to invite Arafat to Moscow for the next two years.[44] For much of the 1980s other Arab allies of the PLO—Iraq and the Gulf monarchies—were heavily committed to the war with Iran, while Egypt had not regained sufficient stature in inter-Arab politics to assist it. Further afield, the Non-Aligned Movement had lost much of its unity of purpose and influence, and the European Community was evidently not ready to replace the US as the broker of Middle East peace. The absence of even a semblance of Arab solidarity deprived the PLO of its main means to build an international consensus on the Palestine issue, and so the credibility of its diplomacy depended on the restoration of Palestinian national unity. For the same reason, Arafat wished to reassert the legitimacy of his leadership by bringing the main opposition groups back into the PLO fold. It was in this context that the USSR had a special advantage, given the influence it had come to enjoy since 1973 with the Palestinian left.

'DOMESTIC' PALESTINIAN POLITICS

As a national liberation movement it was perhaps inevitable that the PLO, or at least significant elements within it, should be influenced by the US–Soviet rivalry and turn towards Marxism-Leninism for their anti-imperialist credo and official ideology. A principal contrast with other comparable movements in the Third World was that the USSR did not share the PLO's starting goals: destruction of Israel and establishment of Arab rule over the whole of mandate Palestine. Indeed, the unavoidable irony was that the Soviet leadership urged the Palestinians (and Arab states) to make a peace that would ultimately require an understanding not only with the Jewish state but also with the rival superpower, the US. Yet the USSR emerged none the less as the predominant influence on the Palestinian left in terms of ideology, organization, and, albeit to a lesser degree, practical politics. In this manner especially, the Cold War was brought to bear

---

[44] Arafat made a point of attending the funeral of Chernenko, during which he was introduced to Mikhail Gorbachev, but he was not received separately in official meetings.

on the internal politics, and through it on the foreign policy, of the PLO. This was evident in the ideological and organizational transformation of the principal guerrilla groups opposed to the mainstream nationalist Fateh, the political influence of the pro-Moscow communists, and the combined challenge posed to the Arafat leadership from within Fateh and the PLO.

Guerrillas on the left

That the USSR should exert significant influence on the internal politics of the PLO and, more specifically, on the evolution of the Palestinian left was by no means a foregone conclusion. Indeed, it had virtually no ideological support among the guerrilla groups until the early 1970s, as militant nationalism predominated as the ideological driving force. Several of the smaller guerrilla groups that joined the PLO in the late 1960s had little formal ideology to speak of, let alone one that looked for social causation or addressed economic issues, examples being the Popular Front for the Liberation of Palestine–General Command (PF–GC), led by Ahmad Jibril, and the Palestine Popular Struggle Front (PPSF). The Vanguards of Popular Liberation War (Sa'iqa) and Arab Liberation Front (ALF) adhered to pan-Arab nationalism and owed allegiance to the rival wings of the Ba'th Party that ruled Syria and Iraq. At another level, the Soviet theory of coexistence between the nuclear-armed socialist and capitalist camps and insistence on the right of Israel to exist clashed with the doctrines of guerrilla war and people's war espoused by the Palestinians. This explains in large measure the political and ideological radicalism of the left as it emerged after 1967—reflected in an eclectic cocktail that drew on the writings of Ernesto 'Che' Guevara, Leon Trotsky, and Mao Zedong—and its initial ambivalence towards the USSR, which it accused of 'bureaucratic socialism'. The Palestinian communists were the only force to diverge sharply, but their opposition to the main goals, military strategy, and ideological leanings of the guerrilla groups led to their formal exclusion from the PLO for at least the first decade of its existence.

Ideological transformations on the left were linked to two factors: major external events that affected the conduct of the overall national struggle—the June 1967 war, Jordanian conflict of 1970–1, October 1973 war, and start of the 'second' Cold War in the late 1970s—and the internal contest for advantage within the PLO.[45] The

---

[45] A useful survey of the politics and ideology of the left is 'Awad Khalil, 'Masar al-Yasar al-Filastini min al-Marksiyya ila al-Biristruyka' [The Course of the Palestinian left from Marxism to Perestroika], *Shu'un Filastiniyya* 212 (Nov. 1990), 19–61.

Cold War gained in importance as a result of the interaction of these factors, and reinforced a third, the statist evolution of PLO politics and structures. This interactive relationship was first demonstrated by the DFLP, the faction of youthful ANM members who had advocated formal adoption of socialism and opposed the alliance with Nasser Egypt and other 'petit bourgeois' Arab governments before 1967 and broke away under Nayif Hawatma in February 1969.[46] The DFLP shed its radical rhetoric after the defeat in Jordan in favour of realignment with the USSR, which it concluded was the best means for it to become a significant force in the Palestinian arena. The shift was reflected in the new emphasis on 'mass action' in the Israeli-occupied West Bank and Gaza Strip: civilian protests, agitation among students and youth, and construction of trade unions and other social associations. This was akin to Soviet-style political strategy, and followed the model offered by the pro-Moscow Palestinian communists since 1967.

The October 1973 war provided the real breakthrough. The DFLP now considered that the Arabs enjoyed 'relative parity' with Israel, and that the USSR held the key to shifting the balance of power further in favour of the Arabs. It argued that a Soviet–Arab alliance could compel Israel to relinquish the Occupied Territories, in which the PLO should establish 'an independent and sovereign national state'.[47] The DFLP played a leading role with Fateh and the Syrian-sponsored Sa'iqa in the adoption by the PNC of the new 'national authority' programme in June 1974, and its leadership was rewarded with an official invitation to Moscow in early November, the first visit by a guerrilla group separately from a wider PLO delegation. The USSR now provided considerable military and material assistance, and continued to do so for many years, while the DFLP cemented ties by liaising regularly with the KGB, coordinating policy during the Lebanese conflict in 1975–6, and later spying on foreign embassies in Beirut.[48]

[46] This was initially the *Popular* Democratic Front for the Liberation of Palestine (PDFLP), but the name was shortened in 1974.

[47] DFLP Central Committee statement in *al-Hurriyya*, 12 Nov. 1973; later reaffirmed in *al-Burnamij al-Siyasi* [The Political Program], modified and approved by the Central Committee, 1975, 27.

[48] The USSR promised in 1974 to provide infantry weapons for 2,000 DFLP guerrillas through its East European allies and military training at its own academies, as well as direct shipments of medical equipment and light industrial machinery. The DFLP was granted an annual quota of 100 places at Soviet military academies (besides 200 places annually for the PLO as a whole), as well as training for intelligence officers and 160–200 seats annually at Soviet universities for its members and supporters. On assistance, see my interviews with Mamduh Nawfal, Abu Mahmud al-Duli, and Suhayl al-Natur, then DFLP military commander, chief of staff, and head of military administration respectively. On intelligence exchange,

A special relationship had clearly developed between the DFLP and USSR by early 1975. In all, DFLP Secretary General Nayif Hawatma made four visits to Moscow in 1974–5; on one notable occasion in December 1975, the Soviets pointedly invited Hawatma after Arafat had deliberately excluded him from a PLO delegation. The DFLP also benefited from the special relationship to win greater political recognition, arms, and financial assistance from Soviet-supplied Arab states. South Yemen and Algeria had offered material aid since 1970–1, but Libya now emerged as a main supplier, offering arms and a $1 million monthly stipend from 1975 onwards.[49] Thanks to Soviet and allied Arab support, the DFLP greatly expanded its Revolutionary Armed Forces and administrative apparatus in 1978–81 and boldly challenged Fateh on a number of occasions. Its ambition to become the foremost Soviet ally within the PLO also prompted a determined drive to broaden its mass base, emulating the Soviet model with 'democratic organizations' for youth, women, workers, and so on. It was in this period, too, that the DFLP decreed the formation of a Leninist party core within its existing structures, and launched a serious effort to develop affiliated workers' unions and associations of students and women in the Occupied Territories.[50]

The DFLP was not the only guerrilla group to seek recognition from the USSR. The PFLP–GC adopted a leftist political programme at its fourth general conference in August 1973, although strenuous objections from Jibril delayed publication until May 1974.[51] The leftist faction responsible for the programme broke away in 1977 to form the Palestinian Liberation Front (PLF), and later frankly adopted Marxism-Leninism as its ideology and hailed the alliance with the socialist countries 'headed by the USSR', as did the PPSF. An added influence was Soviet-backed South Yemen, which offered material aid to both groups starting in 1979.

However, the only serious rival to the DFLP for Soviet support was the Popular Front for the Liberation of Palestine (PFLP), which

see Mamduh Nawfal, *Maghdusha: Qabl an Tafqudaha al-Zakira* [Maghdusha: Before Memory Is Lost], manuscript, written approximately 1992, 132–9.

[49] My interviews with Mamduh Nawfal, Abu Mahmud al-Duli, and Suhayl al-Natur, then DFLP military commander, chief of staff, and head of military administration respectively.

[50] The DFLP had first resolved to become a Marxist-Leninist party at its first national congress in November 1971, but little happened until autumn 1977, when its central committee renewed the impetus. *Al-Taqrir al-Nazari wa al-Siyasi wa al-Tanzimi* [The Theoretical, Political, and Organizational Report] (Beirut: Dar Ibn Khaldun, 1981), 473–83. 'Mass action' was stressed, for instance, by DFLP Deputy Secretary-General Yasi 'Abd-Rabbu in 'Issues of the National Struggle in the West Bank and Gaza Strip', seminar proceedings, *Shu'un Filastiniyya* 119 (Oct. 1981), 26–7.

[51] Programme finally published in *Ila al-Amam*, 17, 24, and 31 May and 7 June 1974.

replaced the Palestinian branch of the ANM under the leadership of George Habash in December 1967. Seeking to 'outbid' the brash young intellectuals of the DFLP who broke away in February 1969, the PFLP immediately adopted Marxism-Leninism formally and decreed its self-transformation into a proletarian party, and took to quoting Mao Zedong liberally in its literature.[52] It also vied with the DFLP in exalting doctrines of guerrilla war and people's war, and echoed its calls for the nationalization of Arab oil, abrogation of treaties with Western powers, and consolidation of friendship with the socialist countries.[53] However, the prospects were remote of establishing close ties with the USSR, which regarded the PFLP as an extremist group guilty of international terrorism.[54] The two parties were also diametrically opposed with respect to most major policy issues: the fate of Israel and the validity of UNSCR 242, resolution of the Lebanese conflict in 1976 and reconciliation with Syria, and PLO diplomacy and advocacy of a Palestinian state in the West Bank and Gaza.

A thaw only occurred after Egypt and Israel signed the Camp David Accords in September 1978. Habash was invited to Moscow in November, and the PFLP central committee called for a 'strategic alliance' between the USSR and the 'progressive' Arab states to foil the separate Egyptian–Israeli peace.[55] With the start of the second Cold War the PFLP, along with the DFLP, adopted the full range of Soviet causes around the world. Both had supported Libya in its border war with Egypt in July 1977, and the PFLP subsequently broke with its principal Arab patron, Iraq, for opposing the Soviet invasion of Afghanistan, aiding North Yemen against the Marxist South, and supporting Morocco in the conflict over the Western Sahara with the Algerian-backed Polisario front. The Palestinian left complicated the PLO's foreign relations by pressing Fateh to adopt similar stands in every instance. The PFLP now looked to Syria, which concluded a defence treaty with the USSR in 1980, as its main Arab ally. It hailed the government's battle against the Muslim Brotherhood, which had targeted Soviet advisers as well as Syrian

---

[52] The PFLP later admitted to its 'Chinese phase' in *al-Istratijiyya al-Siyasiyya wa al-Tanzimiyya* [The Political and Organizational Strategy], 4th edn. (Central Information Committee, al-Hadaf Publications (printed in Damascus), 1983), 25, 30. On the adoption of Marxism-Leninism and the construction of a proletarian party, see *al-Taqrir al-Siyasi wa al-Tanzimi wa al-'Askari li al-Jabhah al-Sha'biyyah li Tahrir Filastin* [The Political, Organizational and Military Report of the PFLP], Feb. 1969.

[53] e.g. the DFLP, *al-Muqawama al-Filastiniyya wa al-Awda' al-'Arabiyya* [The Palestinian Resistance and the Arab Situation], memorandum submitted to the 6th Palestine National Council, Cairo, 1 Sept. 1969, 11, 15, 17, 30, 33.

[54] *Komsomol'skaya Pravda*, 12 Apr. 1970, cited in *Shu'un Filastiniyya* 44.

[55] *Arab Report and Record* 22 (16–30 Nov. 1978).

officials, and castigated the PLO for undermining the much-vaunted, but hollow, strategic alliance with Syria.[56]

The PFLP underwent an ideological transformation in parallel, at least if its rhetoric was to be believed. It professed admiration for the 'persistent successes achieved by the USSR and the socialist bloc countries on the economic, social, and political levels', and expunged remaining reference in its literature to Mao Zedong and the Chinese experience.[57] The PFLP also relaunched the attempt to organize itself as a Leninist party in 1978, looking to the USSR for a model.[58] It sent many senior officials, including Politburo and central committee members, to the USSR and other socialist countries for ideological instruction, and in 1981 proudly declared itself 'as close as possible to becoming a communist party'.[59] This declaration reflected the fond hope of gaining full Soviet recognition and admission to the communist international. The PFLP advocated unification of all Palestinian 'democratic forces' in a united communist party (itself part of a wider Arab communist movement), much as Marxist groups had merged into a single party in Cuba and South Yemen.[60] The DFLP shared this hope, in fact, seeing itself as 'a focal point of the [Palestinian] revolutionary democratic alliance between all the proletarian classes and democratic strata' and expecting to lead the various guerrilla groups professing Marxism-Leninism into a 'united vanguard party'.[61]

Yet the USSR remained reluctant to extend full recognition and maintained certain limits in its support for the Palestinian left. It refused to supply heavy weapons, in keeping with its general policy not to provide the PLO as a whole with the means to destabilize the strategic equilibrium with Israel and trigger an unwanted Syrian–Israeli war. The USSR was distinctly unhappy with Libya for supplying dozens of long-range artillery weapons to the Palestinian opposition in 1979–80, and probably prevented Libyan leader Mu'ammar al-Gadhafi from delivering the long-range Frog-7 heavy

[56] On the attitude towards Iraq, see e.g. *al-Hadaf*, 10 May 1980. On support for Syria, see *al-Bayan al-Siyasi al-Sadir 'an al-Mu'tamar al-Watani al-Rabi'* [Political Report Issued by the 4th National Congress] (Beirut: PFLP, Apr. 1981), 34.

[57] Quote from *Munaqasha li-Taqrir al-Tanzim al-Shuyu'i al-Filastini fi al-Daffa al-Gharbiyya* [A Discussion of the Report by the Palestinian Communist Organization in the West Bank] (al-Hadaf Publications 11, Dar al-Hadaf, n.d. [autumn 1979], 25–6).

[58] e.g. *al-Taqrir al-Tanzimi al-'Askari al-Mali* [The Organizational, Military, and Financial Report], 4th National Congress, Apr. 1981, 76.

[59] *al-Bayan*, 506.

[60] Ibid.; *al-Taqrir al-Tanzimi*, 79; and Mustafa al-Zabri, 'Nadwa: Qadaya al-Nidal al-Watani fi al-Daffa al-Gharbiyya wa Qita' Ghazza [Panel: Issues of the National Struggle in the West Bank and Gaza Strip], *Shu'un Filastiniyya* 119 (Oct. 1981), 50.

[61] First quote from *al-Taqrir al-Tanzimi*, 474. Second quote from 'Abd-Rabbu, 'Nadwa', 49.

bombardment rockets he promised to the PLO in 1981–2.[62] As importantly, the Soviet leadership was careful not to withdraw recognition of Arafat, no matter how hostile it became to the direction of PLO diplomacy. It was willing to signal its displeasure by inviting the leaders of the main opposition groups to visit Moscow or open offices independently of the PLO, but stopped short of issuing joint statements with them or commenting directly on internal PLO affairs, even during the nadir in relations in 1985–6. Ultimately, the main disagreement with the guerrilla left was over its unwillingness to accept unequivocally Israel's right to exist and UNSCR 242 as a basis for negotiation. The contrast was expressed by successful leftist opposition to the inclusion of Palestinian communists in the PNC in March 1977, the lukewarm reception given the Brezhnev peace plan in February 1981, and continued rhetorical insistence on armed struggle.[63] For these reasons the USSR found an identity of views only with the Palestinian communists.

The Palestinian communists

The significance of Soviet support for PLO diplomatic strategy after 1973 was reflected in the growing political influence of the Palestinian communists in the West Bank, who belonged to the Jordanian Communist Party (JCP).[64] Unlike the guerrilla groups after the 1967 war, which it considered guilty of petit bourgeois adventurism typical of Maoism, the JCP opposed armed struggle and the destruction of Israel, urged acceptance of UNSCR 242, criticized 'chauvinistic' Palestinian nationalism, and advocated closer Arab relations with the USSR.[65] The JCP leadership came under pressure from some

[62] On Soviet displeasure with Libya, see my interview with DFLP Central Committee member Suhayl al-Natur. On Frog rockets, see Abu al-Tayyib, *Zilzal Bayrut: al-Qati' al-Thalith* [The Beirut Earthquake: The Third Sector] (Amman: n.p., 1984), 74; and my interview with Khalil al-Wazir.

[63] PFLP politburo member Mustafa al-Zabri in *al-Hadaf*, 18 Apr. 1981; and Habash in *al-Hadaf*, 16 May 1981. On the continued relevance of people's war, see e.g. PFLP, *al-Nizam al-Dakhili* [Internal Statutes] (Information Dept., 1981), 10–11; and PFLP, *al-Istratijiyya al-Siyasiyya wa al-Tanzimiyya* [The Political and Organizational Strategy], 4th edn. (Central Information Committee, al-Hadaf Publications (printed in Damascus), 1983), 106–12.

[64] In Gaza some 200 communists formed an autonomous organization after 1948 but were forced underground by the Egyptian military administration. Their history is related in 'Abdul-Qadir Yasin, *Hizb Shuyu'i Dahruh ila al-Ha'it: Shahada Tarikhiyya 'an al-Haraka al-Shuyu'iyya fi Qita' Ghazza, 1948–1967* [A Party with Its Back to the Wall: A Historical Testimony about the Communist Movement in the Gaza Strip, 1948–1967] (Beirut: Dar Ibn Khaldun, 1978).

[65] Text of official JCP statement issued in Aug. 1967. See also Fahmi al-Salfiti article in *Qadaya al-Silm wa al-Ishtirakiyya* 10/11 (Nov. 1968), reproduced in *Palestinian Arab Documents 1968* (1970), 821–6. On Maoist tendencies, see JCP, *al-Hizb al-Shuyu'i al-Urduni fi al-Nidal min ajl Sad al-'Udwan al-Imbiryali-al-Isra'ili wa Tasfiyatih* [The Jordanian Communist

West Bank members to play an active role in the ongoing guerrilla campaign, but only changed tack in 1969 when the USSR deemed the Palestinians to be engaged in an 'anti-imperialist national liberation struggle'.[66] In March the Soviets approved a JCP request to form a guerrilla wing, al-Ansar, which was invited to participate in some PLO bodies in 1970–1.[67]

What made the communists influential in PLO politics was not their negligible contribution to the armed struggle—Ansar was disbanded by 1972—but their focus on political proselytization and social mobilization in the West Bank. They failed to win PLO support for the Soviet-style national front formed locally under their control in mid-1973, but the main guerrilla groups could no longer ignore them after the October war and joined a revamped Palestinian National Front in 1974. A communist was also co-opted to the PLO Executive Committee in June, albeit not as a formal representative of the JCP. From this point onwards, communist influence grew in proportion to two key factors: the ability to mobilize political support for the PLO in the Occupied Territories, and PLO need for Soviet diplomatic backing. The communist role in mobilizing opposition to the Camp David Accords among West Bank unions, mayors, and other local actors was such that Fateh, the DFLP, and PFLP turned their attention seriously for the first time to the construction of affiliated unions and mass organizations of their own in order to extend their influence.

The USSR was also impressed with the performance of the West Bank communists, but cautiously turned down their requests to form an independent party in 1975 and 1977–8. Their utility was demonstrated in a working alliance with the DFLP and PFLP after 1977 to counter the political domination of Fateh and oppose the PLO's covert flirtation with Egypt and the US. Only in February 1982 did the USSR approve the establishment of the Palestinian Communist Party (PCP), in response both to the collective rise of the Palestinian left and the desire to win Third World allies in the second Cold War. The PLO had already co-opted communists to various bodies since 1974 as a gesture towards the USSR, but carefully limited their numbers and denied them formal representation in the Executive Committee until April

Party in the Struggle to Repel the Imperialist–Israeli Aggression and Liquidate It], report of the Politburo, unanimously approved by the Central Committee of the JCP in its meeting of late Aug. 1968, 19.

[66] Golan, *The Soviet Union and the Palestine Liberation Organization*, 10–11.

[67] The initial approval was supposedly offered in a meeting with Soviet ideologue Mikhail Suslov; Ahmad Sa'd and 'Abdul-Qadir Yasin, *al-Haraka al-Wataniyya al-Filastiniyya 1948–1970* [The Palestinian National Movement 1948–1970], (Jerusalem: Salah-al-Din Press, 1978), 53–4, 113.

1987, when Arafat offered the PCP a seat as part of the double recon-ciliation with the Palestinian left and the USSR.

A Trojan horse?

Although significant, the influence that the USSR exerted over the PLO through its support for the DFLP, PFLP, and Palestinian com-munists was critically dependent on three sources of reinforcement. One, mentioned earlier, was the degree of complementarity between Soviet, Arab, and Palestinian pressures on the Fateh-led mainstream. The second was the statist evolution of the PLO, measured in terms of political institutionalization, social co-optation and the employ-ment of 'rent', and the assertion of particularistic nationalism and its accompanying search for a territorial framework. The USSR could not rely too heavily on the extension of military assistance as a means to promote the political fortunes of its allies, lest it increase the risks of armed conflict with Israel and of undercutting its own hopes of partnership with the US in the peace process; but it could assist its allies to gain ground within the PLO's political, military, and admin-istrative institutions at relatively low cost to itself. This was revealed graphically by the third factor, the emergence of a sizeable leftist fac-tion within Fateh, part of which looked specifically to the USSR as a strategic ally.

As a broadly based national liberation movement, Fateh com-prised many ideological strands, and the emergence of a left wing was natural. The neo-patrimonial nature of its leadership and inter-nal relations lent themselves to organizational fragmentation, despite the formal adoption in the late 1960s of the Leninist principle of 'democratic centralism' and the pyramidal 'cell' structure of com-munist parties. For these reasons, the Fateh leftist faction was deeply fractured for many years, but most significant was the 'Soviet group' led by Majid Abu-Sharar, who doubled as secretary of Fateh's Revolutionary Council and head of the PLO Unified Information Department, and Nimr Salih, member of the Fateh Central Committee and its military General Command. The 'Soviet group' held that the alliance with the USSR would help shift the strategic balance with Israel in favour of the Arab states and PLO, and backed the adoption of a moderate diplomatic strategy by the PLO in 1974.[68] At the same time, its close identification with Soviet pol-icy in the region led it to undermine Arafat's policy, notably during the Lebanese conflict of 1975–6, when the 'Soviet group' first sabo-

[68] An example of their thinking is Nimr Salih, *Nahnu wa Amirka* [We and America] (Beirut: Dar Spartakus, 1981).

taged his attempts to negotiate with the Maronite camp and then opposed reconciliation with Syria in summer 1976.

With the deepening of US–Soviet tensions, the 'Soviet group' and other Fateh leftists moved into secret alliance with other Syrian- and Soviet-backed Palestinian groups. This encouraged PFLP Secretary General Habash, for example, to state in late 1978 that 'the time has come to conduct a serious battle with the aim of correcting conditions in the PLO . . . The battle now is against the Palestinian right wing', and DFLP Secretary General Hawatma to concur that the PLO 'line is dangerous and must be stopped immediately and without hesitation'.[69] It was against this background that the PNC declared a Palestinian alliance with the USSR in January 1979, and Arafat was pushed into adopting public hostility to the US following the signing of the Egyptian–Israeli peace treaty two months later.[70] Over the next year Abu-Sharar and Salih were outspoken in their support for Soviet policy in Afghanistan, obliging Arafat to repair the damage to PLO relations with Saudi Arabia and other Muslim states, and condemned Iraq for launching the war with Iran, violating the stance of official PLO neutrality and aligning themselves publicly with the DFLP, PFLP, and Syria. Leftist influence was strong enough to secure the election of Abu-Sharar to the Central Committee and other figures to the Revolutionary Council at the Fateh general conference in May 1980, and to ensure adoption of a militant political statement. The Marxist tone of the text was unmistakable, and it urged a stronger 'strategic alliance with the socialist states, at the forefront of which is the USSR'.[71]

The extent of Soviet covert ties with the Fateh left is unclear, although Soviet media highlighted statements by its principal figures and lavished special praise on Salih. It is plausible to presume that whatever importance it may have attached to the DFLP, PFLP, and Palestinian communists, the USSR considered that the principal means of exercising significant influence over the PLO ultimately lay in consolidating relations with the dominant Fateh, within which it also cultivated ties with the 'Soviet group'. It was careful not to question Arafat's leadership directly and continued to channel major material support to Fateh until the rupture of 1985, even then permitting Arafat's deputy, Khalil al-Wazir, to maintain close working relations with the military and security staffs of the Warsaw Pact

[69] Habash speech, repro. in *Khitabat wa Maqalat 1977–1979* [Speeches and Articles, 1977–1979], Red Papers series 36 [n.p., n.d. [1979]], 112. Hawatma interview in *al-Hurriyya*, 20 Nov. 1978.

[70] Text in *Journal of Palestine Studies* 8(3)(31) (spring 1979), 168.

[71] Quote from draft text in *Palestinian Arab Documents 1980* (1980), 183.

countries (as well as Cuba and Vietnam). At the same time, the USSR utilized the opportunity to influence the ideological and organizational formation of Fateh by offering training to thousands of members at Soviet military, party, and union academies. Yet Fateh owed far more to neo-patrimonial statist models common in the Third World than to the USSR, and Soviet training proved to have little lasting impact. The 'Soviet group' was dealt a severe blow with the assassination of Abu-Sharar in October 1981, and collapsed following the decision of the ambitious Salih to assume nominal leadership of the military mutiny in May 1983. The USSR encouraged its Palestinian allies not to split from the PLO, and instead encouraged the DFLP, PFLP, PLF, and PCP to form a Democratic Alliance in 1984 as a means of exercising greater influence within it. However, the imminent change of Soviet leadership was to alter the working assumptions of both sides of the PLO divide, and to undermine the residual impact of the Cold War on Palestinian affairs.

THE END OF ILLUSION

The assumption by Mikhail Gorbachev of the Soviet presidency in 1985 and the launch of his 'new thinking' fundamentally altered the strategic environment in which the PLO operated. Early indications were Soviet support for the reunification of the PLO in April 1987 and the gradual thaw in Soviet–Israeli relations in the next two years. The USSR welcomed the start of an official US–PLO dialogue in December 1988, and urged the PLO to respond positively to US proposals in 1989–90, even when it shared Palestinian scepticism about the intentions of the government of Yitzhak Shamir in Israel. Changes in the Soviet attitude were not all welcome, especially the reversal of policy to allow free Jewish emigration to Israel. Most dramatic, however, was the alignment of the USSR with the US-led coalition against Iraq during the Gulf crisis in 1990–1. In the following months the USSR went further, taking it upon itself to persuade the PLO to permit Palestinian participation at the Madrid peace conference on terms dictated by the US and Israel, foremost of which was the exclusion of the PLO. Israel was to recognize the PLO two years later, but by then the USSR had ceased to exist and its main successor state, Russia, had no more than a cosmetic role to play in the peace process.

Despite all evidence to the contrary, the PLO mainstream and the Palestinian left shared the wistful hope until the last moment that the USSR would regain its Cold War stature. Their momentary relief, whether in public or private, at the abortive *coup d'etat* against Gorbachev in August 1991 revealed the extent to which the entire Palestinian political spectrum had come to take the USSR and super-power rivalry for granted. Even Arafat, for whom the USSR was never more than a partner of convenience, shared the universal dis-like of Gorbachev, who was regarded as having single-handedly dis-mantled the USSR. The PLO chairman, as much as anyone else in the PLO, still hoped to utilize Soviet influence in order to obtain acceptable terms for peace from the US, and through it from Israel. He demonstrated the power of this assumption by rapidly establish-ing formal ties with the former Soviet republics of Central Asia and visiting nuclear-armed Kazakhstan, while his colleague Mahmud 'Abbas regularly consulted the Russian leadership about the ongoing peace process. The PLO did not simply abandon its old friends, PLO 'foreign minister' Qaddumi added.

The closing chapter of the Cold War contained several ironies. First and foremost was that by the time the USSR was willing to endorse US-PLO *rapprochement* wholeheartedly, it had lost its abil-ity to offer the PLO more than moral support. As in previous stages of the Cold War, secondly, the degree of freedom that PLO diplo-macy enjoyed was primarily a function of changing priorities in the Soviet global outlook rather than the result of Palestinian initiatives, whether political or military. For decades, thirdly, superpower rivalry had made the Palestinian ambition of destroying Israel unat-tainable, but had also prevented the PLO from gaining a seat at the peace talks. The problem for the PLO was that it needed to assemble a broad coalition in support of its policy objectives, but it was the coalition that also held it back. Only with the demise of the Cold War was the PLO finally able to escape its external and internal con-straints and join the peace process, but then it had to do so on dis-tinctly unfavourable terms.

The end of the Cold War demonstrated vividly the extent to which Palestinian strategic options and politics had been constrained by superpower rivalry. The PLO was particularly vulnerable to external constraints because it was a non-state actor and could not call on truly autonomous sources of power and influence. For the same reason it was more vulnerable than it might otherwise have been to internal opponents. These constraints were especially problematic because the PLO was compelled to operate within a complex Arab state system characterized by patterns of 'balance-of-power politics' and coalition-building, that coincided to damaging effect with the polarization of the wider international system. By the same token, it was perhaps inevitable for the PLO to seek to manipulate superpower rivalry to its own advantage. This came naturally to Arafat and his colleagues in Fateh, who viewed international politics as a 'game of nations' and regarded Palestinian military and political initiatives as means of delivering messages, purchasing influence, or acquiring bargaining cards. The Palestinian left held a normative, ideologically grounded view of politics and alliances in contrast, but it too relied heavily on Soviet support as a means of shifting the strategic balance with Israel. The end of the Cold War and the decline of the USSR therefore dealt both currents of PLO thinking a massive blow.

The disarray of the PLO's diplomatic strategy after the fall of the Berlin Wall revealed the crucial errors of judgement it had made during the Cold War. First and foremost was the belief, held by Arafat and his Fateh colleagues in particular, that the US could impose policy on Israel. This prompted the PLO to direct much of its political effort and diplomatic strategy in the 1970s and 1980s to bring Soviet, European, Third World, and Arab pressure to bear on the US, rather than develop a direct approach towards Israel. A second error was the belief that the PLO, backed by a sufficient international coalition, could compel the US to place Palestinian statehood on the negotiating agenda. The Israeli government would probably have withdrawn from the peace talks even if the PLO had met the prerequisite US conditions for participation in 1977–9, but was not put to that test. Unable to secure rewards sufficient to offset the inevitable costs that the USSR, allied Arab states, and Palestinian opposition would impose, the PLO rejected the option of transitional autonomy and in so doing lost what was probably the only real opportunity of the entire Cold War for Palestinian participation in the peace process.

There were powerful reasons working against PLO flexibility, not least the opposition offered by Palestinian groups and Arab states. Yet the PLO contributed to its dilemma by overestimating three crucial factors: Soviet influence with the US, even during the era of *détente*; Soviet commitment to the PLO, even at the height of the Cold War; and the importance of the PLO itself, whether to the superpowers, to the Arab states, or to peace and stability at the regional and international levels. This explains the attempt to attain a national objective—statehood—within a context—the Cold War—that severely constrained any option more ambitious than autonomy. It also explains the ever-contentious attempt to develop relations with the USSR in order to strike a deal with the US. These implicit tensions in PLO diplomatic strategy dominated its politics, both internal and external, until the end of the Cold War.

That said, it was not errors of judgement but objective realities that constrained Palestinian ability to manipulate Cold War politics.

Above all, the fact that the PLO was a non-state actor limited its ability to maintain a margin for autonomous manouevre within an international system dominated by superpower rivalry. It lacked the material resources and independent capabilities that might have permitted it to switch superpower 'horses' or play one off against the other, and was compelled to play a problematic double-game instead. In retrospect, the most favourable opportunities for the Palestinians occurred during periods of superpower *détente*, but it was then, too, that the PLO most feared US–Soviet agreement at Palestinian expense. Arafat expressed this fear as late as November 1987, when his reaction to the Gorbachev–Reagan summit in the Mediterranean was that 'Malta will not be Yalta'. Yet the growing asymmetry of the Cold War as US power eclipsed that of the USSR meant that when the PLO–Israel peace accord finally came in September 1993, the analogy had lost all meaning. Instead, it offered testimony to the fact that the PLO, despite achieving remarkable diplomatic stature and surviving the vicissitudes of Arab and international politics, had ultimately remained a prisoner of the Cold War so long as it lasted.

7

Israel

EFRAIM KARSH

The Cold War played a secondary, if significant, role in the making of Israel's foreign and defence policies, and virtually no role at all in her domestic politics. Subjected to a concerted Arab attempt to destroy her at birth in 1948, and to a subsequent political, military, and economic siege which began easing only with the conclusion of the peace treaty with Egypt in 1979, Israel's national interests have been predominantly focused on her immediate environment, namely, consolidation of her statehood and security, and the attainment of regional acceptance of her existence, expressed, if possible, in official peace treaties. From the Israeli standpoint, the Cold War was relevant only to the extent that it affected the pursuit of these goals.

This, to be sure, was no small matter. Superpower scramble for allies and assets in the Middle East heavily affected regional dynamics and confronted Israel (as well as her Arab foes) with a multitude of challenges and opportunities. Yet for all their exertions, neither of the two superpowers, let alone the declining imperial powers, Britain and France, gained a decisive say in their smaller allies' grand strategies. They occasionally managed to reinforce existing regional trends and even to bring some of them to fruition; yet they neither charted the general course of the Arab–Israeli conflict, which predated the advent of the Cold War and has outlived its demise, swayed it in new directions, nor even changed its existing currents of flow.

By way of exploring the impact of the Cold War on Israeli policies, this chapter adopts a two-pronged approach. The first part examines the nature and characteristics of the main three phases in Israel's interaction with the Great Powers: association by default with the Soviet Union (the late 1940s); enforced aloofness due to Western lukewarmth (the 1950s to the late 1960s); and the crystallization of the 'special relationship' with the US (the late 1960s to date). The second part discusses some key episodes in this 'special relationship', the only lasting Great Power association Israel has had during her near-five decades of existence, and the delicate bargaining game they involved: the Israeli–Egyptian War of Attrition (1968–70);

the October 1973 war and the ensuing disengagement agreements; and the Israeli–Egyptian peace process of the late 1970s. It does so on the assumption that it is the cardinal questions of war and peace, which stand at the core of the national interest (and, in consequence, generate the sharpest disagreements between allies), that can best delineate the scope of a political relationship. For, 'like breathing, influence becomes especially noticeable when pressure is applied or concern heightens'.[1]

THE HISTORICAL RECORD

Into the bear's embrace

From her earliest days of statehood, indeed from her pre-state existence, Israel strove to escape the unfolding Cold War between the two superpower blocs. Apart from the reluctance to lose potential political, military, and economic gains by being drawn into a struggle which was not hers, and apart from recognizing her limited value for either superpower bloc by comparison with the larger, wealthier, and more populous Arab world, Israel as a Jewish state was anxious not to jeopardize the security and well-being of Jewish communities on both sides of the Iron Curtain; and while the US had come to host the largest Jewish community on earth following the destruction of East European Jewry during the Second World War, there were still some two million Jews in the Soviet Union and approximately 900,000 in Eastern Europe—a third of whom (mainly Polish Jews) lived in the Soviet Union itself.[2]

This is not to say that the Zionist movement, and latterly the State of Israel, were emotionally and ideologically torn between East and West, as is wrongly believed by some Israeli historians.[3] On the contrary, their hearts were with the Western democracies from the outset. Even though the Zionist leaders from the First World War onwards were all Eastern Europeans, or the sons and daughters of Eastern Europeans, and although none of the many national movements in Eastern Europe—Russians, Balts, Poles, Romanians to mention just a few—clung to liberal democracy,[4]

[1] Alvin Z. Rubinstein (ed.), *Soviet and Chinese Influence in the Third World* (New York: Praeger, 1975), 10.

[2] See Yaacov Ro'i, *Soviet Decision-Making in Practice* (New Brunswick, NJ: Transaction Books, 1980).

[3] The foremost exposition of this misconception is Uri Bialer's *Between East and West: Israel's Foreign Policy Orientation 1948–1956* (Cambridge: Cambridge University Press, 1990).

[4] The only notable exception that springs to mind is Finland, which emerged into statehood in 1917, after more than a century of Russian imperial occupation, as a fully-fledged liberal democracy.

the institutions of the Zionist movement—whence the institutions of modern Israel were, for the most part derived—were founded and made to operate on parliamentary-democratic principles from the first. It was all there, set up and running, within a year or two of the calling of the first Congress of Zionists in 1897: free elections on a constituency basis; universal suffrage (i.e., men and women voting and members of the Congress themselves); a fully representative assembly; a political leadership responsible to that assembly; open debate on all major issues; and, before long, what might usefully be called a loyal opposition too.[5]

To their dismay, however, the Zionists found themselves driven into the arms of the Soviet Union, as the British and the American foreign and defence establishments were hostile to their cause and to the creation of a Jewish state. There were many reasons which made Britain better disposed to the Arabs than to the Jews in the wake of the Second World War. For one thing, no imperial power enjoys being ejected from its colonies by a national liberation movement, and in the late 1940s it was the Zionists who were steadily pushing Britain out of Palestine through a combined political and armed struggle. For another thing, there were strong anti-Semitic undercurrents within both the British government and the Palestine administration, coupled with strong patronizing affinity towards the Arabs.[6] Above all, there was the strong conviction that British strategic and economic interests in the Middle East, first and foremost oil, lay with the Arabs, and that 'no solution of the Palestine problem should be proposed which would alienate the Arab states'.[7] These latter considerations were fully shared by the American administration:

The State Department, in general, stressed the importance of continuing good relations with the Arab world and cooperation with the British. The Defense Department, especially Secretary Forrestal, was concerned about

[5] David Vital, 'Some of the Forks in the Road', in Efraim Karsh and Gregory Mahler (eds.), *Israel at the Crossroads: The Challenge of Peace* (London: British Academic Press, 1994), 9–10.
[6] In a note presented to a British Cabinet meeting in Jan. 1947, for example, Sir Alan Cuningham, the High Commissioner for Palestine, described Zionism as a movement where 'the forces of nationalism are accompanied by the psychology of the Jew, which it is important to recognise as something quite abnormal and unresponsive to rational treatment'; 'Palestine: Future Policy', Secret Memorandum by the Secretary of State for the Colonies, 16 Jan. 1947, Annex I, CAB 129/16, C.P. (47)31. See also Richard Crossman, *Palestine Mission: A Personal Record* (New York: Harper, 1947), 130–3.
[7] CAB 128/6, C.M. (46), 71st Conclusions, 22 July 1946. In Jan. 1947 the Chief of the Air Staff told the British Cabinet that if 'one of the two communities had to be antagonized, it was preferable, from the purely military angle, that a solution should be found which did not involve the continuing hostility of the Arabs; for in that event our difficulties would not be confined to Palestine but would extend throughout the whole of the Middle East'; CAB 128/11 C.M. (47), 6th Conclusions, Minute 3, 15 Jan. 1947.

the future availability of Middle Eastern oil. Both were worried about how the Soviet leadership might profit from what was going on.[8]

Indeed, the belief that the Zionist movement was a 'communist stooge' and that, if established, a Jewish state would become a Soviet forward detachment in the Middle East was one of the strongest axioms uniting the British and American foreign and defence establishments. Even President Harry Truman, who overruled the view of his bureaucrats to support the establishment of a Jewish state, and then to render her an immediate *de facto* recognition, was sufficiently alarmed by this misconception to dispatch a special envoy to the Israeli prime minister, David Ben-Gurion, to enquire whether Israel was going to become a 'red state'.[9] That such fears reflected gross ignorance of the essence of Zionism mattered little: it was translated into anti-Zionist and anti-Israeli policy, particularly on the part of Britain.[10]

In these circumstances the Soviet Union became the staunchest champion of the Zionist cause: she endorsed the UN resolution on the partition of Palestine, actively lobbied in support of it, and was the first to extend *de jure* recognition to the newly established state of Israel in May 1948; the Soviets also opposed the attempts to dislodge Israel from her territorial gains in the 1947–9 War (subsequently recognized by the 1949 armistice agreements between Israel and her Arab neighbours), let alone to reduce Israel's territory well beyond that assigned to her by the 1947 Partition Resolution,[11] and supported Israel's admission as a full member of the UN. In the military sphere the Soviets provided vital support in the form of arms supplies and military training, though this was done through a third party, Czechoslovakia. There is little doubt that this support played a key role in saving Israel from a military defeat in the initial

[8] John C. Campbell, *Defense of the Middle East: Problems of American Policy* (New York: Harper, 1958), 37.

[9] David Ben-Gurion, *Yoman Ha-milchama* [War Diary] (Tel Aviv: Ma'arachot, 1982), iii. 846–7. The envoy, Samuel Klaus, reported back that all fears in this respect were groundless and that there was no 'immediate Soviet danger'.

[10] Within this framework the British government was vehemently opposed to the idea of partition; it failed to facilitate the implementation of the UN Partition Resolution of Nov. 1947 and withheld a de facto recognition of the State of Israel for some 8 months. Having realized its inability to prevent partition, the Foreign Office favoured a far smaller and weaker Jewish state than that envisaged by the UN Partition Resolution and did its utmost to bring about such an eventuality, despite its keen awareness that such a minuscule state would scarcely be viable. In fact they went so far as to try to forestall a separate Israeli–Transjordanian peace agreement which did not include the detachment of the Negev from the Israeli state.

[11] Thus e.g. the Soviets were opposed to Count Bernadotte's mission and to his British-inspired suggestion that the Negev, allotted to Israel by the 1947 Partition Resolution, be severed from the Jewish state; they even passed to Israel intelligence information on Egyptian military operations in the Negev to help her retain this area.

stages of the war, and helped her turn the tables on her Arab attack-ers.[12]

Neither East nor West

The Soviet–Israeli honeymoon proved very short-lived. As the 1940s drew to a close, the Soviets were already setting their sights else-where. Having expelled British imperialism from Palestine and dealt Britain's Arab allies a painful blow, Israel no longer served an 'anti-imperialist' role as far as the Soviet Union was concerned; the fur-ther expulsion of Britain from her remaining imperial possessions in the Middle East (e.g. the Suez Canal) could be better achieved by the Arab states, rather than Israel. This trend was reinforced by Stalin's growing realization, particularly after the 1949 parliamentary elec-tions in Israel, that the newly established Jewish state was not going to become a 'popular democracy' after all;[13] hence, from 1949 to Stalin's death in 1953, the Soviets indulged in a ferocious anti-Zionist spree which culminated in the 'Doctors Plot' of January 1953. For her part, Israel facilitated the Soviet decision to disentangle by sup-porting the UN intervention in the Korean War and identifying with the Western powers, to the extent of entertaining the dispatch of Israeli troops to help the UN forces in Korea.[14]

The growing Soviet–Israeli dissociation was brought to a head in 1955, following the establishment of the Western-initiated Baghdad Pact, which not only transformed what had been an effective buffer zone in the prewar period into an important link in the worldwide chain of Western containment strategy but also extended NATO's military power to the USSR's backyard, thus turning it into a poten-tial theatre of war. To stem the West's mounting military power in the Middle East, the Soviets adopted the indirect approach, trying to keep Afghanistan out of the Baghdad Pact and to pool together those Arab countries opposed to the alliance. These attempts struck a responsive chord in Cairo and Damascus: in 1955 the two coun-tries concluded large arms deals with the USSR, thereby giving Moscow her first foothold in the Arab world.

While this Soviet policy was initially motivated by Cold War con-

---

[12] David Ben-Gurion, *Medinat Israel ha-Mehudeshet* [The Restored State of Israel] (Tel Aviv: Am Oved, 1969), i. 103, 109, 128–9, 132, 139; Meir Mardor, *Shlihut Aluma* [Clandestine Mission] (Tel Aviv: Ma'arachot, 1979), 287; Bialer, *Between East and West*, 177–9.

[13] For Stalin's hopes in this respect, see e.g. David Vital, *The Survival of Small States* (Oxford: Oxford University Press, 1971), 74. See also *Pravda*, 21 Sept. 1948; 'Palestine and the United Nations', *New Times* 24 (June 1948), 1–2.

[14] See e.g. Michael Brecher, *Israel, the Korean War and China: Images, Decisions, and Consequences* (Jerusalem: Academic Press, 1974).

siderations, Soviet–Arab relations quickly developed their own distinct momentum. During the Suez War of 1956 the Soviet Union hurried to Egypt's support, going so far as to threaten the invading forces (Britain, France, and Israel) with nuclear retaliation. A year later the Soviet Union shielded Damascus from Turkish military pressures both by threatening that any aggression against Syria 'would not remain limited to this area alone', and by dispatching a small naval unit on an official visit to Syria—a show of force hitherto unprecedented in a Middle Eastern, indeed in a Third World, crisis. Soviet–Iraqi relations, for their part, were dramatically improved in the summer of 1958 following the overthrow of the Hashemite dynasty by a radical *coup d'état*, and soon afterwards the USSR began shipping arms to Morocco, Algeria, and the Sudan.

With her alliance with the Soviet Union a fading memory, Israel intensified her efforts to align herself with the Western powers—to no avail. With the Cold War at its height following the Korean War, and the importance of Persian Gulf oil on a rising curve, the Western powers were anxious not to alienate the Arab states by initiating any move that smelled of support to Israel. Hence they excluded Israel from the Middle Eastern security frameworks they sought to establish in the early 1950s, such as the Middle East Supreme Allied Command (SACME) and the Baghdad Pact.

To Britain, Israel remained a disturbing nuisance that endangered some of her Arab allies, particularly Jordan, which was embroiled in an escalating confrontation with Israel due to sustained terrorist attacks from her territory against Israeli civilian targets and Israel's harsh retaliation. There were some inconclusive explorations in 1951 of the possibility of Anglo-Israeli security cooperation, and there was of course the brief convergence of interests which led to the ad hoc Anglo-Israeli (and French) collaboration in the 1956 Suez War; yet even then Britain was poised to strike at Israel if the latter launched an attack against Jordan, with which London had had a defence pact since 1948.[15]

Similarly, the US administration, since 1952 under the Republican president Dwight Eisenhower, considered Israel an impediment to America's foremost Middle Eastern interests: containing the Soviet Union and ensuring the uninterrupted flow of cheap oil. It gave Israel no American weapons; excluded her from the Western-led regional defence alignments; repeatedly rebuffed her pleas for security guarantees; pressured her to reach an accommodation with Egypt

---

[15] For a succinct discussion of the British plans to attack Israel in the event of an Israeli–Jordanian war, see Zeid Raad, 'A Nightmare Avoided: Jordan and Suez 1956', *Israel Affairs* 1(2) (winter 1994/5), 288–309.

at the price of surrendering her southern part, the Negev, or parts of it; and played the key role in forcing Israel to withdraw from Sinai following the 1956 Suez War. It was only in 1962, during the Kennedy administration, when Israel seemed to be falling behind in the arms race due to a massive influx of Soviet weaponry to the Arab states, that the reluctant president approved an Israeli request for HAWK surface-to-air missiles, pending since the late Eisenhower era. Three years later, overruling the customary opposition of the State Department and the Pentagon, President Lyndon Johnson decided to sell Israel 210 M-48 Patton tanks, and then 48 Skyhawk bombers.[16]

The only Western power willing to give Israel's overtures a receptive ear was France, which since the mid-1950s was increasingly beset by a tidal wave of militant nationalism in Algeria and hoped that the strengthening of Israel would help curb the revolutionary zeal of the Egyptian president, Gamal Abdel Nasser, the staunchest Arab backer of the Algerian insurgents. To Israel this was manna from heaven. Deeply disturbed by the possibility of a second round of hostilities with the Arabs, she had been desperately (and unsuccessfully) searching for sources of weapons while censuring Britain and the US for selling arms to the Arab states while denying them to Israel. Now that France was willing to break ranks with the Western powers' supply policy, Israel did not fail to seize the moment. This resulted in the joint attack on Egypt in 1956 and, more importantly, in the establishment of a multi-faceted procurement relationship, including French support for Israel's nascent nuclear project.

Yet this convergence of interests proved short-lived. With the completion of France's extrication from her Algerian colony in 1962, Israel had outlived her usefulness as far as Charles de Gaulle was concerned. In a slower replay of the Soviet disentanglement from Israel in the late 1940s, the French president began reorienting his country towards the Arab world, while spreading false reassurances of France's unwavering fidelity to Israel, 'her friend and ally'.

Some Israelis were keenly aware of the self-serving nature of French policy. Time and again they pointed to the disquieting symptoms of deterioration in the bilateral relationship: France's growing honeymoon with the Arab states; her dwindling support for Israel in UN debates; her *rapprochement* with the Soviet Union and growing estrangement from her Anglo-Saxon, allies etc. Yet their warnings

---

[16] Contrary to her meagre political and virtually non-existent military support to Israel, the US proved more forthcoming in the economic field. American transfers to Israel between 1950 and 1955 (both public and private) amounted to some $337 million, or 19.4% of Israel's net import of capital.

fell on deaf ears. Eager to cling to this precarious alliance, most Israeli policy-makers saw the 'French connection' as reflecting a deeply rooted amity towards Israel, if not the culmination of a long-standing 'understanding of the Jewish people's needs'; to them France was a friend and an ally, the only Great Power which was not willing to sacrifice Israel's security needs on the altar of the Cold War and its corollary of ensuring Arab loyalties. As long as the tacit Franco-Israeli defence collaboration remained essentially intact, Israeli leaders would not read the increasingly clear writing on the wall.[17]

They were to be brutally disillusioned in June 1967, when de Gaulle used the outbreak of war as a pretext to complete his long-sought policy reversal by imposing an arms embargo on Israel, including on weapons systems that had been already paid for. In the following decades Israel's military relations with France would be completely severed as the latter would become the largest arms supplier of the Arab world after the US and the Soviet Union.

1967 and after

The 1967 Six-Day War was a watershed in Middle Eastern history. It drew the Great Powers deeper into regional affairs, intensified their competition, and transformed their relations with local allies; and it set in train a process of regional disillusionment with the utility of armed force which, decades later, would culminate in peace agreements between Israel and most of her Arab neighbours.[18] As far as Israel's relations with the Great Powers were concerned the war produced a profound change: the substitution of the US for France as Israel's strategic ally and the severance of official relations with the Soviet Union and her East European satellites (with the exception of Romania).

As the only Western-type democracy in the Middle East, Israel had always found more favour with the American public than her Arab neighbours. The immigrant nature of Israeli society, her pioneering spirit, and her commitment to the ideals of individualism and freedom were widely viewed by Americans as a mirror image of their own ethos. To Americans, Israel was a young idealistic nation, fighting with great tenacity against improbable odds, a 'Western' island

---

[17] Walter Eytan, *The First Ten Years: A Diplomatic History of Israel* (New York: Simon & Schuster, 1956), 156–7; Gideon Rafael, *Destination Peace: Three Decades of Israeli Foreign Policy* (New York: Stein & Day, 1981), 79–80; Sylvia K. Crosbie, *A Tacit Alliance: France and Israel From Suez to the Six Day War* (Princeton, NJ: Princeton University Press, 1974).

[18] For discussion of this issue, see my 'Peace Not Love: Towards a Comprehensive Arab–Israeli Settlement', *Washington Quarterly* 17(2) (spring 1994), 143–57.

in a hostile, authoritarian, 'oriental' ocean. This positive image was further fostered by the religious conviction, widespread in particular among Christian fundamentalists in America's Bible Belt areas, that by virtue of her very existence Israel was fulfilling the biblical prophecy of Jewish return to the promised land.[19]

This grass-roots sympathy, as noted earlier, was not matched by political or military support, as the executive branch had always viewed Israel as a political and strategic liability. While the bureaucracy's recommendations were occasionally unheeded by the president—as illustrated by Truman's support for the establishment of Israel against the wishes of the State Department and the Pentagon—Israel was cut out of US Middle East policy throughout the 1950s and the early 1960s.

The 1967 War allowed Israel to dilute these contradictions in the American attitude. By thoroughly defeating Moscow's most prominent regional allies, Egypt, Syria, and Iraq, Israel publicly shamed the Soviets and diminished the pressure of Arab radicalism on the pro-western conservative regimes (the Egyptian withdrawal from Yemen following the war, for example, was received with a sigh of relief by Saudi Arabia). By allowing the US to examine captured Soviet weaponry and sharing operational lessons learnt by the war, Israel contributed to the American military effort in Vietnam. The closure of the Suez Canal was also viewed favourably by the Americans, since it impeded the transfer of Soviet arms to the Indian Ocean and Indochina. In one bold stroke Israel was transformed from an embarrassing strategic liability into a valuable asset.[20] The fear that American troops would have to rush to the rescue of the Jewish state at the expense of wider American interests in the region, a primary argument among opponents of US recognition of Israel in 1948, had been clearly overtaken by events.[21] Even sceptics now grudgingly conceded that Israel no longer hindered the containment of Soviet 'expansionism' but had instead become a formidable barrier to the spread of Soviet influence in the Middle East. Only the 'Arabists' of the State Department and the Pentagon still subscribed to the perception of Israel as a liability to America's relations with

[19] Bernard Reich, *The United States and Israel: Influence in the Special Relationship* (New York: Praeger, 1984), 185–6; William Quandt, *Decade of Decisions* (Berkeley: University of California Press, 1977), 16.

[20] Ibid. 9; Steven Spiegel, *The Other Arab–Israeli Conflict: Making America's Middle East Policy From Truman to Reagan* (Chicago: University of Chicago Press, 1985), 159–60; A. F. K. Organski, *The $36 Billion Bargain: Strategy and Politics in US Assistance to Israel* (New York: Columbia University Press, 1990), 33.

[21] Walter Isaacson and Evan Thomas, *The Wise Men: Six Friends and the World They Made: Acheson, Bohlen, Harriman, Kennan, Lovett, McCloy* (New York: Simon & Schuster, 1986), 452.

the Arab world—though their position was rooted in regional rather than Cold War considerations.

Moreover, the intensification of US–Israeli relations paradoxically strengthened America's hand in the Middle East over the long run and sowed the seeds of discord between the Arabs and their Soviet allies. With pan-Arabism in its death throes and new Arab territories coming under Israeli occupation, it gradually dawned on the Arabs that the US was the only power that could conceivably reverse this disturbing state of affairs: the Soviets had absolutely no political leverage over Israel on account of the severance of bilateral relations following the 1967 War; all Moscow could do was to enhance the Arab war potential and to prepare them for war, something she had always felt half-hearted about. Yet even in this field the Soviets were increasingly outshone, as Israel's military successes were seen as confirmation of the superiority of American (and, by extension, Western) weaponry. Last but not least, the modifications introduced by Israel in American weapons systems, such as the F-4 Phantom, proved immensely beneficial to the American armed forces and military industries; and Israel also offered the Americans valuable intelligence that helped fill vital gaps in their intelligence-gathering capabilities in the Middle East.

These strategic imperatives were highly appreciated by most American presidents from 1967 onwards, most notably Richard Nixon and Ronald Reagan. With Henry Kissinger, who shared his belief in the centrality of the Soviet Union to American global interests, Nixon contrived what came to be known as the linkage policy by which progress in areas of Soviet concern such as strategic arms limitation and increased trade was linked with progress in critical areas for the US such as Vietnam, the Middle East, and Berlin.[22]

Like Iran, and to a lesser extent Saudi Arabia, Israel fitted this strategic concept like a glove. She was not only a formidable military power perfectly capable of defending herself: she was well placed to resist Soviet penetration into the Middle East, either directly or by defeating Arab radicalism and thus underscoring the futility of association with the Soviet Union, or by enhancing American prestige by presenting her as the only superpower capable of 'delivering' Israeli concessions. This newly gained prowess was vividly demonstrated during the Jordanian civil war of September 1970 dubbed the Black September, in which Israel played the key role in warding off an invasion of Jordan by Syria, in support of the Palestinian struggle against King Hussein.

---

[22] Richard Nixon, *RN: The Memoirs of Richard Nixon* (London: Arrow Books, 1978), 346.

To the Nixon administration, the imminent downfall of the king represented not only the loss of one of the West's most reliable Middle Eastern allies but also a major setback in the Cold War context. To Israel, by contrast, the Jordanian conflict had nothing to do with the Cold War but was rather a grave security concern: the Hashemite Kingdom, which had always been more amenable to the Jewish state than the rest of the Arab world, seemed to be on the verge of being overtaken by the Palestinian guerrilla organizations which were overtly committed to the destruction of Israel. Hence, even before the Syrian invasion Israel was prepared to take military action to shore up King Hussein against the possible military intervention by Iraqi forces, deployed in Jordan since the 1967 War. When Iraq failed to move against the king, despite her virulent propaganda attacks on his regime, and Syrian forces entered Jordan, the Israelis moved two armoured brigades to their joint border with Jordan and made preparations for air strikes against the invading Syrian forces. This show of force toughened the Jordanian resistance and allowed those sceptical voices within the Syrian leadership, who had questioned the invasion's wisdom in the first place, to prevail and effect a quick withdrawal from Jordan.

Nixon was elated. Without firing a shot the US had helped defeat two Soviet allies—Syria and the PLO—and underscored the merits of association with the West: 'The Soviets had backed off, raising by another notch the growing Arab disenchantment with Moscow.'[23] Israel had proven her strategic reliability at a critical juncture in Middle Eastern history, and must be strengthened so as to ensure her capability to handle similar future contingencies. American military support to Israel gained considerable momentum, growing from a modest $62 million loan in 1968 to $602 million in 1973. A year later Nixon ordered a $4.4 billion worth of military support, the largest package of its kind until then, as a means to help Israel recuperate from the October 1973 war.[24] In following decades American support for Israel (both in loans and in grants) would stabilize at around $3 billion per annum, approximately two thirds of which was in military aid to be mostly spent in the US.

[23] Henry Kissinger, *White House Years* (Boston: Little, Brown, 1979), 631. See also Rafael, *Destination Peace*, ch. 27.

[24] Agency for International Development, *United States Foreign Assistance and Assistance from International Organizations* (Washington, DC, 1975). The 1974 package was unprecedented in another important respect: it was the first time that part of the military support was given, not in loan form, but as a grant.

Institutionalizing the relationship

An even more Soviet–centric approach was brought to the White House by Ronald Reagan. He viewed international politics as a Manichaean struggle between the forces of light and those of darkness—the Soviet Union and her proxies. This moral crusade was not only about the containment of the 'evil empire', as the Soviet Union was conveniently labelled, but about creating a better and freer world. 'If the democracies maintained their resolve against Communism and encouraged the expansion of democratic rule', Reagan reasoned, 'the rest was inevitable: Marxism-Leninism would be tossed on the ash heap of history, like all other forms of tyranny that preceded it'.[25]

As in the 1950s, the Middle East was seen as a vital link in the worldwide struggle against communism; and as in the 1950s, there were quarters within the executive branch (represented this time by Defence Secretary Caspar Weinberger) who believed that the 'containment' of the Soviet Union should be exclusively predicated on the conservative Arab states. Yet, unlike his 1950s predecessors, President Reagan and his secretary of state, Alexander Haig, viewed Israel as an integral part of the 'strategic consensus' the administration was seeking to forge in the Middle East.

To Israel, this heightened Cold War perspective was a mixed blessing. The perception of Israel as a strategic asset was warmly welcomed by the right-wing Likud government, as was the administration's policy of benign neglect towards the Arab–Israeli conflict due to its overwhelming preoccupation with the 'Second Cold War', as this period of increased East–West tensions is often called. At the same time, Israeli policy-makers were opposed to certain aspects of the American neo-containment policy, primarily the supply of sophisticated weapons systems to the conservative Arab states, Saudi Arabia in particular.

With the appointment of Ariel Sharon as minister of defence in the second Begin government in the summer of 1981, the scales were tilted in favour of the instrumental perception of the American position. Eager to secure America's acquiescence to his plan to uproot the PLO from Lebanon, Sharon capitalized on the administration's strategic benevolence to raise the bilateral relationship to a higher qualitative level. In November 1981, a year after the conclusion of a Syrian–Soviet friendship and cooperation treaty, Sharon paid his first visit to Washington as Israel's minister of defence, where he

---

[25] Ronald Reagan, *An American Life: The Autobiography* (London: Hutchinson, 1990), 556.

signed a joint Memorandum of Strategic Understanding with the reluctant Weinberger. Though the agreement was suspended a month later following the extension of Israeli jurisdiction over the Golan Heights, it was reinstated two years later and was followed by other security-related agreements, such as Israel's inclusion in 1986 in the research programme of the Strategic Defence Initiative (SDI), and, a year later, by her designation as 'a major non-NATO ally'.[26]

A circle had been closed. Within less than two decades, Israel had managed to transform herself from an embarrassing political and strategic liability into a prominent ally of the US in the Middle East, enjoying a multifaceted and institutionalized relationship.

COLLABORATION AND DISCORD: THE DYNAMICS OF THE US–ISRAEL 'SPECIAL RELATIONSHIP'

Not a marriage made in heaven

This is not to say that the newly established 'special relationship' was all bliss. As a superpower with fingers in numerous pies of many flavours, the US was bound to antagonize some of her regional friends at any given moment. She had at once to arm her Arab allies and Israel while leaving neither aggrieved, to promote an acceptable solution to the Middle East problem without appearing self-serving or partial, to woo Arab radicals from the Soviet orbit without alarming the Israelis and the conservative regimes, and to curb Soviet regional influence without rocking the overall edifice of *détente*, let alone triggering a direct superpower confrontation. To juggle so many balls is a difficult task even in the most benign international environment. In the highly charged atmosphere of the Arab–Israeli conflict, where mutual perceptions were light years apart, there was no way for the US to square these many circles.

Nor has Israel been willing to sacrifice her national interests for the sake of America's global or regional objectives, though going at times to great lengths to avoid alienating her major, indeed only, Great Power ally. Consequently, US–Israeli relations, like America's relations with her Arab allies or Moscow's relations with her Arab allies, have followed the all too familiar pattern of strategic interde-

---

[26] Abraham Ben-Zvi, *The United States and Israel: The Limits of the Special Relationship* (New York: Columbia University Press, 1993), 124, 126; Ze'ev Schiff and Ehud Ya'ari, *Israel's Lebanon War* (London: Allen & Unwin, 1984), 63–4.

pendence in which pushing and shoving are the common means of communication and where the junior partner tries to maximize its freedom of manoeuvre and minimize the encroachment of the Cold War (a secondary factor from the regional point of view) on its national interests, and, if possible, to harness its vicissitudes to its advantage.

This behavioural pattern was particularly intense during the Carter (and to a lesser extent the Bush) administration, where the president and the bureaucracy viewed Israel as more of a nuisance than an asset; but it was a recurrent theme in the bilateral relationship even under the most sympathetic presidents, such as Ronald Reagan. A central area of confrontation was military support, where divergences over needs, threats, balances of power, and strategic ramifications abound. The administration often manipulated arms supplies to Israel, either to force her into concessions on the Arab–Israeli conflict (e.g. the 1975 'reassessment') or to score points with the Arab states (e.g. the 1981 destruction of Iraq's nuclear reactor) or because her military requests were deemed politically inconvenient or strategically counterproductive. Conversely, Israel spoiled for confrontation whenever she viewed American arms sales to the Arabs as detrimental to her national security. A ferocious battle raged in 1978 when the Carter administration sought to sell Saudi Arabia 62 of the highly sophisticated F-15 aircraft. Three years later Saudi Arabia formed the stage for yet another confrontation, this time over the sale of five Airborne Warning and Command Systems (AWACS). On both occasions Israel and her American supporters lost out, but not without forcing some tactical concessions on the grudging administration.

This chapter will discuss several critical case studies in the US–Israeli special relationship in an attempt to dissect the dynamics of this delicate balance of interdependence.

Squabbling over the War of Attrition

Interestingly enough, even the Nixon presidency, which saw the forging of the 'special relationship', had its fair amount of severe frictions and stormy confrontations. Though, on the whole, Nixon's Soviet-centric world-view worked in Israel's favour, it also made US–Israeli relations captive to the vicissitudes in superpower relations. As Nixon commented to Kissinger: ' "Even-Handedness" is the right policy— But above all our interest is—what gives the Soviets the most trouble —Don't let Arab–Israeli conflict obscure that interest.'[27]

[27] Henry Kissinger, *Years of Upheaval* (Boston: Little, Brown, 1982), 563.

What this interest actually meant was to become a major bone of contention within the administration. As Egypt and Israel were locked in a prolonged War of Attrition along the Suez Canal (1968–70), policy-makers in Washington diverged over the implications of the war for superpower relations. NSC Adviser Kissinger believed that in the long run the war 'would demonstrate Soviet impotence [and] would persuade Egypt to face the reality that Soviet tutelage and radical foreign policy were obstacles to progress and that only the United States could bring about a settlement'. For their part, Secretary of State William Rogers and his 'Arabists' thought the war worked in favour of Arab radicalism, and advocated a Soviet–American push towards a settlement in which the US would 'deliver' Israeli concessions. Kissinger did not dispute the idea of Israeli concessions but insisted that they should be reciprocated by the Arabs; otherwise the US would be rewarding Soviet clients rather than her own friends and would damage her reputation as a reliable ally. Besides, there was no need to give the Soviets a free ride: since they 'had no means of achieving their objectives except by our cooperation or through a war their clients were to lose', they were bound 'to pay a price for our help, either in the Middle East or elsewhere'.[28]

With some trepidation Nixon gravitated towards the State Department. Eager to end the painful Vietnam saga, he dreaded any regional escalation that could further complicate superpower relations. He shared Kissinger's view that the Arab–Israeli conflict could provide a Soviet quid pro quo in the Far East, but believed that this could be extracted through cooperation rather than confrontation. He therefore agreed, early in 1969, to enter into bilateral negotiations with the Soviet Union over the implementation of UN Security Council Resolution 242. To deflect French accusations of Soviet–American hegemonism in the Middle East, Nixon also agreed to couple the Big Two talks with discussions among the Big Four—the US, the Soviet Union, France, and Britain—at the United Nations level.[29]

This was anathema to the Israelis. As they saw it, they were asked to put their national existence on the line for the sake of American global interests. 'Such a compromise might satisfy the demands of US–Soviet détente', Prime Minister Golda Meir lamented to Rogers,

but it would almost certainly not result in any binding guarantees for Israeli safety. How could it? The Russians were feeding and manipulating the

[28] Kissinger, *White House Years*, 350–1, 368–9; Quandt, *Decade of Decisions*, 103–4.
[29] Nadav Safran, *Israel: The Embattled Ally* (Cambridge, Mass.: Belknap Press, 1981), 432.

entire Egyptian war effort; the British were not far behind the French: only the Americans were at all concerned with Israel's survival. At best it would be three against one, and I couldn't envisage a workable solution ever being achieved under such conditions.[30]

Her attempt to decouple Israel's security from the Cold War was unavailing. The administration was bent on pursuing the multilateral track and on using all necessary means to rein Israel in, not least the manipulation of arms supplies. Shortly before his departure from the political scene, President Johnson had ordered the sale of 50 F-4 Phantom fighters to Israel, to be delivered between late 1969 and late 1970. In the summer of 1969 Israel informally approached the US with a request for an additional 25 Phantoms and 80 Skyhawks, in lieu of 50 Mirage-5 fighters which France refused to supply in violation of signed contracts. As the Americans failed to respond, Meir made a formal pitch for the aircraft on 15 September 1969, during her first visit to Washington as prime minister—to no avail.

But worse was to come for Israel: in a public speech on 7 December 1969, Secretary of State Rogers unveiled his plan for an Arab–Israeli settlement, which envisaged Israel's withdrawal to the pre-1967 borders.[31] Israel quickly dismissed the plan as an act of appeasement and announced her refusal to be sacrificed on the altar of Great Power *Macht Politik*. Even Foreign Minister Abba Eban, the most eloquent voice of Israeli moderation, departed from his detached and measured style and hyperbolically defined the plan as 'undoubtedly one of the major errors of international diplomacy in the postwar era'.[32]

The Rogers Plan was stillborn. Not only was it dismissed out of hand by the Egyptians and the Soviets and given a lukewarm response by President Nixon himself, but it led to a major escalation in the fighting in the form of Israeli air raids on strategic targets deep inside Egyptian territory. It is true that this escalation was predominantly geared to forcing Nasser to end the War of Attrition and, if possible, to bringing about the collapse of his regime; but it was equally motivated by Israel's desire to forestall the imposition of an unfavourable Great Power solution. In the view of the Israeli ambassador in Washington, Yitzhak Rabin, taken at face value by most members of the Israeli cabinet, the Rogers Plan reflected the administration's frustration over Israel's inability to win the War of Attrition; were the conflict to be brought to a swift conclusion, the

[30] Golda Meir, *My Life* (London, Futura, 1976), 320.
[31] For the text of the Rogers Plan, see Yehuda Lukacs (ed.), *The Israeli–Palestinian Conflict: A Documentary Record* (Cambridge: Cambridge University Press, 1992), 55–60.
[32] Abba Eban, *An Autobiography*, 464.

American pressure for political concessions would quickly abate. Rabin believed (reportedly on the basis of tips from official American sources) that, given its outward hostility to Nasser's radical and pro-Soviet stance, the administration would be amenable to the in-depth air raids and might even lend them its tacit support.[33]

What this assessment failed to take into account was the intricate dynamics of superpower relations, both at the global and at the regional levels. Most Israeli policy-makers believed that the Soviets would not come to Egypt's help beyond the familiar parameters of arms supplies and technical and advisory support. Their frame of reference was the Arab–Israeli conflict, not the Soviet–Israeli or Soviet–US rivalries; and to end the disturbing war along the Canal they were willing to overlook the Cold War dimension of Middle Eastern politics and, if necessary, to risk a confrontation with the Soviet Union. Even Minister of Defence Moshe Dayan, who epitomized the minority view that the Soviets would go to great lengths to protect their Egyptian ally, deemed the direct gains of the strategic air raids to outweigh the risks of potential Soviet escalation.[34]

No less importantly, the Israelis misperceived the nature of the American response to the Soviet intervention. Rather than endorse the Israeli attempt to bomb Nasser into submission, the bureaucracy advised Nixon to use Israel's pending arms requests as a lever to halt the air raids on Egyptian strategic targets, which, they claimed, increased the heat on America's regional allies. Neither the massive influx of Soviet weapons to Egypt nor even the mass arrival of Soviet regular units to take part in the fighting seemed sufficiently alarming to change this strategic assessment. The State Department dismissed Israeli allegations of Moscow's new role in the conflict and, even when confronted with indisputable evidence in this regard, tended to downplay its significance. Since Nixon's attention at the time was focused on the Far Eastern crisis, he did not challenge his bureaucrats. On 23 March 1970, less than a week after the administration had reluctantly recognized the existence of large-scale Soviet air defence units in Egypt, Rogers announced that for the time being the US would not sell Israel the requested aircraft since 'in our judgement, Israel's air capacity is sufficient to meet its needs for the time being'.[35]

Not surprisingly, the Israelis were enraged by what they perceived

---

[33] Yitzhak Rabin, *Pinkas Sherut* [Service Notebook] (Tel Aviv: Ma'ariv, 1979), 248–74. Foreign Minister Abba Eban and his chief advisers disputed Rabin's assessment, but their view was rejected by the Cabinet; see Rafael, *Destination Peace*, 205–6.

[34] Yaacov Bar-Siman-Tov, *The Israeli–Egyptian War of Attrition* (New York: Columbia University Press, 1980), 126–30.

[35] Kissinger, *White House Years*, 571; Spiegel, *The Other Arab–Israeli Conflict*, 190–2; Safran, *Israel*, 440–1.

as yet another American attempt to pay with Israeli currency for improved relations with both Soviets and Arabs. In mid-March 1970 they had accepted an American proposal for a cease-fire, which came to naught, only to be rewarded by Rogers's terse statement.[36] Now that their military losses were mounting by the day, the Israelis rolled up their sleeves and moved onto the offensive. In May 1970, seventy-two senators signed a letter to Rogers, protesting that his decision to suspend arms supplies to Israel had produced no similar restraint on the Soviet side.

Nixon was duly impressed. With the counter-Vietcong actions in Cambodia underway, he suddenly realized that the boiling Middle East cauldron was on the verge of explosion. His first reaction, therefore, was to warn the Soviets off escalation while seeking to pre-empt a direct superpower confrontation. In May he met Abba Eban in Washington. 'Was it still Israel's policy that American troops would not be involved in any foreseeable development of the war in the Middle East?' he asked. When given a positive response, Nixon immediately approved the delivery of the remaining planes from the December 1968 arms deal, but made no promise to sell the additional aircraft.[37]

He made good his promise, but not in time to help the Israeli war effort. When a cease-fire along the Canal came into effect on 7 August 1970, the Phantoms had not yet arrived. It was only in October 1970, after Egypt had violated the cease-fire agreement by moving her surface-to-air missiles towards the Canal and the administration feared an Israeli retaliation, that the promised aircraft (from the 1968 deal) eventually arrived in Israel.

This, nevertheless, failed to satisfy the Israelis, who continued to press for the additional aircraft. In a meeting at the White House in December 1970, Defence Minister Dayan protested that the administration was again using arms supplies as a political lever by promising Egypt that such supplies would be suspended for the duration of the Egyptian–Israeli negotiations that were to follow the cease-fire. When Nixon denied the allegation, Dayan cited an official statement to this effect by the Egyptian foreign minister, Mahmoud Riad. Evidently embarrassed, Nixon turned to his secretary of defence, Melvin Laird, and asked whether this was true; Laird confirmed the Israeli complaint. Upon returning home, Dayan learnt that Israel's long-pending request for the Phantoms and the Skyhawks had been approved.[38]

[36] Kissinger, *White House Years*, 569; Meir, *My Life*, 321–2.
[37] Eban, *An Autobiography*, 466; Quandt, *Decade of Decisions*, 99.
[38] Moshe Dayan, *Story of My Life*, 456–7.

Yom Kippur and after

The precariousness of the US–Israeli relationship was further under-scored by the October 1973 war. From the outset it was evident to Nixon and Kissinger, who on 22 September 1973 became secretary of state in addition to his position as NSC adviser, that a battlefield stalemate would provide the foundation on which American-led negotiations between Israel and the Arabs could ensue.[39] They there-fore opposed an early cease-fire that would leave the Arabs with their initial gains—a rather simple task since Sadat (and to a lesser extent Asad) would not stop fighting as long as they were winning. At the same time the administration sought to prevent a dramatic Israeli comeback by dragging their heels on her arms requests.

To the Israelis this was a step short of betrayal. Shortly before the outbreak of hostilities the Israeli cabinet had declined a request by Chief of Staff David Elazar to launch a pre-emptive air strike against the Egyptian and Syrian armies, which were about to attack the Jewish state within a matter of hours. Though this decision was partly motivated by the desperate hope for a last-minute miracle that would avert war—which, in turn, was bound to tarnish the government's smug election campaign that was under way at the time—it was essen-tially designed to prevent the portrayal of Israel as an aggressor, so as to buy America's goodwill and support in the event of war.

Now that these hopes were shattered, the Israelis rang the loudest alarm bells in Washington. In the predawn hours of 9 October, the Israeli ambassador to Washington, Simcha Dinitz, was woken by a phone call by Prime Minister Meir, who instructed him to contact Kissinger with a request for an immediate airlift. 'I can't speak to anyone now, Golda,' protested Dinitz, 'it's much too early.' 'I don't care what time it is,' Meir snapped back. 'Call Kissinger now. In the middle of the night. We need help today because tomorrow it may be too late.'[40]

A few hours later Dinitz informed Kissinger of Israel's staggering losses and told him that Meir was prepared to come to Washington incognito, if only for an hour, to plead with Nixon for arms supplies. Kissinger dismissed the idea out of hand. Yet he was sufficiently alarmed to take the Israeli request to the Washington Special Action Group (WSAG), the inter-departmental senior crisis management group, only to find his colleagues reluctant to meet Israel's requests, since 'turning around a battle that the Arabs were winning might blight our relations with the Arabs'. All that the WSAG was willing

---

[39] Nixon, *RN*, 921.   [40] Meir, *My Life*, 362.

to do was to allow an El Al jet to pick up bombs and air-to-air missiles from Oceana Naval Air Station, near Norfolk, Virginia, and to give Israel two Phantom aircraft from her annual quota:[41] a far cry from Israel's minimal expectations, particularly since the Soviets had already initiated a massive sealift to replace Arab war losses; the first ships left the Black Sea ports on 7 October, arriving in Syria and Egypt three days later.

Later that day Kissinger discussed the situation with Nixon. The president had thus far given the crisis only passing attention. He had been immersed in his own Watergate quagmire and the imminent downfall of his deputy, Spiro Agnew, over a corruption scandal. His initial inclination upon the start of the war had been to be tough with Israel, in order to prevent those Arab states that had stayed out from entering the war. 'Were the Israelis to win quickly,' he told Kissinger, 'they would be even more impossible to deal with than before.' But now the story was completely different. Israel looked to be in the eye of the storm and Nixon was the last person to allow a close American friend be defeated by Soviet allies. 'The Israelis must not be allowed to lose,' he said. 'Let them know that we would replace all their supplies.' As a first step he ordered a low-key resupply of aircraft and consumer items such as ordnance and electronic equipment. This decision was immediately conveyed to Dinitz.[42]

The promised arms, though, failed to arrive. Nixon was too absorbed in his personal predicament to follow his order through, and the bureaucracy was all too happy to take advantage of this. For Israel these were critical days. Having recaptured the Golan Heights and driven a few miles into Syrian territory, on 11 October Israel began moving some of her tanks southwards. Whether she could move onto the offensive in the Sinai peninsula without a major resupply remained questionable. And to make things worse, on 10 October scores of Soviet transporters landed in Egypt and Syria, in what was to become the largest ever Soviet airlift to a combatant Third World ally. Even though Soviet arms were already reaching the Arab states by sea, and although the amount of sea-borne supplies during the war was sevenfold those delivered by air, the conspicuousness of the airlift made it a potent symbol of Soviet support for the Arabs.[43]

[41] Kissinger, *Years of Upheaval*, 492–5; Dayan, *Story of My Life*, 518; Quandt, *Decade of Decisions*, 179; *Sunday Times* Insight Team, *Insight on the Middle East War* (London: André Deutsch, 1974), 134.

[42] Kissinger, *Years of Upheaval*, 495–6; Nixon, *RN*, 922; Walter Isaacson, *Kissinger: A Biography* (London: Faber & Faber, 1993), 516–17.

[43] During the war the Soviets airlifted the Arabs some 10,740 tons of military equipment, compared with 71,260 delivered by sea. Samuel S. Roberts, 'The October 1973 Arab–Israeli

In these circumstances, the Israelis and their supporters in Washington were bombarding the administration with appeals for arms. In a terse phone conversation with Nixon on 11 October, Meir attacked the administration's indifference to Israel's desperate needs at a time when the Soviets were heavily arming the Arabs. Nixon called Kissinger. Why had his order of two days earlier not been implemented? Kissinger blamed the Pentagon. 'I'm pissed off about the business of not getting the planes through,' said Nixon. 'Tell [Minister of Defence] Schlesinger to speed it up.'[44]

The following day Kissinger met Dinitz. The ambassador complained that Schlesinger and his aides were avoiding him, and warned that if Israel's supplies were not replenished immediately she would exhaust them in two or three days. Whether or not Dinitz insinuated that Israel might go nuclear rather than face a certain destruction, as some observers have claimed, Kissinger was sufficiently alarmed to phone Schlesinger at about midnight and to urge him to get the airlift off the ground. Schlesinger would not damage America's relations with the Arabs, especially since the latter were rattling the oil sabre; he called the White House, and only after receiving the go-ahead agreed with Kissinger on the preliminaries of the airlift. The following morning, 13 October, precisely a week from the start of the war, Nixon officially approved the full-scale resupply of Israel. A day later, 30 C-130 American transporters landed in Israel.

In his memoirs Kissinger denies the 'canard that the Nixon Administration deliberately withheld supplies from Israel to make it more tractable in negotiations'.[45] Yet for all this feigned innocence the situation on the ground was crystal clear: 'Israel was losing, the Soviets were supplying their clients, the Americans were not.'[46] Secretary of Defense Schlesinger had no qualms about admitting that 'the US delayed, deliberately delayed, the start of its resupply operation, hoping that a ceasefire would be implemented quickly'.[47] Nixon confirms the Pentagon's prevarication in his memoirs,[48] and even Kissinger himself would seem to contradict his own assertion by accusing the Pentagon of procrastination—had Israel been adequately resupplied there would conceivably have been no need for

War', in B. Dismukes and J. McConnell (eds.), *Soviet Naval Diplomacy* (New York: Pergamon, 1979), 208.

[44] Isaacson, *Kissinger*, 519; Nixon, *RN*, 924, 926.

[45] Kissinger, *Years of Upheaval*, 496.

[46] Stephen E. Ambrose, *Nixon*, iii: *Ruin and Recovery, 1973–1990* (New York: Simon & Schuster, 1991), 234.

[47] Schlesinger's press conference on 26 Oct. 1973, reported in the *Department of State Bulletin*, 19 Nov. 1973, 624.

[48] Nixon, *RN*, 924–7.

such accusations. On 25 October, the day a lasting cease-fire came into effect, Kissinger came close to direct admission of such heel-dragging by telling a press conference that 'throughout the first week we attempted to bring about a moderation in the level of outside supplies that were introduced into the area'.[49] The truth of the matter is that while the Israelis were turning every stone in Washington in a desperate bid for arms, Kissinger was already jockeying for position in the postwar negotiations. Having grasped the full scope of Israel's plight following his 9 October meeting with Dinitz, he began pressuring her to accept a cease-fire 'in place' while exploring with the Soviets the acceptability of such an idea.

This was, of course, unacceptable to the Israelis. A cease-fire in place meant that the Arabs would be able to retain most of their initial gains, something Israel was unwilling to countenance at the time. For a couple of days she resisted Kissinger's pressures but, with the worsening of her situation, began to give ground. Starved of American military supplies, the Israelis saw no early prospect for a breakthrough on the Egyptian front. At the same time, the recovery of the Golan and the seizure of modest Syrian territory kindled hopes of a possible trade-off between the gains in Syria and the setbacks in Sinai. On 12 October Israel gave her grudging consent to a cease-fire in place, only to be let off the hook by Anwar Sadat, who dismissed the idea out of hand.[50] Sadat's rejection of a cease-fire was the last straw that broke Washington's prevarication over Israel's arms requests. By way of ensuring that the war ended inconclusively, the administration was ready to starve Israel of weapons. Once Israel was brought to her knees and the Soviets were openly rearming the Arabs, that policy had lost its rationale. Only a resurgent yet tightly controlled Israel now seemed able to drive the buoyant Arabs to accept a cease-fire in place; contain the outburst of Soviet activism; and pave the way for postwar negotiations. 'I don't want the Israelis to get too cocky by our airlift,' Nixon told Kissinger. 'We have to squeeze the Israelis when this is over and the Russians have got to know it. We have to squeeze them goddamn hard.'[51]

Squeeze indeed they did, and much earlier than Nixon anticipated. As a dramatic reversal of fortunes on the battlefield took place, when

---

[49] *Department of State Bulletin*, 12 Nov. 1973, 586.

[50] Eban, *An Autobiography*, 514–15; *Sunday Times, Insight on the Middle East War*, 134–7; Spiegel, *The Other Arab–Israeli Conflict*, 251; Quandt, *Decade of Decisions*, 177–83; Edward N. Luttwak and Walter Laqueur, 'Kissinger and the Yom Kippur War', *Commentary* 58(3) (Sept. 1974). Kissinger himself admitted the pressures on Israel to accept a cease-fire in place in an interview with Muhammad Hassanein Heikal (*al-Anwar*, Beirut, 7 Nov. 1973; English version, *Journal of Palestine Studies* 3(2) (winter 1974), 210–15).

[51] Isaacson, *Kissinger*, 522.

Israel managed to move onto the offensive and to cross the Canal in strength, the Americans quickly moved to Egypt's succour. With the Soviets they masterminded a cease-fire proposal, had it passed at the UN as Security Council Resolution 338, and pressured the by now victorious Israelis to accept it. When the cease-fire broke down and the Soviets seemed poised to intervene militarily on Egypt's behalf, the administration reined them in by declaring a worldwide nuclear alert. It then forced Israel, which conducted a breathless race to complete the envelopment of the Egyptian forces in the Sinai, to halt her advance. This was achieved on 25 October 1973.

By now Kissinger was determined to win Egypt away from the Soviet Union come what may, even if the price had to be paid in Israeli currency. As a first step he sought to allow Egypt to retain the spoils of war by preventing Israel from starving the Egyptian 3rd Army, deployed in previously held Israeli territory on the eastern bank of the Canal, into surrender. He then travelled to Cairo in November 1973, for his first ever Middle East visit, where he established close rapport with Anwar Sadat. The two shared a strategic vision predicated on weakening the influence of, and ideally the exclusion of, the Soviet Union from Middle Eastern affairs. This culminated in the two disengagement agreements of 1974 and 1975, which put Egypt on course to regaining her lost territories and transformed her into a cornerstone in the edifice of US Middle Eastern strategy. Kissinger's trump card for effecting this about-face in Egyptian–American relations was America's 'special relationship' with Israel.

'Reassessment'

In order to achieve the second agreement the administration did not shy from applying brutal pressure on Israel. In August 1974 Vice President Gerald Ford succeeded Richard Nixon in the White House following the latter's resignation over the Watergate affair. A lacklustre figure who had reached his country's top political post by default, Ford was thirsty for instant successes that would endow him with a much-needed presidential aura. With the ghosts of Watergate still hovering over the political scene, economic recovery from the oil shock not in sight, superpower *détente* on the wane, and Indochina falling under communist domination, an interim agreement between Egypt and Israel presented itself as a realistic target. The anxiety for an immediate success of sorts was fully shared by Kissinger, who retained his cabinet portfolio under the new president, and who seemed to have lost his magic touch as his main achievements were being progressively undone. In February 1975, and again in March, he visited Egypt and Israel, only to reach the frustrating conclusion that, for all their interest in another agreement, the gap between the two countries remained too wide to bridge.

In Israel he found a young and indecisive leadership. In April 1974 Golda Meir resigned the premiership, to be succeeded by Yitzhak Rabin, former army chief of staff and ambassador to the US. Defence Minister Moshe Dayan, who resigned along with Mrs Meir, was replaced by Shimon Peres, while Israel's foremost diplomat, Abba Eban, lost his post to Yigal Allon, who also served as deputy prime minister.

From the outset the new leadership was beset by a deep personal animosity between Rabin and Peres. The two had vied for the national leadership following Meir's departure, and although Rabin won by a narrow margin, Peres would not resign himself to playing second fiddle. This rivalry was to last for decades, playing a key role in Labour's fall from power in 1977 and its consequent failure to regain it until 1992. In the early months of 1975 it played a significant role in condemning Kissinger's mediation attempts to failure, as the newly installed government would not entertain any concessions for fear that this would threaten its fragile basis. If Israel were to withdraw to the strategic passes, some forty kilometres east of the Suez Canal, Rabin told Kissinger, then she would have to be generously rewarded. At the very least, Egypt could be expected to end the state of belligerency and the economic boycott of Israel, and to allow free passage of Israeli goods through the Suez Canal, as well as free movement of people between the two countries.

As these demands went far beyond what Sadat was willing to concede, and as Israel remained unmoved by the growing American pressures, including a tough letter from Ford to Rabin threatening that the US 'would not finance a state of deadlock that would damage its political interests', Kissinger returned empty-handed to Washington. Soon afterwards Ford made good his threat by declaring a 'reassessment' of US–Israeli relations. Economic and military contacts with Israel were suspended, including Israeli requests for an aid package of some $2.5 billion and for the supply of the modern F-15 fighting aircraft. Senior Israeli ministers, scheduled to visit Washington, were advised to stay home. Kissinger embarked on a series of consultations with prominent figures from the foreign policy establishment, most of whom were viewed by Israel as hostile to her cause.

In the summer Israel informed the administration of her readiness to re-enter into negotiations with Egypt. Sadat quickly reciprocated

by reopening the Suez Canal to international navigation and agree-
ing to extend the mandate of the UN Emergency Force (UNEF),
deployed in Sinai as part of the first disengagement agreement. On
20 August, having laid the ground for nearly two months, Kissinger
flew to the Middle East for another round of shuttle diplomacy.
Eleven days later he announced the attainment of a second disengagement agreement between Israel and Egypt; this was signed in
Geneva on 4 September 1975.[52]

This was a shining victory for American diplomacy, made possible
by the close relationship established with Israel following the 1967
war. By demonstrating that the key to resolving the Arab–Israeli
conflict resided in Washington, rather than in Moscow, Kissinger
dealt the Soviets their most caustic Middle Eastern blow since the
mid-1950s—luring their prime regional ally from their fold (though
Sadat was very much a 'willing infidel') and excluding them from the
nascent regional political process. Yet a closer examination of the
'reassessment' process would easily reveal a qualified American success, which owed more to Israel's post-1973 trauma than to the
administration's prowess, and was bought at the political, military,
and economic price exacted by Israel (and, for that matter, by Egypt
as well).

The October war was for Israel what the Six-Day War had been
for the Arabs: a national shock. The hubris that had permeated the
Israeli psyche following the astounding victory of 1967 was replaced
by the painful realization that negotiations were the only way to
resolve the Middle East conflict. It was this humbled state of mind
which, more than anything else, enabled the 1975 agreement; but it
by no means implied that Israel was willing to accept an American
dictate. On the contrary: for all the political infighting within the
Israeli cabinet which narrowed its room for manoeuvre, and despite
Rabin's predilection for cooperation with the US, developed during
his Washington tenure, he was not deterred from fighting back the
administration's pressure. The most vivid demonstration of the
Israeli resistance was afforded on 21 May 1975, when, at the initiat-

---

[52] The agreement provided for an Israeli withdrawal to the eastern side of the strategic
passes, and for the return to Egypt of the Abu Rudeis oil-fields, located on the south-western
coast of the Gulf of Suez. For her part Egypt agreed to the passage of 'non-military cargoes
destined for or coming from Israel' through the Suez Canal. A new UN buffer zone was established between the two armies, and Egypt and Israel were each allowed a surveillance station
in the passes, for early-warning purposes. American civilian personnel were to be attached to
these stations, 'to verify the nature of the[ir] operations', and the US was to establish three
early-warning stations, as well as three unmanned electronic sensor fields, in the passes to monitor the agreement. No less importantly, Egypt and Israel undertook 'not to resort to the threat
or use of force or military blockade against each other', and to seek a comprehensive peace,
based on Security Council Resolution 338 of 22 Oct. 1973.

ive of the American–Israel Public Affairs Committee (AIPAC), sev-
enty-six senators sent a strongly worded letter to the president, urging a greater responsiveness to 'Israel's economic and military needs'
and emphasizing that 'a strong Israel constitutes the most reliable
barrier to the domination of the area by other parties'. A week later,
in another unmistakable signal to the administration to ease the pressure on Israel, the US Senate blocked the sale of Hawk anti-aircraft
to Jordan. A series of public opinion polls taken at the time found
that 'a solid majority of the American people felt that the current
Israeli government was reasonable and wanting to work for a peace
settlement'.[53]

It was only after the administration had given Israel (and Egypt)
a series of secret written far-reaching commitments that the road to
the Egyptian–Israeli disengagement agreement was finally cleared.
Within this framework, the administration promised that

the United States government will make every effort to be fully responsive,
within the limits of its resources and congressional authorization and appro-
priation, on an on-going and long-term basis to Israel's military equipment
and other defense requirements, to its energy requirements, and to its economic needs.

This statement of intent was accompanied by a number of significant
political commitments, including an understanding that the next
agreement with Egypt (and Jordan) should be a final peace treaty,
and a pledge to continue the existing American policy 'whereby it
will not recognize or negotiate with the Palestine Liberation
Organization (PLO) so long as the Palestine Liberation Organization
does not recognize Israel's right to exist and does not accept Security
Council Resolutions 242 and 338.'[54]

The Egyptian–Israeli peace

Contrary to the standard (mis)perception,[55] it was the local protagonists themselves, mainly the Egyptian president Anwar Sadat and
the Israeli prime minister Menachem Begin, who played the key role
in kicking off the Egyptian–Israeli peace process of the late 1970s

[53] Ben-Zvi, *The United States and Israel*, 99–100.

[54] The Egyptian gains were similarly significant. These included *inter alia* a promise that the
agreement would be followed by 'a serious effort to help bring about further negotiations
between Syria and Israel' and, most importantly, a pledge 'to assist the economy of Egypt, subject to the approval of the United States Congress'; this laid the basis of the long-standing
American support to Egypt which turned the latter within less than a decade into the largest
recipient of US non-military aid in the Third World.

[55] For this standard misconception, see e.g. William Quandt, *Camp David: Peacemaking and
Politics* (Washington, DC: Brookings Institution, 1986).

and bringing it to fruition—not the US administration and the naïve president Jimmy Carter. That Sadat was geared towards peace, which would extricate Egypt from the vicious circle of the Arab–Israeli conflict and would heal her many wounds, was indicated already prior to the 1973 war; but Begin was equally intent on reconciliation, so as to redeem his image as 'warmonger and terrorist' and to go down in history as a great peacemaker.

Had it been up to Jimmy Carter, Sadat would have never come to Jerusalem. The American president believed that Kissinger's step-by-step approach had outlived its usefulness, and that his efforts at excluding Moscow from the Arab–Israeli peace process were misconceived. Hence, rather than encourage a direct Egyptian–Israeli dialogue, Carter sought to reactivate the peace process on a multilateral basis and in collaboration with the Soviet Union.[56] On 1 October 1977, Secretary of State Cyrus Vance and the Soviet foreign minister Andrei Gromyko issued a joint statement calling for the reconvening of the Geneva Conference within two months, under UN auspices and US–Soviet chairmanship, and set out the general agenda for negotiation.

This backfired in grand style. Both Begin and Sadat were aware of the reverse correlation between the state of global *détente* and the room for manoeuvre for the smaller actors: the warmer Great Power relations, the narrower the lesser actors' freedom of action; for this reason they were both wary of Carter's courtship of the Soviets. Hence, not only did the Vance–Gromyko Statement fail to lead to Geneva, but it reinforced Begin's and Sadat's determination to go it alone. Though in his first official meeting with Carter in mid-July 1977, Begin agreed to participate in an international peace conference on the basis of UNSCR 242 and 338, accepted comprehensive settlement as the ultimate goal of the conference, expressed readiness for a territorial compromise on the Egyptian and the Syrian fronts, and agreed to limit the building of new settlements in the West Bank and the Gaza Strip,[57] he preferred to negotiate peace on a bilateral basis with each of Israel's neighbours. In August 1977 he sent his foreign minister, Moshe Dayan, to London for a secret meeting with King Hussein. When the king refused to take the plunge, rebuffing

---

[56] Cyrus Vance, *Hard Choices: Critical Years in America's Foreign Policy* (New York: Simon & Schuster, 1983), 163.

[57] Jimmy Carter, *Keeping Faith: Memoirs of a President* (New York: Bantam Books, 1982), 290–1; and his *The Blood of Abraham* (Boston: Houghton Mifflin, 1985), 42. See also Zbigniew Brzezinski, *Power and Principle: Memoirs of the National Security Adviser 1977–1981* (London: Weidenfeld & Nicolson, 1983), 99; Vance, *Hard Choices*, 180–4; Moshe Dayan, *Breakthrough: A Personal Account of the Egyptian–Israeli Peace Negotiations* (London: Weidenfeld & Nicolson, 1981), 18–21.

Dayan's exploration of the possibility of a territorial compromise that would divide the West Bank between Jordan and Israel, Begin turned his sights to the largest and most powerful Arab state— Egypt. In late August 1977, during an official visit to Romania, Begin informed President Nicolae Ceausescu of his interest in a direct dialogue with Egypt, and requested his help in this respect. A similar message was relayed to King Hassan of Morocco a week later, at a secret meeting with Dayan.[58]

This time the Israeli peace overture fell on fertile soil. Like Israel, Sadat was wary of the reactivation of the Geneva peace conference. For one thing, he would not make Egyptian national interest hostage to the whims of the smaller Arab players by coming to Geneva in a unified Arab delegation. For another thing, he had serious misgivings about Carter, whose image in the Arab world was one of weakness and indecision.[59] To make things worse, the American eagerness to give the Soviets a focal role in the peace process, demonstrated most vividly by the Vance–Gromyko Statement, was anathema to Sadat, who viewed Moscow as a major disruptive force in the Middle East. Hence, since the US seemed unable to sustain the peace process on her own, Egypt had no choice but to establish a direct dialogue with Israel. This was done already before the Vance–Gromyko Statement in the form of a secret meeting in Rabat between Dayan and the Egyptian deputy prime minister, Hassan Tohami, on 16–17 September 1977, and the road from there to Sadat's Jerusalem visit was short.

This visit took the administration by complete surprise, though it was tipped off by Sadat about an impending dramatic move.[60] Apparently oblivious of the visit, Under-Secretary of State Warren Christopher voiced support for the joint Soviet–American statement of 1 October and for Moscow's participation in the peace process— as if this approach had not been instrumental in bringing Sadat to Jerusalem. Carter himself, reluctant to concede the collapse of his Middle East strategy, kept a resentful calm for a few days before issuing a half-hearted endorsement for the evolving Egyptian–Israeli peace dialogue.

While it is true that the administration's later integration into the Egyptian–Israeli dialogue was helpful in narrowing the gaps between the two parties, it should be kept in mind that the process was

[58] Ibid. 35–7, 41, 47, 87.

[59] See e.g. Ismail Fahmi, *Negotiating for Peace in the Middle East* (London: Croom Helm, 1983), 189, 194, 196, 207.

[60] Carter, *Keeping Faith*, 296; Brzezinski, *Power and Principle*, 111; Vance, *Hard Choices*, 194; Fahmy, *Negotiating for Peace*, 255–63.

generated, fuelled, and sustained by Israeli and Egyptian determination to reach peace. Indeed, when the administration tried to expand
the Egyptian–Israeli deal to the Palestinian realm, it ran into a brick
wall, as the PLO, which had not yet reconciled itself to the inevitabil-
ity of the historic compromise over the Holy Land, refused to accept
'a fraction of [Palestinian] rights in a fraction of their homeland', as
Palestinian intellectual Fayez Sayigh put it.[61] This allowed
Menachem Begin to drag his feet in the bilateral negotiations with
Egypt over the implementation of the Camp David Accords in the
West Bank and Gaza, where a Palestinian self-governing authority
was to be established for an interim period of up to five years until
the attainment of a permanent solution, predicated on Resolutions
242 and 338.

All in all, if the Cold War—or in this case, its temporary abating—
did in fact play any role in triggering the Egyptian–Israeli peace
process, it was of a limited and indirect nature, namely, reinforcing
the Israeli and the Egyptian conviction that if they did not look after
their own affairs nobody else would, since both superpowers were
pursuing their own agendas, which had little to do with concern for
the well-being of their junior allies.

EPILOGUE

There is little doubt that Israel has been one of the main beneficiaries of the end of the Cold War and the collapse of the communist
bloc. The absence of diplomatic relations with the Soviet Union and
her East European satellites since the Six-Day War, though more
hurtful to Moscow (in terms of diminished power and influence in
the Middle East) than to Israel, was a reflection of Israel's international isolation that policy-makers in Jerusalem would have readily
lived without, all the more so since the Soviet Union still hosted the
second largest Jewish diaspora community worldwide; indeed, the
normalization of relations with the former communist states was
accompanied by a tidal wave of Jewish immigration, which increased
Israel's population by more than 10 per cent.

Yet since the Cold War played a secondary role in Israel's definition of her national interest, which, not unlike many other small
states, has always been focused on her immediate environment, the

---

[61] Cited in Howard M. Sachar, *A History of Israel*, ii: *From the Aftermath of the Yom Kippur
War* (New York: Oxford University Press, 1987), 86. For the Palestinian rebuff of the
American suggestion to join the peace process, see also Edward Said's 'The Morning After',
London Review of Books, 21 Oct. 1993.

end of this half-a-century-long chapter in international politics will probably have a smaller impact on the making of Israel's future policies than was believed at the euphoric moments of the late 1980s or the early 1990s. Israel's existential problem, as her leaders have always been painfully aware, has been her intractable conflict with the Arab world; and since the origins of this conflict and its stubborn persistence have nothing to do with the Cold War but with deeply rooted indigenous factors, its resolution can only stem from regional hopes, interests, and perceptions rather than from external pressures.

Indeed, while the end of the Cold War has certainly contributed to the nascent peace between Israel and her Arab neighbours, this development is above all the culmination of a prolonged and painful process of mutual disillusionment with the utility of armed force, among Arabs and Israelis alike, begun with the 1967 Six-Day War. It is no mere chance that the Israeli–Palestinian–Jordanian peace agreements of 1993–4 were negotiated outside Washington, with the US administration kept in the dark; Warren Christopher's snappy reaction to the announcement of the 1993 Oslo Accord, not unlike his disorientated response to Sadat's Jerusalem visit sixteen years earlier, spoke volumes on America's frustration at being side-stepped by her junior partners. As 'the only remaining superpower' the US can help consolidate and expand this process by economic, political, and military means—but it cannot impose a *pax Americana* on either Israel or the Arabs. President Asad, or any of his likely successors, will not make peace unless this serves the Syrian national interest as they see it; nor will the militant Islamic movements such as Hamas or Hizballah discard their rejection of Israel's right to exist because of American pressure; nor will any Israeli leader be coerced into a withdrawal from the occupied territories unless this is done within an arrangement that satisfies Israel's security needs, as she sees them, with or without the Cold War.

8
Iraq

CHARLES TRIPP

INTRODUCTION

The intention of this chapter is to assess the ways in which two different 'logics' or dynamics interacted in shaping Iraqi politics and the policies pursued by Iraqi governments during the period of the Cold War. The first came from domestic political processes in Iraq. For any ruler of Iraq, there have been certain recurrent preoccupations associated with the regional position of Iraq as a state and with the various forces working in Iraqi society. Their capacity to generate conflict or to produce support has shaped the policies of successive Iraqi governments, leading to the distinctive patterns of Iraqi politics.

The second 'logic', however, was that of the Cold War in its various guises: as ideological conflict, as competition between different models of economic development, and as rivalry between two massively powerful states and their systems of alliances. The power, the resources, and the global reach of the US and the USSR were naturally taken into account by Iraqi governments when assessing dangers to their position or opportunities for furthering their interests. In this sense, therefore, Iraqi politics and the policies of the Iraqi state were not unaffected by the Cold War. The challenge, however, is to understand the ways in which the Cold War made a difference to the choices of successive Iraqi governments, without necessarily suggesting that those choices were dictated by purely Cold War considerations.

This chapter argues that it was only in the realm of regional or international order that Iraqi policies were significantly affected by the logic or the dynamics of the Cold War—and that even in this area many of the moves made by Iraqi governments owed as much to domestic political considerations beyond the concerns of a distinctively Cold War logic. A closer examination of the period of Ba'thist rule in Iraq will demonstrate the ways in which these different preoccupations interacted with each other. During this same period the force of the logic of the Cold War became progressively weaker in its effects upon Iraqi policies. More specifically, however, it will be argued that the Iraqi government, during the war against Iran in the 1980s, became increasingly determined to escape from the fateful antitheses of the Cold War in order to enlist the support of both superpowers for its own purposes. The fact that Saddam Hussein was largely successful in doing so was due to a number of developments within Iraq, in the region, and in the changing relationship between the superpowers which prefigured the end of the Cold War itself.

THE COLD WAR IN THE REALM OF SYMBOLIC POLITICS

There are a number of ways in which the Cold War can be characterized in international relations, stemming in part from the self-representation of the actors themselves and in part from the very structure of the conflict. First, the Cold War can be seen from the perspective of symbolic politics as a mythical construct providing opposing discourses of legitimation. On the one side was an idealized representation of liberal democracy, carrying in its train all the values and beliefs associated with such an idea of desirable order. On the other was the equally idealized projection of the Marxist-Leninist vision, with its associated values and aspirations. In both cases, although mythical, these ideals were not purely imaginary. Each had fierce adherents, individuals and groups committed to their propagation, and thus political systems and structures of power which revolved around the interpretation and implementation of these ideals. As symbolic or mythical creations, however, both thrived— and for some of their adherents defined themselves—in contradistinction to the other. Thus, one of the more colourful aspects of the so-called ideological competition that marked the Cold War was the projected representation of the other in which all parties indulged. It was this polemical and rhetorical exchange which provided the language of the Cold War, and which was taken by many to be a true representation of the identities, sentiments, and philosophies which underpinned the conflict.

Precisely because of the ease with which these languages could be used, they tended to be deployed extensively across the world, including the Middle East, often giving the erroneous impression that they signified that various actors had 'taken sides' or committed themselves, through conviction, to one side or another of the ideological competition that was the Cold War. In the Iraqi case, if one looks at the forty or so years of the duration of the Cold War, it becomes apparent that the chief function of these symbolic antitheses was to provide successive Iraqi leaders with a language with which to inter-act with the dominant global powers. It seems, therefore, that the mythical constructs of the Cold War did not have much purchase on the imaginations of those who shaped and directed Iraqi policy dur-ing this period. Rather, they were seen by them principally as a set of conventions which demanded conformity if the rewards and pro-tection of the system were to be unlocked. Thus, as in many other parts of the world, the use of the languages of 'anti-communism' or of 'anti-imperialism' became devices employed to persuade the Great Powers to part with subsidies, development assistance, military hard-ware, diplomatic support, and an element of international protec-tion.

This local use of a global or universalizing vocabulary was as much a characteristic of Iraqi politics prior to the revolution of 1958 as it was thereafter. A couple of cases may serve to illustrate this theme. Nuri al-Said, the dominant figure of Iraqi politics in the period 1945–58, has often been characterized as 'anti-communist'— a label which he embraced wholeheartedly and for good reason. As the actions of his administration in the late 1940s and the 1950s demonstrated, he was clearly a bitter enemy of the Iraqi Communist Party, initiating its suppression with particular ferocity. In that sense, therefore, it could be argued that Nuri al-Said's ideological proclivi-ties, his values, and his political ideas inclined him more to one side rather than the other in the Cold War. However, a closer examina-tion of his political position and the values he appeared to espouse through his political activities soon shows that he was not simply anti-communist.

Nor, by being anti-communist, did he fall into the camp of the lib-eral democrats, projected as the 'other side' in the Cold War. On the contrary, it could be plausibly argued that Nuri al-Said was as fiercely anti-liberal and anti-democratic as he was anti-communist.[1] The fact that he sought to label many of those who opposed him on a number of issues as 'communists' during this period showed merely that he found it a useful language of denunciation in a world where a degree of uncritical international support might be forthcoming if one could thus characterize one's domestic opponents. Consequently,

---

[1] P. Marr, *The Modern History of Iraq* (Boulder, Colo.: Westview, 1985), 108–16. The pic-ture of Nuri al-Said that emerges even from the account of a favourable commentator is sig-nificant in this regard—see W. J. Gallman, *Iraq under General Nuri: My Recollection of Nuri al-Said 1954–1958* (Baltimore: Johns Hopkins University Press, 1964), ch. 6.

it would be difficult to sustain the argument that the Cold War as a struggle between opposing ideas of the good life and its proper conduct engaged either the sympathies or the imagination of Nuri al-Said. He was only interested in it in so far as the brandishing of the symbolic apparatus associated with the struggle might bring him resources and advantage in his domination of Iraqi politics.

A similar set of observations might be made of the more recent experiences of Iraq under the rule of the Ba'th Party—or, more accurately, under those who rule in the name of the Ba'th Party. Saddam Hussein and others around the late President Ahmad Hasan al-Bakr adopted a distinctively 'anti-imperialist' vocabulary after the coup which brought them to power in 1968. In the public declarations of the regime, this was associated with all the other symbolic markers of what was misleadingly called at the time 'progressive' thought, encompassing such things as 'anti-feudalism', national liberation, Arab socialism, and collectivization. As a result, the regime gave the impression that it was driven during those early years by a distinctive, 'leftist' ideology, amply illustrated in the public pronouncements and the mythical projections of the state. On this basis, it could be suggested that the symbolic antitheses of the Cold War did indeed have some relevance for understanding the impulses behind Iraqi policies during this period.

However, as in the case of Nuri al-Said, caution is needed before making any such inferences. It was certainly true that Hasan al-Bakr, Saddam Hussein, and others were anti-imperialist, but for them imperialism was simply one among many foes. They were equally vehemently anti-Marxist, in the double sense of having no ideological sympathy with the ideals of Marxism and of being ruthless and bitter opponents of the Iraqi Communist Party (ICP). This did not preclude the appearance of solidarity with the ICP and its incorporation into a 'National Front' with the Ba'th Party whenever it seemed tactically prudent to signal such a symbolic *rapprochement*. This development was most obvious in the early years of the new regime, when it appeared both that domestic and regional isolation, as well as internal Ba'th Party manoeuvres, required the cultivation of the ICP.

Given these circumstances, dictated by strategic considerations rather than by ideological conviction, it was not surprising that during the years 1968–71 the ruling Ba'thists pursued an ambiguous policy towards the ICP. On the one hand, there were sporadic attacks on its personnel and offices, as well as arrests of its members and persecution of its associated organizations. At the same time, however, the regime was advocating dialogue with the ICP and proclaiming its readiness to establish a 'national front' of progressive forces. Domestically, the Ba'thist regime was making it clear to the ICP that they could only operate on the restricted terms offered by the regime itself. But it was also signalling that the post-1968 variant of Ba'thism did not harbour the vindictive hatred of the ICP which had been responsible for the terrible persecutions of its members during the brief nine months of Ba'thi rule in 1963.[2]

These trends were to produce the National Action Charter in November 1971. This was a long programmatic document which unequivocally stated the Ba'th Party's determination to remain in full control of Iraq, but which also suggested much common ideological ground with other leftist forces in Iraq, most notably the ICP. Its promulgation came in the middle of the process of Iraqi cultivation of the USSR, spearheaded by Saddam Hussein, at that time Secretary-General of the Iraqi Ba'th party. The Charter had been preceded by the invitation to the Ba'th party to attend the 24th Congress of the CPSU in March 1971, during which Saddam Hussein had been singled out by the Soviet press for praise because of his encouragement of the formation of a front with the ICP. It was followed by Saddam Hussein's own visit to the USSR in February 1972, which can be seen as a prelude to the signing of the Treaty of Friendship and Cooperation between the USSR and Iraq in April 1972. This, in turn, gave the signal for the appointment of two members of the ICP as cabinet ministers in the Iraqi government. The publication of the National Action Charter and the ending of the repression of the ICP were thus clearly related to the concern of the Iraqi leadership to establish ever closer relations with the USSR.[3]

However, it was also part of another initiative for which Saddam Hussein was largely responsible: the outflanking and eventual neutralizing of the left wing of the Ba'th party itself. Saddam Hussein had effectively destroyed a rival centre of power in the clannish, military section of the Ba'th, through engineering the dismissal and murder of General Hardan al-Takriti, originally one of the decisive figures of the coup of 1968. In order to do this, he had sought allies in the party who were themselves mistrustful of the overweening role of the military officer Ba'thists. In many cases, these allies were figures on the left of the Ba'th party, representing those who shared, through ideological conviction, a number of the preoccupations and

    [2] A. Yodfat, *Arab Politics in the Soviet Mirror* (Jerusalem: Israel University Press for the Shiloah Centre, 1973), 165–71.

    [3] H. Shemesh, *Soviet–Iraqi Relations 1968–1988* (Boulder, Colo.: Lynne Rienner, 1992), 37–40, 63–9; O. M. and B. M. Smolansky, *The USSR and Iraq: The Soviet Quest for Influence* (Durham, NC: Duke University Press, 1991), 111–17.

beliefs of the 'left' more generally during the Cold War. For them, the symbols and mythology of the Cold War were of genuine concern, encapsulating their world-view and their vision of how Iraqi society should develop.

Such people were useful to Saddam Hussein at the time. They reinforced him against the military Ba'thists and could be used to signal to the USSR the 'progressive' nature of the Ba'thist regime in Iraq and thus its suitability as an object of support. At the same time, he could rely upon them to be on their guard against any encroachment on their ruling prerogatives by the ICP. Sympathetic as the left of the Ba'th may have been to a number of the beliefs and values of the ICP, they were nevertheless deeply mistrustful of it as an organization, seeing it as a rival for power, competing for the same constituencies and prepared to use the same methods.

The left of the party was also dangerous to Saddam Hussein's ambitions. They were mistrusted by many of the clannish Ba'thists in the military who formed the ultimate guarantee of the regime's continued existence. The left, therefore, had the capacity to provoke the kind of rift in the party which had destroyed the Ba'thist regime in 1963. Secondly, and more importantly for this argument, they represented those who may have joined the party for reasons of ideological conviction and who adhered therefore to a particular interpretation of the ideological direction and the obligations of its leadership. Thus, they represented a possible forum for the indictment of the senior members of the regime, such as Saddam Hussein, should the latter decide at any time that it was more prudent or profitable to steer a different ideological course.

In the light of these calculations, it was not surprising that Saddam Hussein should have concentrated in the following years on the subordination of all aspects of party and state to his own direction, culminating in his assumption of the presidency in 1979. Because of the National Action Charter and the National Front which was formed in 1973, the ICP found itself drawn into this process and was eventually subjected to the repression which such a strategy required. Thus an abortive *coup d'état* in the summer of 1973 by the head of the intelligence services, Nadhim Kazzar, provided Saddam Hussein with the opportunity not only to bring these services under his own personal control but also to implicate one of the principal theoreticians of the Iraqi Ba'th, Abd al-Khaliq al-Samarra'i, associated with the left of the party. This was followed almost immediately by the legalization of the ICP and the formation of the National Front, which brought the Ba'th and the ICP into even closer public alignment. He thereby placated the left of the Ba'th, concerned about the fate of al-Samarra'i, but also ensured that the activities of the ICP and of Ba'thist ideological sympathizers came out into the open.[4]

The ICP's freedom to publish its newspaper, *Tariq al-Sha'b*, and to organize within certain limits seemed to show that the National Front was working and really did represent the significant leftist ideological sympathies of the regime. However, it was also providing evidence for Saddam Hussein of a different kind. As he became increasingly confident about his control over the state apparatus and as the opportunities for increasing that control grew with the massive increases in Iraq's oil revenues in 1973–4, so the ICP began to feel once again the forms of intimidation to which it had been subjected before. From 1976 onwards, although the National Front remained in existence, members of the ICP were harrassed with increasing frequency. By 1978 hostility between the two parties came out into the open: the ICP newspaper criticized the political and economic direction of the regime; for its part, the regime uncovered a 'communist conspiracy' in the armed forces. A number of ICP members in the military were executed, and a decree was introduced proscribing all non-Ba'thi political activity for anyone who was serving, or who had ever served, in the Iraqi armed forces.

These moves were accompanied by purges in the Ba'th as well, culminating in the great purges of 1979 when potential ideological opponents of Saddam Hussein were eliminated. This was the same year in which the ICP newspaper *Tariq al-Sha'b* was closed down, the two ICP cabinet members were dismissed, and the arrests and executions of ICP members increased. Nevertheless, the senior leadership of the ICP were allowed to leave the country unharmed and the ICP remained a legal organization, even if membership clearly brought with it increased risks. It seems quite possible that Saddam Hussein stopped short of outright suppression of the ICP precisely because he believed that this might cause an unwelcome rift with the USSR. However, he cannot have failed to notice that the persecutions of the ICP in 1978 and 1979 had evoked little response from the USSR. It was true that they seem to have led to a sundering of relations between the CPSU and the Ba'th party, but this symbolic relationship was no longer important to Saddam Hussein, since he now dominated the Ba'th in an unprecedented way. More to the

---

[4] See e.g. the 8th Ba'th Party Regional Congress in 1974: Ministry of Information, Iraq, *The 1968 Revolution in Iraq: Experience and Prospects* (London: Ithaca Press, 1979). Some have taken its strongly leftist tone to mean that the ICP alliance was indeed having an effect on the direction of the regime. It could also be seen, however, as a device for the identification of which members of the party stood where on which issues. The fact that the 'direction' provided by the final report would be so rapidly and thoroughly flouted by the government would suggest that other ends were indeed being served.

point, Moscow's reaction to the conflict between the Iraqi regime and the ICP seemed to be one of sorrow rather than anger. In this regard, it seemed that Saddam Hussein would not have to pay any price for the increasingly important symbolic separation between the Ba'th and the ICP and for the repressive measures taken against the latter.[5]

In sum, therefore, the brief interludes when the ICP was not being actively persecuted by the Ba'thi regime coincided with the years when the regime found it useful to deploy the language of the 'solidarity of progressive forces' for reasons of external aid and domestic expediency. Similarly, the development of the Ba'thi regime demonstrated, under the guidance of Hasan al-Bakr, but particularly under Saddam Hussein, that there was little sympathy for socialism or collectivism as properly understood. The vocabulary was used as part of a legitimizing discourse internally, since a professed attachment to socialism was taken to imply a commitment to the lavish funding of a welfare state. However, as the fate of all the self-confessed socialists within the Ba'th party itself demonstrated, it was not the intention of Saddam Hussein to become beholden to any ideology if it appeared that it might impinge on his own freedom of action.

It is this consideration which was bound to weaken any incorporation of Iraq into the symbolic or mythic polarization of the Cold War. Whilst it was certainly true that during this period there were genuine and ideologically committed liberal democrats, as well as Marxist-Leninists, active in Iraq, it was equally true that they rarely, if at all, had any significant impact on the course of the policies pursued by those who ruled the Iraqi state—unless it was to provoke their own suppression. Instead, throughout this period, a succession of Iraqi regimes made a series of rhetorical flourishes, suggesting sympathy for one 'side' or tendency whilst at the same time doing their utmost to ensure that any set of symbolic beliefs independent of their own control were effectively neutered.

Irrespective of the genuine differences in outlook between the various regimes which have ruled Iraq during the period of the Cold War, they have all used indigenous symbolic political languages with which the ideological constructs of the Cold War simply did not intersect. The Hashemite loyalism of Nuri al-Said, the Iraqi nationalism of Abd al-Karim Qasim, the Arab nationalism, tinged with Islamic pietism, of Abd al-Salam Aref, or the various themes combined in the personalism of Saddam Hussein were all off the scale or

---

[5] Smolansky and Smolansky, *USSR and Iraq*, 127–37; Shemesh, *Soviet–Iraqi Relations*, 164–70.

out of the continuum of the mythical antitheses of the Cold War. None of these owed anything either to liberal democracy or to Marxism.

Furthermore, all of these regimes, in addition to their distinctive public rhetoric, more or less consistently voiced, have also used languages of greater symbolic effectiveness, addressed to the crucial domestic constituencies which matter for their survival. These are the languages of power, resourcefulness, ruthlessness, obligation, honour, and identity which are used in the distinctive setting of Iraqi political society to carry conviction among those whose support is vital for the survival of the regime. The power bases of these regimes have each been different, requiring particular combinations of elements and stress on certain aspects of social identity and organization. Nevertheless, the common feature has been their largely parochial resonance, central to the preoccupations and the value systems of Iraqi political actors, but remote from the projected symbolic constructions of the Cold War.

THE COLD WAR IN THE REALM
OF POLITICAL ECONOMY

A second way in which the Cold War can be viewed is from the perspective of political economy. In this reading, the Cold War becomes a contest between two different and fundamentally opposed prescriptions for politico-economic development and between the systems of economic power identified with these prescriptions. On one side, therefore, the Western model of liberal private-enterprise capitalism was held out as the most effective and productive model of economic development. It was claimed not only that this was materially the most successful form of economic life, but also that it created the conditions for the exercise of free will and in that sense, regardless of the inequalities it generated, provided mankind with the opportunity for complete and sustained development. This was met, of course, by the Marxist critique of capitalism on one level but also, in the context of the Cold War, by the advocacy of a model of state planned, collectivist socialism. Against the capitalist model, it was argued that only this would provide the rational and sustainable growth necessary for the establishment of a developed economy. Centralized state planning in investment and production, public ownership of the means of production, the nationalization of land, and a strategy of autarkic economic self-sufficiency were to be the hallmarks of various attempts to escape from the effects of international capitalism and to 'build socialism'.

If one tries to study and to explain the development of the Iraqi political economy through these antithetical models, it becomes clear, as in the case of symbolic politics, that there is little significant intersection with the preoccupations of Iraqi governments. Deceptively similar labels and symbolic associations were deployed, but it becomes difficult to interpret the political economy of Iraq as lying on one side or the other of these diametrically opposed models. Not only was the experience of Iraq as a developing country bound to be far more mixed than this Cold War dualism allowed, but also there were other things going on. Under the regime that existed prior to the revolution of 1958 there were certainly capitalists who thrived within certain sectors of the Iraqi economy. However, the important rural sector of the economy was marked by a pattern of landownership bordering on feudalism. There also existed a vast network of patronage and favouritism exercised by those who occupied powerful positions within the state, creating a state-dependent patrimonial economy. In addition, there was the legacy of British imperialism in the shape of economic and oil interests. Consequently, there were significant and perhaps decisive elements within the political economy of Iraq which could not be easily fitted into the polar opposites of the Cold War.[6] Thus, when it came to the ordering of the economy and to making economic decisions, it would be difficult to argue that the choices were bounded or shaped by the sorts of consideration that were thought to be at the heart of the Cold War.

After 1958, when economic policy began to move more towards the concentration of planning and economic power in the hands of the state, this was due to a number of indigenous preoccupations in Iraq. First, the regimes which ruled Iraq in the wake of the 1958 revolution were determined, as a political strategy, to disempower the pre-1958 élites. In many cases, this meant not simply seizing the reins of state power, but also extending that power into the economic realm which had been such a source of strength and privilege for the élites in question. Secondly, the shape of the political economy in Iraq under Abd al-Salam Aref, in particular, was following closely—and often consciously—the model laid down by Gamal Abdel Nasser in Egypt. Not only did this conform with certain Third World development models fashionable at the time, but it also served the purpose of concentrating more power by bringing more patronage

---

[6] A valuable insight into the diversity of the pre-1958 political economy of Iraq is provided in H. Batatu, *The Old Social Classes and the Revolutionary Movements of Iraq* (Princeton, NJ: Princeton University Press, 1978), chs. 5, 6, 9.

resources into the hands of the president and of those whom he favoured.

This was no less the case after the Ba'thist coup of 1968, despite the radical rhetoric and the token efforts at limited forms of collectivization in agriculture. In practice, the economic power of the country lay concentrated in the state and, most importantly, in the hands of the distinctive clan that came to control the state. This was visible prior to the mid-1970s, although the tenor of the rhetoric may have suggested to some that a determined ideological model of development, based on that apparently being advocated by the USSR, was being consciously established. The truth seems to have been more piecemeal, more pragmatic, and far less homogeneous. This became especially visible with the massive rise in oil revenues after 1974 which greatly increased the purchasing and patronage power in the hands of the narrow group of individuals who now ruled Iraq, effectively under the direction of Saddam Hussein.[7]

With these resources at the disposal of the central government, a rather different model of development emerged, corresponding to neither of the models characterizing the competition between opposing systems associated with the Cold War. Perhaps the best designation of this pattern which was indigenous (but not unique) to Iraq is that of 'patrimonial development' Essentially, this encompasses two strategies, deployed simultaneously, the principal intention of which is to benefit those in power whilst conforming with some of the conventionally accepted formulae for 'national development'.

The first of these, visible throughout Iraq, has been the strategy of patrimonial 'state' development. Under this programme, largesse is distributed to clients and favourites, consumerist preferences are catered to among the mass public, a vast network of importers and licensees is sustained, and the economic infrastructure of the state is built up on an impressive scale. At the same time, a large bureaucratic apparatus is developed in order to provide the regulatory and distributive system in which the exercise of patrimonial power can take place. In this manner, a large and sophisticated state sector emerged in Iraq, encompassing a vast range of productive enterprises, service organisations, and research institutes. This sector came under the aegis of both civilian and military ministries, depending upon the strategic nature of the activity in which the various organs were engaged.

---

[7] Iraq's oil revenues jumped from $575 m. in 1972 to $5,700 m. in 1974, rising steadily thereafter to $7,500 m. (1975), $8,500 m. (1976), $9,631 m. (1977), $10,200 m. (1978), $21,291 m. (1979), and $25,981 m. (1980); *Middle East Economic Survey* 25(1) (19 Oct. 1981), supplement, p. vii.

The details of this rapid and massive development of the state sector in the Iraqi political economy can be found elsewhere.[8] Its relevance here is that it may have given the impression that the Iraqi leadership was committed to a distinctive, collectivist model of political economy, suggesting that the leadership had indeed chosen one model over another in the competitive environment delineated by the antitheses of the Cold War. In practice, this state sector was being established according to a model and backed by an impulse that had little to do with the alleged virtues of collectivism over free enterprise. The purpose was to retain the commanding elements of the economy in the hands of or at the disposal of the rulers of the state. As the state enterprises grew, so did the many private enterprises to which the state contracted out much of the business. This was most marked in the construction sector, where great fortunes were made by those who were well connected to senior figures in the regime. State patronage thus assured the government of a growing class of beneficiaries, as well as giving the government the means to ensure the continued dependence of these people.[9] These were the preoccupations which led to a certain pattern of economic development. In some contexts and under some circumstances, these could be furthered by the advocacy of 'state-led' development.

In other circumstances, as the 1980s and the war with Iran were to demonstrate, they could also be responsible for the advocacy of something which might be called patrimonial 'capitalist' development. The impulse behind this set of policies was identical to that which had given rise to the forms of 'state'-led development, namely the reinforcement of the patrimonial system which had formed the foundation for the particular kind of rule controlled by Saddam Hussein. Under this system, licences to trade were given to favourites and permits were issued through various descending networks of clients. Strategically selected or well-connected sectors of society were given greater access than others to the new freedoms to trade that were being granted. The language with which these new measures were introduced was appropriately that which seemed to speak to the dominant liberal economic ideologies of the period, concerned with 'privatization' or with the 'retreat of the state'. [10]

[8] See e.g. A. Alkazaz, 'The Distribution of National Income in Iraq, with Particular Reference to the Development of Policies Applied by the State', in D. Hopwood, H. Ishow, and T. Koszinowski (eds.), *Iraq: Power and Society* (Reading, Berks.: Ithaca Press for St Antony's College, Oxford, 1993), 193–256; M. Farouk-Sluglett and P. Sluglett, *Iraq Since 1958: From Revolution to Dictatorship* (London: I.B. Tauris, 1990), 227–54; M. Sader, *Le Développement industriel de l'Irak* (Beirut: Centre d'Études et de Recherches sur le Moyen-Orient Contemporain, 1983).   [9] Farouk-Sluglett and Sluglett, *Iraq Since 1958*, 228–42.

[10] R. Springborg, 'Iraqi *Infitah*: Agrarian Transformation and the Growth of the Private Sector', *Middle East Journal* 40(1) (1986), 33–52.

However, it would be misleading to see these choices as having been determined by a decision to favour one model of economic development over another. On the contrary, as Saddam Hussein repeatedly made clear to those who had begun to profit from the new encouragement of private enterprise, there was a 'state' logic behind this which meant that the framework of discipline and control remained unambiguously in the hands of those who ruled the state. Any attempt to step beyond this or any failure to attend to the other preoccupations of the ruling regime would be met by fierce coercive measures. As in the case of 'state'-led development, the guiding principle appears to have been the concern to establish a productive economy which would ensure the distribution of rewards and resources to those who mattered, but under the close and watchful eye (and hand) of the ruling regime, in whose interest the system was established in the first place.[11]

It is possible to conclude, therefore, that in the matter of political economy, the competing models of the Cold War were largely irrelevant as far as the rulers of Iraq were concerned. As with the symbolic or mythical antitheses of the Cold War, the languages appropriate to one or other of these models may have been deployed—for reasons of relative advantage or for the simple reason that no other language of political economy appeared to exist. In this context, however, it is worth noting that precisely such an attempt to formulate an alternative language of political economy was initiated in Iraq by Ayatollah Muhammad Baqir al-Sadr. In the 1960s he sought to elucidate the notion of a distinctively 'Islamic economics', arguing that the polar opposites of the Cold War did not have to encompass all of human aspiration and activity: to be anti-communist, did not mean that you had to be pro-capitalist.[12] His attempt was not wholly successful, in the sense that it became clear that the formulation of arguments about the very notion of 'the economy' involved the writer in systems of thought and of value possibly antithetical to his purpose.

More importantly, in the light of the development of the Iraqi political economy, al-Sadr's arguments had no visible effect on the policies of those who ruled the Iraqi state. For these rulers, another logic, largely patrimonial in nature, dominated their thinking about the political economy. It lay outside the binary scale established by the polar opposites of the Cold War models of political economy. As

[11] Isam al-Khafaji, 'State Incubation of Iraqi Capitalism', *Middle East Report* 142 (Sept.–Oct. 1986), 4–9.

[12] See Muhammad Baqir al-Sadr, *Iqtisaduna* [Our Economy] (Beirut: Dar al-Kitab al-Lubnani, 1982).

such, other than in merely rhetorical terms, it was not touched by this competition. Instead, it corresponded to an internal set of values and to systems of meaning and power which had their origins and found their impulses within Iraqi society.

THE COLD WAR AND INTERNATIONAL ORDER

The third principal way in which the Cold War can be usefully represented is to see it as a competition between two powerful states for strategic alliances on a global scale. This contained a neo-imperialist logic whereby the measure of a state's prestige and power was taken to lie in the extent of its global influence and reach. In so far as the Cold War competition was also supposed to be about rival constructions in political philosophy and in political economy, success in the sphere of alliance-building was also taken to be a token of the relative merits of rival systems of belief. Global competition for local allies was also based on the premiss that the Cold War might one day erupt into armed conflict between the two superpowers. From this perspective, therefore, local allies across the world were also seen as strategically useful and potentially central to the military planning of one side or another. Consequently, this is the logic of the Cold War as a competition between two power blocs, East and West, both of which sought and to some degree demanded of a variety of states that they be willing to play a part in a larger game of strategic advantage.

It was this logic which produced such grand strategies as that of containment, pursued by successive American administrations during the period of the Cold War. It also produced the counter-strategies deployed by the USSR of 'leapfrogging' or of undermining the governments of states which had committed their countries to play a part in American containment strategies. Underlying this logic and closely related to the strategies which characterized the Cold War was the mental construct of the 'zero-sum game', whereby any loss of influence by one bloc was seen as an inevitable gain for the other. In so far as it corresponded to the ways in which those at the heads of the opposing alliance systems looked at the rest of the world, seeing its component states as of lesser or greater utility for their own purposes, this thinking and the logic that lay behind it were powerful shapers of policy and, as such, had a marked impact on the Middle East, as elsewhere.

It can plausibly be argued that, of all the aspects of the Cold War, this had the greatest influence on the calculations of successive Iraqi governments. Under the monarchical regime and under the various regimes which followed the 1958 revolution, Iraqi rulers, like those of most of the weak, post-imperial states of Asia and Africa, could scarcely ignore the global dominance of the Great Powers. Most had an awareness of—sometimes an oversensitivity to—the vulnerability of their own state and their own position in the hierarchy of global power, whether the threat was seen as coming directly from one superpower or another, or from regional states which enjoyed the backing of Great Power patronage. Consequently, the Cold War as a particular configuration of global power involved and implicated governments in Iraq as they sought to play by and to profit from its rules. This did not mean, however, that they did not try to bend those rules to their purposes, or that they subscribed to the strategic views of the world advocated by their patrons of the moment. In this respect one might argue that, influential as the Cold War logic may have been in helping to explain certain policies pursued by successive Iraqi governments, there was always an ambiguity about their involvement—an ambiguity stemming from the domestic and regional concerns which they were simultaneously seeking to address.

The Baghdad Pact

The most obvious apparent example of Iraqi involvement in the Cold War was the adherence of Iraq, under the premiership of Nuri al-Said, to the Baghdad Pact. This Pact brought together Turkey, Iraq, Iran, Pakistan, and Great Britain under the benevolent patronage of the US, and has been regarded as pre-eminently a device of the Cold War, aimed at the containment of the USSR in the strategic thinking of the time. Because of the hostility it provoked in parts of the Middle East and because adherence to it was cited—eventually—as part of the Free Officers' indictment of the Iraqi *ancien régime* which they overthrew in 1958, the Pact has also been seen as an example of the 'distorting' effect which Cold War logic could have on Iraqi politics. The argument here implies that adherence to the Baghdad Pact indicated the degree to which Nuri al-Said had become mesmerized by the strategic logic of the Cold War, losing touch thereby with both regional and domestic 'realities' and making his downfall inevitable.

This argument must be treated with caution, in so far as it suggests that Nuri al-Said did not know what he was doing in the context of Iraqi politics by signing the Baghdad Pact. It is certainly true that the alliance structure of the Baghdad Pact was a product of the Cold War and of the strategic thinking of that particular phase of the Cold War. It is also possible that Nuri al-Said, as an ex-Ottoman officer, was always more sensitive to and apprehensive of Russia's alleged historical designs on the Middle East than most of his contemporaries elsewhere in the Arab world. He could thus be said to have shared a strategic outlook not dissimilar to the political élites in Turkey and Iran, making sense therefore of his own country's participation in a containment strategy such as that implied by the Baghdad Pact.

However, it can also be plausibly argued that Nuri al-Said was influenced by a number of other factors in his decision to bring Iraq into the Baghdad Pact. None of these owed anything to the logic of the Cold War. On the contrary, they sprang directly from the regional and domestic concerns of the government of Iraq at the time. One such concern was the perennial one which still plagues governments of Iraq, namely how best to organize Iraq's relations with its two powerful neighbours, Turkey and Iran. For Nuri al-Said, one of the advantages of the Baghdad Pact was that it appeared to provide not simply a defensive alliance against the USSR but also a collective security pact which would help to regularize and manage a vital part of Iraq's regional security. Under the aegis of Great Britain and—indirectly—of the US, Iraq could be confident that its relations with Turkey and Iran would be based on a degree of mutual trust. Given the poor relations between successive post-revolutionary Iraqi governments and the governments of both Turkey and Iran—and the often disastrous consequences of these strained relations for Iraq— the regionalist logic which was at work in the formation of the Baghdad Pact cannot be discounted.

Of equal importance for Nuri al-Said at the time was the potentially explosive question of relations with the former imperial power, Great Britain. Nuri al-Said had been ambivalent about the rather clumsy attempt to renegotiate the Treaty with Great Britain which took shape in 1948 in the Portsmouth Treaty. The massive and violent demonstrations which had erupted as a result of the signing of this treaty made a lasting impression on him. They alerted him to the need for a more flexible and a more ambiguous framework within which the advantages of a treaty could be retained for Iraq, without having to become entangled in the divisive issue of treaty negotiations prior to its expiry in 1957. It seems that he believed that he had found such a framework in the Baghdad Pact. By linking regional alliances with the anti-communist theme, he seems to have diluted the question of the role of Great Britain and obviated any need for a bruising round of negotiations over a new treaty.

The public reaction in 1955 to the signing of the Baghdad Pact was very different to that of the signing of the Portsmouth Treaty. Part of the mutedness of the public response was undoubtedly due to Nuri al-Said's thorough and effective use of the repressive apparatus of the state, but part seems to have been due to genuine confusion among some sectors of the political world about the relative merits of the Baghdad Pact. Although there were many who opposed it for a variety of reasons, the very variety of these reasons tended to give the Pact a rather more confused resonance in Iraq than the apparently more clear-cut question of a treaty with Great Britain. It is possible, therefore, to see yet another logic at work than that of the Cold War in understanding Nuri al-Said's decision to bring Iraq into the framework of the Baghdad Pact.

It is not to be denied that Iraqi policies were to some degree subjected to a Cold War logic in this respect—after all, it provided the framework and the rationale in which groupings such as the Baghdad Pact could be constructed. Nevertheless, even here, other motives and impulses were clearly at work, and it would be unwise to ascribe to Nuri al-Said reasons which are unproblematically 'read off' the international text of the Cold War. The same observation applies to his successors as rulers of Iraq. It is, therefore, worth examining in more detail the ways in which Iraq under the Ba'th— and more particularly under Saddam Hussein—has attempted to grapple with the logic of the Cold War in the light of more local preoccupations of regional and domestic political security. For Saddam Hussein, as for other Iraqi rulers, the challenge seems to have come from the need to derive material benefits from the particular international configuration of the Cold War without, however, paying the penalty of abiding by its rules, if adherence to those rules seemed to complicate a more local domestic or regional project. It would, after all, be the outcome of these projects which would have the more immediate effect on his tenure of power.

The Iraq–USSR Treaty of Friendship and Cooperation

Just as with the Baghdad Pact and Nuri al-Said, so the Ba'thi government's signing of the Treaty of Friendship and Cooperation with the USSR in 1972 has been taken to be an indicator of Iraqi involvement in the Cold War. The Treaty itself had a rather formulaic aspect, emphasizing the general principle of cooperation between the two countries in a large number of fields, including defence. It also contained expressions of the two countries' joint stands *vis-à-vis* 'international peace and security'. This was not, therefore, a treaty of alliance or an agreement which drew Iraq in any very significant operational way into the strategic plans of the USSR.[13] As the language which accompanied it at the time tended to suggest (and as Saddam Hussein, to his claimed annoyance, was later to discover), this Treaty was largely of symbolic significance.

In the game of alleged 'influence', the USSR had apparently made a 'gain' in Iraq, as the language of the time would have described it. Consequently, although insubstantial, the Treaty was regarded as part of the symbolic apparatus of international relations in the Cold War, and for that reason it appears that the USSR was willing to enter into it. In addition, the agreement took place at the very time when the Soviet relationship with Egypt was running into difficulties. Consequently, it was undoubtedly seen by the USSR as useful, since a close relationship with Iraq might be important in the event of a loss of influence in Egypt. Furthermore, it appears to have come as a culmination of an increased Soviet interest in Iraq which antedated the coming to power of the Ba'thist regime. This new interest was undoubtedly stimulated by the 1966 announcement by the British government that it would be withdrawing from the Persian Gulf in 1971, and by the growing Soviet interest in the Indian Ocean. Consequently, the cultivation of close relations with Iraq, particularly an Iraq which seemed to be willing to align itself with the USSR on a number of international issues, was thought important enough to merit the expenditure of considerable Soviet effort.

For the Iraqi part, the Treaty appears to have had regional and domestic significance for the Ba'thist regime, or more particularly for the ascending faction of Saddam Hussein within that regime. It was, in part, an attempt to deal with the consequences of the regional isolation of the Ba'thi regime since 1968. Friendless among the Arab states of the Gulf because of the mistrust which existed concerning the regime in Baghdad, the new government in Iraq was also increasingly apprehensive about the threat from Iran. Armed clashes had already erupted in 1969 and 1970. With British withdrawal from the Gulf and the assertion of Iranian primacy there with the full backing of the US, it appeared to the Iraqi regime that it would be subjected to increasing pressure from Iran and from the Western powers behind Iran. Indeed, there are indications that the USSR feared precisely that Iraq might use the encouragement of the Treaty to pursue a more aggressive or at least defiant policy *vis-à-vis* Iran and sought to discourage this by developing its relationship with Iran simultaneously.

[13] For the text of the Treaty, see Yaacov Ro'i, *From Encroachment to Involvement* (Jerusalem: Israel University Press for the Shiloah Centre, 1974), 566–9.

Another consideration for the Iraqi government revolved around the problem of the Iraq Petroleum Company. The USSR had already been invited by the Iraqi government to help develop the North Rumailah oil field, establishing thereby the first substantial Soviet involvement in the Gulf oil industry. By the early 1970s, with the possibility emerging once again in the Middle East of the nationalization of foreign-owned oil companies, the thoughts of the Iraqi government had turned to the possible nationalization of the Iraq Petroleum Company (owned by a consortium of Western companies). Clearly, in the event of such a strategy being carried out, a close relationship with the USSR would have been an asset. Indeed, it was only a couple of months after the signing of the Treaty of Friendship and Cooperation that Iraq went ahead with its nationalization of the IPC, involving itself in considerable litigation and depriving itself of an immediate source of hard currency. The day after this occurred, the Iraqi minister of foreign affairs flew to Moscow and received assurances of Soviet assistance in the export of Iraq's oil and in the development of its own refining capacity.[14]

A further concern of the Iraqi government appears to have been the Kurdish question. This had not been resolved, although the 1970 accord had temporarily reduced the pressure. However, for the Ba'thist regime, it was clear that such pressures would build once more, since they themselves were responsible for ensuring that the 1970 accord should not erode the power of the central government. This was an aspect of Iraqi politics ever vulnerable to regional exploitation, particularly by Iran, and in such circumstances Soviet support for Iraq would have been helpful. Furthermore, if as seemed likely, the government in Baghdad sought to resolve the Kurdish issue in its favour by military means, Soviet military supply would be vital.

It was at this time, as well, that Saddam Hussein was seeking to strengthen his hand against the 'left' within the Ba'th—that is, against those Ba'thists who held to a predominently socialist interpretation of the Ba'thist ideology. The Treaty with the USSR may have been designed in part to win for Saddam Hussein this symbolic prize, by cutting the ground from under the feet of the left in the party. As explained above, the simultaneous cultivation of the Iraqi Communist Party may have been due in part to similar motives, as well as having the useful effect of facilitating relations with the USSR. It was noticeable that when Kosygin visited Baghdad for the signing of the Treaty in April 1972, he had a meeting with an ICP

[14] Shemesh, *Soviet–Iraqi Relations*, 78–80.

delegation at the Soviet embassy (as well as with a delegation from the Kurdish Democratic Party) in which he is supposed to have encouraged their cooperation in the suggested National Front with the Ba'th.[15] This may well have facilitated Saddam Hussein's task of incorporating the ICP symbolically into the regime—an incorporation which was part of an internal party strategy at the time.

It is possible, therefore, to argue that Saddam Hussein's actions in initiating the process which brought about the 1972 Treaty with the USSR were in part due to the working out of a certain Cold War logic in Iraqi politics. Above all, the notion that the kind of association established with the USSR in the Treaty would act as a form of protection against Iran, the principal regional ally of the US, would have been a powerful one. Alliance systems and the invocation of superpower protection to ensure the maintenance of a certain regional order were very much part of the understanding of the management of regional conflict during the Cold War. However, other considerations also played their part in the calculations of the relative utility of such a form of association. They did not owe anything in particular to the conditions of the Cold War, but, as was the case with the Baghdad Pact, they found expression in the specific form of the Treaty of Friendship—a form which made sense in the structural and normative universe of the Cold War.

However, within a few years it was obvious that, whatever the circumstances which had induced the Iraqi government to enter into the Treaty of Friendship with the USSR, distinctively Cold War considerations were playing less and less part in their calculations. Two factors in particular seem to have been responsible for this. The first was the Kurdish war which broke out in 1974 and was only ended through the Algiers agreement with Iran in 1975. The inevitable explosion of resentment in Kurdistan over Baghdad's bad faith and the frustrations with the 1970 agreement developed into an armed insurrection in 1974. The Kurdish rebels looked to Iran for sanctuary and for help, and this presented the Shah with an instrument of considerable value with which to exert pressure on Baghdad. It could be argued that a certain Cold War logic came into play here, since the direct and indirect assistance of the US to the Kurdish rebels through Iran may have been due in part to Washington's perception of Iraq, since the 1972 Treaty, as a Soviet ally in the region and therefore an appropriate target for debilitation through internal war.

As the Baghdad government discovered, this logic did not, however, work in its favour. In subsequent years Saddam Hussein was to

[15] Smolansky and Smolansky, *USSR and Iraq*, 115; Shemesh, *Soviet–Iraqi Relations*, 76.

denounce the USSR for its failure either to restrain Iran in its assistance to the Kurds or to provide Baghdad with sufficient ammunition
to make a military defeat of the Kurds imaginable. Whatever the
truth of this (and in the case of the alleged 'shortage' of ammunition
this appears to have been a later fabrication, designed for other
reasons),[16] it seems to point to a certain disappointment in Iraq concerning the relationship with the USSR. The 1972 Treaty was clearly
of limited utility in the regional calculations of the Iraqi regime.
Instead, Saddam evidently realized that, unless greater damage were
to be borne, he would have to swallow his pride and arrange a
regional deal with Iran which would ensure an end to its support for
the Kurdish rebels. Since Iraq could not match the military strength
of Iran and since it seemed unlikely that the USSR would do much
to assist Iraq if fighting along the border were to escalate, Iraq was
obliged to make a number of concessions to Iran. These were embod-
ied in the Algiers Agreement of 1975, leaving lingering resentments
in the Iraqi leadership at the unfought war it had just lost to Iran
and at the unwillingness of the USSR to help Iraq.

The second major factor which allowed or perhaps induced Iraq
to escape in large measure from the logic of the Cold War in its
regional relations was the effect of the explosion in the price of oil in
1973–4. The massive oil revenues which the Iraqi government now
controlled meant that it had a degree of power and autonomy
unavailable to it before. In some respects Iraq could now dictate the
pattern of its relations with much of the rest of the world, since it
became a target of cultivation by those powers which wished simultaneously to assure their energy supplies and to find a market for
their goods. Consequently, it was during this period that the Iraqi
pattern of trade changed dramatically, away from the USSR and the
Eastern bloc and towards Japan and Western Europe, in particular.[17] At the same time there was a diversification of arms suppliers,
particularly towards France, although the bulk of the Iraqi armed
forces continued to be supplied by the USSR. In the context of arms
acquisition, it also appears to have been during the second half of
the 1970s that the Iraqi government set up its programmes for the
acquisition of non-conventional weapons. With massive financial
resources at its back, the Iraqi government appeared to have made a
determined and often successful attempt to escape from the pattern
of Cold War policing of non-conventional arms supply.

Regionally, the emergence of Iraq as one of the major oil-
producers and financial powers of the Gulf meant that it had much

---

[16] Shemesh, *Soviet–Iraqi Relations*, 125.   [17] Ibid. 257.

more in common than hitherto with similarly situated states. It is in this context that, despite the humiliations of the early 1970s, relations with Iran became remarkably stable, if not necessarily cordial. More importantly, as far as the preoccupations of the Iraqi government were concerned, the growing links with the Arab states of the Gulf and the rest of the Arab world meant that the government had ambitions to become a significant regional player in inter-Arab politics. It is in this context that the years 1978 and 1979 become so significant for the Iraqi government.

Saddam Hussein's presidency and the war with Iran

Domestically, it is the period of Saddam Hussein's formal elevation to the presidency of the republic, accompanied by the purges of the Ba'th—of Arab nationalists and of socialists—which put the finishing touches to his ideological domination of the party. In the region, two important developments occurred. In the first place, President Sadat's pursuit of negotiations with Israel during 1978, resulting in the Washington Treaty of 1979, had led to Egypt's ostracism by much of the rest of the Arab world. As the Iraqi government's calling of the Baghdad Summit in 1978 had demonstrated, this was seen as an opportunity by Saddam Hussein to assert the role of Iraq as a potential leader of the Arab world. Playing much upon the independence of the Arabs, the importance of non-alignment, and the capacity of the Arab states to determine their own future, if necessary against the interests of the superpowers, he seemed to be preparing the ground for a distancing of Iraq and the Arab states from heavy reliance on one side or the other in the Cold War. If this was indeed the time when he decided to authorize the systematic beginning of Iraq's nuclear weapons programme, this would also suggest that he was determined to escape from Cold War logic which, in his view, strengthened Israel but refused to allow the Arab states to acquire the weapons which would give them meaningful strategic parity with Israel by matching its nuclear deterrent. In short, the economic power granted by oil wealth and the opportunity of Egypt's apparent elimination from the game seemed to allow Iraq to escape from Cold War logic and to assert its regional hegemony.

Indeed, this was to be particularly important if Iraq was to become an increasingly influential player in Gulf politics. To be seen as in some sense associated with the 'Soviet interest' in the Gulf would have constituted a barrier to Iraqi influence, since it would have alarmed both the Gulf sheikhdoms and the Western interests that lay behind them. It is partly in this context that the significance of the

Iranian revolution should be seen. The revolution which overthrew the Shah brought to power a regime whose very ideology was marked by a repudiation of the game of Cold War politics. The slogan 'Neither East nor West' was intended to demonstrate the illegitimacy of the models which had hitherto dominated world politics, and to suggest that the new Islamic republic had a third way, of greater legitimacy and authenticity. From the perspective of Saddam Hussein in Baghdad, the alternative of the Islamic republic might look threatening in one sense. However, it also made it clear that Iran, as a regional power, was repudiating its global alliances and was not likely to construct any others of equal significance, given the colour of its ideology. Iran, by consciously tossing aside the logic of the Cold War, also looked as if it had lost its protection. At the same time Iran's military strength was being run down by the post-revolutionary upheavals.

As a consequence of these developments, an opportunity, even a compulsion seemed to have been created for Saddam to initiate military action in order to regain that which he had lost in 1975. In doing so, he might have hoped to assert Iraq's role as protector of the Gulf, as well as to resolve matters relating to his authority within Iraq itself. During this period, therefore, it is possible to argue that an awareness of the logic of the Cold War influenced Saddam Hussein's thinking about what he could achieve in the region. Crucially, his ambitions and the incentive to act were internally generated, stemming from the forces at work in Iraqi political society. However, in so far as these expectations and ambitions required a regional field for their realization, there was an awareness of the rules of the Cold War in two senses which seem relevant to this argument.

In the first place, independent economic power through oil revenues seemed to open up the possibility that Iraq could escape from the binary opposites of the Cold War and rediscover, through action on an Arab stage vacated by Egypt, the power of regional hegemony, if necessary by acting against the logic of the Cold War in such matters as the acquisition of weapons of mass destruction. Secondly, the repudiation of Cold War logic by the Iranian revolutionary regime suddenly made Iran seem supremely vulnerable to precisely the kind of military action which would have been unthinkable had its foreign relations still been governed by the rules of the Cold War game. The path seemed to be open in 1980 for Iraq to act decisively and ruthlessly to assert its regional supremacy by using military force against Iran.

It is fairly common wisdom that the war against Iran did not proceed as Saddam Hussein had hoped. Initially, however, he was full of optimism about what he thought the Iranian government would be obliged to concede by the force of Iraqi arms. A quick victory was conceivable because he thought that the Iranian government would recognize the hopelessness of its position, with Iran's armed forces in a shambles and bereft of the support of any of the Great Powers. To this end Saddam Hussein dispatched Tariq Aziz to Moscow, reportedly with the task of persuading the USSR not to cheat Iraq of victory by demanding a cease-fire before Iraq had achieved its objectives. At the United Nations, Iraqi efforts were also channelled in the same direction, contributing to the notorious paralysis of the UN in the face of the Iraqi invasion of its neighbour's territory.

The Iraqi government could be confident of the inaction of the US, but there was evidently some concern about the attitude of the USSR, not simply because the USSR signalled its disapproval of Baghdad's actions by suspending arms shipments to Iraq, but also because the Iraqi government recognized that an anti-American Iran might be seen, from the perspective of Cold War logic, as a potentially pro-Soviet Iran. Nevertheless, Iran had repudiated such logic and, although it maintained relations with the USSR, its government consciously refused any closer entanglement with the Eastern bloc. Indeed, for much of the war it was supremely confident in the power, not simply the virtue, of its revolutionary Islamic message, believing that it would triumph on the basis of its own human resources. Consequently, Saddam Hussein, during the first year or so of the war, could be confident in turn about Iraq's capacity to achieve its objectives without intervention by either superpower. Characteristically, he made a virtue of this, declaring in 1981 that this was the 'first time in contemporary history that a Third World country has been able to wage a successful defensive war . . . without being forced to place itself under the umbrella of a military alliance or the influence of a Great Power'.[18] In other words, he believed that the power of Iraq, founded on its financial and military might, had allowed it to break out of the logic of the Cold War and to pursue its own strategic objectives, free of subordination to the Great Powers.

It was not long, of course, before Saddam Hussein realized that Iraq's power, great as he may have imagined it to be, was not up to the task. The forces of the Islamic republic rallied and launched a devastating series of counter-offensives in 1982. Not only did the Iranian government make a mockery of the Iraqi expectation of victory, but they also made demands of their own, involving the dismantling of the whole system of power in Iraq—and seemed on the

[18] Saddam Hussein's 17 July Revolution Anniversary speech, Baghdad Home Service, 17 July 1981, in BBC Summary of World Broadcasts (SWB) ME/6779/A/1, 20 July 1981.

verge of carrying this through by force of arms. Iraqi forces were routed and expelled from the territory of Iran, and the Iranian armies seemed poised to invade Iraq. Realizing that he was fighting a very different kind of war, Saddam Hussein was also aware of the danger he now faced in having asserted Iraq's independence and freedom from superpower protection. In the light of his boast of 1981, it is instructive to compare his complaint of 1982:

It is strange that the superpowers kept maintaining the position of onlooker towards the bloody conflict between Iraq and Iran. They made no tangible effort to stop the war . . . a conflict has been left raging for two years without any serious attempt to stop it, although it is raging in one of the most dangerous and vital regions of the world.'[19]

Thereafter, it became one of the pillars of Iraqi strategy to ensure that the superpowers should both become aware of the vital nature of this region and the disastrous consequences for the interests of both the USSR and the US of an Iraqi defeat at the hands of Iran. In other words, it was now Saddam Hussein's ambition to go against Cold War logic, not by asserting the autonomy of Iraq, but by bringing both superpowers into the war on the side of Iraq. In this task he was largely successful: Iraq ended the war with, effectively, two superpower protectors. He tried a number of ploys to achieve this result. First, he played upon the fears in both the USSR and the US of the Iranian revolution and of the consequences for the Middle East and for their own interests in the event of an Iranian victory. He thereby turned Iran's own slogan of 'Neither East nor West' against it, by suggesting that Iran was fundamentally hostile to the interests of both East and West.

Secondly, Saddam Hussein went to some lengths to persuade the outside world, and the superpowers in particular, both that Iraq was a solid proposition and that it was a paying one. During the years of the war there is evidence of a nagging fear in Iraq that the Great Powers might look upon Iran—whatever the colour of its regime—as the better proposition in the long run, meriting its cultivation at the expense of Iraq. It was Saddam Hussein's intention to convince them of the solidity, unity, and stability of Iraq. In this, he was considerably helped not simply by the financial resources of the Iraqi state (which were soon exhausted) but by the financial backing of the Arab states of the Gulf. This allowed him to begin a programme of massive arms acquisition, from France and from the USSR principally, but also from a range of other countries. It also allowed him

---

[19] Saddam Hussein's speech of 20 June 1982, Baghdad Home Service, 20 June 1982, SWB ME/7058/A/1, 22 June 1982.

to supplement the conventional weapons programme with a number of programmes for the acquisition of chemical, biological, and nuclear technologies—and, indeed, to use the chemical weapons with relative impunity.

Thirdly, Saddam Hussein shamelessly used the language of Cold War flirtation when seeking to stimulate greater Soviet interest in the fate of Iraq or when trying to titillate the US into more effective forms of support. Thus, when he was seeking a greater degree of Soviet support at critical moments in the war, or when he wanted to warn them against supplying arms to Iran through Syria, he would feign 'principled condemnation' of the USSR and make moves in the direction of the US. He established a lavishly funded and active public relations exercise in Washington which lobbied effectively for greater American support, enticing Americans with the prospects of a stable, secular, prosperous Iraq, in favour of the status quo in the Middle East and displaying all the symptoms of 'moderation'.[20]

More decisively, as far as the prosecution of the war itself was concerned, Saddam Hussein ensured that eventually the US navy and air force were effectively fighting on the side of Iraq and against Iran in the waters of the Gulf. Through the strategy of the long-distance destruction of Iran's oil assets along the shores of the Gulf and in the attacks on shipping involved in trade with Iran, Iraq provoked Iran into a series of reprisal attacks against shipping doing business with Iraq's Gulf allies. This escalation of what became known as the 'Tanker War' led eventually to direct confrontation between Iranian forces and various Western naval forces anxious to protect the vital oil routes from the Gulf. It also led to the curious spectacle of both the USSR and the US becoming involved in the shipping of Kuwaiti oil in their own or reflagged tankers. It can be plausibly argued that the open-ended escalation of this conflict in 1988 led the Iranian government to believe that it would soon be engaged in a full-scale war with the US, as well as Iraq, and that in such circumstances it would have no resources, domestic or international, with which to defend itself. It was in these circumstances that Ayatollah Khomeini agreed to the terms of the cease-fire resolution which would bring the war to an end.

Looking back over this sequence of events, it is therefore possible to argue that Iraq did indeed succeed in escaping from the logic of the Cold War entirely during the 1980s. Whereas in the 1960s and 1970s a certain set of rules governing the Cold War had significantly affected Iraq's regional and international behaviour, during the

[20] For a good discussion of these developments, see B. W. Jentleson, *With Friends Like These: Reagan, Bush and Saddam 1982–1990* (New York: Norton, 1994).

1980s these no longer applied. In some respects, the ground had been prepared for this by the late 1970s emergence of Iraq as a regional power of some military and financial weight, based upon its massive oil wealth. However, during the 1980s two further factors were at work which served to weaken the rules of the Cold War game in this setting. In the first place, it was evident that those rules found it difficult to accommodate revolutionary Iran. It was not simply that the new revolutionary regime consciously repudiated the polar opposites of the Cold War; it was also clear that the rules of the 'zero-sum game' and other Cold War calculations simply did not apply to a confident and determinedly autonomous regime such as that of Iran after 1979. The second major factor undermining those rules was, of course, the change that was taking place in the USSR itself after the coming to power of Mikhail Gorbachev in1985. Although the full implications of these changes took some time to become apparent, it was clear from 1985 onwards that, even assuming that the Cold War would continue in some form, the ground rules underpinning it were likely to change significantly. For a country like Iraq, therefore, this made it easier to escape from the consequences of that particular configuration of global power in the conduct of its own international relations.

CONCLUSION

The Cold War did not originate in states such as Iraq, nor were the issues at stake—whether symbolic or material—intrinsic to the formations of these societies. However, Iraq, like most other states, could not ignore the impact of the Cold War on the configurations of power in international relations. The preoccupations of the superpowers and of their powerful allies led to the construction of a certain kind of international order, governed by distinctive rules and justified by a specific set of rationales which no government could afford to ignore entirely. In the Iraqi case, the challenge facing successive governments was how best to derive benefit from these rules, whilst at the same time ensuring that they and the forces at their back intruded as little as possible on the jealously guarded sphere of autonomous decision-making. In the final analysis, the consequences of these decisions would depend upon the working out of domestic political processes which owed little, if anything, to the dynamics of the Cold War.

It was perhaps scarcely surprising, therefore, that the dimension of the Cold War which so preoccupied successive Iraqi leaders was that which derived from the competition and suppressed conflict of the superpowers as leaders of bloc alliances, capable of materially affecting Iraq's regional ambitions and its regional security. The other dimensions of the Cold War—as symbolic competition between different political philosophies or as rivalry between different models of political economy—had little grip on Iraqi politics. They may have provided a language of politics, useful for the conduct of international relations in so far as the granting or withholding of resources might have depended upon such usages, but their 'logics' were not as compelling as that of the strategic competition between the superpowers.

In respect of the latter, the case of Saddam Hussein demonstrated the determination of the Iraqi government to escape from the set of rules and expectations which constituted the 'logic' of the Cold War in the regulation of international relations. This only became imaginable and actually possible under the particular conditions of the late 1970s, when Iraq began to emerge as an independent power of some substance in the Middle East. Nevertheless, the impulse to do so had almost certainly always existed, even if the incentive or the opportunity had until that period been largely lacking. These opportunities, as well as the pressing incentives, seemed to bear in on Saddam in quick succession during the late 1970s and during the war with Iran. Indeed, this war was itself, to some degree, the outcome of Saddam's opportunistic perception that the Iranian revolution had placed Iran beyond the rules of the Cold War game. Although this did not mean that Iran was as immediately vulnerable as he had supposed in 1980, it did mean that it was vulnerable in the long run to the kind of attrition of which Iraq was capable, having successfully engaged the support not only of regional states but also of both the superpowers. Iran discovered that, having repudiated one set of rules, it did not have the power to make its own rules thereafter. Instead, it found itself having to compete in a game not of its own making and which it had neither the strength nor the resources to win.

The problem for Saddam Hussein was not dissimilar, although the consequences took slightly longer to manifest themselves. He had succeeded in escaping the logic of the Cold War and had thereby enlisted the support of both superpowers on his side in the war against Iran. This did not mean, however, either that he was the master of the game or that another set of rules, another logic had failed to replace that of the Cold War in international relations. As he discovered after the ending of the war with Iran, emerging as the leader of a bankrupt country, the Cold War rules which he had so opportunely evaded were in any case breaking down and a new set of rules were beginning to form, which he regarded as deeply hostile to his style of government and thus to his political survival.

Increasingly in the post-Cold War world that was developing at the end of the 1980s and the beginning of the 1990s two other 'logics' were making themselves felt. The first was the heartless logic of the market. The Iraqi government found itself bereft of resources, massively in debt, and unable to raise the kind of finance regionally or internationally which had once been the foundation of Iraq's power. With the end of the war and the subsiding of the presumed Iranian threat to oil and other commercial interests, the fate of the Iraqi government was clearly a matter of indifference to much of the international community. In so far as states were interested in Iraq, it was directly connected with the ability of Iraq to repay the massive debts it had incurred during the previous decade and to find the finance for the purchases it was continuing to make. In the absence of a Cold War logic or of the more regional logic engendered by the fears of the Iranian revolution, there seemed to most of the creditor states to be no pressing strategic reason to bail out Iraq.

This was combined with the re-emergence of another set of impulses in the shaping of Great Power policies towards states in Asia and Africa—another 'logic'—which had largely been held in abeyance during the Cold War. This derived from the newly self-confident interventionist liberalism of the US and its Western allies. Events in Eastern Europe in 1989 and the continuing turmoil in the USSR at the time were seen as having been due in large measure to the principles enunciated at Helsinki and elsewhere. Precisely because of the strategic logic of the Cold War, these had not been insisted upon to any great degree amongst the actual or potential regional allies of the West. In 1989–90, however, insistence upon such principles seemed to have a strategic purpose in itself, in so far as the collapse of one side in the Cold War could have been partially attributed to the seriousness with which populations and governments throughout the Eastern bloc took these principles.

For governments such as that of Saddam Hussein, this development meant the learning of a new language, rather unconvincingly practised in the 'open' elections for the Iraqi national assembly in 1989. However, of greater concern for Saddam Hussein, it also seemed to mean increasingly intrusive criticism of the organization of power within Iraq itself. When this came from the same states which also held the material and financial resources to which Saddam Hussein desperately wanted access, the prospects were bleak and threatening. Some measure of his anxiety in this respect can be taken from a speech he made in early 1990 at a time when these pressures were being brought to bear on Iraq. In it he acknowledged that the old 'balance' between the superpowers had now disappeared, giving the US unmatched power. The consequences of this development clearly filled him with alarm, especially since he detected a new tendency to 'inerfere in the internal affairs' of the Arab states under the cover of 'human rights slogans'.[21]

It is in the light of the working out of these two 'logics' of the post-Cold War dispensation that the invasion of Kuwait and the second Gulf War should be seen. The government of Iraq had discovered that, even though it had the resources to enable it to escape from the confining logic of the Cold War, it could not escape the new languages and rules that were emerging after the end of the Cold War. Ironically, as Saddam Hussein tried in vain to deal with the consequences of the strategic miscalculation of invading Kuwait in 1990, he sought to invoke the language and the now defunct logic of the Cold War. Up to the very last moment of the crisis, prior to the reconquest of Kuwait by the allied forces, the Iraqi regime appeared to have had a misplaced confidence in the ability of the USSR to extricate Iraq from its situation, through mediation or deterrence. The fact that the USSR had neither the capacity nor the inclination to do so in what was effectively a post-Cold War order seemed to exasperate and enfuriate Saddam Hussein, despite his own efforts to escape from the confining logic of that order during the preceding decade.

The end of the particular configuration of global power implied by the competitive structures of the Cold War did not mean that a vacuum had thereby been created. On the contrary, it only meant that new rules and new preoccupations were coming into play, dominating the emerging forms of international order and obliging states such as Iraq to abide by them or to suffer the consequences. Iraq's present predicament is in some sense, therefore, a testimony to its inability either to escape from the rules of this game or to muster the resources which would allow it to play that game with some hope of advantage.

[21] Speech by Saddam Hussein at the summit meeting of the Arab Cooperation Council, Amman, 24 Feb. 1990, quoted in O. Bengio, *Saddam Speaks on the Gulf Crisis* (Tel Aviv: Moshe Dayan Centre for Middle East and African Studies, 1992), 41–4.

9

Iran

SHAHRAM CHUBIN

INTRODUCTION

Iran was located at the very core of the Cold War in the Middle East. In 1945 it had to choose whether to seek the protection of a friendly distant state or risk annexation by a hostile neighbour. It chose an informal alignment with the West. This ensured its security against external aggression; but the corollary of this was the strengthening of the state under the Shah. Western support aided the centralization of power and reinforced the authoritarian inclinations of the monarch. As the acute threat to the country diminished, Iranians came to take its security for granted. However, increasingly, they viewed the political system under the Shah as repressive, arbitrary, and an affront as well as a source of personal insecurity. By the time they had organized to overthrow a now intolerable regime in the late 1970s, many Iranians saw the country's alignment with the West as having served the Shah's political interests more than those of Iran's national security.

The Cold War, which from the Western perspective was about containing Soviet military power, coincided with Iran's national security interests. Moreover the nature of the ensuing relationship that developed between the Shah and the US, also served Iran's interests. The Cold War inverted power relationships by allowing the weaker party to cash in on weakness. This made the local player more independent and influential than it looked locked in an unequal embrace: the weak and vulnerable partner was able to use its leverage to get its way more often than might have been expected from the respective power of the two parties. The Shah's opponents none the less successfully depicted the relationship as one of subservience, serving only US interests. Given its historical experience, the Cold War had ominous and powerful connotations in Iran. Despite the very real threat posed by the Soviet Union to Iran in the wake of the Second World War, necessitating the protection of some countervailing power, Iran was unready, psychologically and politically, for the fully-fledged relationship that soon developed between Tehran and Washington. Persia had for long been the object of imperial contention between Russia and Britain. This had created frustration and humiliation among Iranians and great sensitivity about the country's trampled sovereignty; consequently *any* relationship with a foreign power was scrutinized for evidence that it compromised the nation's interests. In this nationalist perspective, the Cold War was only the latest chapter in a long-standing rivalry of outside powers over and around Persia. In this view, Iran would be well advised to stand apart from it.

The Cold War was not only competition between two blocs over power but, perhaps more centrally, a contest between two ideologies, over their values and the bases on which society ought to be organized and run. To Iran, politically weak and socially fractured, with weak political institutions of doubtful legitimacy, the Soviet Union represented a double threat: a direct military threat, and an indirect threat through subversion and exploitation of the country's social and political weaknesses.

Given the dual nature of the superpower rivalry, alliances during the Cold War had a double function: to reassure and buttress allies domestically and to help deter external threats. Due to the Shah's tireless efforts, as well as the logic of the situation, US support for Iran was practically indistinguishable from support for the Shah. Support of allies inevitably entailed concern for the type of regime being defended and hence intruded into domestic politics. The alignment of Iran with the West reinforced the power of the throne against its domestic rivals and identified the West with the regime. This meant that the Shah's shortcomings were blamed on his allies; that opposition to the monarch entailed opposition to his backers, and that a major domestic upheaval would have corresponding consequences for Iran's foreign relations. This was to have explosive consequences for a country with Iran's past. Persian sensitivity about equality, independence, sovereignty, and domestic autonomy clashed with the requirements of defence and alignment. The needs of security in the era of the Cold War did not mix well with imperialism's legacy in Persia.

The period under review, divided into two phases, reflects the tensions inherent between the two orientations and the requirements of security versus independence. The first phase corresponds to the era of the Shah's rule, 1945–79, the second with that of the Islamic republic, 1979–89. The two are not exactly comparable; one included the beginning and the zenith of Cold War rivalry, while the second was an era in which superpower relations had been essentially stabilized, although tensions continued. Iran's domestic and foreign policies under the Shah, shaped by and during the Cold War, continue to animate politics in the Islamic republic.

Because of its contiguity to the USSR, Iran felt directly menaced and was thus intimately concerned by the territorial issues at stake in the Cold War. As a result of this external condition, its choices were more limited than those of geographically remote states like Egypt, for which non-alignment was a viable option. Because of the the nature of the relationships entailed in Iran's decision, and the historical context in which it unfolded, the impact of the Cold War on Iran was necessarily profound. However, Soviet proximity and its military threat also increased Iran's strategic importance and leverage. The Cold War was thus a period of fluctuating insecurity for Iran, but it was not without its benefits. How far in this context Iran was able to achieve its own aims internationally and regionally, how far they were distorted by the Cold War, is another focus of this chapter.

The key relationship was with the US, the leader of the Western bloc and a new player in Iran. Three areas call for emphasis: the decision to align and its impact; the military aid relationship; and the impact of the relationship with the US on domestic politics. Throughout all of these, I examine the degree to which plausible expectations about the dependency of the weaker party conform to the evidence flowing from the relationship. In general, the relationship with the US was altogether more varied, and more characterized by a two-way influence, than is often suggested. Iran was not as subservient as the Shah's detractors have sought to depict, and US support of the Shah was neither inevitable nor unwitting. Rather, it evolved over time in the absence of better alternatives; it was never total, unwavering, or characterized by illusions. Ironically, this support became most solid when the Shah appeared most secure (and indispensable), and it was precisely at that point that things began to unravel.

The first era, 1945–79, was a mixed one, with Iran able to secure some of its interests, aided by the imperatives of the Cold War. Iran was free to pursue its own interests in regional politics, largely unconstrained and to some extent assisted by the Cold War. Ultimately it was on domestic politics that the Cold War connection had the most impact. It was there that the US influence was felt or perceived most directly. US support for the Shah led in time to his assumption of absolute power; this in turn entailed political stagnation. Combined with rapid economic modernization and social disruption, this created revolutionary conditions which the monarchy was unable either to assuage or contain.

The Islamic Republic of Iran (IRI), established in February 1979, though still in a world dominated by the Cold War, chose to ignore or at least subordinate it to other considerations. How it defined and pursued its interests sharply contrasts with the Shah's Iran. This is attributable in part to different values and orientations, but in part also to a changed strategic context. By 1979 the acute national security threat to Iran from the USSR had diminished or been contained. The stabilization of the blocs during the Cold War meant that the Shah's successors had more leeway and greater freedom of choice in the identification of, and the pursual of, their interests. Second, the Iran of the Islamic republic was less dependent than postwar Iran; it inherited a stronger economy, foreign exchange reserves, considerable military equipment and annual oil revenues in the early 1980s of some \$20 billion.

On the other hand, with the decline of the Cold War, the IRI lost some of its influence. Especially as the superpower rivalry wound down in the late 1980s, Iran was less able to manoeuvre between the blocs and use its geopolitical importance to enhance its diplomatic leverage. Iran under the clerics is thus a study in contrasting reactions to changing circumstances, domestic and strategic.

A related point is the attention paid to regional politics. At the height of the Cold War, the state exposed to a direct superpower threat would be expected to consider regional issues as of secondary importance. As the primary threat diminished, there would be more room for choice. I will examine this by dividing the Cold War into periods corresponding to its intensity: (i) 1945–62; (ii) 1962–79; (iii) 1979–85; (iv) 1985–9. Phases (i) and (iii) correspond to eras of tension, and periods (iii) and (iv) to chapters of *détente*. We would expect more focus on regional concerns in the periods of thaw and less in periods of tension. However, given the differences in conditions noted earlier, and given the Islamic republic's rejection of the Cold War as irrevelant, the focus on regional foreign policy is much greater throughout the entire period of the Islamic republic than it was under the Shah. This stemmed in part from choice, in part from the different conditions of Iran in the two periods.

For our purposes, it is sufficient to ask how Iran's regional foreign policies were influenced by the Cold War? How far were they congruent with the interests of the friendly superpower? In general, the Islamic republic pursued regional policies while its predecessor focused on broader international politics. The common link for both regimes has been the relationship with the US, in the case of the former, of friendship, in the latter, of rivalry. It is in support of, or in opposition to, the US that Iran has been drawn into wider international political relationships. Domestically too, political differences in Iran today can be gauged by attitudes to 'normalization' of relations with the US. Iran's encounter with the US has been traumatic for both parties. It remains so, and is a continuing legacy of the Cold War.

IRAN UNDER THE SHAH

Cold War alignment in perspective

The Cold War was not the first experience by Iran of Russo-Soviet imperialism; this had been a recurring feature of relations for the past century. Soviet reluctance to leave Azerbaijan was to be expected. Whether dressed up as concern for border security or, more frankly, as the extension of Soviet influence in a belt of adjacent countries, the common denominator in Russo-Soviet behaviour was territorial expansion. However, Iran's distrust was not exclusively focused on the north. Britain too, for plausible reasons to do with the defence of India, competition with Russia, and interest in Persian Gulf oil, had carved out an area of influence in southern Iran and of paramountcy in the Persian Gulf.

Britain and Russia had intervened in Persia at will, promoting their own political candidates, trampling its sovereignty, and otherwise stunting its independence. Iranians had reason to suspect the ambitions of Great Powers. When they competed, Iran had to choose sides and pay the costs of that rivalry. When they collaborated, it was no better; for it was usually at Iran's expense, like the agreement of 1907, driven by European political considerations, concluded by Britain and Russia, to limit their rivalry and share power by dividing Persia into a northern and southern zone. Dissatisfied with Iran's neutrality in 1942, these two powers jointly agreed to invade the country. Even when the Soviet Union proved reluctant to withdraw from Azerbaijan after the war, Britain was not very concerned. Its priority was the extension or at least retention of its own influence in southern Iran. Hence Britain considered Soviet actions from that standpoint.[1] It was very nearly politics-as-usual.

In light of such experiences, Iranians were sceptical of a new round of Great Power rivalry, even if this time it included a new power—the US. The Iranian perspective was coloured by the past, characterized by a pervasive external interference that had left the country

---

[1] See L. Fawcett, *Iran and the Cold War: The Azerbaijan Crisis of 1946* (Cambridge: Cambridge University Press, 1992), 141–76, esp. 146–51.

politically penetrated to a degree that made its élites incapable of acting without getting permission from either the British or the Soviet
embassy; unable to take responsibility, and with a tendency to see all,
even local events, as the result of the plots and machinations of external powers. In this atmosphere, the fact that the USSR appeared the
most pressing threat, and that the US sought a global coalition to
contain it, would be taken with a grain of salt.

Despite the apparent fit between Iran's security imperatives and
those of the US, between Iran's vulnerability as a state exposed in
the front line to Soviet menace and US interest in supporting it, the
past was bound to cloud this relationship. For Iranians the implications of such a relationship for politics within the country were far
from clear. There were also risks for Iran if the superpowers were
reconciled. The balance between risks and costs of alignment versus
non-alignment were not by any means a subject of national or élite
consensus. Would the Cold War enable Iran to reclaim, or would it
further reduce, its sovereignty?

Iran thus entered into a security relationship with the US more
sceptically than its objective situation might have suggested.
However, though exposed to Soviet power, Iran's strategic importance gave it some bargaining power. Iran could neither meet the
Soviet threat by itself nor reliably count on its traditional policy of
neutrality. Soviet behaviour in Iran during and after the war suggested that a country geopolitically situated like Iran could not
expect to be neutral or non-aligned.[2]

In the past Iran had followed other strategies. It had sought to balance outside powers, negatively by symmetrical exclusion and positively by conceding influence to each in different parts of the country,
in order to keep the remainder for Iran. Another approach had been
to seek a third power as a balance to offset the two competing
powers; this had been tried at various times with Germany, and some
had hoped that the US might one day play such a role. None of these
approaches appeared workable at the start of the Cold War. Like
Turkey and Norway, also neighbours of the USSR, Iran exchanged
its (failed) neutrality policy for one offering more assurance; hence
alignment appeared a prudent response to Iran as well as other states
on the Soviet periphery.

Because superpower competition was ideological rather than territorial or specific, it brooked little compromise. In the old contest for
power between Russia and Britian, both had preferred a weak, com-
pliant Persia. In the Cold War, because the Soviet menace came from

[2] Ibid. 107, 180.

subversion as much as from crossing frontiers, there was a corresponding need for a strong centre. Allies had to be strong enough to resist subversion and intimidation. They needed to be dependably pro-Western politically. The resilience and dependability of the domestic political system in friendly states like Iran assumed strategic importance. Inevitably the question of alignment raised the question of the domestic political system and the nature of the state, bringing the US directly, as it were, into the Iranian political arena. Support for Iran meant support for a regime that would be strong and dependably pro-Western in alignment. The Shah quickly recognized the twofold potential benefits of alignment, and played on it to increase his own power.

Alignment with the US had immediate benefits for Iran, but was unprecedented and incremental. During the Azerbaijan crisis in 1945–6 and again during the oil nationalization dispute with Britain in 1952–3, when it appeared that Britain was, first, indifferent to Soviet designs and, later, unconcerned about the impact of pressure on Tehran and Iran's political stability, the US became involved. Unlike Britain, the US wanted an independent, intact, and sovereign Iran. In the oil nationalization crisis, US officials accused Britain of putting their own interests in Iran above the risks of that country's collapse. US envoy George McGhee observed that if the US was sympathetic to Iran during its dispute with Britain, 'It is only because we didn't want during the Cold War to run the risk of losing Iran'.[3]

US concern for Iran's territorial integrity was reassuring, and alone would have justified Iran's policy of alignment. But recognition by the Shah from an early date in the relationship that US interest in a strong and predictable centre in Iran coincided with his own dynastic interests also accounts for Iran's movement toward alignment. The Shah emerged from the Azerbaijan affair (when the USSR had proven reluctant to withdraw its forces from northern Iran) with a strong disposition to become the champion of alignment. This was a departure from traditional policy, and was not neutral in its domestic political ramifications. In seeking alignment to gain security guarantees and economic and military assistance, the Shah also wanted to enhance his own power and standing within Iran. He could do this if he could get the major powers to equate the stability of his regime with the security of Iran.

Iran's major politicians, like Gavam Saltaneh or Mohammed Mossadegh, by contrast, sought to rely on traditional policies, espe-

---

[3] R. W. Louis, *The British Empire in the Middle East 1945–1951* (Oxford: Clarendon Press, 1984), 664, 655, 636. For the US reaction to Britain in the earlier period cited, see Fawcett, *Iran and the Cold War*, 145–9.

cially that of negative equilibrium, relying on virtuoso statesmanship, guile, subtlety, and ingenuity to make up for the military power that Iran lacked. This type of neutralism was anathema to the US, which saw it as a misguided nationalism that flirted with communism.[4] Mossadegh, for his part, argued that Iranians saw alignment as endangering their security.[5] While Iran sought to meet the requirements to qualify for military assistance, the Shah was sensitive to the possible charge that he had sold out the country for his own ambitions. He could only take the risk if the returns were to justify it.[6]

The US for its part came to see, during the internal upheaval associated with the oil nationalization crisis, how much it relied on the Shah in the absence of political institutions, democratic traditions, or parties worthy of the name. A National Security Council (NSC) evaluation which became the basis of policy in March 1951 observed: 'The primary objective of our policy is to prevent the domination of the country by the USSR.' This meant that the US was unwilling to accept non-alignment. It concluded that if 'Iran assumes an attitude of neutrality in the "Cold War", political steps by the US and the UK to restore alignment with the free world would be required'. This conclusion was reiterated in a further NSC appraisal three months later, which noted that in the Anglo-Iranian dispute the US should adopt a position which 'will provide for the continued orientation of Iran towards the Western world', which it called an 'overriding priority'.[7] Later in the year, the secretary of state contrasted British and American policy thus: while the US wanted to prevent that country from going communist, the British wanted to 'preserve what they believe to be the last remaining bulwark of Brit. solvency; that is their overseas investment and property position'.[8] A year later, the acting secretary of state advised the US embassy in Tehran that the key question was 'how to support a non-Commie Govt. so that it can remain in control of Iran affairs'.[9]

Iran's domestic political crisis was aggravated by the oil dispute which saw groups competing in their nationalistic opposition to Britain and, in so doing, arousing popular emotions. With factions

[4] Ibid. 140; Louis, *The British Empire*, 656, quotes Dean Acheson on Mossadegh to that effect.

[5] Loy Henderson, US Ambassador in Tehran, reported to the State Dept. in a cable on 19 Jan. 1952, *The Foreign Relations of the United States, 1952–1954*, x: *Iran 1951–54* (Washington, DC: US Govt. Printing Office,1989) (henceforth *FRUS* x), 334–5.

[6] For the Shah's sensitivity about appearing to be subject to US influence, see Henderson's report in *FRUS* x, 19 Apr. 1952, No. 170, 371–4.

[7] Undated NSC study No. 107 (Mar. 1951), *FRUS* x, No. 6, 11–21; NSC 107/2, 27 June, in *FRUS* x, No. 32, 71–6.

[8] Secretary of State to the State Dept., *FRUS* x, 10 Nov. 1951, No. 129, 279.

[9] Bruce, *FRUS* x, 31 Oct. 1952, No. 233, 510.

outbidding each other and refusing compromise or mediation, the political situation looked fluid and Iran's orientation in the Cold War correspondingly uncertain. In this context the US National Security Council, in a major analysis of policy, fixed on certain points: first, it saw a priority need for a non-communist regime; second, it saw current trends as 'unfavorable to the maintenance of control by a non-Communist regime for an extended period of time', the National Front having eliminated every alternative to the communist (Tudeh) party. Third, in the event of a communist seizure of power, the US should support a non-communist government to replace it.[10]

A major restatement of US policy after the restoration of the Shah in 1954 reiterated the priorities: to keep Iran independent and free from Soviet domination and 'communist control'. Because of its location and resources, it was assumed that Iran was a target of Soviet pressure; the US objective therefore became the establishment of 'A strong stable government in Iran capable of maintaining internal security and providing some resistance to external aggression'.[11] In short, Iran's alignment required support from the US for its government and military. In aligning Iran with the US, the Shah was entitled to expect support for his political role as ruler. What else could a 'strong stable government' mean? The decision to take sides with the West in the Cold War, understandable from a national security perspective, was not neutral in its domestic political implications.

While the Shah sought a firm commitment from the US, to obtain funding and support, the process of formal alignment proved lengthy and uneven. For one thing, the departure from traditional policy that alignment entailed left the Shah open to the charge of trading US support for the throne for Iranian independence. For another, the US itself proved less than enthusiastic to embark on any new formal commitments. US adherence to the Baghdad Pact signed shortly after the oil nationalization crisis in 1955 was only as an associate member. (It was renamed CENTO after Iraq's withdrawal in 1958.) It was followed by the Eisenhower Doctrine in 1957, which promised US support to any Middle Eastern state under threat from international communism. A declaration rather than a treaty, this was hardly binding and was open to unilateral US interpretation.

The Shah was unhappy with the rewards or reassurance being offered for the risks (domestic and international) that he felt he was running by committing Iran unequivocally to the West. Turkey, by

10 NSC/136/1, *FRUS* x, 20 Nov. 1952, No. 240, 529–32.
11 NSC/5402, *FRUS* x, 2 Jan. 1954, No. 403, 865–90.

contrast, was covered by an effective guarantee in NATO, and was receiving far more substantial assistance. To strengthen Iran's hand the Shah resorted to a tactic of playing off the two superpowers against each other. In 1958 he invited Soviet officials to Tehran to discuss a non-aggression pact, suggesting a willingness to revert to neutrality or a more balanced posture between the two superpowers. This ploy had the intended effect; the US quickly offered Iran a direct commitment, in the form of an bilateral security agreement. This assurance remained weak, however, being an executive agreement rather than a treaty, and therefore lacking full political and legal weight.

The Shah's manoeuvring over a defence agreement reflected both the controversial nature of alignment in Iranian politics and the less than complete or enthusiastic US commitment to Iran. While there was a Soviet threat, Iran's interests overlapped with those of the US; but they were never completely congruent. The Shah wanted a firmer commitment, more aid and freedom of manoeuvre.

Cold War, détente, *and regional politics*

Contiguous with the USSR and with a weak security guarantee, Iran's policies needed continuous adaptation as the Cold War evolved. Iran had to consider how much its security continued to be threatened, thus requiring external assistance, and how much that defence relationship now impeded a normalization of relations with, or provoked, its neighbour. The balance between deterrence and engagement had to be continuously recalibrated in accordance with trends in international politics. For a state like Iran there was an additional consideration, etched into the national consciousness by history; the need to anticipate and be one step ahead of a Great Power *rapprochement*, which could come at its expense.

Under the monarchy, the Cold War era breaks down conveniently into two periods: 1945–62 and 1963–79. These roughly correspond to phases of tension and *détente*, although within each period there were fluctuations. The two phases respectively also correspond to periods when Iran was more concerned with the Cold War, and to a preoccupation with regional affairs. They also reflect differences in Iran's capabilities; in the first it was weaker, in the second richer and more confident.

The first period was one of progressive US involvement with Iran. US aid under the Point 4 programme and limited military assistance encouraged Iran to take the plunge and make a decision about its stance. The intensity of the threat from the USSR at this time claimed almost exclusive attention. The threat was urgent and direct and, in the first phase, military. The US appeared as the salvation. By the early 1950s the direct military threat gave way to that of subversion, and exploitation of indigenous discontent through local communist parties or agents. The Iranian Communist Party, the Tudeh, was the largest such party in the Middle East. It was supported by urban elements and intellectuals, and benefited from the absence of other political parties and festering social and political discontent. The Tudeh used hostility toward British imperialism to oppose any pro-Western alignment. It clearly also had Soviet support, and appeared intent on infiltrating the armed forces. Soviet threats and heavy-handedness from 1945 to 1962, with very few intervals, virtually pushed Iran into the Western camp and kept it there throughout this period.

The Cuban missile crisis in October 1962 was a seminal event in the Cold War. The superpowers were clearly edging toward a limited *détente*. Iran acted promptly and gave the Soviets formal assurances that Iranian territory would not be used for hostile activity against the USSR. Reflecting a certain disllusionment with President Kennedy (see below) the Shah also sought to reactivate contacts with the USSR, to improve his security and his leverage on the US. However, Iran repositioned itself between the superpowers primarily to anticipate events lest it be caught out if the US–USSR *détente* deepened.

After 1962, Iran concentrated on building bridges to its northern neighbour, without relinquishing its security ties with the US. Cooperation with the USSR centred on border projects at first, but then expanded in the mid-1960s to a steel mill complex and deeper commercial relations. Visits of delegations and exchanges were stepped up. In 1965 the Shah told his hosts on a visit to Moscow, without a trace of irony, that if Iran could have chosen its neighbours it would have chosen the USSR. Differences on strategic issues and Iran's general support for the West (or the status quo) continued, but in a more cordial way. Trade which had grown to $1 billon a year now included gas sales, and were set to double by the end of the 1970's.

The Shah's strategy was deliberate to bind the USSR into a pattern of peaceful transactions and to give it a stake in a prosperous Iran. He continued to distrust Soviet regional ambitions: its support for Iraq, for south Yemen, for communists in Afghanistan, and for 'liberation movements'. The USSR, in turn, was concerned by Iran's military programmes and the Shah's ambitions to play a leading role in regional affairs. The Soviet leaders were none the less impressed by his staying power and his pragmatism. By 1978, Iran's relations with the Soviet Union were excellent; the Shah's strategy appeared to be working. Moscow, despite a Treaty of Friendship concluded in 1972, had not supported Iraq against Iran in their rivalry from 1969 to 1975. By the time of the revolution the Soviets, like the Americans, had come around to believing that there really was no realistic alternative to the Shah.

Iran's relations with the US changed considerably after the mid-1960s. Embroiled in Vietnam, the US came to appreciate loyal, uncritical, and helpful allies like Iran. As Iran increased its oil revenues it became less dependent on the US, which permitted a more balanced and healthy relationship to develop. Increasingly from the late 1960s, Iran was singled out as a success story, the Shah treated as an elder statesman, and Iran seen as a dependable regional asset rather than a weak Cold War client.

As the period of intense Cold War rivalry receded and the superpower relationship became stabilized, the danger of a military confrontation arising from a deliberate act of aggression by the USSR also diminished. Cold War politics and priorities which had dominated the concerns of the superpowers and their allies, including Iran, were no longer as pressing. After the mid-1960s, even for states that considered the Cold War a priority, regional politics and concerns resurfaced. Hitherto Iran's primary security concern had been to balance Soviet power. The Cold War which arose from the West's decision to check Soviet expansion exactly reflected Iran's priorities.

Were Iran's regional policies dictated by the Cold War and did the passing of the Cold War affect Iran's regional policies? While the Cold War may have distorted regional politics and alignments for others, it did not have such an effect on Iran. Unlike more distant Middle Eastern states which focused on Israel or on an 'Arab Cold War', but like Turkey, for Iran the Cold War took priority over regional politics. To some extent Iran viewed regional politics from this standpoint. It could not afford to treat states inclining toward the USSR with indifference, or to see regional alignments as separate from the overarching US–Soviet rivalry.

During the early, tense phase of the Cold War, Iran was so preoccupied with the Soviet threat that its 'regional' policies were very much a function of that dominant conflict. Its cooperation with Turkey, Iraq, and Pakistan was based on this. By the late 1950s, after the revolution in Iraq and the rise of Arab nationalism, Iran became concerned by the spread of radicalism in the region under the aegis of ambitious regional states. The Shah was particularly concerned that the US might be unable or unwilling to deal with this threat, for which its alliance systems had not been devised. Between 1958 and 1963 it had become clear first in Iraq and later in the Yemen (1963–4), when the US had sought good relations with Abdul Nasser, that Washington might prefer to accommodate radical trends in the region rather than confront them. Thereafter, regional affairs claimed more of the Shah's attention.

To deal with the gap between the existing security mechanism (CENTO) and the probable threats from regional sources, the Shah devised two responses. First, in 1965 he sought to institutionalize cooperation with Pakistan and Turkey in the Regional Cooperation for Development organization (RCD) and extended military assistance to these states in 1965 and 1974 respectively. Second, to contain Nasser in Yemen, he improved relations with Saudi Arabia, on the basis of Islamic solidarity.

It was clear that the Shah's definition of security encompassed a policy supportive of the status quo and was antagonistic to radical change. It was also evident that as long as they were genuinely regional in origin and inspiration, the US did not automatically oppose these or define them as threats in the same way as the Shah. There was thus a gap between Iran's view of regional politics and those of the US. This difference was evident between 1965 and 1969. Thereafter the advent of the Nixon administration brought a shift to a more geopolitical perspective, stressing the importance of containing the local allies of the USSR, and denying Moscow any momentum in the Third World.

After 1969, the Shah had no need to emphasize the Soviet dimension of regional threats to the Americans, for President Nixon was receptive, and the impending withdrawal of Britain from the sensitive Persian Gulf underlined the geostrategic importance of Iran. The impending 'vacuum', as some referred to it, combined with the recognition that the US would be unable to replace the British presence, led to the enunciation of the Nixon Doctrine in Guam in June 1969. In this the US looked to its regional allies in important parts of the world to do more for regional security. The Shah was willing, and also had the money to finance the means, to do so. The intersection of US strategic needs and the Shah's ambitions for Iran in regional affairs made Iran a major strategic asset for the US in the 1970s. This time, though, it was not to contain a Soviet military threat but to assure regional security from threats from all sources, including those from Soviet allies.

Thus after 1969 priorities shifted to regional politics, and to the Persian Gulf in particular. In this period there was a close parallelism of interest between Iran and the US. (It was so close and so evident that even a sceptical President like Jimmy Carter was unable to gainsay it.) If Iran under the Shah in this period acted as a 'regional gendarme', it was not because it was paid to do so, or was assigned the mission, but rather because it defined its interests in this way. These interests happened to coincide with those of the US and the West more generally. Iran's good relations with the pro-Western states of the Persian Gulf and its poor relations with Iraq and South Yemen were due to Iran's own views, not those of Washington. Similarly, the *rapprochement* with Egypt after 1970 was in Iran's own interests, anticipated that of the US, and was not dictated by Washington.

In the case of Iran's border conflict with Iraq, it appears that the local state, Iran, used the superpower's interest in good ties to obtain assistance in pursuing a local dispute. Despite the Iraq–Soviet treaty of 1972, and Soviet arms supplies, there was little reason to believe that the USSR in fact supported Iraq in its dispute with Iran, or that this conflict had anything much to do with the superpowers. Nevertheless, the Shah was able to obtain US assistance (for the Iraqi Kurds fighting their government) by depicting Iraq as a potential agent probing Western responses and testing its resolve. In this one case it seems that Iran as a regional state was able to use 'Cold War thinking' as a means of, and justification for, obtaining assistance. There is no evidence of the reverse situation, i.e. where the Cold War or its alignments created regional antagonisms or sparked conflicts. However, differing orientations in the Cold War did tend to obstruct reconciliation between states and to exacerbate rivalries, for example Iran and Egypt, and possibly Iran and Iraq. However, Iran chose its regional policies and friends according to its interests. That these often tended to be states that were moderate, conservative, and pro-Western was not especially surprising.

Iran's regional ambitions, its relationship with its neighbours, and its interaction with a wide variety of states were the products of its own leader's decisions and judgements. To a considerable extent they coincided with the interests of the Western states. This was not necessarily deliberate: within the alignment that the Shah had chosen, he had every incentive to play an independent role. Sensitivity about being labelled a dependent of the West (or a 'puppet') was not simply an issue of pride; in terms of domestic politics it was a liability weakening the monarch's legitimacy. The Shah therefore sought, when this was feasible, to put a maximum distance between his own and Western policies or initiatives. In 1965 he inaugurated what he referred to as his 'independent national policy', emphasizing in foreign policy what he needed to get across domestically— that he was his own man.

US military assistance: intervention and independence

Reza Shah, a military officer, had taken pains to build up Iran's military as the loyal instrument of the monarchy rather than as a genuinely national institution. His son, Mohammed Reza, determined to do likewise. His enthusiasm for military modernization and, some would say, arms technology in general was such that he set the pace in the expansion of Iran's military establishment. His ambitions, however, exceeded Iran's resources, and propelled him to increase his demands on the US. While the Cold War required the defence of allies and prudence dictated that allies be made relatively self-reliant, the Shah's demands were still usually in excess of what the US was willing to provide. While the US could afford to take a more detached attitude, Iran as the small state adjacent to the superpower threat could afford to take no chances. In the domain of military assistance then, the stage was set for a tug-of-war between the Shah and various administrations. Instructive in this relationship is

that it was usually Iran that sought arms while the US tried to set limits on these;

that in the unequal relationship, in which Iran was notionally the 'client', it was more often Tehran that was able to have its way by using the leverage afforded it by its geopolitical importance, room for manoeuvre, and weakness;

that the concentration on the military relationship necessitated by the Cold War was bound to have political implications within Iran.

The arms relationship between the US and Iran started on a small scale in the Second World War and grew slowly. The US showed no enthusiasm for assisting in building Iran's military beyond a bare minimum. It preferred to encourage military cooperation regionally, and was concerned that any arms supplied to Iran would be wasted—lost if the Soviets should attack. So it was the Shah who was the driving force behind the programme. In the earlier period of real dependency, the impecunious monarch cajoled, pleaded, complained, and threatened to reconsider Iran's alignment if the US did not stop treating Iran 'like a stepchild'.[12]

As Iran's bargaining power and importance increased, it was able to acquire more and better arms, often against the inclination of sections of the US governmental bureaucracy. To the argument that the US fed the Shah's appetite or was responsible for Iran's militariza-

---

[12] The US Ambassador in Tehran (Henderson) reported a conversation with the Shah in which he made this reference; *FRUS* x, 8 Mar. 1954, No. 434, 956.

tion, there was a plausible defence: as a supplier the US could exercise a restraining influence which would be absent if it renounced any relationship.[13]

The US started the training of the Iranian army and gendarmerie to reduce the pretext for foreign powers to intervene. By 1945 'only the Shah–military alliance' (in the words of a historian of the period) appeared able to offer the security that was necessary for the Cold War.[14] The Shah exploited his apparent indispensability. In 1953 he told the US ambassador that with a loyal army he could create order in Iran and ride out its difficulties.[15]

After his restoration with US and British help in 1953, the Shah took the initiative in asking the US to fund an army that could do more than maintain internal security. He argued that without some capacity to defend itself from external threats, such an army would be too demoralized to stand up to Soviet intimidation. He wanted a capability that would at least impose a 'delaying action' on an aggressor. The Shah saw the importance of the military more broadly, arguing that by strengthening it

Iran would become a self-respecting country with enough confidence in its future to develop its economy, to play an appropriate political and economic role in the world and overcome an inferiority complex which has plagued and weakened it for so many years.[16]

With strong support from the US ambassador, the Shah was able to increase Iran's share of military assistance after 1954. This was due to changed thinking in Washington. After the Shah's struggle for power with radical nationalists like Mossadegh, which the US saw as indistinguishable from communists, Iran's political stability assumed new importance. Washington now saw military aid as a means of political influence as well as an investment in the defence of the 'free world'. In a major restatement of US policy, it was acknowledged that Iran was under pressure and that it was of 'critical importance to the US that Iran remain an independent nation'. Thus one report concluded:

[13] This was an argument Secretary of Defence Robert McNamara made to Congress, International Development and Security, Senate Committee on Foreign Relations, 14 June 1961, in *Executive Sessions of the Senate Foreign Relations Committee* (Historical Series), vol. xiii, pt. 2, 87th Congress, 1st Session, 1961 (henceforth *Executive Sessions 1961*) (Washington, DC: US Govt. Printing Office, made public Dec. 1984), 124.

[14] Fawcett, *Iran and the Cold War*, 131–2,140.

[15] See Henderson's report to the Dept. of State, *FRUS* x, 18 Sept. 1953, No. 368, 799, and 797–801.

[16] Henderson to Dept. of State, *FRUS* x, 14 Mar. 1954, No. 439, 957, 955–8. Illustrative of many exchanges on military requests by Tehran of Washington; see *FRUS* x, 29 Sept. 1953, No. 307, 805; 14 Nov. 1953, No. 385, 831–4; 17 Dec. 1953, No. 396, 851–3.

Military aid to Iran has a great political importance apart from its military impact. Over the long term, the most effective instrument for maintaining Iran's orientation towards the West is the monarch [*sic*] which in turn has the army as its only real source of power. US military aid serves to improve army morale, cement army loyalty to the Shah and thus consolidate the present regime and provide some assurance that Iran's current orientation towards the West will be perpetuated.[17]

Later that year, the Secretary of State sought to convince his counterpart in the Defence Department on the need for more aid to Iran, observing, 'Additional assistance to the armed forces will offer a means of influencing the Shah and other leaders.'[18]

In deciding to expand military assistance, the US did not then or later ignore the need to avoid burdening or straining the Iranian economy. Judging from US documents, the question whether a military that weighed heavily on society might itself constitute a threat to stability and order was one frequently considered by the US government. Washington acknowleged the need to expand Iran's military, 'while bearing in mind the need to stabilize Iran's economy'.[19] The US ambassador, Henderson, advised the State Department that the US should emphasize to the Iranians that the army should not be such as to make demands on the budget in the future or to 'retard the development of Iran's national economy'. During the Shah's visit to Washington in 1954, the president was advised to tell him: 'we do not want to develop a military establishment in Iran that would be an undue burden on the national economy.'[20]

The Shah's insistence on 'more', and US reluctance to provide it, are a continuing theme in the Cold War relationship of the two countries until about 1969. How significant was US aid in this period in absolute terms and compared to aid to other countries? It is worth recalling that initially the Iranian politicians, suspicious that it might compromise their independence, were reluctant to accept even the small amounts on offer. In 1948 the Majlis (parliament) considered the terms of a *loan* from the US for the purchase of war surplus, and after heated debate grudgingly approved acceptance of only $10 million of the $25 million on offer. From 1946 to 1951 military aid *credits* totalled $16 million; there was no economic assistance. In May 1950 an agreement made Iran eligible for *grant* aid. Four years later this had amounted to a total of $101.4 million in military aid allo-

---

[17] NSC Statement of Policy toward Iran, *FRUS* x, 2 Jan. 1954, No. 403, 868–70.
[18] Foster Dulles to Secretary Wilson, *FRUS* x, 8 Nov. 1954, No. 503, 1063.
[19] Acting Secretary of State to US Embassy in Tehran, *FRUS* x, 1 Mar. 1954, No. 430, 933.
[20] Cable in *FRUS* x, 4 Mar. 1954, No. 431, 937. See also Secretary of State to Tehran Embassy, *FRUS* x, 13 Dec. 1954, No. 505, 1072.

cated to Iran, of which only half had been delivered. This figure included training and transportation. Compared to Iran's annual total of some $11.5 million, Turkey's annual average (1950–60) was some $100 million. After 1954 the Shah requested increased military assistance (and was supported in this by the US military mission in Iran). For the next three years the total was raised to $360 million.[21] In fact, total military aid during 1950–7 amounted to $400 million, not an extravagant sum considering the state of Iran's military after the Second World War. Ill-equipped and undermanned (87,000), Iranian armed forces had lacked basic infrastructure as well as housing.

After the crises of 1957–8 in Iraq and Lebanon, the Shah was able to obtain more aid. However, to do so he had to indulge in brinksmanship, threatening to come to terms with the USSR if his defence needs were not met by the West. As noted earlier, the Shah wanted a firmer defence commitment and more aid. The US embassy in Tehran reported that 'the Shah's motive in entering negotiations with the USSR was primarily blackmail for more US aid and resentment against what he believes to have been US niggardliness and unfairness over the years re. aid'. It continued that the core of the problem was the Shah's 'insatiable appetite' for arms, and noted that the Baghdad Pact 'meant nothing to people or Gov. of Iran other than strong hope of massive aid and/or territorial guarantee from the US in return for Iranian adherence pact'.[22] The tone of exasperation suggests the writer's incomprehension that Iran's motives for alignment were based on a cost–benefit calculus.

By 1961 Iran had expanded its forces to roughly 200,000 and had absorbed some $530 million in US aid. The US advisory group had also increased from 200 to 700 people.[23] It appeared that Iran had convinced the US of the need for expanded assistance. However, this was shortlived. With the Kennedy administration, the US attitude again changed, resulting in a cutback in military assistance. Concern for the economic burden of Iran's military expenditures resurfaced, but this time the message was more brusque. Iran's military assistance was cut from $72 to $60 million and supporting assistance from $22 to $15 million. A senior official told Congress confidentially:

---

[21] The amount is less impressive if it is considered that this was to include ammunition reserves, defence support (roads, airfields), housing, reception facilities, and relocation; *FRUS* x, 884, 1052.

[22] Tehran Embassy to Secretary of State, No. 1425, 30 Jan. 1959 [declassified 29 Aug. 1979; photocopy].

[23] See testimony of Admiral Grantham to US Senate Foreign Relations Committee, *Executive Sessions 1961*, 141.

I think the Shah now understands that we are now more concerned with economic and social development . . . than with other criteria. . . . The word is getting through to him that we are not interested in maintaining his prestige [through military expenditures] at the cost of doing these constructive things.[24]

Repeatedly the question arose: what was the right size for the Iranian armed forces? A recurring US argument, that whatever it did Iran could not stop a Soviet advance and therefore it should not bother to try, was somewhat less self-evident and attractive to the Iranian nationalist than to the foreign strategist. But the argument that the burden of a large military could aggravate Iran's political and economic problems, and hence her security, could not be dismissed as easily. To justify their expansion, the Shah referred in 1959 to armed forces too large for internal security and too small to assure security against an external threat. The same phrase was used by Senator William Fulbright to justify their contraction. President Kennedy's biographer, Ted Sorenson, was to use the same image in criticism of the Shah's fixation on the military.[25]

Fluctuations in the level of military aid to Iran reflected changing assessments in Washington of the contribution of arms to security, and the state of the Cold War itself, as well as the importance of Iran in the Cold War. But they also reflected the Iran–US relationship and the bargaining power of the two parties. The phases in the relationship and Iran's military expenditures are revelatory.

1. In the first phase, 1946–64, Iran was dependent on US generosity. Military assistance extended until 1954 was intended for internal security, with some provision thereafter for external threats. *Grant* aid became significant only after crises and pressure from Iran in 1958. It came to a halt during 1961–3 with the Kennedy administration, which put emphasis on political reform and developmental assistance. Concerned by US reluctance to underwrite the cost of upgrading Iranian forces, the Shah now also felt it necessary to match those of regional adversaries.[26]

2. From 1964 grant aid was reduced, terminating in December 1965 when Iran was declared a 'developed' country. Thereafter mil-

---

[24] Phillips Talbott, Assistant Secretary of State for Near East Affairs, to Senators Church and Humphrey, *Executive Sessions 1961*, 157–60.

[25] See respectively the Shah to US Ambassador Wailes, in the telegram from Wailes in Tehran to Secretary of State, 30 Jan. 1959; declassified 29 Aug. 1979 (TS) (No. 1425, 30 Jan. 1959). Fulbright, *Executive Sessions 1961*, 26 June 1961, 277; and T. Sorenson, *Kennedy* (New York: Harper & Row, 1965), 628.

[26] J. C. Hurewitz, *Middle East Politics: The Military Dimension* (New York: Praeger, 1969), 265–95.

itary *sales* replaced military assistance. With Iran paying, the Shah had more say in the amounts and the content of what Iran obtained. Iran's military expenditures grew as its oil revenues soared, rising *tenfold* from 2.5 billion rials (1953–4) to 14.2 billion rials (1960–1) to 23.9 billion rials (1966–7). Even so, military expenditures were unable to keep pace with oil revenues, which rose *sixtyfold* between 1954 ($10 million) to 1966 ($600 million). The US 'contribution' continued now, in the form of sales: $48 million in 1965; $90 million in 1966; $161 million in 1967; $100 million in 1968; and $104 million in 1969.[27]

3. The third period, 1970–4, saw a shift to a more commercial relationship, with cash purchases guaranteed by the export/import bank. These amounted to $120 million in 1971, $200 million in 1972, $300 million in 1973, and $200 million in 1974. Thereafter Iran's purchases were strictly cash, and therefore unconstrained by any US controls. In (fiscal years) 1972–5, sales increased sevenfold from $525 million to $3.91 billion. Overall sales 1972–6 totalled $10.4 billion.[28]

These phases correspond to Iran's capabilities and relative bargaining power. In the first (1945–58) Iran was poor and weak, dependent on its Cold War patron to expand its armed forces and seeking a firm security commitment. It had few options and was thus essentially subject to the preferences of the US. Even after the expansion of military assistance in 1954 and again in 1958, the Shah wanted larger forces than the US was willing to underwrite. There was little he could do about it, except to manoeuvre as in 1958 to get better terms.

The second phase saw a change in the relationship reflected in the shift from grant to credit and then to cash. The 'client' now had greater freedom of choice as to how much and what to buy. In 1966 the Shah had already given a preview of his determination to have a say in the type of military equipment Iran should have. Replaying his tactic of 1958, he again used the threat of moving closer to the Soviet bloc to gain better terms from Washington, in this case to obtain Phantom F4 aircraft.[29]

[27] Ibid. 284–6.
[28] 'US Military Sales to Iran', Staff Report to the Subcommitteee on Foreign Assistance of the Committee on Foreign Relations, US Senate, 94th Congress, 2nd Session (Washington, DC: US Govt. Printing Office, 1976), vii. 38–54 and esp. 58.
[29] The Shah was concerned that Iraq had received the supersonic MIG-21 and that Washington was heedless of Iran's regional defence needs. In making overtures to the USSR the Shah was careful this time not to leave the Soviets without some compensation. (In 1958 his use of the Soviet connection to improve bargaining power with the US had been cynical in the extreme, leaving Moscow nothing for the exercise and leading to worsened relations with Tehran.) In 1966, by contrast, the Shah was careful not to antagonize the USSR, and went

Iran had demonstrated that in an unequal relationship the stronger power did not always get its way: there was scope for reverse leverage, in which the weaker partner acquired bargaining power. Once Iran was able to buy for credit or cash, it was no longer as subject to US restraining influence. Increased revenues gave Iran greater autonomy to decide its own level of military spending, subject to neither US strategic priorities, nor congressional lecturing, moralizing, or vacillation. As its oil revenues increased, Iran appeared more stable. Its contribution to regional security, especially in the Persian Gulf, now came to be valued rather than discouraged. Arguments for arms appeared more persuasive in Washington, when they were being paid for.

In 1972 President Nixon reduced the bureaucratic obstacles to Iran's arms purchases. The relationship between Iran and the US depended on the rhythms of the Cold War, on the personal relations between heads of state, and on the respective leverage of the two states. By the mid-1970s the client–patron relationship had become closer to one of partnership. But the acquisition of arms, however justifiable in terms of Cold War threats, did not necessarily deal with threats closer to home.

Domestic politics during the Cold War

As a struggle between two systems, the Cold War was not only about military security or alliances but also about the viability and vitality of two distinct political-economic systems. It was in large part a contest about the future political and economic direction of countries like Iran. As a revolutionary state, the USSR served as a model for politically disenchanted Iranians, who might count on practical assistance as well as inspiration from it. Iran's alignment with the West was thus a double engagement, which sought to compensate for its military weakness and to tie itself firmly to US support of the status quo.

The logic of the Cold War, which saw the superpowers seek allies in their competition, was well adapted to Iran's needs. While one superpower sought commitment against the other, the regional state sought as wide a commitment as possible, including against regional threats and domestic enemies. Because of the interconnection between the external and internal dimensions of security, the domestic politics of Iran were inextricably tied up with the Cold War. The

through with a largely symbolic arms purchase (of jeeps, and armoured carriers.) Iran also received the Phantom aircraft, the only Middle East country other than Israel to do so. Some remain, barely operational, in 1996.

US could not escape association with the regime or government with which it cooperated. US commitment to Iran as a state could not, as a matter of practical politics, be separated from support for the incumbent regime, i.e. the Shah. The US could scarcely be expected to create or discover strong institutions or a tradition of healthy and vigorous politics where none existed. Inevitably, in the absence of institutions, it fell back on personalities. Yet this was not without trepidation, doubt, and reluctance most noticeably in the Kennedy and Carter administrations. The Shah for his part used the absence of mediating institutions to press for a personal link and commitment.

The impact of the Cold War was profound in Iran's domestic politics. By strengthening Iran the West (principally the US) reinforced the Shah's power. This meant support for one of several political players and identification with his (authoritiarian) policies. It also meant a domestic polarization of politics in which the Shah's opponents became hostile to his foreign supporters, the Western powers. The strains of the Cold War required a strong leader in Iran. It need not have been the Shah. Historically the US had little affinity with monarchs. The Shah's defects were known. The prime consideration was the unity of the country and he came to be seen as the best bet to keep the country and military together under central control. In 1944 the US ambassador, Leland Morris, noted that the weakness at the top needed to be eliminated 'either through the hand of the Shah or by the rise of a strong man.'[30]

The US came to favour the Shah, for, compared to the politician-nationalists, he appeared more predictable and cooperative, spoke the language of the Cold war more persuasively than others, and seemed more likely to bring order to the country. US commitment to the Shah still only came slowly, remained conditional and subject to fluctuations, and was entered into tentatively with few illusions. The Shah's political stature grew only slowly, in part as a consequence of the decline in credibility of other politicians. In 1945–7 he appeared 'almost an inconsequential figure', yet by 1949–51 he seemed to be someone to be reckoned with, 'not least as a willing collaborator'.[31] After the assassination of the prime minister, Razmara, in 1951, an official US assessment was that there was a need for a 'firm hand and forceful direction if situation is not to become so unsettled that Communists can take over with relatively little difficulty'. It concluded: 'Only person in [State] Department opinion who could provide this direction under present circumstances is [the] Shah

---

[30] Quoted in Fawcett, *Iran and the Cold War*, 130.
[31] Louis, *The British Empire*, 636.

and we believe that US and Britain should support him in every feasible way and encourage him to act with force and vigor in (this) crisis.'[32] This was confirmed by an NSC directive that concluded that Iran needed a government that could keep internal order and that was determined to resist Soviet aggression. It suggested that the US should extend political support, 'primarily to the Shah as the only present source of continuity of leadership'.[33]

During the oil nationalization crisis with Britain, the emergence of Mossadegh as a populist figure, and the Shah's palpable weakness in competing with or resisting him in the political struggle, strained the emerging US commitment. Mossadegh's popularity in opposing Britain led to the US ambassador's estimate of him as 'the outstanding political figure'. In contrast, the Shah was depicted during the crisis as using the US 'like a security blanket' in seeking advice and approval for every act.[34] During this crisis the Department of State doubted the Shah's political survival, a judgement shared by the embassy with the qualification that 'he might still emerge with a certain vestige of influence'.[35] Again and again US officials referred to the Shah's defects, in particular his refusal to tolerate a strong prime minister or to support his prime ministers.[36] This was not balanced by a willingness to exercise 'positive leadership'. Indeed, 'his habitual vacillation' made his own or other leadership impossible.[37] Instead the Shah played on his principal asset, the weakness of political institutions, which he judged or hoped made him indispensable. In 1951 he told the US ambassador that if Britain turned against him personally, 'our monarchial system which in my opinion, is the main stabilising influence in this country, can collapse'. Two years later he declared: 'If I fail, [there is] no alternative but communism.'[38]

In light of the revolution it sometimes appears that US support for the Shah was inevitable and firm. In fact it was more tenuous than

[32] Acting Secretary of State Webb to US Embassy, Tehran, *FRUS* x, 7 Mar. 1951, No. 4, 8.

[33] NSC Proposal for Statement of Policy, NSC 107/2, *FRUS* x, 27 June 1951, No. 31, 73.

[34] See US Ambassador to Tehran Henderson's report to the State Dept., *FRUS* x, 10 Mar. 1953, No. 316, 706–8. Earlier, the ambassador had reported that he had 'leaned over backwards not to get involved in Iranian internal affairs' (28 May 1952, No. 176, 386).

[35] *FRUS* x, 7 Mar. 1953, No. 314, 703.

[36] See Henry Grady, *FRUS* x, 23 Jan. 1951, No. 2, 4; Henderson, *FRUS* x, 23 Feb. 1953, No. 303, 679; 7 Mar. 1953, No. 314, 702–3.

[37] See Office of National Estimates, *FRUS* x, 1 Mar. 1953, No. 310, 689; Secretary of State to US Embassy, Tehran, 3 Mar. 1953, No. 311, 691.

[38] Reported by Ambassador Henderson, *FRUS* x, 30 Sept. 1951, No. 98, 187; 23 Aug. 1953, No. 353, 763. Later on, when under pressure from the US, the Shah demonstrated 'the power of the weak' by pointedly observing that 'this kingship business has given me nothing personally but a headache', implying a willingess to abdicate and leave the US with a headless ally. For this episode and similar tactics, see S. Chubin and S. Zabih, *Iran's Foreign Relations: A Small State in a Zone of Great Power Conflict* (Berkeley: University of California Press, 1974).

it appeared. His personal weakness was known; his political ineptitude, vanity, and procrastination were all recognized, and it was even anticipated that his political base would in time be eroded and become vulnerable.[39] Nevertheless, over time the Shah became a fixture: he saw off all his potential rivals, Iran's economy prospered, and he grew more in confidence and correspondingly in stature. Above all, as he became stronger he became more resistant to US influence and the US more reluctant to antagonize him. The Cold War thrust the question of national security into the forefront of priorities for Iran. The Shah was able to convince the US that the monarchy and the military were the only bulwarks against communism that merited support. In the absence of much competition from Iran's politicians, whose nationalism veered toward neutralism, the US settled for the monarchy less out of conviction than by default.

In building up the military, the US contributed to a distortion of Iran's political system in favour of the monarchy. Where Mossadegh had seen alignment as a danger to Iran's independence and rejected it, the Shah, emphasizing the Soviet threat, embraced it. In strengthening the military under the Shah, ostensibly for national security purposes, the US and the Shah contributed to the perpetuation of a royal absolutism. They skewed Iran's political development by building up institutions for repression rather than contributing to the creation or strengthening of representative institutions or groups, or to the pluralism necessary for a civil society.

As the Shah became more confident (itself in part a product of US backing) he overrode the constitutional restraints on him. By the late 1950s he no longer accounted to the Majlis in detail for military affairs, and had abolished the legislative restraints on the size of the American military and gendarmerie missions. In 1964 he signed a status of forces agreement (SOFA) with the US exempting US soldiers, in cases of infractions of the law, from trial in Iranian courts. This gave an obscure cleric named Khomeini the kind of symbolic issue, redolent of capitulations and subservience, which could be used to tap into the frustration of the people and their sense of injury.[40]

In building up the military, the Shah created a powerful force at considerable expense. How effective it would have been in combat was never tested. It was at least as important in terms of domestic

[39] See the text of an anonymous British memorandum in the US files discussing the events of 1953 and noting the political and social forces present in Iran that would in time weaken the Shah, *FRUS* x, 2 Sept. 1953, No. 362, 780–8; see also Memorandum from Acting Special Assistant to Secretary of State for Intelligence, (Fisher Howe) to the Secretary of State (Dulles), 'Political Prospects in Iran: Intelligence Note', 30 July 1954, No. 485, 1041–2.

[40] See Roy Mottahedeh, 'Iran's Foreign Devils', *Foreign Policy* 38 (spring 1980), 19–34.

politics, where its loyalty to the Shah was unquestioned. Unlike other military forces, it was never a competitor for power (as in the Arab states) or a custodian of democracy (as in Turkey). It was never autonomous enough to become an interest group, but the Shah's determination to keep it loyal made it the object of special favours. The Iranian military symbolized the connection with the US, not least by the image of an 'umbilical relationship' of logistical dependence.[41] By the late 1970s over 12,000 officers had been trained (since 1947), attesting to the close ties with the US.[42] It was this tie that made the Shah's successors distrustful of the armed forces and determined to sever its link with the US.

Iran's alignment may have been prudent policy against the Soviet threat; it was certainly good politics for the monarchy. US support for Iran came to mean in practice support for the Shah and the military. Before the Cold War, Iran's domestic politics had been penetrated by outside powers; politicians were supported by, and on the payroll of, Russia and Britain. The displacement of that imperial rivalry was to replace a two-sided competition with one even less representative. It ended the process of political evolution that had started after the Second World War, which might have led to a more plural system of quasi-parliamentary democracy. The dominant position of the US in Iran had the effect of reinforcing the Shah and marginalizing his critics as well as his opponents. It squeezed and eliminated the political centre and reinforced royal absolutism.

The Cold War tended to encourage polarization. In Iran the Soviet/Tudeh threat appeared to loom large, both because of Soviet proximity and Iran's apparent vulnerability. As late as 1961 Khrushchev told Walter Lippman, a US journalist, that Iran was like a 'rotten apple' ready to fall into the Soviet lap. The Shah banned the Tudeh party in 1953. It was at that time the largest communist party in the Middle East, with roughly 25 per cent support. It was using Iranian nationalism to promote anti-Western (principally anti-British) policies, implicitly favouring the USSR. The Shah saw the Tudeh and the Soviet threat as linked. They constituted a threat both on the streets with mobs and in the potential infiltration of the armed forces. The Shah was as concerned about this dimension as much as by a direct military threat. He foresaw Soviet intimidation and subversion to which, without US support, he would be powerless to respond. He therefore viewed the Soviet/Tudeh menace as marching hand in hand, requiring a joint response. One part of the response

---

[41] A phrase used in a famous report of arms sales to Iran: 'US Military Sales to Iran', 51.

[42] See S. Chubin, *Security in the Persian Gulf: The Role of the Outside Powers* (Aldershot, Hants: Gower, 1981), 5, 17.

was harsh repression, the second was normalization of relations with Moscow. From the mid-1960s the Shah sought to give the USSR a stake in a stable Iran, and an incentive to prefer his regime to any other Iranian interlocutor.

In the tense early Cold War period, the threat of insurrection and mob activity during periods of domestic crisis, of national coalitions including communist parties, that were quickly subverted and made into instruments of communist domination, were real threats. In Iran the Shah early determined not to tolerate 'fellow travellers' like the National Front, which would make common cause with the communists and become first their ally and then their unwitting dupe. In such a context it was easy to fall into an 'us and them' mentality, in which domestic politics took on the polarization of international politics.

The Shah's pronounced preference for the status quo made him distrustful of the Soviet Union and its allies. It also made him aware of the need to neutralize the domestic threat by weakening the link between the USSR and his domestic enemies. He did this in part by the improvement of relations with Moscow. Commercial ties, stable borders, and predictability were all welcome to the USSR. Moscow showed that it had no compunction about selling out its local allies for improved relations with the Shah. The USSR had not shown any inclination to support the Tudeh in the critical period in 1953, an opportunity that was not to be repeated. This suggested that the USSR viewed the Tudeh more as an instrument for spying and perhaps bargaining than as the principal vehicle for gaining control over the government or seizing power in Iran. As a consequence, the Tudeh party languished as a minority or fringe group, never regaining the popular support it had enjoyed in the early 1950s.

The other element in neutralizing the threat of radical change from any quarter was to appropriate its programme. The Shah simply became a radical reformer, the promoter of revolution from the top down, the bloodless or 'white revolution'. From 1960 onwards the Shah promoted land reform and sought to weaken the power of traditional landowners, while giving the peasantry a stake in the land they worked. Opinions differ whether the Shah was motivated by genuine commitment or by the threat that the new Kennedy administration posed to the United States by now traditional support of the monarchy. President John Kennedy saw the Cold War broadly in terms of the social and political struggle in developing countries, and alliances with dictators and oligarchs as a distinct liability for the democratic states. Kennedy therefore put pressure on the Shah to appoint a strong and reformist prime minister, Ali Amini. Under compulsion the Shah, who, saw a strong prime minister as a personal threat, acceded, but dismissed him as soon as politic. The monarch nevertheless embarked on a programme of social and economic reform to defuse any unrest, and to strengthen the monarchy. The resultant modernization programme, primed by oil revenues, was to embrace all aspects of society but the political.

During the Carter presidency (1976–9) the US again re-examined relations with Iran. Again, the president wanted to encourage a more democratic and institutionalized system in Iran and to disengage from the embrace of the Shah. Carter saw preoccupation with the Cold War as distorting and something that could be transcended. Both presidents' attempts to shift the emphasis of US policy failed in the absence of an alternative, and in light of Iran's undoubted importance as an ally first *vis-à-vis* the USSR and later as a force for stablility regionally. These periods demonstrated, however, that US policy in the Cold War after the oil nationalization dispute was never as consistent and unwavering as sometimes depicted.

While the West initially saw the Shah as vain and weak (although by the 1970s he had almost become assimilated into the ranks of world-class statesman), the Shah was sceptical about the West's dependability. He never lost his distrust of the Western powers, most marked when he was most reliant on them, but continuing even when Iran had achieved a modicum of stability and greater bargaining power.[43] The more the Shah gained confidence, the less he promoted politics, or encouraged the expression of different ideas or criticism. He reduced the political space available for other groups. Increasingly politics revolved around two poles: the Shah's men and the others. Political parties, groups, and individuals were co-opted, repressed, or emptied of content, leaving the monarch alone on the political stage.

The Cold War, with the premium it attached to security and predictability, gave the Shah the opportunity to strengthen the monarchy, centralize power, and dominate the military at the expense of the healthy development of other institutions. Increasingly remote from society, the government no longer felt accountable to the Majlis or the population. While an enlightened royal autocracy or sternly paternalistic regime were not foreign to the country's traditions, this was a new era. The Shah's authoritarian policies at home increas-

---

[43] He especially mistrusted Britain, and held it responsible for the assassination of at least one prime minister, Razmara (1951). As late as 1975 he wondered about possible US military responses to Iran's increase in the oil prices, and whether he might use the possiblility of a Soviet response as a deterrent to it. See, A. Assadollah Alam, *The Shah and I: The Confidential Diary of Iran's Royal Court 1969–1977* (New York: St. Martin's Press, 1992), 122, 440.

ingly amplified the country's contradictions; political blockage was at odds with the demands of a growing and dynamic economy (fueled from the mid-1960's by oil revenues) which demanded a modicum of personal and financial security and freedom. The Shah was unwilling to concede to his subjects the latitude his own policies demanded.[44] As the threat from the north declined and the Cold War stabilized, the Shah's jealous monopolization of political power appeared more and more anachronistic, especially for a regime professing to want to imitate and eventually outpace the West. It also worked against the Shah's own ambitions for Iran. Moreover, to what was becoming a diverse, politically mobilized populace—urban poor or middle class—the frozen political landscape appeared increasingly intolerable.

US support for the Shah meant that it was associated with his policies, internal and external, whether or not they represented US policy. This close identification worked both ways: initially it served to bolster the Shah domestically. Later it came to implicate the US in the Shah's unpopular domestic policies. Iran's alignment with the West had reinforced the state's power. This had led neither to political liberalization nor to the decentralization of power, but to renewed authoritarianism. The West's identification with this state of affairs stimulated a cultural backlash against things Western. The regime's élites, identified with Western values and techniques, were rejected along with the Westernization they were thought to represent (materialism, individualism over society, etc.) which were now discredited. It remained for the the regime's opponents to discard the trappings of Western thought (and values) and enlist Islam as the ideology and symbol in whose name they would confront the Shah and his foreign supporters.

Thus by the time of the revolution the identification of the Shah with the West (the reverse side of the identification of Iran with the Shah, by *both* the US and the USSR) had alienated the Shah's opponents from the West. Ignoring the more complicated reality (including the Shah's genuine popularity earlier when things were going well), Iranians came to see the Shah as the West's creature, merely a puppet controlled from a distance. In constructing the revolutionary mythology they also came to deny the objective threat that Iran had faced, during the Cold War, which had required a strategic choice. Instead they argued that the superpowers were equally dangerous.

[44] See R. Graham, *Iran: Dictatorship and Development* (London: Penguin, 1979), and M. Gasiorowski, *US Foreign Policy and the Shah: Building a Client State in Iran* (Ithaca, NY: Cornell University Press, 1991).

The Shah's successors, in seeking to repudiate his legacy, ascribed Iran's relationship with the West to subservience rather than to a consideration of Iran's security interests at a time of acute threat. This revisionism about Iran's foreign policy had become almost conventional wisdom before the end of the Cold War. In seeing the Shah as motivated wholly by dynastic or regime considerations, this interpretation minimized the existence of a Soviet threat or implicitly supported the view that it could have been met otherwise, e.g. by non-alignment. In reality Iran had few easy choices regarding its security in the early Cold War. Neither historical experience nor geography gave it much latitude. Between uncertain non-alignment and untried alignment, the choice was relatively clear. The consequences of that choice were not foreordained. A more enlightened policy of political liberalization might have avoided the ensuing débâcle.

The revolution was a product of internal Iranian conditions, primarily the political blockage which a now politically mobilized populace found so frustrating. Iran's foreign and defence policies, on which the populace were rarely consulted, did not rank very high in in its causes, though admittedly military expenditures appeared to many as extravagant. Opposition to the Shah regime's domestic policies was the principal motor for the revolution. Inevitably this came to include its foreign orientation and alignment, which were seen as the factors which enabled the regime to stay in power so long. This meant that Iran's allies were implicated in any domestic upheaval, and were consequently the first targets for any regime replacing the Shah. In at least one sense this was deserved, for these outside powers had long since abdicated any sense of strategic responsibility for the country and had begun to see it merely as a commercial market. These powers' deference to the Shah, and their inability to act as a corrective to his increasingly authoritarian rule, implicated them in the upheaval that followed.

THE ISLAMIC REPUBLIC: NON-ALIGNMENT AND INDEPENDENCE

The Shah's successors sought to depict him as an 'American agent' and his regime as one which allowed Britain and the US to loot Iran and take 'as much as they possibly could'.[45] In this view the Islamic

---

[45] This view is still repeated 16 years after the revolution. For a recent reference, see Ayatollah Khamenei, the Rahbar's broadcast Voice of the Islamic Republic of Iran (provincial network), in Persian, 3 Feb. 1995, in BBC Summary of World Broadcasts (henceforth SWB), Middle East, ME/2222 MED/11–14, 8 Feb. 1995.

republic 'stood up to the world's colonialists, hegemonists and bullies'. Iran rejected the notion of alignment, and Khomeini 'set up a government in confrontation with the East and the West. With his action . . . he disintegrated the Marxists' thesis. . . . He frightened Western capitalism which was led by America . . .'[46] In pursuing a foreign policy based on 'Neither East nor West', Iran was denying the neccessity for choice, rejecting the notion that the Cold War had anything to do with Iran. In so far as they felt Iran's security threatened by superpower rivalry, the Shah's successors preferred to rely on means other than alignment. For them this had the connotation of dependence and loss of autonomy. They believed that a policy of balancing and exclusion could serve Iran's interests better, and that the formula: 'Islam is the solution' applied to all questions, including those relating to security in the Cold War. Defining security as absolute independence, revolutionary Iran made much of self-reliance, commitment, and morale as sources of power for a state. Facing 'arrogant and domineering powers', Iran now wanted to rely on its willpower and on the 'authenticity' of its message, rejecting the traditional calculus of power. Suspicious of any unequal relationship as 'enslaving', Iran sought to minimize its contacts with the superpowers.

Revolutionary Iran's foreign orientation was thus in marked contrast to that of its predecessor. It became an article of faith in Islamic Iran that it had gained true independence rather than its mere form. Yet it bound itself in terms of its very legitimacy to pursue a policy that rejected any engagement with the superpowers and the US in particular. This limited its room for manoeuvre, though it provided Iran with an all-purpose scapegoat for its failings. Futhermore the independence was illusory: as long as the Cold War persisted, Iran simply benefited from a 'free ride'; the West's security umbrella would be extended whether Iran sought it or not. Without doing anything, Islamic Iran was a beneficiary of its predecessor's prudence.

In denying the importance of military power, the Iranian authorities immediately cancelled $11 billion of arms ordered from the US by the Shah. They subsequently spent much of the next decade scrambling for arms on the international market, paying high prices for inferior armaments, all the time using the well-stocked warehouses of arms left by the Shah, whom they continued to excoriate.

The Cold War continued unabated until at least 1985. The Soviet invasion and war in Afghanistan was an indirect though proximate

[46] See the Majles Speaker Nateq Nouri's eulogy of Khomeini's contribution, 'Vision of Islamic Republic of Iran', Network 1, Tehran in Persian, 27 Apr., in SWB ME/2290 MED/1–3, 29 Apr. 1995.

threat to Iran. In assisting the Afghans, Iran and the US were on the same side, a reflection of strategic realities, not ideological preferences. Superpower rivalry continued during the Iran–Iraq war. However, reflecting the maturation of the Cold War, each superpower was concerned to deny any advantage to the other rather than to make any gains itself. This reflected the regional setting, where Iran had shaken itself loose from alignment with the US and Iraq had drifted away from the USSR. Thus neither state was closely tied to a superpower. This gave the superpowers an incentive to pursue policies of damage limitation rather than opportunism or exploitation.

The Iran–Iraq war demonstrated another, new phenomenon, indicative of the passing of the Cold War and of conditions more common in the period after it. During the Cold War, the superpowers had had the influence to contain local conflicts.[47] By the 1980s this was no longer the case; they no longer had the leverage nor the will to get involved in conflict management. They therefore limited themselves to seeking to deny the other any breakthrough—hence Moscow's shrill warnings when the US fleet entered the Persian Gulf in 1984. Traditional rivalry persisted. Washington was concerned by the prospect of Soviet advances. Together with Britain in 1983, it was instrumental in getting information about Soviet–Tudeh espionage in Iran to the Iranian authorities and in getting the party banned. A similar motivation was evident in the US in 1985 in the genesis of the 'Irangate' affair. US intelligence officials argued that the US and the USSR 'lack preferred access to Iran. Whoever gets there first is in a strong position to work towards the exclusion of the other.'[48]

To differentiate itself from its predecessor, revolutionary Iran set a high priority on reversing its course. Accordingly Iran withdrew from CENTO and joined the non-aligned. It shut down gas exports to the USSR and flared the gas; it cancelled the Shah's nuclear programme and his order for submarines; it reduced oil production, and emphasized barter trade, subsidies, and state involvement in the economy. It cultivated ties with the state trading nations of the Eastern bloc, the 'oppressed' in Africa, and the marginal states of Romania and North Korea. The decision of Islamic Iran to depict the US, the victor of the Cold War, as the major enemy appeared at best quixotic.

---

[47] Often by manipulating arms supplies. Saddam Hussein complained that the USSR denied him arms in his conflict with the Kurds and Iran in 1974; see Chubin, *Security in the Persian Gulf*, 166.

[48] *Report of the President's Review Board*, Tower Commission (Washington, DC: US Govt. Printing Office 1985), B-6.

However strident its ideological claims, Iran's foreign policy during 1979–89 was dominated by the reality of the needs of the war with Iraq. This saw the spectacle of a decidedly pragmatic Iran ready to deal with the 'Great Satan' in order to gain access to arms, which it had itself earlier refused. Iran's dead-end diplomacy in that costly war, which left Iraq on Iran's territory, were only effaced by Saddam Hussein's *folie de grandeur* in 1990, which gave the Islamic republic a second chance.

The revolution in Iran ushered in a 'return of regional politics'. Prior to this, global forces had relegated the regional to a secondary role; thereafter, as the Cold War wound down, the positions were reversed and regional forces became dominant. Iran's regional policies were based on the assumption of an 'Islamic axis' or cooperation on an Islamic basis, transcending differences whether sectarian or based on national interest. After the Iran–Iraq and Iraq–Kuwait wars, this assumption turned out to be a lacking in much support regionally. Iran's support for radical Palestinians and Islamist groups and opposition to the Arab–Israeli 'peace process' set it on a conflict course with most of its Arab neighbours. This was compounded by Iran's tendency to see Saudi Arabia as the follower of 'American Islam', and by efforts to use the annual pilgrimage for political purposes which its host considered politically destabilizing.

A decade and a half after the revolution, with the breakup of the Soviet Union and the passing of the Cold War, Islamic Iran was still unclear whether to pursue revolutionary projects or national interests. Its refusal, or inability due to internal divisions, to choose unequivocally hurt its relations with its Arab neighbours and caused Israel to consider Iran as an emerging strategic threat. In broader terms, Iran's foreign policy remained a relic of the Cold War. Its emphasis on non-alignment in an era when there were no remaining blocs, its hostility towards the only remaining superpower, the US, its insistence on independence when interdependence and economic competition had become inescapable—all reflected an inability to adapt to the new world after the Cold War. Islamic Iran was also unable to compensate for the reduction in its strategic leverage resulting from the passing of the Cold War. Islamic Iran was still searching for a role. It emphasized 'cultural' rather than military threats to its revolution. The 'Islamic axis' was a poor substitute, not only because of divisions within Islam but because Iran, as a Sh'ia (Sh'iis constituting barely 15 per cent of Islam) and non-Arab state, was scarcely acceptable in a leadership role. Its rhetoric has antagonized the Arab states of the Persian Gulf, and brought US forces formally into the region, for the first time on a quasi-permanent basis.

Iran sought to demonstrate solidarity with Muslims as far afield as Bosnia. Yet it had unstable borders in an arc from Iraq in the west to the Kurdish areas of Turkey, to Azerbaijan, Tadjikstan, and Afghanistan. Here its support for fellow Muslims was tempered by pragmatic considerations of *realpolitik*. Indeed Iran's support for oppressed Muslims was selective. Foremost was the desire not to offend Russia, on whom the Islamic republic now relied for technology. As Iran's relations with the US deteriorated steadily after 1995, it become correspondingly more solicitous of Russia's sensitivities. Iran seldom referred to the hapless Tadjiks, still less the embattled Chechens.

In domestic politics, the Islamic republic could point to some achievements. It permitted elections of the Majlis and of the president. Within the limits imposed by the authorities, these were relatively free; they were, however, limited by the fact that candidates had been vetted and approved, not always on non-political grounds. The early experiments with parties, giving rise to the regime's own vehicle, the Islamic Republican Party, were disbanded in the mid-1980s. Differences within the regime itself, as represented by factions (the Ruhaniyat and Ruhaniyoun) each with their own newspapers (e.g. *Salaam* for the Ruhaniyoun) and able to criticize the government, were given freer rein. The Majlis too was able to debate, exercise criticism, block appointments, and delay legistlation. As long as the framework of the Islamic republic itself was accepted, there was leeway for political discussion.[49]

For those wanting a secular state however, there was no tolerance. The same criteria applied to publications; within the regime's specified limits there was lively debate. Many Iranians did not agree with those limits and were hence excluded. Two million fled the country, among them the best-educated. Periodic attempts by the regime to revive the zeal of the faithful by crusades against moral laxness, economic exploiters, or Western ideas could not alter the fact that the regime lacked any sort of programme other than criticism of its predecessor. This meant that hostility toward the US continued to serve as a benchmark for the regime's revolutionary credentials. It became the 'easiest' issue on which to rally the faithful, an infallible source of consensus when unity on other issues was proving elusive. How long this will last is less certain. The US as the all-purpose bogey, the source of all Iran's troubles, rings less and less true to a youthful population that sees the past as distant history and holds the regime

---

[49] The Minister of the Interior, Ali Mohammad Besharati, proudly reported that 80 political parties had been incorporated and officially recognized as such in Iran; IRNA, Tehran, 10 May, in SWB ME/2301 MED/13, 12 May 1995.

accountable for current failures. At the same time, the compensating tilt towards Russia, a country with a defunct ideology, inferior technology, and an imitative culture of materialism scarcely inspires any support within Iran.

The overthrow of the monarchy and the expulsion of the 'Great Satan' were symbolic acts of liberation, which reclaimed politics for Iranians. The fact that the revolution took place during the Cold War also symbolized an act of defiance and self-assertion *vis-à-vis* 'oppressive' foreign powers, and may in time act to purge Iranians of their sense of helplessness and instil in them a new sense of constructive responsibility for their own destiny.

The Cold War was a product and consequence of the Second World War. In a broader sense it was part of the period of inter-western politics that has been largely superseded by a more global and multi-faceted competition. Decolonization and the problems associated with intervention were already at work parallel with the Cold War. By the time Iran left the Western camp, the bipolar competition was nearly over. The end of the Cold War closed the period of Western imperialism and intervention in Iran's domestic life. It was the last chapter of a sustained saga of interference that had taken place in a Persia/Iran too weak or disunited to resist. Earlier, it had been competitive intervention; in the Cold War, the pattern was the same, but Iran chose one side. With the passing of an era in international relations in which the West and its rivalries were the central and controlling factors of international politics, and with political mobilization in Iran, Iranians are now free to organize their own affairs and their relations with their neighbours and the world, independently, for good or ill.

10

Turkey

WILLIAM HALE

In a study of the impact of the Cold War on the politics of the Middle East, one has to start by making the obvious point that, between 1945 and 1990, Turkey's international position was fundamentally different from those of the other Middle Eastern countries, bar Iran, in that it was a front-line participant in the Cold War. Accordingly, the global conflict normally took precedence over regional conflicts in its foreign policy, and it could not afford the luxury of non-alignment. This reinforced the Kemalist perception that Turkey was, or ought to be, part of Europe—or (in Cold War terms) part of the first rather than the Third World. The Cyprus problem was the only regional conflict in which Turkey was directly involved, but this was a contest in which the other Middle Eastern states were no more than bystanders. For most of the period, Turkey was only a peripheral actor in Middle Eastern politics.

This chapter examines Turkey's position in the Cold War under two headings—first, its relations with the superpowers and Cold War alliance blocs, and second, its role in regional conflicts. It is evident that the first heading demands far more space than the second, and this is reflected in the structure of this chapter. The Cyprus conflict is discussed under the first heading since, for present purposes, its most important aspect was its effects on Turkey's relations with the superpowers. The final section of conclusions tries to assess the degree of independence which Turkey enjoyed during the Cold War, and to compare its position with those of other Middle Eastern countries.

The effects of the Cold War on each country's domestic politics are a third focus of attention in this book. However, in the Turkish case, it is hard to devote a separate section to this, since it seems that Turkey's foreign relations had little effect on domestic politics, except possibly during the initial period of 1945–50. This is discussed at an appropriate point in the chronological narrative. For the rest, it seems very doubtful that outside powers had more than a marginal impact on internal developments. Certainly, the US did not instigate the three military interventions of 1960, 1971, and 1980. On the other hand, the need to maintain good relations with the West probably strengthened the Generals' decision to go back to their barracks, on each occasion.[1] By the 1980s, most of Turkey's top military commanders had been trained in the US, and maintained regular contacts with their NATO colleagues, so they were fairly well aware of thinking in Western capitals. At the same time there were some powerful reciprocal influences, in the sense that domestic politics had an important role in determining foreign policy shifts, especially during the 1960s and at the beginning of the 1980s. Since these vitally affected Turkey's position in the Cold War, they are explained in the course of the first section.

In this context, something should also be said about the process of foreign policy-making in Ankara. Unlike most of the other Middle Eastern states, Turkey has had a democratic system of government for most of the postwar period, so one would expect that this process would have been relatively open. Unfortunately, this is not the case. All the government archives for the period since the end of the Ottoman empire have been closed to researchers, and little information is available from other sources. Generally, it is assumed that policy-making was confined to a restricted circle of élite actors, including the president and prime minister, the foreign minister and his senior officials, and the chiefs of the armed services. None the less, it is also clear that at certain points—for instance, during the Cyprus crises of 1964, 1967, and 1974—public opinion, expressed by the press and members of parliament, did have a significant effect on policy. However, there have apparently been no detailed attempts to examine or illustrate this process, which remains one of the least explored aspects of Turkish politics.

TURKEY AND THE GLOBAL CONFLICT, 1945–1990

To simplify and systematize a long and complicated story, the evolution of Turkey's position in the Cold War can be broken down into five chronological phases. Within the Cold War period, a crucial watershed was passed in 1962–4, when the Cuban missile crisis demonstrated that uncritical membership of the Western alliance could pose catastrophic risks for Turkey, and the Cyprus crisis of

---

[1] See William Hale, *Turkish Politics and the Military* (London: Routledge, 1994), 239, 323. For details on the US reaction to the 1980 coup, see James W. Spain, *American Diplomacy in Turkey* (New York: Praeger, 1984), 233–6, and Kenan Evren, *Kenan Evren'in Anıları* (Istanbul: Milliyet Yayınları, 1990), ii. 92–3.

1964 showed that Turkish national interests could contradict those of NATO. The five phases correspond fairly closely to successive phases in the Cold War at the global level, though the turning-points do not correspond exactly. They can be summarized as:

1945–52: the transition phase (corresponding to the emergence of the Cold War)

1952–64: the full engagement phase (corresponding to the zenith of the first Cold War)

1964–80: the phase of partial disengagement (corresponding to the period of superpower *détente*)

1980–5: the re-engagement phase (corresponding to the second Cold War)

1985–90: the final phase (corresponding to the Gorbachev era in East–West relations)

The choice of a terminal date is not simple, since it is not easy to say precisely when the Cold War ended. Nevertheless, 1990, which saw the signature of the CFE and CSCE treaties, seems the most appropriate date. To go further, into 1991, would take one into a discussion of Turkish policy during the second Gulf War, and in central Asia and the Balkans, which were essentially a product of the post-Cold War transformation.

1945–1952: the transition phase

Since the foundation of the republic in 1923, Turkey had been committed to cultural and ideological Westernization. However, this did not imply a military alliance with any one of the Western powers, unless the security situation necessitated it. Hence, the new Turkish state had no such alliances, until a tripartite treaty was signed with Britain and France on the eve of the Second World War in 1939. Up to that time, Turkey had enjoyed friendly relations with the Soviets. Ankara's involvement in the Cold War essentially came about as a reaction to policy initiatives from the USSR, rather than from Turkey itself, or from the Western powers. In March 1945 the Soviet foreign minister, Vyacheslav Molotov, told Selim Sarper, the Turkish ambassador in Moscow, that the 1925 Soviet–Turkish Treaty of Friendship and Neutrality, which was due for renewal in November 1945, could not be extended without important revisions. In the following June, Molotov expanded this point by laying down three principal conditions for renewal: first, the retrocession of the frontier provinces of Kars and Ardahan to the USSR; second, permission for the establishment of Soviet bases at the straits of the Bosporus and

Dardanelles; third, the revision of the Montreux Convention, governing the passage of warships through the straits, in favour of the USSR. This was accompanied by a press propaganda campaign, rumours of troop movements in Bulgaria, and the like—in effect, an overall war of nerves against Turkey.[2]

For the Turks, the Soviet demands meant that 'the old eastern question has risen from its grave'.[3] As in the nineteenth century, they faced a direct security threat from Russia, and were unable to counter it unaided. They rejected the Soviet demands, but they needed an alliance with the West and were uncertain as to whether they could secure one, since they had effectively been neutral during the Second World War.[4] The alliance with Britain of 1939 was still officially in force, but it soon became clear that Britain was too weak to render the assistance which Turkey needed, and that the USA was initially reluctant to fill the gap.[5] The problem was not overcome until President Truman's address to Congress of March 1947 (the 'Truman Doctrine') calling for $400 m. in military aid to Greece and Turkey in the period to June 1948. This was accepted by both Houses of Congress in April–May 1947.[6] In 1948 Turkey began to receive Marshall Aid. By this stage it had obtained American diplomatic and military support, but no firm security commitment from the West.

The North Atlantic Treaty was signed in April 1949. Turkey was keen to be included, since it felt that otherwise the wrong signal would be sent to the USSR (in effect, that the USA would defend Western Europe, but not Turkey) and that it would be treated as a second-class member of the international community. However, the admission of Greece and Turkey to NATO was delayed by several factors. Among them were initial arguments by the US joint chiefs of staff that Greece and Turkey should only be given associate status in NATO, as the primary military commitment of the alliance should be to the north Atlantic. Similar arguments were advanced by the Scandinavian member states. Additionally, Britain was anxious to incorporate Turkey in a proposed Middle East Command, rather

[2] Bruce R. Kuniholm, *The Origins of the Cold War in the Near East*, 2nd edn. (Princeton, NJ: Princeton University Press, 1994), 255–8; Harry N. Howard, *Turkey, the Straits and US Policy* (Baltimore: Johns Hopkins University Press, 1974), 216–19.

[3] Ahmet Emin Yalman, *Vatan*, 18 July 1945, quoted in Kuniholm, *Origins*, 255.

[4] Turkey had officially declared war on Germany and Japan in Feb. 1945, but played no direct part in the hostilities; the declaration was designed to ensure participation in the forthcoming San Francisco conference, establishing the United Nations.

[5] At the Potsdam conference of July–Aug. 1945, President Truman pressed for the internationalization of all waterways, but he does not seem to have been ready at this stage to consider direct action in favour of Turkey: Kuniholm, *Origins*, 263.

[6] Ibid. 413–14.

than in NATO. Eventually, the allies took the decision to admit Greece and Turkey in July 1951, and this was formalized in February 1952.[7] The outbreak of the Korean War, and Turkey's participation in the UN forces in 1950, probably played a role in this change of heart. By joining the UN forces in Korea, Turkey increased its moral claim to Western assistance—though how much practical effect this had can be debated, given that gratitude is not usually a ruling emotion in international politics. More materially, the Korean War demonstrated the need for global containment of the USSR (rather than one limited to central Europe), and showed that containment was impossible without a manifest will and capacity to fight a limited war. It also induced Congress to accept a fourfold increase in the US defence budget. These considerations overcame objections to the admission of Turkey, most of whose territory lies outside Europe.[8]

In retrospect, certain points about this process are striking. In the first place, Turkey was the suitor: it was not Turkey which had to be persuaded to join the Western alliance (as in the case of most of the other Middle Eastern states) but the Western powers who had to be persuaded to admit Turkey. This derived from the fact that Turkey was much more directly faced with the risk of Soviet aggression than were the Arab countries. It was virtually uninvolved in the Palestine question, where the sympathies of the Arabs ran directly contrary to those of the US. Machiavelli advises the ruler of a small state not to enter an alliance with a big one unless he is forced to.[9] In this instance, however, Turkey could not have preserved its security without such an alliance. Admittedly, it is likely that the USSR was not actually prepared to invade Turkey in 1945–6, and that the Turks realized this.[10] Instead, what Stalin apparently aimed to do was to establish a military presence at the Straits, and to coerce an isolated Turkey into a bilateral deal which would have left it under Soviet domination. Hence, Turkey needed the alliance for diplomatic support, and for the ultimate guarantee of military backup if this became necessary. A campaign of diplomatic resistance would not have been convincing or effective if the Western powers had not shown that such resistance had military teeth. Certainly, part of

[7] George McGhee, *The US–Turkish–NATO Middle East Connection* (London: Macmillan, 1990), 54, 72–3, 87–9; John C. Campbell, *Defense of the Middle East* (New York: Praeger, 1960), 40–5.

[8] Duygu Bazoğlu Sezer, 'Turkey's Security Policies', in Jonathan Alford (ed.), *Greece and Turkey: Adversity in Alliance* (London: Gower, for International Institute of Strategic Studies, 1984), 62; Bruce R. Kuniholm, 'Turkey and the West Since World War II', in Vojtech Mastny and R. Craig (eds.), *Turkey between East and West: New Challenges for a Rising Regional Power* (Boulder: Westview, 1996), 45–70.

[9] Niccolò Machiavelli, *The Prince*, ch. 21.

[10] Howard, *Turkey, the Straits and US Policy*, 249.

Turkey's motivation for joining NATO was the desire for recognition of its status as a European power (the 'Kemalist ideological imperative', perhaps) and for the benefits of Western economic aid. However, this can only be a partial explanation, and is far from sufficient. As has been argued earlier, cultural Westernization did not necessarily imply attachment to the Western alliance. Turkey's main motivation for joining NATO was the existence of a distinct Soviet threat to its security and independence.[11]

The impact of the alliance with the West on domestic politics at this time is also an important but problematic issue. Frequently, it is suggested that President İsmet İnönü took the decision to abandon the single-party system, and allow Turkey's first free elections in 1950, mainly because he realized that if it retained a patently undemocratic internal regime, his government would never win the favours of the West. This explanation is not without substance, but it is only partial, and virtually impossible to prove. In the first place, there is no hard evidence to show that the Western powers demanded democratic credentials, as a condition for Turkey's admission to NATO. Secondly, there were some powerful internal pressures, which would probably have led İnönü to his actual decision, whatever the external circumstances. Even if foreign policy considerations were important, İnönü was certainly reluctant to admit them, probably because this would have damaged his domestic credibility. His position was summed up several years later in a conversation with the American scholar Dankwart A. Rustow, in which he first denied the foreign policy motive: ' "all that slander about me, as if I had been swimming with the stream". Then he visibly relaxed, and with a shrewd smile added "and suppose I had been swimming with the stream, that too is a virtue." '[12]

1952–1964: the full engagement phase

The early 1950s marked the height of the first Cold War, and Turkey's engagement in it. None the less, its commitment to the West remained unshaken for many years after the death of Stalin and the end of the Korean War in 1953. In May 1953 the USSR formally

[11] For discussion of these points, see Melvyn Leffler, 'The American Conception of National Security and the Beginnings of the Cold War, 1945–48', *American Historical Review* 89 (1984), 346–81, and Bruce Kuniholm's 'Reply' in the same volume, 385–90.

[12] Dankwart A. Rustow, 'Transitions to Democracy: Turkey's Experience in Historical and Comparative Perspective', in Metin Heper and Ahmet Evin (eds.), *State, Democracy and the Military: Turkey in the 1980s* (Berlin: de Gruyter, 1988), 245 n. 10. On a related point, see George S. Harris, *Troubled Alliance: Turkish–American Problems in Historical Perspective, 1945–1971* (Washington, DC: American Enterprise for Public Policy Research, 1972), 39.

withdrew its territorial claims, though its position on the Straits still seemed ambiguous.[13] Ankara accepted this retreat 'with satisfaction' but made no attempt to pick up the olive branch. In April 1960 it was announced that Premiers Adnan Menderes and Nikita Khrushchev would exchange visits, but Menderes was overthrown by a *coup d'état* on 27 May 1960, before anything could be achieved. On 28 June Khrushchev wrote to General Cemal Gürsel, the head of the post-coup junta, urging that Turkey should opt for neutrality, but met with a determined refusal—apparently because the military regime was uncertain of the US government's attitude towards the coup, and wished to assure Washington of its loyalty to the alliance. Both the military government and its civilian successor, under İsmet İnönü, refused an offer of $500 m. in aid from Moscow, since they believed it would be linked to political concessions by Turkey.[14]

Turkey's strategic importance to the Western alliance was outlined by General Dwight Eisenhower to President Truman in January 1951. Eisenhower described Europe as a long bottleneck, with Russia as the wide part of the bottle at one end, Western Europe the narrow neck, and Spain at the Western end. If the Western powers controlled both sides of the bottle (that is, the North Sea and the Mediterranean) then they could prevent a Soviet advance in the centre, by hitting Soviet forces hard on both flanks. On the southern flank, arms and the support of Western forces should be given to Turkey and Yugoslavia. Accordingly, Turkey was closely integrated into Western defence planning. Three-quarters of its land forces were earmarked for NATO, under the Commander-in-Chief of Allied Forces, Southern Europe (CINCSOUTH) based in Naples. Its air force was also earmarked for assignment to Supreme Allied Command, Europe (SACEUR), as was its navy. During the 1950s the Turkish and US authorities reached a series of secret bilateral agreements, giving the US armed forces extensive facilities in Turkey. These came to include, most notably, the İncirlik air-base, near Adana, with other bases at Karamürsel, Ciğli, and Diyarbakır, intelligence-gathering facilities at Karamürsel, Sinop, Samsun, Belbaşı, and Diyarbakır, and naval facilities and storage centres at İskenderun and Yumurtalık. Under an agreement signed in 1957, the

---

[13] Ferenc A. Vali, *Bridge Across the Bosporus: The Foreign Policy of Turkey* (Baltimore: Johns Hopkins University Press, 1971), 174–5.

[14] Sezer, 'Turkey's Security Policies', 56–7; Kemal H. Karpat, 'Turkish–Soviet Relations', in Karpat et al., *Turkey's Foreign Policy in Transition, 1950–1974* (Leiden: Brill, 1975), 86–7; Suha Bölükbaşı, *Turkish–American Relations and Cyprus* (Lanham, Md.: University Press of America, for White Burkett Miller Center of Public Affairs, University of Virginia, 1988), 48–9.

US air force stationed strike aircraft armed with tactical nuclear weapons in Turkey. By 1968 there were about 24,000 US defence personnel in the country. Turkish forces were substantially modernized with US hardware: between 1948 and 1964, authorized US military assistance to Turkey totalled $2,445.3 m., with actual deliveries or expenditures of $2,271 m. plus $32.8 m. in deliveries of surplus equipment. In addition, between 1950 and 1962, Turkey received around $1,380 m. in programme and project economic aid (apart from PL480 wheat deliveries), the vast majority of which came from US sources.[15]

Turkey's commitment to the West was put to a severe test at the time of the Cuban missile crisis of October 1962. The position of Turkey was crucial, although the full extent of this was not apparent at the time: in fact, it might be more appropriate to speak of the 'Cuban–Turkish missile crisis'. The Menderes government had agreed with the US to locate 15 Jupiter intermediate range missiles, armed with nuclear warheads, on Turkish territory (actually near İzmir) in October 1959. Some officers of the Turkish foreign ministry and the general staff opposed the deployment of the Jupiters, on the grounds that they would provoke the USSR, but were overruled by the government and the general staff commanders.[16] The missiles were not actually installed until late 1961, and did not become operational until March or April 1962—only a few months before the Cuban crisis broke. By this stage, the US authorities had realized that they were inaccurate and vulnerable to a Soviet first strike. The Jupiters had anyway become outdated by the Polaris submarine-launched system. They had also been the subject of several complaints by Khrushchev before October 1962.[17] In May 1961, Secretary of State Dean Rusk raised the issue of their withdrawal with Selim Sarper, now the Turkish foreign minister. He received a negative response, on the grounds that 'their parliament' had only just passed appropriations for the cost of installing the Jupiters, and that 'it would be very embarrassing to go right back to them and say that they were being taken out. And then he said it would be very bad for the morale of Turkey as a member of NATO if they were taken out before a Polaris submarine were in the Mediterranean to

---

[15] Sezer, 'Turkey's Security Policies', 64–5; Kuniholm, 'Turkey and the West Since World War II'; Harris, *Troubled Alliance*, 54–5, 155, 167; William Hale, *The Political and Economic Development of Modern Turkey* (London: Croom Helm, 1981), 104, 230.

[16] Information from Mr İsmail Soysal.

[17] Barton J. Bernstein, 'The Cuban Missile Crisis: Trading the Jupiters in Turkey?', *Political Science Quarterly* 95 (1980), 99–100, and 'Reconsidering the Missile Crisis: Dealing with the Problems of the American Jupiters in Turkey', in James A. Nathan (ed.), *The Cuban Missile Crisis Revisited* (New York: St. Martin's Press, 1992), 58–60.

take their place' (which was then the case).[18] Similarly, George McGhee, then the Chairman of the Policy Planning Council, reported to the president in June 1961 that removal of the Jupiters would be seen as a sign of weakness, following Khrushchev's tough stance at the Vienna summit earlier that month. McGhee also believed that it would be difficult to persuade the Turkish government to accept removal, since General Lauris Norstad, the Supreme Commander of Allied Forces in Europe, had previously stressed their military value in conversations with Sarper. Later, during the spring and summer of 1962, Rusk twice raised the question again with Turkish representatives, but they continued to object, and President Kennedy was told by the State Department that it would be unwise to press the matter.[19]

The turning-point in the missile crisis came on the evening of 26 October, when Khrushchev sent a long personal letter to President Kennedy, suggesting that he would remove the Soviet missiles from Cuba if the blockade on the island were lifted and the US did not attack Cuba. However, a second letter from Khrushchev, delivered on the morning of 27 October, specifically linked a withdrawal of the Cuban missiles to parallel withdrawal of the Jupiters from Turkey.[20] In Washington, the idea of a Turkey-for-Cuba trade was much discussed, but was resisted on the grounds that it could lead to further demands from the USSR and that, as the US ambassador in Ankara, Raymond Hare, put it, the Turks would much resent the idea that 'their interests were being traded off in order to appease an enemy'.[21] Accordingly, President Kennedy responded to Khrushchev by replying only to his first letter (that is, proposing withdrawal of the Soviet missiles without a trade). Khrushchev accepted this formula on 28 October, and the crisis was over.[22]

After October 1962, Washington moved fast to secure the removal of the Jupiters. On 17 February 1963 the new Turkish foreign minister, Feridun Cemal Erkin, told parliament that the government had agreed that they would be replaced by Polaris submarines in the Mediterranean. The last of the Jupiters was removed on 24 April.

[18] Dean Rusk, interviewed in James G. Blight and David A. Welch, *On the Brink: Americans and Soviets Reexamine the Cuban Missile Crisis* (New York: Noonday Press, 1989), 173. See also McGhee, *The US–Turkish–NATO Middle East Connection*, 166. The reference to 'their parliament' is presumably to the then Constituent Assembly (Turkey was under military government at the time).

[19] Kuniholm, 'Turkey and the West Since World War II'; Robert F. Kennedy, *Thirteen Days: A Memoir of the Cuban Missile Crisis* (New York: Norton, 1971), 72–3; Bernstein, 'Reconsidering the Missile Crisis', 62–3.

[20] Kennedy, *Thirteen Days*, 64–8, 71–2, 160–4.

[21] Quoted in Bernstein, 'Reconsidering the Missile Crisis', 76.

[22] Kennedy, *Thirteen Days*, 80–2, 88.

Meanwhile, US spokesmen categorically denied that there had been any Turkey-for-Cuba trade. This line was repeated by Erkin to the Turkish parliament and by Prime Minister İsmet İnönü in a press interview in August 1963.[23] However, Robert Kennedy later revealed in his posthumously published memoirs that on the evening of 27 October, on his brother's instructions, he had told Soviet Ambassador Anatoli Dobrynin that, if Moscow removed its missiles from Cuba, 'it was our judgement that, within a short time after the crisis was over, these [Jupiter] missiles would be gone'.[24] Subsequently, it appeared that Robert Kennedy's commitment to Dobrynin had actually been more explicit than he had stated in his memoirs, and that the administration would have been ready to make it public if Khrushchev had not backed down first.[25]

The main immediate effect of the crisis on the Turkish government was evidently the realization that the stationing of the Jupiters on Turkish territory had created severe risks for Turkey, and that Polaris was a far more effective safeguard of its security. Had Khrushchev not agreed to withdraw the Cuban missiles, then the US could well have decided to destroy them by air attack. The Turkish Jupiters would then have been the target for a Soviet nuclear counter-strike, and İzmir would have become the Hiroshima of the Third World War.[26] In the long run the crisis severely weakened Turkey's faith in the alliance, since it showed that the USA could make a secret deal sacrificing its ally's interests to protect its own. However, it has to be remembered that knowledge of the secret offer to Dobrynin did not become public until some time later. By this time, its effects on Turkish opinion had been overshadowed by the far more open clash between Turkey and the USA over Cyprus in 1964.

1964–1980: the partial disengagement phase

In 1964, Turkey's attitude towards the Western alliance (especially the USA) entered a much more critical phase. Subsequently, successive Turkish governments tried to move away from exclusive reliance

[23] Nasuh Uslu, 'Turkey's Relationship with the United States, 1960–1975' (Ph.D. thesis, University of Durham, 1994), 185–7; Bernstein, 'Reconsidering the Missile Crisis', 98–9; James A. Nathan, 'The Heyday of the New Strategy', in Nathan (ed.), *The Cuban Missile Crisis Revisited*, 23; Mehmet Gönlübol and Haluk Ülman, '27 Mayis 1960 Devrimi ve Sonrası' [The Revolution of 27 May 1960 and Afterwards] in A. Suat Bilge et al., *Olaylarla Türk Dış Politikası* [Turkish Foreign Policy in the Light of Events] (Ankara: Ankara University, Political Science Faculty, 1969), 352.
[24] Kennedy, *Thirteen Days*, 86–7.
[25] Bernstein, 'Reconsidering the Missile Crisis', 96; Blight and Welch, *On the Brink*, 83–4.
[26] Uslu, 'Turkey's Relationship with the United States', 184–5.

on NATO, and to adopt a more independent and 'multi-faceted' foreign policy—improving their relations with the USSR and its satellites, and trying to develop new links with the Arab countries and the Third World generally. However, this shift was fairly limited and hesitant. It failed to pay many dividends, and was never developed to the point of opting for outright neutrality.

Global and internal developments played their part in this process. On the first score, the establishment of *détente* between the superpowers manifestly reduced the risk of direct aggression by the USSR, and probably enhanced a Turkish perception that Turkey could take the risk of clashes with the USA. In fact, by the 1970s some Turkish authorities were already speaking of the Cold War as having ended.[27] Meanwhile, growing diversity in the domestic party spectrum developed, following the introduction of a new and more liberal constitution in 1961. In particular, the 1960s saw the emergence of a vocal left wing—hitherto almost entirely absent—in the shape of the Turkish Workers' Party. This failed to capture more than a tiny fraction of the vote in the 1965 and 1969 elections, and was closed down by court order in 1971. However, it was able to mount large public demonstrations, and had some influence in shaping press and intellectual opinion. More importantly, after Bülent Ecevit's election to the leadership of the Republican People's Party in May 1972, the party moved over to a more anti-American and 'third worldist' foreign policy position.

In line with this change, a debate developed among academics and other foreign policy professionals during 1966–8 as to whether Turkey should remain in NATO. On the one side, critics like Professor Haluk Ülman, who later served as Ecevit's foreign policy adviser, urged that Turkey should opt for neutrality. Ülman argued that NATO membership could drag Turkey into a conventional war anywhere in Europe, where it might not have direct national interests, and restricted its ability to intervene in conflicts in which it did, such as that over Cyprus. If the USSR were to attack Turkey, he suggested, then the Western powers would still come to its aid, even if it were not in NATO, to prevent a Soviet conquest of the Middle East. On the other side, supporters of NATO membership, like retired admiral Sezai Orkunt and the then foreign minister, İhsan Sabri Çağlayangil, argued that Turkey still needed NATO, as the most secure deterrent against aggression, and a source of military aid

---

[27] e.g. the then Prime Minister, Bülent Ecevit, in a paper delivered in 1978, remarked that 'we have to realize the fact that the cold-war period ended . . . quite a few years ago': 'Turkey's Security Policies', in Alford, *Greece and Turkey*, 136. Similarly, writing slightly later, Duygu Sezer refers to the cold war as 'a thing of the past': 'Turkey's Security Policies', 43.

and equipment. Admiral Orkunt also pointed out that if Turkey left NATO then this could weaken its position in the Cyprus dispute, since there was the risk that the West would then increase aid to Greece, tipping the balance of power in favour of Athens. Accordingly, in 1968, a report prepared for the Republican People's Party, which was then in opposition, concluded that Turkey should remain in NATO, but should try to adopt a more flexible and independent stance within it.[28] This effectively became the basis of Ecevit's policies during the 1970s.

The Cyprus crises of 1964, 1967, and 1974 were undoubtedly the major cause, and manifestation, of the revised approach. In June 1964 there appeared to be a serious danger that Turkey might invade Cyprus, following President Makarios' announcement of the withdrawal of the special constitutional rights of the Turkish Cypriots in November 1963, and subsequent widespread attacks on the Turkish community by the Greek Cypriots. On 5 June 1964 President Johnson sent premier İnönü what became a notorious letter warning him that his NATO allies had not had a chance to consider whether they had an obligation to protect Turkey against the Soviet Union 'if Turkey takes a step which results in Soviet intervention', and that the US could not agree to the use of American supplied military equipment for an invasion of Cyprus 'in present circumstances'.[29] The full text of the letter was not released until 1966, but at the time somewhat distorted and tendentious versions of it reached the Turkish press.[30]

It is not certain that the letter did actually prevent a Turkish invasion of Cyprus in 1964, since it appears that İnönü was extremely anxious to avoid such action. His innate caution apart, he was well aware that the USSR strongly supported President Makarios, and that the Turkish armed forces were very ill-prepared for a landing.[31] However, what is certain is that the letter prompted a staff official response from İnönü and a sharp reaction in public opinion. Turks

[28] Vali, *Bridge Across the Bosporus*, 157–64.

[29] For the text of the 'Johnson letter', see *Middle East Journal*, 20 (1966), 386–8. İsmet İnönü's reply is in the same volume, 388–93.

[30] Uslu, 'Turkey's Relationship with the United States', 205; Harris, *Troubled Alliance*, 115.

[31] Bölükbaşı, *Turkish–American Relations and Cyprus*, 66–8. Turkey had no landing-craft at the time, and would have had to use cargo ships and small boats to land troops on Cyprus: ibid. 88. In an interview given on 12 June, İnönü stated that the invasion had been fixed for 4 June, but 'one day before I was warned by Washington not to use American arms for purposes not approved by America. Mr Johnson said that if the Russians took action, our NATO guarantees might not hold.' However, this merely deepens the mystery, since the 'Johnson letter' was not delivered until 5 June. Quoted in Jacob M. Landau, *Johnson's 1964 Letter to İnönü and Greek Lobbying of the White House* (Jerusalem: Hebrew University of Jerusalem, Jerusalem Papers on Peace Problems 28, 1979), 6–7.

now concluded that, since the US was preventing them from intervening militarily to protect the Turkish Cypriots, it was in effect
favouring the Greeks. Over the following years, parts of the Turkish
press began to take a much more critical (sometimes almost para-
noid) attitude towards the US, and left-wing sympathizers launched
large demonstrations against US establishments, fleet visits, and the
like.[32]

The second crisis in Cyprus, in 1967, was more effectively handled
by the US government, and less damaging in its effects on
Turkish–American relations. Attacks on Turkish Cypriot villages in
November 1967, allegedly directed by the EOKA terrorist leader
General Grivas, triggered off renewed fear of a Turkish invasion
(though whether Turkey was actually prepared to invade is again
open to question, as in the case of the 1964 crisis).[33] President
Johnson held back from a formal *démarche* similar to his 1964 letter,
and sent the former secretary for defence, Cyrus Vance, on a diplomatic mission to both sides. Vance persuaded Greece to withdraw
the troops it had illegally introduced into Cyprus, though he did not
induce Makarios to disband the Greek Cypriot national guard. The
Turkish left again used the occasion to mount demonstrations
against the US, but most Turkish opinion concluded that since
Washington had pressured Greece to accept some of Turkey's
demands, it had now moved closer to the Turkish view.[34] It was also
noticed that the USSR conspicuously failed to support the Greeks,
apparently due to the takeover in Athens by the Colonels' junta in
April 1967: in fact, the Soviet ambassador secretly assured the
Turkish government that Moscow would not oppose a Turkish landing in Cyprus.[35]

During the early 1970s, Turkish–US relations were further upset
by a dispute over cultivation of the opium poppy, which was an
important source of income for Turkish farmers in certain provinces
and had long been used for medicinal purposes, both in Turkey and
abroad. The rapid spread of heroin addiction in the US in the late
1960s induced Washington to press the Turkish government to ban
the crop. Eventually, in June 1971, the military-controlled government under Nihat Erim announced a total ban, effective from the

[32] Uslu, 'Turkey's Relationship with the United States', 224–8: Harris, *Troubled Alliance*,
128–44.
[33] Bölükbaşı, *Turkish–American Relations and Cyprus*, 133–8. In 1967, Turkey still had only
2 landing-craft and 150 parachutes. The US Sixth Fleet was also deployed close to Cyprus,
though it is not known whether it would have intercepted a landing: ibid. 135, 137.
[34] Ibid. 138–42; Uslu, 'Turkey's Relationship with the United States', 238.
[35] Bölükbaşı, *Turkish–American Relations and Cyprus*, 144–5.

autumn of 1972. This provoked strong populist opposition in Turkey, mainly on grounds of injured pride, since it was argued that Turkey had made a serious sacrifice merely to please its superpower ally. Accordingly, the succeeding coalition government under Bülent Ecevit revoked the ban in July 1974. Turkey had previously been the world's largest legal exporter of opium, and the ban had produced a severe shortage of the drug in the international pharmaceutical industry. The Ecevit government also introduced strict measures to prevent the diversion of opium into the illegal trade, by enforcing what was known as the 'poppy straw process' of harvesting. Hence, it was hard for the US government to insist on the reintroduction of the ban: in fact, in September 1974 the Ford administration actively encouraged Ankara in its new approach.[36] By this stage, however, the main focus of Turkish–US relations had shifted back to the renewed conflict in Cyprus.

The 1974 Cyprus crisis differed from its two predecessors, in that the Greek junta had clearly put itself in the wrong, in the eyes of international opinion, by temporarily overthrowing the legally elected president of Cyprus, and was evidently aiming to bring about *enosis*, which was expressly forbidden by the Treaty of Guarantee of 1960. The Nixon administration was in disarray, thanks to the Watergate scandal and Secretary of State Henry Kissinger's preoccupation with Middle East peacemaking. Nor was Kissinger inclined to protect Makarios, whom he described as the 'Castro of the Mediterranean'. Equally, the USSR was prepared to accept a Turkish military intervention, provided the independence of Cyprus was assured. Hence, Moscow did not actively oppose either the initial invasion of 20 July or the second Turkish advance of 14 August. Crucially, the Turkish armed forces now had enough specialist equipment to carry out a landing relatively easily.[37] Before the first landings, the decision-makers in Ankara decided that the only event which would cause them to cancel the operation were clear signs that it would be physically opposed by a third party—notably the US. Since there was no clear evidence of such opposition, they went ahead with the landings on the originally planned date of 20 July. They realized that the invasion could have provoked a war with Greece, but believed that they could handle this (in fact, 70 per cent of their landing-craft were kept in the Aegean—presumably in readi-

---

[36] James W. Spain, 'The United States, Turkey and the Poppy', *Middle East Journal* 29 (1975), 295–309; Uslu, 'Turkey's Relationship with the United States', 268–314.

[37] Bölükbaşı, *Turkish–American Relations and Cyprus*, 184, 187, 194, 211, 221. By 1974, Turkish shipyards had constructed 100 landing-craft, and the army had 15,000 parachutes and 100 helicopters: ibid. 189.

ness to invade the nearby Greek islands).[38] Prime Minister Ecevit
was able to claim that Turkey had now broken away from its
American leading-reins. On the morning of the invasion he told
Under-Secretary of State Joseph Sisco: 'we have done it your way for
ten years . . . and now we are going to do it our way.'[39] However,
there is no evidence that the USA had seriously tried to oblige
Turkey to do it *its* way in 1974.

The 1974 invasion established Ecevit as a nationalist champion,
and he later tried to build on this by developing a more independent
foreign policy. In a 1978 address, he suggested that Turkey was
adopting 'a new national security concept and new defence and foreign policies'.[40] What these amounted to was hard to say, however.
Certainly, Turkey adopted a far less cooperative attitude towards the
US, by preventing it from using its military facilities in Turkey for
anything other than strictly NATO purposes, mainly in the Middle
East. It also tried to rebuild its bridges with the Arab countries, and
the non-aligned states generally, in the hope of winning greater support for its cause in the United Nations.

The most serious test of Turkey's relationship with the US in the
1970s came in September 1974, when the House of Representatives,
acting under strong pressure from the pro-Greek lobby in Congress,
passed a resolution banning military aid and sales to Turkey until the
president certified that Turkey had made substantial progress
towards an agreement on Cyprus. After unsuccessful opposition
from the White House, the embargo came into effect on 5 February
1975. In response, the Turkish government suspended the Defence
Co-operation Agreement (DECA) with the US which it had signed
in July 1969. On 25 July Süleyman Demirel's government, which had
now succeeded that of Ecevit, suspended all operations at all US
facilities in Turkey, other than those having a purely NATO function (in effect, İncirlik). This continued until August 1978, when
Congress reversed the embargo decision. Operation of the major US
facilities was resumed in October 1978, and a new DECA was signed
in March 1980.[41]

In retrospect, what is surprising about the embargo is how little
damage it did to Turkish–American political relations in either the

[38] Information from a senior member of the Turkish Foreign Ministry at the time; see also
Mehmet Ali Birand, *30 Sıcak Gün* [Thirty Sweltering Days] (Istanbul: Milliyet Yayınları, 1975),
59.

[39] Quoted in Theodore A. Couloumbis, *The United States, Greece and Turkey: The Troubled
Triangle* (New York: Praeger, 1983), 93.

[40] Ecevit, 'Turkey's Security Policies', 138.

[41] Richard C. Campany, Jnr., *Turkey and the United States: The Arms Embargo Period*
(New York: Praeger, 1986), 55–6, 63–4; Sezer, 'Turkey's Security Policies', 64–5.

short or longer term. In the circumstances, and given the public reaction to the Johnson letter of 1964, one could have expected massive public protests, furious reactions from the government, and, in all likelihood, Turkish withdrawal from the Western alliance. In fact, the public reaction was extraordinarily muted, and Turkey did not even withdraw from NATO's military wing (as France and Greece had previously done)—let alone from NATO as a whole. Part of the reason probably was that Turkish domestic politics were entering a phase of deep crisis at this time, so that the question tended to be overshadowed by other, far more pressing problems. Apart from this, it was clear from the start that the US government was very half-hearted and divided on the embargo issue, since the embargo was opposed by both the Ford and Carter administrations. During the 1976 presidential election campaign, Jimmy Carter indulged in some pro-Greek rhetoric, in an attempt to appeal to Greek–American voters, but by early 1978 he had moved back to supporting a total and unconditional lifting of the embargo.[42] Congress itself partially lifted the embargo as early as October 1975, when commercial arms sales to Turkey were resumed. Moreover, throughout the embargo period Turkey was able to continue deliveries of US-made weapons from other NATO partners—a loophole of which Washington must have been fully aware.[43]

As this account of the Cyprus story has suggested, the serious upsets in Turkish–US relations were accompanied by a vast improvement in Ankara's relationship with the USSR. This corresponded to a change in thinking by policy-makers in Moscow, who began to recognize that the Third World states of socialist orientation were not necessarily progressing towards socialism. Accordingly, the 'national capitalism' school of thought argued that the USSR should develop relations with non-socialist developing countries, which were relatively prosperous and likely to be important regional actors. This strategy would also aim to exploit contradictions between these countries and the Western capitalist states, on the assumption that their leaders would wish to develop 'nationalist' capitalism as an alternative to dependency. They could then become socialist after passing through the capitalist phase. Turkey appeared to meet the criteria assumed by this strategy quite closely.[44]

---

[42] Couloumbis, *The United States, Greece and Turkey*, 106.

[43] Campany, *Turkey and the United States*, 63; Sezer, 'Turkey's Security Policies', 67.

[44] Gareth Winrow, 'Gorbachev's New Political Thinking and Turkey', paper delivered to Conference of British International Studies Association. University of Warwick, Dec. 1991, 2–4. Winrow's analysis follows that of David Albright, but argues that, in the case of Soviet policy towards Turkey, the shift began earlier than Albright suggests.

On the Turkish side, the *rapprochement* with the USSR was emphasized by Ecevit, but it was also pursued by the several Demirel governments of the time. The process had actually begun during the 1960s. It started before the Cyprus crisis of 1964, though was naturally strengthened by it. In May 1963 a Turkish parliamentary delegation visited Moscow, to be told by Khrushchev that Stalin's policy towards Turkey had been 'idiotic', and that the USSR now desired cooperation and friendship. There was a round of mutual visits in the following years, culminating in a visit by Soviet Premier Alexei Kosygin to Ankara in December 1966, and by Prime Minister Demirel to the USSR in October 1967. The most striking effect was the beginning of a substantial Soviet aid programme to Turkey. According to CIA estimates, between the 1960s and the 1980s Turkey received a total of around $3.4 bn. in Soviet aid—more than any non-communist state, except for India and Afghanistan.[45]

One has to conclude, however, that the USSR received remarkably little political return for this economic largesse. It thus appears that the 'national capitalism' school of Soviet strategists were over-optimistic in their assumption that the national capitalist states would be clearly weaned away from the West. By the 1960s, as Khrushchev's letter to Gürsel of 1960 had indicated, Moscow had given up the aim of trying to turn Turkey into a Soviet satellite. Instead, it simply urged that it should adopt unarmed neutrality. In 1972 the two countries signed a Declaration of the Principles of Good Neighbourly Relations, to be followed by a Political Document on the Principles of Good Neighbourly and Friendly Cooperation in 1978. Though each of these referred to the prohibition of the use of force, they fell well short of the fully-fledged non-aggression pact which the Soviet side had been seeking.[46] In spite of the Soviet friendship offensive, Turkey resolutely refused to leave NATO by opting for neutrality.

It also has to be remembered that while the Soviet Union's diplomats were trying to woo Turkey, its generals, admirals, and secret service were frequently doing the opposite—intentionally, or otherwise. The invasion of Czechoslovakia in 1968 caused a sharp anti-Soviet reaction in Turkey, since it suggested that the Turks might suffer the same fate if they left the Western alliance. As İnönü put it soon afterwards, 'we have examined the NATO agreement and announced our stand. The recent Czech events have shown how correct this stand was.'[47] Similarly, the extension of Soviet naval power

---

[45] Winrow, 'Gorbachev's New Political Thinking and Turkey', 4; Vali, *Bridge Across the Bosporus*, 176–80.
[46] Winrow, 'Gorbachev's New Political Thinking and Turkey', 7.
[47] Quoted in Vali, *Bridge Across the Bosporus*, 83.

into the Mediterranean in the 1960s alarmed the Turks and strengthened anti-Soviet opinion, since it suggested that the USSR was trying to squeeze Turkey between a Mediterranean and Black Sea
Soviet presence.[48] Extensive Soviet underground activities to aid ter-
rorists of both the extreme right and extreme left during the late
1970s also heightened Turkish suspicions of Moscow, though the
exact extent and effect of these activities remain somewhat obscure
and contested.[49] On all these grounds, the changes of the 1960s and
1970s raised questions about Turkey's attachment to the West which
had been absent during the previous phase, but no clear alternative
was apparently available, or pursued.

1980–1985: the re-engagement phase

After 1980, Turkish foreign policy returned to a distinctly more pro-
Western orientation. As part of this process, Turkey moved firmly
back to the aspiration of a first world rather than Third World identity. Domestic political changes, in particular, contributed to this
result. The coup of 12 September 1980, which put Turkey under a
military regime until December 1983, totally suppressed the radical
left internally. Moreover, the terrorism which had almost brought the
state to its knees in the late 1970s left leftist radicalism severely discredited, so that it failed to re-emerge after the return to multi-party
politics in 1983. Bülent Ecevit refused to withdraw entirely from politics, as the military regime had planned, but even so he was not much
more than a marginal player on the political stage after 1983. The
mantle of the Republican People's Party was effectively inherited by
the Social Democracy Party (after 1985, the Social Democrat Populist
Party) headed by İsmet İnönü's son, Professor Erdal İnönü. The
social democrats inherited much of the Republican People's Party's
domestic political agenda, but not Ecevit's attempt to reorient
Turkish foreign policy towards a more non-aligned position, or his
role as the leader of the nationalist cause over Cyprus. Meanwhile,
the dominant force was that of Turgut Özal's Motherland party,
which won an absolute majority in two general elections (in 1983 and
1987) and remained in government until 1991. Özal was an outspoken and effective advocate of free-market economic policies, which
radically altered much of the Turkish economy during the 1980s. This
was combined with a determination to strengthen links with the
Western powers, both in America and Europe. Özal had Reaganite

---

[48] Sezer, 'Turkey's Security Policies', 57.
[49] Paul Henze, *The Plot to Kill the Pope* (London: Croom Helm, 1984), 61–4, 101–2, 132;
Hale, *Turkish Politics and the Military*, 226–7.

(or Thatcherite) economic objectives, and a good personal relationship with both these leaders. In short, domestic politics worked strongly in favour of the re-strengthening of the Western alliance.[50]

Global politics also helped to determine this swing of the pendulum. The Soviet invasion of Afghanistan at the end of 1979 destroyed the case for neutrality, since it clearly showed that a neutral neighbour of the USSR—however hard it tried to avoid foreign policy clashes with Moscow—had no security against Soviet aggression. With the onset of the second Cold War, Turkey gravitated back into the Western camp. The invasion of Afghanistan was firmly denounced by Ankara. The fate of the Afghans, as fellow Muslims, awakened strong resonances in Turkey, which were reinforced by the fact that Turkey received several thousand Afghan refugees (that is, Turkic Kazakhs, from the extreme north-east of the country). Immediately after 1980, Soviet economic aid dried up.[51] Meanwhile, Turkey's relations with the USA and the other Western powers stabilized, after the upsets of the 1960s and 1970s. The DECA was duly renewed in 1980, and at annual intervals thereafter, the only points of friction being wrangling over the exact amount of US assistance to Turkey, and some attempts by the pro-Armenian lobby in Congress to block the aid flow. Özal was also determined to press ahead towards the ultimate goal of Turkish accession to the European Community, even though this was recognized as a fairly distant objective.

Meanwhile, Greek–Turkish relations were improved by the military regime's decision, in October 1980, to accept Greek readmission to NATO's military wing.[52] However, bilateral contests with Greece over Aegean offshore oil rights and the related question of territorial waters remained unsettled. Seemingly endless talks, and talks about talks, between the Greek and Turkish Cypriot leaders continued with no results. Nevertheless, by the mid-1980s, Greek–Turkish relations had effectively drifted into a relatively stable state of mutual stand-off.[53]

1985–1990: the final phase

The beginning of the end of the Cold War was marked by the death of Konstantin Chernenko and his succession as General Secretary of the CPSU by Mikhail Gorbachev in March 1985. Essentially,

[50] For a detailed analysis of Turkish domestic policies at this time, see C. H. Dodd, *The Crisis of Turkish Democracy*, 2nd edn. (Wistow, UK: Eothen Press, 1990).

[51] Winrow, 'Gorbachev's New Political Thinking and Turkey', 7.

[52] Couloumbis, *The United States, Greece and Turkey*, 162.   [53] See ibid. 117–32.

Gorbachev's foreign policies were based on the proposition that global security as well as economic advance would be enhanced by economic cooperation, rather than competition, between East and West. In effect, the strategy of supporting the 'national capitalist' states was abandoned, in favour of the assumption of economic interdependence between the two sides in the former Cold War. This transformed Turkey's international position, since it meant that, for the first time since the 1930s, Turkey could simultaneously enjoy good relations with both the USA and USSR. Paradoxically, Ankara's relationship with Moscow at this time was better than it was to become after the constitutional dissolution of the USSR, when the eruption of the nationalities question within the former Soviet Union, and conflicts in the Balkans, gave rise to a host of mutual conflicts and suspicions.

A full Turkish–Soviet non-aggression pact—the unrealized aim of Khrushchev's policies of the 1960s—was not achieved until March 1991, when a Treaty of Friendship and Good Neighbourliness was signed by Presidents Gorbachev and Özal. However, this was after the end of the Cold War, and a result rather than a cause of it. During the 1980s, the most striking change in Turkish–Soviet relations was a dramatic growth in economic relations. Bilateral trade turnover nearly quadrupled between 1987 and 1990, from $476 m. to $1.8 bn. The most important element in this was the supply of natural gas from Russia to Turkey, through a pipeline constructed in 1987 and crossing Bulgaria and Romania. The project was the result of an agreement signed in September 1984—just before the advent of Gorbachev to power. The same year saw the conclusion of separate agreements on trade, and on economic and scientific cooperation. Another, and equally striking change was that Turkey now became a source of credits to the USSR, rather than the other way round. In 1989 the Turkish Export–Import Bank extended two $150 m. credits to the USSR for the purchase of consumer goods, to be followed by another credit of $350 m. in 1990.[54]

A crucial effect of the new global environment was that this vast improvement in Turkey's relations with Moscow had virtually no effect on its relations with the Western powers. The relationship with the USA continued on the even keel established during the first half

[54] Winrow, 'Gorbachev's New Political Thinking and Turkey', 2, 10–11. The timing of these agreements raises the question whether the succession of Gorbachev was as distinct a turning-point as the foregoing argument implies. Two possible explanations may be relevant. First, by 1984 Turkey badly needed reliable and substantial supplies of natural gas—mainly for environmental reasons—and Russia was the obvious source. Second, policies in Moscow (or perceptions of them in Ankara) may have been altering just before the death of Chernenko. Further research on this point seems to be needed.

of the decade, the only serious upset occurring in 1987, when Congress cut the proposed aid package to Turkey for 1988 from $914 m. to around $570 m. This was accompanied by moves by a group of pro-Armenian congressmen who prepared a resolution declaring 24 April an official day of commemoration for the 1.5 m. Armenians whom they claimed had been killed by the Turks during the First World War. A new DECA, signed in March 1987, remained unratified by the Turkish parliament, although both governments agreed to put it into effect. Problems deriving from pro-Armenian pressure in Congress were not overcome until 1990. Meanwhile, in 1987, Turkey submitted a formal application to Brussels for full membership of the EC. The Community's response, delivered in 1989, was negative, since it declared that negotiations for full membership could not even be considered until after 1992. However, this reply had virtually no connection with the broader global environment, since it almost entirely derived from the Community's awareness of the economic problems involved, as well as shortcomings in the civil rights regime in Turkey and the Cyprus problem. During the same period, Turkish–Greek relations continued their previous and virtually independent course of stalemate, punctuated by a renewed clash over offshore oil rights in the Aegean in March 1987. This was defused in January 1988, at a meeting in Switzerland between Turgut Özal and the Greek premier, Andreas Papandreou. Relations between Athens and Ankara then returned to their normally suspicious but sub-critical state.[55]

TURKEY AND REGIONAL CONFLICTS

As was suggested at the beginning of this chapter, Turkey's policy in the Middle East has almost always been secondary, in the minds of its architects, to its relations with the superpowers. Equally, Turkey's influence on the politics of the region was nearly always peripheral until the end of the Cold War, when the Gulf crisis of 1990–1 unexpectedly pushed it into a front-line position in the confrontation with

[55] For further material on recent Turkey–EC/EU relations, see Canan Balkir and Allan M. Williams (eds.), *Turkey and Europe* (London: Francis Pinter, 1993), and William Hale, 'Turkey: A Crucial but Problematic Applicant', in John Redmond (ed.), *Prospective Europeans* (London: Harvester Wheatsheaf, 1994), 113–32. Other information in this paragraph is derived from the writer's contributions to *Middle East Contemporary Survey* (Boulder, Colo.: Westview) for 1987, 1988, and 1990, and Andrew Mango's contribution to the 1989 edn. For a valuable summary of the evolution of the Cyprus dispute in the 1980s, see Suha Bölükbaşı, 'The Cyprus Dispute in the Post-Cold War Era', *Turkish Studies Association Bulletin* 18 (1994), 4–6.

Iraq. This sense of distance partly derived from historical memories on both sides—the Turks' perception that the Arabs had 'betrayed' them during the First World War, and the Arabs' unhappy memories of the last days of the Ottoman empire. An oft-quoted speech by Ataturk, and a popular song referring to the miseries and losses of the Ottoman empire's seemingly endless and pointless wars in the Yemen, illustrated the general conviction that Turkey should stay out of Middle Eastern entanglements, especially military ones. Adnan Menderes' break with this tradition by joining the Baghdad Pact was later regarded as a serious mistake.[56] The official commitment to secularism also meant that, until the late 1960s, Turkey studiously avoided any commitment to its Middle Eastern neighbours which might have smacked of pan-Islamism. More immediately, the gap between Turkey and the Middle East was determined by the fact that, except for Iran, the Middle Eastern states had relatively few strategic interests which were shared by the Turks.

On the Arab–Israeli dispute, Turkey has consistently adopted a policy of effective neutrality, with periodic verbal support for the Palestinians. Ankara recognized the state of Israel in 1949, and has never withdrawn this recognition. It reduced its representation in Tel Aviv to the minimum second secretary level in 1980, following the Israeli annexation of East Jerusalem, but upgraded this in 1986, and has since restored full ambassadorial representation. On the other hand, since the 1970s, it has regularly supported pro-Palestinian resolutions at the United Nations, and allowed the PLO to open an office in Ankara in 1979.[57] This policy was almost entirely the result of its broader foreign policy interests. It had no good reason to provoke the US government or the pro-Israeli lobby in Congress on what was, for Turkey, a subsidiary issue. Common opposition to Syria—given the long-standing Turkish–Syrian tension over Alexandretta—was also an important link with Israel, which resulted in a good deal of intelligence cooperation between the two countries. At the same time, the need to win more support for its Cyprus policy at the UN, especially during the 1960s and 1970s, induced Turkey to take a more pro-Palestinian stance, at least in public. This had little effect, however, as most of the Arab states continued to support Makarios: in fact, Iran and Pakistan were the only prominent supporters of Turkey over Cyprus (see Shahram Chubin's contribution to this volume, pp. 216–49).

---

[56] See William Hale, 'Turkey, the Middle East and the Gulf Crisis', *International Affairs* 68 (1992), 681.

[57] Michael M. Bishku, 'Turkey and Its Middle Eastern Neighbours Since 1945', *Journal of South Asian and Middle Eastern Studies* 15 (1992), 59, 67, 69.

More broadly, Turkey's policy towards the Middle East during the Cold War era can be divided into two sub-periods. These roughly corresponded to the second and third phases in its relations with the superpowers, outlined earlier. The first, lasting from 1952 to 1960, was dominated by the signature of the Baghdad Pact, and the subordination of Turkey's regional interests to the perceived need to maintain and strengthen its links with the Western powers. When Turkey joined NATO in 1952, it also accepted that it would play a part in the proposed Middle East Defence Organization (MEDO), originally sponsored by Britain. However, this project fizzled out during 1953, following the Egyptian revolution.[58] The idea was then partially resurrected by the Baghdad Pact, originally a pact of mutual cooperation between Turkey and Iraq, signed in February 1955. Britain, Iran, and Pakistan became full members of the Baghdad Pact organization later in the same year, with the US as its principal patron and paymaster. In 1959, after the Iraqi revolution, the Pact was renamed as the Central Treaty Organization (CENTO). It thus became a 'northern tier' rather than a Middle Eastern alliance, and lingered on as such until the Iranian revolution of 1979.

Clearly, the main weakness of the Baghdad Pact project was that it never attracted the support of the main Arab states, bar Iraq, who saw no reason to stand up and be counted in a Cold War conflict in which they did not feel involved. Moreover, even for those states which were members, it was of questionable defence value. It had no unified military command structure (as in the case of NATO) and amounted to little more than a pledge of mutual assistance if any member state were attacked by the USSR, which Iraq and Pakistan were hardly likely to be. There is also some mystery as to what the Turkish attitude towards it was. Such information as is available suggests that Adnan Menderes was enthusiastic—in fact, that he had a more-Dullesian-than-Dulles phobia about the danger of communist penetration in the Middle East. On the other hand, President Celal Bayar seems to have been far more lukewarm in his approach. George McGhee, the US ambassador in Ankara at the time, relates a conversation between Bayar and John Foster Dulles in March 1953, when the MEDO project was under discussion, in which 'Bayar pledged to go forward with the efforts to build MEDO, if that were the policy of Turkey's allies, despite the belief that it would be a wasted effort'.[59] This reinforces the impression that Bayar, for one,

---

[58] McGhee, *The US–Turkish–NATO Middle East Connection*, 148–56; Campbell, *Defense of the Middle East*, 45.

[59] McGhee, *The US–Turkish–NATO Middle East Connection*, 156.

was very doubtful about the value of the Baghdad Pact, but agreed to support it out of loyalty to the USA.

This uncertainty is reflected in a controversy about Turkey's policy towards Syria and Iraq during the critical period of 1957–8. In the summer of 1957 Menderes became worried about the possibility of a communist takeover of Syria, and massed troops on Turkey's southern border. According to a British Foreign Office report, Turkey 'seems to have considered "going it alone" against Syria', even though this would have played into Soviet hands.[60] It is well established, however, that Ankara allowed the USA the use of the İncirlik base in support of its intervention in Lebanon in 1958, although this was quite clearly outside İncirlik's NATO functions. More crucially, it appears that Menderes pressed hard for military action against Iraq after the overthrow of the Iraqi monarchy in 1958, and again in 1959, but desisted only after strong pressure from the US.[61]

During the 1960s it was widely recognized in Ankara that the Baghdad Pact project had been seriously misguided, since it had actually aided the rise of Soviet influence in the region. By the middle of the decade, the need to wean the Arab states away from supporting Makarios was also apparent.[62] This opened up a second phase in Turkish policy towards the Middle East, which lasted until the Gulf crisis of 1990. In effect, Turkey now sought to uncouple its membership of the Western alliance from its policy towards the Middle Eastern states, and to develop as good relations as possible with all its southern neighbours. Two further guidelines influenced this approach: first, that links were established on a bilateral, not multilateral, basis and second, that Ankara would not take sides in inter-Arab or Arab–Iranian disputes. This strategy was unaffected by the pendular swings in Turkey's relations with the superpowers during the 1980s, so that Turkish regional policy was essentially a continuum right through this period.

Apart from the general move towards more independent policies, which were part of the broader changes of the 1960s, this new strategy had an important economic dimension. After the oil price rises

---

[60] Quoted in Philip Robins, *Turkey and the Middle East* (London: Frances Pinter, for Royal Institute of International Affairs, 1991), 26.

[61] Ibid. 27. Richard D. Robinson agrees that it 'was only by the most vigorous American arguments' that Menderes was persuaded not to invade Iraq in 1958: *The First Turkish Republic* (Cambridge, Mass.: Harvard University Press, 1963), 187. On the other hand, George S. Harris argues that it was not the US which dissuaded Menderes from engaging in this adventure, but the fact that the Turkish army would have been physically unable to invade Iraq, given the lack of roads in the border area: Harris, *Troubled Alliance*, 65–6.

[62] Kemal H. Karpat, 'Turkish and Arab–Israeli Relations', in Karpat et al., *Turkey's Foreign Policy in Transition*, 122–3, 125.

of 1973–4, the Middle East came to play a far more important role in Turkey's external economic relations than had hitherto been the case. This effect was enhanced by the Iran–Iraq war of 1980–8, since Ankara's strictly neutral position, and the periodic closure of the Gulf sea route, vastly increased Turkey's trade with both countries. Between 1970 and 1982, Turkish exports to the Middle East rose from a trifling $54 m. to $1.9 bn. per year, and its imports from $64 m. to $2.6 bn.[63] As a proportion of total foreign trade, trade with the Middle East declined during the second half of the 1980s, in line with the fall in oil prices, but nevertheless retained a substantial role.

Ideologically, a striking sign of the Turkish *rapprochement* with the Middle Eastern states during the 1960s was the decision to partici-pate in the initiation of the Organization of the Islamic Conference (OIC) in 1969. Hitherto, this would have been thought of as an unac-ceptable infringement of Kemalist secularism, and the decision was only taken by the then Demirel government after a great deal of deliberation. As it is, Turkey has never ratified the OIC's charter, and participates in its activities on condition that these may not run counter to the provisions of the Turkish constitution,[64] which lists secularism as one of the basic principles of the state.

The effects of changes in the Turkish relationship with the US were also evident in Turkey's Middle Eastern policy at this time. In the October 1973 war, the government specifically forbade the use of İncirlik for non-NATO missions, though it did allow the use of Turkish bases for the evacuation of US civilians from Jordan in 1970, and from Iran in 1979.[65] Nor did it cooperate in the abortive mission to rescue the US hostages in Tehran in 1980. During the 1980s, it also appears that Turkey fought shy of providing bases for the proposed Western Rapid Deployment Force in the Middle East. In 1982 Ankara signed a 'co-locator operating bases agreement' with the USA for the modernization of ten airfields in Eastern Turkey, and the building of two new ones.[66] However, it was emphasized that these bases would be used purely for NATO operations. In its approaches to the West, Turkey was constantly emphasizing its sup-posed position as a 'bridge' to the Middle East. Until 1990, however, it was clear that this would not involve any military commitments. As in other respects, Turkey avoided taking on external commit-ments which did not closely correspond to its own national interests and capacities.

[63] Bishku, 'Turkey and Its Middle Eastern Neighbours Since 1945', 66.   [64] Ibid. 65.
[65] Bruce R. Kuniholm, 'Turkey and NATO: Past, Present and Future', *Orbis* 27 (1983), 426.
[66] Ibid. 438.

CONCLUSIONS

Perhaps the most striking feature of Turkey's position in the Cold War is that its alliance with the West lasted throughout. The fundamental reason for this was that it met the needs of both sides. Of course, the Turks would have fought hard against a Soviet military attack on their territory, even if they had not been in NATO. Nevertheless, they needed the alliance since, unaided, they would probably not have been able to hold off the superior Soviet forces for long. In spite of the problems in the Turkish–US relationship which emerged during the 1960s and 1970s, the balance of the argument was still in favour of remaining in NATO. On the Western side, at the height of the Cold War, Eisenhower's 'bottleneck' strategy underlined the value of Turkey to the West in preventing a possible Soviet advance into Western Europe. In the Middle East, Turkey was a virtually irreplaceable asset for the Western powers, since it provided a strong insulating barrier between the USSR and the Arab world. Admittedly, Khrushchev and his successors were able to leap over the northern tier by building up their political and military links with key Arab states; however, these links were far from dependable. In the long run, this tactic proved a wasted effort, which overstretched Soviet resources. Without actual military occupation, which was virtually ruled out by Turkish membership of NATO, the Soviet Union found it impossible to exercise effective control over its Arab clients. The fact that Turkey was a firm Western ally also had a fundamental effect on the international position of the northern Arab states since, if Turkey had fallen under Soviet control, they would probably have been unable to opt out of the Cold War, or choose the option of non-alignment.

Clearly, Turkey's stance was closer to that of Iran than to those of the Arab states. Nevertheless, there were two important differences between the Turkish and Iranian positions. First, Turkey's defence forces formed part of a unified command structure, which was never applied in the Baghdad Pact organization, or by CENTO. Second, the Shah's alignment with the West was largely determined by domestic political factors (in particular, the assumed strength of the pro-Soviet Tudeh party and other oppositional forces) which were absent in the Turkish case. For Turkey, the main reason for alliance with the West was the perceived military threat from the Soviet Union, rather than a need to bolster the government against its domestic opponents. Hence, its commitment to the alliance was stronger and more stable.

Of the various themes in the Turkish–US relationship, the strategic and military factor was easily the most important, for reasons that have been explained earlier. Turkey also received substantial economic aid from the US, but it is likely that, for most of the period, the economic element was only of subsidiary importance for both sides. The economic policies of successive Turkish governments were normally determined quite independently of foreign policy considerations, and were not necessarily helpful to Western interests. Given the size of the Turkish economy, direct US investment in Turkey was quite insignificant. Even by 1991, when the economy had been substantially liberalized, total net foreign investment in Turkey was equivalent to no more than 0.6 per cent of GNP, compared with 1.6 per cent in the case of the USA. Of the total foreign capital stock in 1992, US firms accounted for only 11.6 per cent, being exceeded by countries on which Turkey had no political or military dependence, like Switzerland and the Netherlands.[67] During the 1950s, US aid to Turkey was an important factor in the country's economic growth. However, its significance tailed off during the 1960s and 1970s, as the domestic economy gathered momentum. Moreover, after 1963, the USA was only one member of an OECD aid consortium, which also included West Germany, Japan, France, and the UK. Turkey's most serious external economic problems were the debt crises which it faced in 1957–9, and again in 1978–80. On both occasions, however, the most important actors on the Western side were the IMF and the OECD, whose policies were mainly determined by technical economic criteria rather than political considerations.[68] In short, the linkage between Turkey's foreign policy, and its economic development, seems to have been quite weak.

As Robert Rothstein remarks, the danger for a small power in seeking alliance with a big power is that it may move from insecurity to the status of a satellite.[69] The question is raised as to whether its alliance with the West reduced Turkey to this status, or something like it. Adapting the definition of state power suggested by David Vital, we may define control as the ability of one state to force a second state to follow lines of policy which it might not otherwise pursue, and the ability of the second state to implement its own agenda, even if this conflicts with that of the first state.[70] As we have seen, the USA had relatively little influence on the course of Turkey's

[67] Data from *Doing Business in Turkey* (Istanbul: IBS Research and Consultancy, 1993), sect. 6.5.1.
[68] Hale, *The Political and Economic Development of Modern Turkey*, 107–8, 240.
[69] Robert L. Rothstein, *Alliances and Small Powers* (New York: Columbia University Press, 1968), 61.
[70] David Vital, *The Inequality of States* (Oxford: Clarendon Press, 1967), 87.

domestic politics during the Cold War, so on these grounds the argument that Turkey was no more than a satellite seems quite unjustified. In its foreign policy, it seems fair to conclude that Turkey could be strongly influenced by policy initiatives from the US, but that Washington never exercised anything like total control. The fact that Turkey was a member of a multilateral defence organization, rather than having a bilateral alliance with the USA, probably contributed to this result, since it meant that power on the Western side was more dispersed.

Certainly, the strategic importance of the NATO alliance meant that it was a crucial factor in the determination of Turkish foreign policy. Even when the Cyprus crises of 1964 and 1974 put Turkey on a potential collision course with the US, the need to maintain the alliance was a vital consideration for Ankara. Admittedly, it appears that the İnönü government would have been very reluctant (and maybe unable) to invade Cyprus in 1964, even if the US had not actively opposed it. Nevertheless, the 'Johnson letter' seems to have been a conclusive determinant of İnönü's policy. Later on, the invasion of Cyprus in 1974 was presented by Ecevit as an escape from American tutelage. However, it appears that the Nixon administration had made no real attempt to prevent the invasion, and that Ecevit would have abandoned the idea if it had done so.

On the other hand, there were also some striking limitations to US power over Turkey. For example, the arms embargo of 1975–8 had virtually no effect on Turkish policy towards Cyprus—in fact, it probably encouraged the Turks to dig their heels in, rather than make concessions to the Greeks, as Congress had intended. Similarly, the Turkish government was able to resist pressure from the Kennedy administration to dismantle the Jupiter missiles on its territory, prior to the Cuban missile crisis of October 1962. Significantly, opinions in Washington were divided in both cases, and the Turks knew this. Admittedly, the Erim government was persuaded by Washington to introduce the opium ban in 1971. However, when Ecevit rescinded it unilaterally in 1974, there was little that the US government could do to stop him, and it eventually accepted the logic of his decision.

In the Middle East, Britain and the US had encouraged Turkey to play a leading role in the formation of the Baghdad Pact in 1955, but it appears that Prime Minister Menderes was as keen on the project as they were, so there is no clear evidence that Washington pushed Ankara into a policy which it would not otherwise have followed. US pressure may have been instrumental in persuading Turkey not to intervene in Iraq in 1958–9, but the case is far from proven. During the 1960s and afterwards, it seems that the USA was much less forth-right in encouraging Turkey to play an active role in the Middle East. On occasions when the US wished to use the NATO bases in Turkey for regional interventions—such as during the October 1973 war, or the attempted rescue of the Tehran hostages in 1980—then the Turkish government successfully withheld its permission. Similarly, it refused to cooperate in the formation of the proposed Rapid Deployment Force in 1982. To sum up, it appears that Turkey could not take steps which the US would probably have opposed by direct military intervention but, in conditions short of this, it preserved considerable freedom of action.

The successive changes in the global climate of the Cold War also had some significant effects on Turkey's position. In particular, it can be argued that the gradual deconstruction of the Cold War during the Gorbachev era weakened the position of most Third World states, since it significantly reduced the marginal value of their friend-ship to both the superpowers. In the Turkish case, however, it seems to have had opposite effects: in fact, it appears that Turkey was a substantial net gainer from the transformation. The end of the direct Soviet military threat was an undeniable advantage for a country on NATO's front line. In addition, the improvement in relations with Moscow opened up economic opportunities for Turkey which had been firmly closed at the height of the Cold War.

Finally, it seems reasonable to conclude that for Turkey the Cold War was primarily territorial, rather than ideological. Ideology was not entirely absent in the formation of foreign policy, but its most striking feature was the conviction of most Turks that they had an inescapable moral duty to protect their ethnic brethren in Cyprus. This was a commitment which had virtually nothing to do with the ideological contest of the Cold War. In Turkey's relations with the superpowers, İnönü and Menderes were fiercely anti-communist, as were most of their successors. Nevertheless, the overwhelmingly important determinant of their foreign policy was the fact that Turkey possessed a piece of strategic real estate, in the Bosporus and Dardanelles, which the USSR coveted, and which Turkey could not defend unaided. In most of Turkey's later foreign policy decisions, material and territorial interests took precedence over ideological alignments. On these grounds, Turkey could be said to have con-ducted its foreign policy during the Cold War with a remarkable degree of pragmatism and success.

Conclusion

AVI SHLAIM

The history of the Middle East in the second half of the twentieth century evolved in the shadow of the Cold War and its aftermath. It is generally accepted that the relationship between external powers and local powers is one of the keys to understanding the politics of the Middle East. Most students have approached this relationship from the perspective of the external powers. These students have tended to conclude that the external environment in general, and the Cold War in particular, played a decisive role in shaping developments in the Middle East.

In this book the relationship between external powers and local powers during the Cold War era is studied from the perspective of the latter. The aim of the book has been to examine the international politics of the Middle East from the 'inside out' rather than from the 'outside in'. Each chapter treated one local actor and tried to assess the impact of the Cold War on its behaviour at the international, regional, and domestic levels. This approach yielded many fresh and valuable insights. The main conclusion to emerge from the country studies is that the impact of the Cold War on Middle East politics was much more limited than is generally believed. In all the chapters, with the possible exception of those on Iran, Turkey, and the Palestinians, the conclusion is the same: the primary impulse for the behaviour of the actor under consideration was internal and the Cold War was only a secondary factor. In this respect, the book poses a challenge to the conventional wisdom on the relationship between the Cold War and Middle East politics.

Political scientists use some jargon which just possibly may help to clarify the difference between the conventional view and the view advanced in this book, namely, system dominance and subsystem dominance. System dominance implies that the international system is the primary factor in shaping the politics of a particular region or subsystem, in this case the Middle East. Subsystem dominance implies that the politics of the region are shaped primarily by internal forces. All the contributors to this book would probably come down on the side of subsystem dominance even if, like the present writer, they do not like the jargon. But the distinction between system dominance and subsystem dominance should not be pushed beyond a certain point. For, as Fred Halliday argues in the opening chapter, an abstract contraposition of two positions is an unsound way in which to grasp complex political processes.

One of the reasons for the complexity is that Great Powers and small powers tend to have rather different perspectives. Great Powers, as a rule, are more interested in their relations with other Great Powers and in the global balance of power than they are in their relationship with a small ally. They may therefore be tempted, in extreme cases, to sacrifice the small ally on the altar of their own overriding global interests. A small power, on the other hand, is usually more concerned with its immediate neighbours, whether friends or foes, and with the regional balance of power. It would therefore tend to be less sensitive to the global consequences of its actions, and to resist any attempts by a Great Power ally to curtail its freedom of action.

In the aftermath of the Second World War four Great Powers competed for influence in the Middle East: Britain, France, the US, and the Soviet Union. But whereas the two European powers steadily lost influence, the two extra-European powers steadily gained influence. What both of the superpowers had in common was a globalist approach to the Middle East. Both the US and the Soviet Union approached the Middle East from the perspective of the global rivalry between West and East. Both displayed a zero-sum mentality in which a gain by one side was regarded as being necessarily at the expense of the other. For both, specific policies towards the Middle East were an extension of their global strategy in the Cold War. In the case of the Soviet Union, however, policy towards the Middle East was also influenced to a significant degree by regional considerations. The reason for this is that the Middle East lay along the southern border of the Soviet Union and therefore impinged on its own security much more directly than it did on the security of the US. In other words, whereas the US had a pronounced globalist outlook on the Middle East during the Cold War, the globalist outlook of the Soviet Union was modified by some concerns of a regionalist kind.

If the outlook of the two superpowers was similar but not identical, their position in the Middle East was profoundly dissimilar. The position of the US was deeply entrenched and broadly based and the Americans were on the offensive most of the time, trying to expel the Soviets from the Middle East. The Soviets, on the other hand, were in a weak and vulnerable position and could never entertain any serious hope of expelling the Americans from the Middle East. It is true that the Soviets made some spectacular gains in the Middle East in the aftermath of the Second World War. They penetrated the region and became a major player in what had previously been an exclusive Western preserve. They built some of the big monuments in the region, like the Aswan Dam. They acquired allies, leapfrogged over the Baghdad Pact, and extended their military presence in the region. Nevertheless, it would be a mistake to regard the Cold War in the Middle East as an equal contest between the two outside powers. Both of these powers relied on the supply of arms, the giving of economic aid, and the promotion of their respective ideologies to bolster their position in the Middle East. The US, however, had far greater ideological appeal, more political clout in world politics, greater economic resources, and superior military technology.

The position of the Soviet Union was tenuous in the Middle East for the same reason that it was tenuous in the rest of the Third World: it relied very heavily on the supply of arms. Since there was so little cultural affinity, and since economic aid was strictly rationed, the relationship between Moscow and its Third World clients revolved very largely round the supply of arms. In the Middle East, Moscow was able to score some striking victories in the contest with the West through the supply of arms. The Czech arms deal of September 1955 broke the Western monopoly over the supply of arms to the region, enshrined in the Tripartite Declaration of May 1950, and laid the foundation for Moscow's alliance with Egypt. But Moscow also suffered setbacks as a result of its reluctance to supply arms, the most devastating of which was Anwar Sadat's expulsion of the Soviet advisers from Egypt in May 1972.

What the country studies in this book reveal are the two sides of the same coin: the jealousy with which the local powers guarded their independence during the Cold War and the difficulty that the superpowers encountered in controlling the behaviour of their clients. The local powers invariably had their own agenda and they employed various tactics, some subtle and some not so subtle, to mobilize their superpower ally behind this agenda. One tactic was to play off the superpowers against one another, to threaten, for example, that if the West refused to supply them the arms they required, they would turn to the Soviet Union. Even staunch pro-Western leaders like the Shah of Iran and King Hussein of Jordan were not above using this tactic. Another common tactic was to paint local crises with Cold War colours. Thus in 1958 President Camille Chamoun of Lebanon requested and obtained American help under the Eisenhower

Doctrine, although he was engaged not in a Cold War contest against Moscow and her allies but in a domestic struggle for power against Arab nationalist opponents. Similarly, in 1982, in the context of the second Cold War, Israel embroiled the Reagan administration in its ill-fated war in Lebanon by promising Washington that such a war would tilt the balance of power in the Levant against Moscow and its proxies.

The predicament of the superpowers in dealing with their Middle Eastern allies may be summed up as commitment without control. This predicament is clearly illustrated by the Soviet–Syrian alliance after the June 1967 War. Syria was widely regarded as a loyal Soviet client but, as Patrick Seale points out, this was a classic Cold War misunderstanding. Cold War considerations were relatively unimportant in shaping the policies of this key regional player. It was the other way round: the alliance with the Soviet Union was put to work in the service of local needs and ambitions. The Syrians wanted Moscow's help against Israel while holding the Soviets at arm's length. They gave Moscow no control over their decision-making either in war or in peace. Moscow was placed in the awkward position of having to supply arms to an ally whose aims it considered unrealistic and over whose policies it had no real control. Moscow was in fact interested in maintaining a 'no peace, no war' situation in the Middle East. But in October 1973 Syria and Egypt went to war against Israel without consulting Moscow. The war dragged Moscow to the brink of a nuclear confrontation with the US and yet it continued to experience the utmost difficulty in controlling the actions of its Arab allies. The 1982 Lebanon war highlighted yet again the inherent contradiction in Soviet–Syrian relations. President Asad wanted Soviet weapons and protection but also insisted on preserving his autonomy. In general, Syria's relations with Moscow were characterized more by muddle and mutual frustration than by real friendship and cooperation.

Washington's relationship with Israel, while much more intimate than the relationship between Moscow and its Arab friends, was not without its trials and tribulations for the senior partner. Washington's predicament after 1967, rather like Moscow's, consisted of giving Israel economic and military aid on an ever-increasing scale without gaining a major say in Israeli decision-making, either in war or in peace. As Efraim Karsh notes, the Cold War played only a secondary role in the making of Israeli foreign and defence policies, the primary concern being the conflict with the Arabs. During the presidency of Richard Nixon the American–Israeli relationship developed into a close strategic partnership, while under Ronald Reagan the relationship was institutionalized in a Memorandum of Strategic Understanding and Israel was embraced within the 'strategic consensus' that his administration sought to foster in the Middle East against the 'evil empire'. But Israel had a much clearer, firmer, and more consistent conception of her own national interest than was the case on the American side of the special relationship. And when the interests of the two countries diverged, Israel strenuously resisted sacrificing her own regional interests for the sake of America's global interests. The 1969–70 War of Attrition and the October 1973 Yom Kippur War provide examples of Israel's capacity to act independently, even provocatively, and in defiance of American wishes. But the 1982 Lebanon War provides the best example of the tail wagging the dog.

If most of the above examples relate to war, it is because wars have a way of bringing the Cold War logic to the fore. But the superpowers fared only slightly better when it came to peacemaking in the Middle East. It used to be said that while the Soviet Union held the key to war in the Middle East, the US held the key to peace. This was true in the sense that the Soviet Union was the only superpower willing to supply arms to the radical Arab states, while the US was the only superpower with leverage over Israel. In fact, both superpowers laboured under severe handicaps in the international diplomacy surrounding the Arab–Israeli conflict after 1967. The Soviet Union was allied to the radical Arab states and to the PLO but it did not share their rejectionist programme. This rejectionist stand was used by the US and Israel to rebuff Soviet calls for the convening of an international conference on the Arab–Israeli dispute.

The US was committed to a settlement of this dispute along the lines of UN Resolution 242, to Israeli withdrawal from the occupied territories in exchange for peace, but it had no say in the making of Israeli foreign policy. The Americans had no way of 'delivering' Israel even if they had wanted to. They gave the Israelis money, they gave them arms, and they gave them advice. The Israelis took the money, took the arms, and rejected the advice. Attempts by America to put pressure on Israel to moderate her diplomatic stand usually evoked strong and strident protests in Jerusalem. When the US proposed Four Power talks on the Middle East in early 1969, the Israelis refused to put their national existence on the line for the sake of American global interests. When later in the year Secretary of State William Rogers unveiled his plan for an Arab–Israeli settlement which envisaged Israel's withdrawal to the pre-1967 borders, Israel announced her refusal to be sacrificed on the altar of Great Power *Macht Politik*. Efraim Karsh's chapter provides many more examples of American–Israeli differences over peace plans but not a single example of the mighty superpower successfully twisting the arm of its small ally.

The conclusion of the Egyptian–Israeli peace treaty in 1979 did represent a major breakthrough in the conflict, and President Jimmy Carter received much of the credit for this breakthrough. This standard view is called into question by Efraim Karsh. According to Karsh, it was the local protagonists themselves, Egyptian President Anwar Sadat and Israeli Prime Minister Menachem Begin, who played the key role in kicking off the Egyptian–Israeli peace process in the late 1970s and in bringing it to fruition. The abating of the Cold War led both leaders to suspect that the superpowers were pursuing their own agendas and to conclude that if they did not look after their own interests, nobody would. The Egyptian–Israeli peace treaty thus belied the widely held view that the local protagonists could not reach a settlement on their own, and that only the superpowers could impose a settlement on them.

The subsequent history of the peace process in the Middle East conveys the same lesson: the US could help the local protagonists to reach a settlement; it could not impose a settlement on them. Fifteen years elapsed between the Camp David Accords and the next major landmark, the Oslo Accord between Israel and the PLO signed in September 1993. The Bush administration, in the aftermath of the 1991 Gulf War, set up two tracks for negotiations, an Israeli–Arab track and an Israeli–Palestinian track, but it could not induce the Israeli government headed by Yitzhak Shamir to proceed along either track. The agreement signed by Prime Minister Yitzhak Rabin and PLO Chairman Yasser Arafat on 13 September 1993 was the result of secret negotiations in Oslo. True, the agreement was signed in the White House in the presence of President Bill Clinton, but the Clinton administration had done nothing to bring about this agreement and did not even know about the secret negotiations in the Norwegian capital until the very last moment. Similarly, the Jordan–Israel Peace Treaty signed on 26 October 1994 was the result of local initiative, albeit one that enjoyed the encouragement and support of the US. The conclusion is clear: the local protagonists jealously protected their independence in peace as well as in war, relegating the superpowers to a secondary and supportive role.

So far we have spoken of the Cold War as if it were a single and fixed phenomenon, whereas in reality it was more complex and changing. There were different phases in the evolution of the Cold War and each phase had different implications for the relationship between each superpower and its respective allies in the Middle East.

Broadly speaking, bad relations between the superpowers enhanced the bargaining power of their local allies whereas good relations reduced the bargaining power of the local allies. Thus, during the period of *détente* in the early 1970s the superpowers undertook to exercise mutual restraint in the Middle East and to discourage their clients from rocking the boat. The message that Anwar Sadat and Hafiz al-Asad received very clearly was that Moscow wanted to preserve its good relations with Washington and would therefore not support any attempt to try to eject Israel from the occupied territories by force. *Détente* thus marginalized Egypt and Syria and had the effect of freezing the political and territorial status quo in the Middle East. Since Sadat and Asad found this status quo intolerable, they embarked independently of the Soviet Union on the road to war.

Decisions on war and peace inevitably engage the attention of international relations experts, and they are treated extensively in the chapters that make up this book. But the contributors to this book were also asked to pay particular attention to the impact of the Cold War at three levels of national decision-making: the international, the regional, and the domestic. An attempt will therefore be made in the final section of this concluding chapter to see if any general patterns emerge.

At the international level, in terms of their general foreign policy orientation, most Middle Eastern states preferred to remain non-aligned during the Cold War. The Arabs were particularly jealous of their recently won independence, and they were anxious to get rid of the last vestiges of Western imperialism like the British occupation of the Suez Canal Zone. The Cold War was seen as a struggle between East and West which did not directly concern them. They resented pressures on them to take sides, and opted to stay out of this external struggle if they possibly could. But if they could not opt out of the Cold War, they tried to exploit it to their own advantage, notably by trading their allegiance for arms and money. President Nasser of Egypt was a past master at exploiting the rivalry between the superpowers. Although he became one of the leaders of the Afro-Asian bloc, his brand of non-alignment was blatantly opportunistic. Syria, by contrast, remained firmly aligned to the Soviet Union during the Cold War because it had no other option. Hafiz al-Asad regarded Soviet support as the bedrock of Arab nationalism and of the Arab struggle against Israel. That is why he was so shocked when Sadat expelled the Soviet advisers from Egypt and moved his country from the Soviet camp into the American camp. Asad himself made no move to desert the Soviet ship until it started sinking. During the 1990–1 Gulf crisis he cautiously began to climb aboard the American bandwagon, but not before securing a free hand in Lebanon in return for joining the American-led coalition against Iraq.

Iraq was aligned during the Cold War, with the West until the 1958 revolution which overthrew the monarchy, and with the Soviet Union afterwards. Nuri al-Said was one of the staunchest pro-Western leaders in the Arab world in the 1950s and the chief recruiting agent for the Western-inspired Baghdad Pact. The other Arab states, led by Egypt, declined to join the Pact, largely because they wanted to stay out of the Cold War but partly because of inter-Arab rivalries. Saddam Hussein became president of Iraq in 1979, just as the second Cold War was about to be launched by President Ronald Reagan. Saddam played the Cold War card, as he played all other cards, for all it was worth. During the Iran–Iraq War he scored one of his most remarkable achievements by involving both superpowers on Iraq's side against revolutionary Iran. For a while, Saddam managed to escape the logic of the Cold War. But, as Charles Tripp shows, during the presidency of Mikhail Gorbachev, the Cold War rules began to change in a way that was inimical to Saddam's regime. In early 1990 Saddam warned his fellow Arabs against the dangers of American hegemony in the region, but he himself made a major miscalculation in annexing Kuwait: he placed Iraq on a collision course with the West at a time when the Soviet Union was no longer able or willing to bail out Iraq.

Lebanon, Jordan, and Israel, in their different ways, all sought to benefit from the Cold War. Lebanon, as Fawaz Gerges shows, always played the Cold War card and always lost. King Hussein, on the other hand, played the Cold War card much more skilfully and more successfully. As Lawrence Tal demonstrates, the Cold War allowed the king to obtain much-needed Western aid and to shore up his regime against its Israeli, pan-Arab, and domestic opponents. In the longer term, it helped him transform Jordan from a precarious entity into a durable state. In the case of Israel there was never any real doubt about the country's pro-Western orientation, although in the years 1948–50 the official posture was one of 'non-identification' in the Cold War. The real turning-point for Israel was her stunning victory in the Six-Day War of June 1967. Until then she was seen as an impediment to the American strategy of containment, especially by the Eisenhower administration. After 1967 Israel presented herself, and was increasingly accepted, as a major strategic asset for the US in the battle against Soviet expansionism and Arab radicalism. The 1991 Gulf War, during which Israel was attacked by Iraqi missiles, dented Israel's reputation as a strategic asset. Vital American interests were at stake, and the best service Israel could provide was to keep a low profile, to take punches on the chin without responding. Nevertheless, following the election of Bill Clinton, Israel succeeded in restoring the special relationship with the US. Once again it was the tail that wagged the dog.

Iran and Turkey form a special category because they had a common border with the Soviet Union and this made them front-line states in the Cold War. Their position was thus fundamentally different from that of the other Middle Eastern states. For both countries the Cold War was a real rather than a hypothetical concern and for both of them, consequently, the global conflict took precedence over regional conflicts. Iranian and Turkish policy in the Middle East was usually secondary, in the minds of its architects, to their relations with the superpowers. But whereas for Turkey the Cold War was primarily territorial, for Iran it was both territorial and ideological.

Iran was the site of the first Cold War confrontation in 1946. In this confrontation Stalin backed down in the face of firm Western support for Iran. Western support and assistance remained critical after this crisis, given Iran's weak and exposed position on the front line of the Cold War. The Soviet Union remained the principal threat to Iran's security, and containing this threat remained her dominant security concern. In addition, as Shahram Chubin suggests, the Shah's alignment with the West was determined by ideological factors. He was fiercely anti-communist and he had to contend with the strong pro-Soviet Tudeh party and other oppositional forces at home. Alignment with the West during the Cold War thus reflected rather than distorted the Shah's priorities. These priorities were abruptly reversed following the Islamic revolution and the fall of the Shah in 1979. The dominant security concern was no longer the containment of the USSR but the containment of Iraq, which attacked Iran in 1980 and engaged it in a gruelling eight-year war. Ideological priorities also changed from alignment with the West to a strict policy of non-alignment, of 'neither East nor West'.

The most striking feature of Turkey's position in the Cold War is that its alliance with the West lasted throughout. The reason for this is that the alliance served the needs of both sides. Turkey needed Western support in resisting Soviet claims on its territory. For the West, Turkey, which became a member of NATO in 1952, was an irreplaceable asset; it provided a strong insulating barrier between the USSR and the Arab world. As William Hale points out, for Turkey the Cold War was primarily territorial rather than ideological. Most of Turkey's leaders were fiercely anti-communist. But the chief determinant of their foreign policy was the fact that Turkey possessed a piece of strategic real estate, in the Bosporus and the Dardanelles, which the Soviet Union coveted and which Turkey could not defend unaided.

Turning to the impact of the Cold War on the regional policies of the Middle Eastern states, it is convenient to begin with Iran and Turkey because, once again, they constitute a special category. As we have just argued, for both of these countries Cold War concerns usually took precedence over regional concerns. As part of the projected 'northern tier' Iran and Turkey were essential to Western plans for the defence of the Middle East and both joined the Baghdad Pact. But for both countries, for most of the Cold War, the main threat was the Soviet Union, not the countries further south. The Shah did try to assert Iran as the policeman of the Persian Gulf, but this was in addition to rather than in place of Iran's role as a front-line state in the Cold War. Moreover, the Shah enjoyed strong American backing in playing the policeman of the Gulf because he fitted so neatly into the framework of the Nixon Doctrine, a doctrine of avoiding direct American military involvement and relying on allies to sustain a regional balance of power favourable to American interests. Turkey regarded itself as a European country. It had no vital interests in the Middle East and preferred to put some distance between herself and the Arab countries. It joined the Baghdad Pact largely to please the West and it came to regret its decision to join. Despite its membership of the Baghdad Pact, Turkey remained a peripheral player on the Middle East scene until the end of the Cold War, when the 1990–1 Gulf crisis unexpectedly pushed it into a front-line position in the confrontation with Iraq.

For the rest of the local actors—Israeli, Palestinian, and Arab— regional conflicts took precedence over the global conflict. This, indeed, is one of the clearest conclusions to emerge from this book. For Israel, ever since its inception, the Arab states have posed an existential threat and her national interest has focused predominantly on her immediate environment, on coping with this threat. From the Israeli standpoint, the Cold War was relevant only to the extent that it affected the pursuit of her own vital interests. In time Israel became a skilful player of the Cold War game, but she did so only in pursuit of regional interests and regional ambitions. For the Palestinians, too, the struggle for national liberation took precedence over the East–West struggle. The PLO tried to enlist the support of the Soviet Union but as a weak national liberation movement it had very little to offer. To the US the PLO had even less to offer, so playing off the Cold War protagonists against one another was never a real option. The fact that the PLO was a non-state actor made it all the more dependent on the Arab states and greatly constrained its ability to pursue an independent foreign policy. Essentially, the PLO was a microcosm of inter-Arab politics rather than an independent actor on the international stage. The position of the PLO changed fundamentally with the Oslo Accord of 13 September 1993, but this accord was brought about neither by the Arab states nor by outside powers but by direct negotiations between the PLO and Israel. The end of the Cold War may have facilitated this agreement, but the primary impetus came from within the region itself.

The energies of the Arab states through much of the postwar era were consumed by two regional conflicts: the conflict with Israel and the conflict between themselves, the Arab Cold War as it is sometimes called. For the Arab leaders, the global Cold War was of interest mainly as a means of strengthening their own position *vis-à-vis* their Israeli foe and their Arab rivals. The radical Arab leaders naturally turned to Moscow for help against Israel, while Israel and the conservative Arab regimes turned to Washington. The fact that America had friends on both sides of the Arab–Israeli divide complicated the politics of the conflict. In the Arab Cold War, on the other hand, the battle lines corresponded more closely to those of the global Cold War: the radical regimes were allied to Moscow whereas the conservative regimes were allied to the West.

In the 1950s and 1960s the Cold War helped to create the conditions for Egyptian dominance in the Arab world. Nasser capitalized on the conflict between the superpowers and their respective ideologies to promote his own radical brand of pan-Arabism. But he was also the beneficiary of the Western tendency to view the Middle East from a Cold War perspective, and of Western errors in trying to dragoon a reluctant Arab world to join in a pact against the Soviet Union. Nasser's defiance of the West greatly enhanced his popularity in the Arab world.

In the eyes of the masses, Nasser moved from one success to another in his struggle to assert Arab independence against Western imperialism. The assault on the Baghdad Pact, the Czech arms deal, the nationalization of the Suez Canal Company, his 'victory' in the Suez War, the creation of the United Arab Republic, and the Iraqi Revolution were all manifestations of Nasser's growing power and reach during the Cold War. Only with the June 1967 War did the tide begin to turn. Significantly, it was not his old Western enemies but a local one, Israel, which inflicted on Nasser the most devastating defeat of his entire political career.

The smaller Arab states were, for the most part, at the receiving end of the Arab Cold War. Facing a challenge from radical pan-Arabism, on top of the challenge represented by Israel, forced them to keep a vigilant eye on the regional balance of power. Their relations with the superpowers were dominated by their local fears, local security concerns, and local needs. Syria was the prize in the contest for regional hegemony after the Second World War. It was not a major actor until much later but a political football, kicked back and forth between rival Arab and international players. Jordan, caught between Israel and the radical forces in the Arab world, had to manoeuvre constantly on the regional scene, with whatever outside help it could get, to protect its independence. The key to King Hussein's strategy during the Cold War was survival and in this he was outstandingly successful. Lebanon was much less successful in preserving its independence and territorial integrity. Lebanon is a weak state beset by deep internal divisions and surrounded by powerful and ambitious neighbours. Opinions vary as to whether the disintegration of Lebanon was due primarily to internal or external causes. What is clear is that since the mid-1970s Lebanon has been in the grip of civil war, inter-state war, and foreign occupation. What is equally clear is that the global Cold War did nothing to enhance Lebanon's ability to withstand either the internal or the external pressures. Lebanon is thus a prominent victim of the cruel geopolitics of the region.

Finally, contributors were asked to assess the impact of the Cold War on the domestic politics of their country. A fairly broad consensus emerged for downplaying the role of the Cold War in the domestic politics of the countries examined in this book. In the case of Israel the Cold War is said to have played virtually no role at all in domestic politics, while in the case of Turkey, Iraq, and Syria it played only a limited role. Only in the case of Iran under the Shah was there a direct link between the Cold War and domestic politics: the Shah's alignment with the West reinforced the anti-communist orientation of his domestic policy.

The Shah's case raises broader questions about the relationship between the Cold War and authoritarianism in the Middle East. There can be no doubt that authoritarianism is the product of Arab history and Arab political culture, but the Cold War created an international climate which, at the very least, did not discourage authoritarianism. The Arab countries that were allied to the USSR came under no pressure to democratize because the USSR itself was a one-party state. Even the suppression of local communist states by Arab regimes elicited only the mildest of protests from the leader of the communist bloc. In Egypt, the communist party was suppressed, along with the other political parties, and parliament was abolished after the Free Officers' revolution of 1952 for reasons that had very little to do with the Cold War. But, as Adeed Dawisha notes, the Cold War did provide a convenient excuse for anti-democratic practices: political parties were denounced as serving the interest of foreign powers.

That the USSR did not promote democracy in the Middle East is hardly surprising. America's failure to promote democracy and pluralism or even basic human rights in the Middle East is much more difficult to reconcile with her official ideology. Some American leaders extol Israel as a shining example of democracy in a sea of authoritarianism, but no American president, with the exception of Jimmy Carter, actually tried to promote democracy and human rights in the rest of the region. Whenever America's strategic interests in the Cold War clashed with the values she espoused, it was the latter that were sacrificed. Iran under the Shah was a primary example. Not only did the Americans refrain from criticizing the Shah's regime; they provided training and equipment that enabled the regime to step up internal repression. King Hussein of Jordan presided over another undemocratic regime, but as long as his foreign policy remained pro-Western he could be assured of America's backing. But the worst case of American double standards concerned Iraq under the rule of Saddam Hussein. Saddam's methods of dealing with domestic opponents were extraordinarily brutal and abhorrent and included the use of chemical weapons against the Kurds. Yet as long as he kept revolutionary Iran mired down in a costly and debilitating war, the Americans turned a blind eye to his excesses. It was only when Saddam started treading on American toes by invading Kuwait that American leaders belatedly began to draw attention to the undemocratic character of Saddam's regime.

The most general conclusion suggested by this book is that the Cold War was less important in explaining the politics of the Middle East than we have previously been led to believe. Local actors had their own domestic and regional agendas and they tried, in their different ways and with varying degrees of success, to make the Cold War serve these national agendas. That the Cold War protagonists tried to control the behaviour of their local clients is not in question, but the degree of control they achieved ranged between the limited and the non-existent. It would be a mistake, therefore, to try to explain the international politics of the Middle East by focusing on the Cold War dynamics and ignoring the regional dynamics, and it would be an equally great mistake to write a history of this period in which the Great Powers alone feature as the leading actors.

So did the Cold War make any difference? In the first chapter of this book, Fred Halliday points out that it may be argued that most of what occurred in the Middle East in the post-1945 period could have taken place without the Cold War at all: the Arab–Israeli dispute, the rise of Arab nationalism, the emergence of the oil-producing states, the Islamic challenge to the Shah and other regimes. It may indeed be argued that none of these was centrally reliant on the Cold War for its emergence and development. But Halliday himself does not argue that. On the contrary, he recognizes the importance of the Cold War as a context—a military, political, and ideological context—that affected these processes in a variety of ways.

Halliday goes on to suggest that perhaps the greatest function of the Cold War in the Middle East was that it served as a distraction: it diverted attention from other pressing problems within the societies concerned, and froze positive developments that might otherwise have accelerated. From this conclusion none of the contributors to this book is likely to dissent. The Middle East is assailed by a bewildering array of social, economic, and political problems. The Cold War not only diverted attention from these problems but also pre-empted for the regional arms race the lion's share of the resources that could have been put to more productive uses. The end of the Cold War provides a favourable context for the countries of the region to start tackling some of these problems; it does not provide solutions and it certainly does not guarantee success. The fate of the Middle East will be shaped in the future, as it has been in the past, primarily by regional rather than international forces.

INDEX

Notes 1. Most references are to the Middle East, unless otherwise indicated.
   2. Names with the prefix al- are listed under the following name.